MAY - 4 1987

TCHAIKOVSKY:
A Biographical and Critical Study

THE YEARS OF WANDERING
(1878–1885)

TCHAIKOVSKY:

THE YEARS OF WANDERING
1878–1885

Volume III

by

DAVID BROWN

W·W·NORTON & COMPANY

NEW YORK   LONDON

1986

ISBN 0-393-02311-7

W. W. Norton & Company, Inc., 500 Fifth Avenue, New York, NY 10110.
W. W. Norton & Company, Ltd., 37 Great Russell Street, London WC1B 3NU.
Printed in Great Britain
1 2 3 4 5 6 7 8 9 0

To Elizabeth

CONTENTS

ILLUSTRATIONS

PREFACE

THIS VOLUME COVERS the seven years of Tchaikovsky's life following his resignation from the Moscow Conservatoire in 1878. His existence during this period was almost rootless; insofar as he had a home, it was with his sister Sasha and her family at Kamenka in the Ukraine. Otherwise he spent his time in the seclusion of country estates, or wandering restlessly in Western Europe until, in 1885, he took a house at Maidanovo, and settled into the first of a series of homes outside Moscow upon which he was to centre the rest of his life.

It was almost inevitable that a hypersensitive man, as emotionally ravaged as Tchaikovsky had been by the devastating experience of his marriage, should have retreated into an existence as solitary as he could make it. On a personal level he sought only the love of his intimate family and the companionship of his closest friends, and in such an existence the course of his life became correspondingly constricted. For the biographer this poses something of a dilemma: in how much detail should he record a day-to-day existence comprising so many events of a minor nature? It is a problem exacerbated by the ever-increasing abundance of information which survives as the composer's list of works lengthens and his reputation grows. Yet there is, in fact, a very positive value in chronicling this phase, for it is precisely in the slight events of a man's life, and in his routine intercourse with those close to him, that his most fundamental characteristics will emerge. In this present volume, perhaps more than in any of the remaining three, Tchaikovsky is at his most exposed; in his responses to ordinary occurrences and situations we may observe most clearly his idiosyncrasies and rapidly changing moods, his likes and dislikes, loves and hates, his common sense which could rise to wisdom, his kindness and compassion, his improvidence, pettiness, prejudices, his perceptiveness and blindness in assessing personality and behaviour, his openhanded generosity and calculating deviousness, his gentle but constant envy of those whose sexual nature permitted them the experiences and joys of normal family life.

And in the music, too, there is more than one might expect of works conceived within a period when their creator was so emotionally withdrawn, even impaired. Even in these difficult years his lively inventiveness did not desert him, and though few pieces from this phase belong within the first rank of his compositions, even those which are second rank must command our grateful attention when their composer has remained as tuneful and resourceful as Tchaikovsky. Indeed, on occasions he showed himself still capable of matching the quality of his best earlier works and of those yet to come: in portions of the Piano Trio, for instance, or of the opera *Mazepa* – while in the Manfred Symphony, which closes this volume, he triumphantly regained a richness of inspiration and an emotional fullness which proclaimed unequivocally that he was completely and confidently himself again.

The editorial principles and practices of the preceding two volumes are maintained in this one. So, too, I owe a continuing debt to several people who helped in practical ways in those volumes: to Dr Anthea Baird and Mr A. Helliwell (now retired) of London University, and to my undaunted typist, Mrs Miriam Phillips, whose oft-challenged powers of comprehension still so readily solve the calligraphic riddles confronting her on my typescript. As before, my wife receives the dedication, which can be no more than a partial recompense for the help she has given in checking and proof-reading. And, again, the earlier pages of this volume contain material from the Soviet-suppressed volume, *Pisma k rodnïm* (Moscow, 1940), a photo-copy of which has been so generously made available to me by Mrs Alexandra Orlova. To all these, and the others who have contributed in various ways to this volume, my most grateful thanks.

UNIVERSITY OF SOUTHAMPTON   DAVID BROWN
MAY 1985

Main Literary Sources for Volume III

with abbreviations

TLP 1–17 Tchaikovsky (P.), *Polnoye sobraniye sochineny: literaturnïye proizvedeniya i perepiska* [Complete edition: literary works and correspondence], 17 vols. (Moscow, 1953–81)

TD Tchaikovsky (P.), *Dnevniki* [Diaries] (Moscow/Petrograd, 1923)

TPB Tchaikovsky (P.), *Pisma k blizkim* [Letters to his family] (Moscow, 1955)

TPJ 1–2 Tchaikovsky (P.), *Perepiska s P. I. Jurgensonom* [Correspondence with Jurgenson], 2 vols. (Moscow, 1938–52)

TPM 1–3 Tchaikovsky (P.), *Perepiska s N. F. von Meck* [Correspondence with Nadezhda von Meck], 3 vols. (Moscow/Leningrad, 1934–6)

TPR Tchaikovsky (P.), *Pisma k rodnïm* [Letters to his relatives] (Moscow, 1940)

TTP *P. I. Chaykovsky: S. I. Taneyev. Pisma* [Tchaikovsky/Taneyev Letters] (Moscow, 1951)

BVP Balakirev (M.), *Perepiska s P. I. Chaykovskim* [Correspondence with Tchaikovsky], reprinted in Frid (E.) [ed.], *M. A. Balakirev: vospominaniya i pisma* [Balakirev: Recollections and letters] (Leningrad, 1962)

DTC Dombayev (G.), *Tvorchestvo P. I. Chaykovskovo* [Tchaikovsky's works] (Moscow, 1958)

TZC 1–3 Tchaikovsky (M.), *Zhizn P. I. Chaykovskovo* [Tchaikovsky's life], 3 vols. (Moscow, 1900–2)

YDGC Yakovlev (V.) [ed.], *Dni i godï P. I. Chaykovskovo* [The days and years of Tchaikovsky] (Moscow/Leningrad, 1940)

One musical source is also abbreviated in references:

T50RF Tchaikovsky (P.), *50 Russian Folksongs*, arranged for piano duet by Tchaikovsky (Moscow, 1869)

I

FIRST SUITE AND
THE MAID OF ORLEANS

WHEN TCHAIKOVSKY ARRIVED in St Petersburg on 20 October 1878
he had hoped to resume work on his First Suite and to decide the subject
of his next opera, but on the very day of his arrival Alexey Apukhtin's
brother died, and Tchaikovsky, himself much upset by this, spent the
first days trying to console and distract his old friend. Otherwise he
confined his visiting to the numerous members of his family, but this he
found a great strain, for by now he had grown far away from most of
them. They welcomed him warmly and he tried to be an agreeable
guest, but he found very wearing the perpetual requests that he should
play the piano and talk about music with people who had little or no
understanding of it. Few of these relatives seemed able to grasp why he
had left the Conservatoire. As for the many acquaintances he met on
the streets, they, so he said, always wanted to probe into his private
affairs with questions which made his longing to get away from Russia
the stronger. He saw the revival of *Vakula*, was angry with himself for
what he saw as its faults, and his discontent increased. Only with his
father and twin brothers did he feel really at ease, and but for the fear of
hurting them, he would have fled St Petersburg forthwith.

His declared intention was to leave for Clarens in mid-November as
soon as a passport could be arranged for his valet, Alexey, but an
invitation from his sister Sasha to visit Kamenka before going abroad
proved irresistible. He would stay there a month, he decided, perhaps
even two, and would then go straight to Italy. Yet again his plans were
to be revised. Nadezhda von Meck, his benefactress, was in Florence,
and was pressing him to come so that he might spend some time within
the same city as she. Since she offered to make all the necessary
arrangements for his visit Tchaikovsky could not decline and he
entrusted everything to her. He had only one requirement: the accommodation she selected for him must be out of range of those extraneous
musical sounds which had so irritated him in Florence on his previous
visit, for he was determined to work. His stay with Sasha would be

curtailed to one week, but he would appease his sister by promising to return to Kamenka in the spring. On 13 November he was again in Moscow to tie up his affairs and complete the disposal of his apartment and furniture. Having dined some of his closest friends and dropped incognito into a rehearsal of the First Piano Concerto which Nikolay Rubinstein was about to perform yet again at an RMS concert, he collected Alexey and left the next day for the Ukraine.

Tchaikovsky had found himself quite unable to work during his three weeks in St Petersburg, and he hoped that at Kamenka he might resume composition. He was the more irritated, therefore, to discover that the sketches which he had already made for the first three movements of his First Suite had not been packed into his luggage when he left the Russian capital. Being unable to work upon these, he pressed ahead with the projected movements, and when he left his sister's home on 27 November, two more had been outlined, thus completing the suite as he had first envisaged it. During his eleven days at his sister's he joined heartily in her wedding anniversary celebrations and in hunting expeditions. Before his departure he asked Anatoly to forward the missing sketches to Florence, and he had already begun to look ahead to a new project. Browsing through Lev's library he came across Zhukovsky's translation of Schiller's *Die Jungfrau von Orleans*, skimmed through it, and the seed of a new work was sown. In Florence he would first score the suite, 'and then I shall begin to think about an opera, and I think I've finally settled upon Joan of Arc,' he confided to Modest.[1] Having asked Jurgenson to discover whether the libretto of Auguste Mermet's *Jeanne d'Arc*, produced at the Paris Opéra in 1876, was published, he set off for Vienna. Here he forwent an opportunity of hearing Verdi's *Les Vêpres siciliennes* because that opera did not interest him, but the next evening he revelled in a performance of Meyerbeer's *Robert le Diable*. Before leaving the Austrian capital he purchased a copy of another Verdi opera, *Giovanna d'Arco*, for though he considered it a poor work, he thought it might be worth examining the libretto even though this had been drawn only loosely from Schiller. His spirits had plummeted on leaving Kamenka, but when he arrived in Florence on 2 December and saw the splendid accommodation Mrs von Meck had placed at his disposal, with its new grand piano, writing material – even a supply of his favourite cigarettes – he found his morale completely restored.

The tenor of Tchaikovsky's life in Florence was relaxed yet purposeful. As usual he went for walks and read a great deal. Two things marred the idyll. The first was the lack of any music worth hearing in

[1] *TLP7*, p. 457; *TPR*, p. 458; *TPB*, p. 180; *DTC*, p. 99.

Florence; almost the only musical pleasure he found came from the vocal score he had purchased there of Massenet's recent opera, *Le Roi de Lahore*. The second was the condition of his twin brothers in St Petersburg. Anatoly would not write, and Tchaikovsky assumed there must be something seriously wrong, while Modest had been plunged into a further bout of self-doubting by Tchaikovsky's friend, Laroche, to whom he had read his unfinished novel, and who had criticized it tactlessly. But the peace and calm of his Florentine abode afforded Tchaikovsky unqualified satisfaction. Out of a sense of duty he wrote his patroness at least one letter a day until she left Florence. She replied with equal zeal, sharing his delight in the great success which 'their symphony' enjoyed when it was performed for the first time in St Petersburg on 7 December, but differing strongly over the merits of Lalo's Violin Concerto which Tchaikovsky felt to be weak ('you are *too much* a musician for him to be able to please you. . . . I like Lalo more than Bizet,' she declared obstinately – and a little aggressively, since she knew perfectly well Tchaikovsky's passionate admiration for the composer of *Carmen*).[2] Kotek's successor as her resident violinist, Wladislaw Pachulski, had ambitions to turn composer, and Tchaikovsky, again out of a sense of duty, coached him twice a week.

So that there should be no danger of their encountering one another accidentally on their separate excursions, Nadezhda von Meck had quietly provided Tchaikovsky with a timetable of her regular routes and outings. At her request he went to see where she was staying, approaching her house close enough to hear the chatter of children's voices from the garden. When she and her family entourage passed his apartment the next day he glimpsed her from a distance. Next she invited him to visit her villa: Pachulski would show him round and he would have to meet no one. No doubt she looked forward to receiving from him an account of his tour so that she could imagine him in her present house, just as she had been able to envisage him in her Moscow home. But he declined the invitation, saying that he would feel embarrassed to think that everybody was hiding because of him. He began, in fact, to feel a growing apprehension at the dangers within these close approaches. 'What if we should meet? How should I behave?' he wrote anxiously to Anatoly on 5 December. 'She apparently isn't in the least afraid of this, for she's even sent me a ticket for the theatre on Saturday, and she'll be there also. . . . Sometimes I even wonder whether now she indeed wants a personal acquaintance, although there's no hint of this in her daily letters. All this makes me

[2] *TPM*1, p. 509.

less than free and, to tell the truth, in the depth of my heart I very much wish she would leave sooner.'[3] Six days later he was expressing even greater alarm. 'N[adezhda] F[ilaretovna] was also in the theatre, and this embarrassed me, just as her proximity in general also constantly embarrasses me. . . . For instance, every morning I see how, when she passes my villa, she stops and tries to see me! [She was, mercifully, very short-sighted.] How ought I to behave? Go to the window and bow? But in such circumstances should I not call out from the window: "Hullo!"?'[4] Yet he had at all costs to keep his uneasiness to himself, and in his letters to her he continued to profess his passionate unqualified joy at her nearness.

Thus encouraged, Mrs von Meck made a further proposal: that Tchaikovsky should postpone the trip he was preparing to make imminently to Paris until February, when she herself intended to visit the French capital. Tchaikovsky was quick to see how, by agreeing to such a close concurrence of itineraries, he was likely to become chained to her. 'There have already been hints in several of her letters that she would like it *always* to be as it is now, that she would *always* take upon herself all concern for my welfare,' he wrote to Modest on 18 December. '. . . Today, she writes to me that she has decided, after Vienna, to go to Paris early in February, and asks me not to go there now, and that if I do not want to go to Vienna (she suggested to me that I should), then that I should now proceed to Clarens, and visit Paris by 13 February. In other words, she wishes me not to live independently in Paris but in a flat which she has rented and provided with all that's necessary. I replied that I have to obtain in Paris materials for an opera (this is true) and that therefore I shall now still go to Paris for several days, but that afterwards I'm prepared to go to Clarens and be in Paris on 13 February. And now, having written this, I'm in a bad temper. You'll say I'm being fussy. That's true, but it's also true that, however tactfully and delicately she may go about it, N[adezhda] F[ilaretovna] still somewhat inhibits my freedom, and that I'd with pleasure turn down her apartment if it were possible, for the money which she gives me is fully adequate for me to flourish.'[5]

Tchaikovsky held to his resolve. On 27 December Nadezhda von Meck and her suite left Florence for Vienna. By this time he had become accustomed to her close presence and to seeing her, and being seen, across a theatre. Even so, he was surprised at his own reaction to

---

[3] *TLP*7, p. 479; *TPM*1, pp. 598–9; *TPR*, p. 463; *TPB*, p. 182; *YDGC*, p. 193 (last sentence only).

[4] *TLP*7, p. 492; *TPM*1, p. 601; *TPR*, p. 467; *TPB*, p. 184.

[5] *TLP*7, p. 519; *TPM*1, p. 605; *TPR*, pp. 473–4.

her going. 'I feel a great longing for her and a great void beyond my expectations. I pass her uninhabited villa with tears in my eyes. . . . What had at first embarrassed and confused me now forms a subject for the most sincere regret,' he admitted to Modest later that day.[6] With her she carried away Tchaikovsky's profuse thanks for all the joy she had made possible for him in Florence, and also a full preliminary assessment of Pachulski's abilities. For the latter he provided a letter of introduction to Anton Door, his old colleague at the Moscow Conservatoire; for Modest he penned a poem on the lily of the valley in remembrance of an expedition they had made together in Florence during the spring to pick Tchaikovsky's favourite flower. 'For the first time in my life I've succeeded in writing some really tolerable verses which are, moreover, *deeply felt*,' he added proudly in his covering letter.[7] On 28 December he set out for Paris.

From the day of his arrival in Florence nearly four weeks earlier Tchaikovsky had determined to establish a creative momentum, and he had wasted no time in scoring the two movements he had with him of his First Suite upon which he had started in the Ukraine during the summer. He had begun the scherzo on 27 August, and by 2 September he could inform Modest that he had set about a second movement. 'I'm writing an *Introduzione e Fuga*. Both these pieces [the Scherzo, and the Introduction and Fugue] will become part of a suite which I want to compose so that I may have a good rest from symphonic music.'[8] Four days more, and he was confessing the extent of his labours to Nadezhda von Meck, and defining clearly the shape which this '*suite* in the style of Lachner' would take.

When I arrived in Verbovka I felt I simply could not resist my inner compulsion, and I therefore hastened to set down on paper sketches of this suite. I worked with such enjoyment, such enthusiasm, that I literally did not notice how the hours flew by. At this moment three movements of this future orchestral piece are ready, a fourth is roughly sketched, while the fifth is in my head. . . . The suite will consist of five movements: (1) Introduction and Fugue, (2) Scherzo, (3) Andante [these were the three movements which were fully sketched], (4) Intermezzo (*Echo du bal*), (5) Rondo. Because I was constantly thinking of you while I was composing this piece, at every stage was asking myself whether this or that bit would please you,

[6] *TLP*7, p. 541; *TPM*1, p. 607; *TPR*, p. 483.

[7] *TLP*7, p. 541; *TPM*1, p. 608; *TPR*, p. 483; *TZC*2, p. 241; *TPB*, p. 191; *YDGC*, p. 198.

[8] *TLP*7, p. 374; *TPB*, p. 173; *DTC*, p. 385.

whether this or that melody would touch you, I cannot dedicate it to anyone other than *my best friend*.[9]

Though the suite's ultimate shape had seemed clear to Tchaikovsky at this early stage, it was to be much modified. Within a week of beginning scoring it in Florence, the two movements he had by him were finished. Unfortunately the rest was still in Russia, and there followed a long period of anxiety and frustration which he filled by setting to work on his new opera, *The Maid of Orléans*. It was the middle of January before at last a much-frayed Tchaikovsky received the missing package, and by then he was so engrossed in the opera that there was no question of redirecting his attention to the orchestral piece. On 6 March, having the day before finished sketching the opera, he at last began some preliminary work on putting the sketches in order, but his labours were only sporadic, and it was 26 April before he could announce that the scoring was completed. At this stage the work still consisted of only five movements, and their sequence was quite different from that in which they were later to appear. In addition, the last two movements (Nos. 4 and 6 in the final order) had titles. Tchaikovsky had listed the work's intended content to Modest while at Kamenka in November:

(1) Introduction and Fugue
(2) Scherzo
(3) Andante melanconico
(4) *March of the Lilliputians*
(5) *Dance of the Giants*

Then in August 1879, when Jurgenson was actually engraving the suite, Tchaikovsky perceived a fundamental defect and wrote urgently to his publisher:

If you haven't yet got to No. 4 I shall be happy in the extreme. Only now has it suddenly occurred to me that all five movements of the suite are in duple time. *This is impossible!* And because No. 4 is of doubtful merit, I have hastened to compose another piece in waltz time to replace this; this is incomparably better. As soon as I've finished the opera, and this will be done in a week, I'll score this new number and will bring it to you by September, together with all the

[9] *TPM*1, p. 421; *TLP*7, pp. 375–6; *TZC*2, p. 200; *DTC*, p. 385 (partial).

rest. Is this possible? Shall I be in time? . . . If it's already too late, I ask you all the same to append the new number, for it's impossible to leave the whole suite in one metre. . . . But it would be best of all to cross out No. 4 (the very doubtful one) and insert the new one instead.[10]

The March, however, was to be reprieved, though only after outside intervention. 'You write that the *Marche miniature* ought to be left,' Tchaikovsky observed to Jurgenson on 5 September 1879 from Simaki. '. . . Speaking frankly, I would wish to throw out this rubbish altogether. Moreover, I find *six* movements too many. . . . But the point is that I'm a poor judge of my own pieces until they have been performed. I think *Taneyev* is familiar with the suite. I rely *entirely* upon his judgement. Please send him a note asking him to state his opinion *frankly*.'[11] If Taneyev decided the March was to be retained, the Andante was to be dropped and the order would be Introduction and Fugue, Divertimento (the new movement), Scherzo, March, Gavotte. It was now the Andante's turn to be saved, and when the suite was first performed on 20 December 1879 at an RMS concert in Moscow conducted by Nikolay Rubinstein, the order of the six movements was the one finally established.

Tchaikovsky did not attend the première, for he was in Rome, and Jurgenson must have taken some sly pleasure in reporting to the composer on the reception accorded the new work. 'The first movement went off without fervent expressions of delight. The second evidently pleased. The Andante pleased very much, but the March drew applause which wouldn't stop until it was repeated. The Scherzo was very well received. The Gavotte found the audience by now fatigued and bursting to get away.'[12] Rubinstein claimed that the orchestra found the work difficult, but Tchaikovsky, who was very upset by this report, refused to accept that the objections were valid. '[This complaint] exasperates me, drives me to despair. The more I try to be simple and easy, the less successful are my efforts,' he lamented to Taneyev on 31 December.[13] The suite was heard – and very enthusiastically received – in St Petersburg on 6 April 1880, when again it was the March which scored the greatest success. In fact this movement was to be played frequently as a separate item because of its popularity.

None of Tchaikovsky's three original orchestral suites can count

---

[10] *TLP8*, pp. 315–16; *TZC2*, p. 301; *TPJ1*, p. 109; *DTC*, p. 387.
[11] *TLP8*, p. 335; *TZC2*, p. 305; *TPJ1*, p. 111.
[12] *DTC*, p. 388.
[13] *TLP8*, p. 473; *DTC*, p. 388; *TTP*, p. 41.

among his most important works. By the time he came to compose the
third, and by far the best of them, he believed that he could fully
understand what had most strongly drawn him to the form. '[The suite]
has for some time been particularly attractive to me because of the
freedom it affords the composer not to be inhibited by any traditions, by
conventional methods and established rules,' he told Nadezhda von
Meck on 28 April 1884.[14] This was a very retrospective view, accurate
to a certain point, but one in which Tchaikovsky had forgotten that
what had impelled him to essay his first suite some six years before was
that it absolved him not only from certain compositional responsibilities but from expressive ones as well. By the summer of 1878 he
was quite incapable of finding within himself those reserves of
titanic emotional force from which he had forged the first movement of
the Fourth Symphony only a year earlier. Deciding that he needed 'a
good rest from symphonic music', as he told Modest, he yet did not
wish, in shedding the heavier expressive responsibilities, to negate
himself to the degree he had done in the Rococo Variations. Instead
that same polish and poise he heard as a property of eighteenth-century
music was to be achieved within his own idiom; it was to be his
equivalent of what he had identified in *Carmen* as *le joli*. But whereas
Bizet's music had drawn in full measure upon the passion and violence
of a tumultuous tale, Tchaikovsky's First Suite is rooted primarily in
the decorative world of the ballet divertissement. However, lest this
should all seem too light, even frivolous, a measure of self-conscious
highmindedness is afforded by the opening fugue with its earnest
introduction (to give the whole suite a frame this opening fugal material
returns to close the piece). Tchaikovsky had several times before used
extensive fugato sections, notably in the finales of the Second String
Quartet and Third Symphony, but only once before, among the Piano
Pieces, Op. 21, had he included a full-blown example of the form. The
fugue of the First Suite is a thoroughly pedantic specimen in its earlier
stretches, impressive as a demonstration of resourcefulness in devising
new contrapuntal webs to accompany successive entries of the subject,
but ineffably dull as music, despite the Tchaikovskyan rhetoric which
begins to tear through the mesh of the contrapuntal net in the latter half
of the piece. The mild spicing of the coda merely serves to emphasize
how stodgy has been the preceding fare.

What follows in the other five movements is far more palatable, yet
rather second-rate, despite some undeniable charm. By now
Tchaikovsky knew his own technique and style so well that he could,

[14] *TPM*3, p. 272; *TLP*12, p. 352; *DTC*, p. 403.

when genuine creativity remained unstirred, 'invent himself'. Admittedly there are some nice things in this suite – for example, the first main division of the Divertimento with its halting clarinet opening, and the section which begins with the wistful, slightly folky E flat minor theme in the middle of the Scherzo (otherwise a very pedestrian movement) – but the overall impression is of inconsequence, for here the lightness is not a necessary phase of relaxation to set off or complement more portentous matters, but instead projects a lack of real commitment, a point emphasized when, near the end of the Intermezzo, the watery flow finally thickens into a new più mosso melody of some real emotional allegiance. Otherwise this Intermezzo is little more than blandly melancholy, despite all Tchaikovsky's undeniable skill at melody spinning. It is the only movement susceptible to any kind of sonata interpretation (here exposition and recapitulation without development, but with a markedly extensive coda). As for the other movements, they rely for their effect heavily (the Gavotte) or entirely (the March) upon the exploitation of a particular, arresting kind of scoring. If the Gavotte puts us a little in mind of the debt Prokofiev was to owe Tchaikovsky, the March foretells even more affirmatively the world of Tchaikovsky's own last ballet, *The Nutcracker*, in which he was to exploit so scintillatingly yet excessively his flair for orchestral confectionery. Scored only for treble instruments (violins, bells, triangle and upper woodwind), this trifle lives entirely through its perky, sugar-coated timbres. Glinka had envisaged a similarly delicate, ear-tickling world in the women's chorus that precedes Chernomor's March (and in the trio of the march itself) in Act 4 of *Ruslan*. But whereas that silvery music had been alluringly persuasive, this is merely cute. A foreshadowing of the mirlitons of *The Nutcracker* is detectable also in the passage for three flutes in the Divertimento. Since the suites were not concerned with major expressive issues, there was no problem in listening to them, and they swiftly enjoyed an audience success which did more to spread their composer's fame than many of his more serious, far finer pieces.

As we have seen, within a week of his arrival in Florence Tchaikovsky had exhausted the work he could do upon the First Suite. After a further week of inactivity he could bear it no longer, and he focused his attention upon his other creative project, the opera on Joan of Arc. His determination to compose this had consolidated since leaving Kamenka, and after three days in Florence he was making plans to begin. He would even make a special trip to Paris to collect relevant literary materials, above all Mermet's libretto. So much did his enthusiasm grow that finally, despite the lack of a scenario, let alone a libretto, he could restrain himself no longer and started to devise his own text from Zhukovsky's translation of Schiller. 'Fearfully, excitedly, and not without some diffidence, I have set about the opera,' he announced to his benefactress on 17 December, having that very morning begun composition.[15] She responded by promptly sending him a copy of Henri Wallon's *Jeanne d'Arc* to aid his work. Within four days he had composed the entire scene of Joan's recognition towards the end of Act 2. In fact, so gripped was he by this new subject, so overwhelmed with ideas, and so moved by reading Wallon's account of Joan's terrible end (the only bit in this book which at all impressed him) that it induced a nervous attack which persuaded him he must break off composition. It also gave him an added reason for going to Paris; as he explained to Jurgenson, the excitements and pressures in composing an opera were such 'that I am simply afraid of living in a quiet corner where I have always to be alone with myself. I must have a ready opportunity, by means of the theatre, music, walking along noisy streets, and so on, to divert and distract myself from the exclusive concentration of all my powers upon one subject.'[16] Thus he did no more work on *The Maid of Orléans* until after his visit to Paris.

When he arrived in the French capital he found the noise and bustle of everyone preparing for the New Year in the sharpest contrast to the tranquillity of Florence. Equally contrasted was the cultural fare on offer, and he sampled to the full what Paris could provide during his ten-day stay. Mostly with Alexey or Kotek, who had travelled especially from Berlin and whose expenses Tchaikovsky defrayed, he visited a variety of entertainments, including several performances at the Comédie-Française, where he was vastly impressed by Sarah Bernhardt in Racine's *Andromaque*. At the opposite end of the enjoyment scale was a performance of Gounod's recent *Polyeucte* at the Opéra.

But by far the most distasteful experience of his Paris stay was to receive, via both Jurgenson and Anatoly, intelligence of Antonina's activities. His brother had been approached by an unknown man, claiming to be a relative of Tchaikovsky's wife, who now, the stranger said, wanted a divorce; what were Tchaikovsky's terms? Mindful of Antonina's past vacillations, a deeply distrustful Tchaikovsky stipulated that he was prepared to be divorced on the grounds of '*adultery, impotence*, or whatever you like',[17] but that he would do nothing until he returned to Russia, and that would be in his own good time. But for a

---

[15] *TPM1*, p. 530; *TLP7*, p. 512; *TCZ2*, pp. 236 and 314; *YDGC*, p. 195; *DTC*, p. 99.
[16] *TLP7*, p. 527; *TPJ1*, p. 60.
[17] *TPR*, p. 489.

while he was badly upset. In Florence, he said, he had sometimes thought of Antonina, but there his whole marriage episode had seemed so remote that it might have been no more than a bad dream. Now reality confronted him again, and a nightmare rose up before him. 'What did I not imagine to myself! Amongst other things I had already decided in my own mind that she was instituting criminal proceedings against me, and wished to charge me. Vividly I saw myself in the dock, and though I routed the public prosecutor with my concluding speech, I still perished under the weight of the shameful indictment. In my letters to you I tried not to appear afraid, but in fact I considered myself already quite ruined,' he confessed to Anatoly on 7 January 1879,[18] by which time he had recovered his composure a little. Nevertheless his stay in Paris was poisoned. He became annoyed by Kotek's foibles – and felt ashamed of himself. To Anatoly he admitted that Kotek's 'fondness for women'[19] was irritating him.

While the theatres afforded Tchaikovsky much pleasure, he found the musical life in Paris altogether deplorable on this visit. The one event which might have given him pleasure was the festival concert at the massive Hippodrome at which various celebrated French composers, including Saint-Saëns, Massenet, Gounod and Delibes, were to conduct their own works. But Tchaikovsky mistook the date by one week, and when he arrived he discovered his ticket admitted him to a horse show instead! As for his own operatic enterprises, he obtained a copy of the Mermet libretto, but found it of less use than he had hoped. 'In the end I have come to the conclusion that Schiller's tragedy, although it is not consistent with historical accuracy, still outstrips all other artistic presentations of *Joan* in its depth of psychological truth,' he concluded to Nadezhda von Meck.[20] Having equipped himself with all the literary materials he felt he needed for his opera, including Jules Michelet's *Jeanne d'Arc* and at least one of Jules Barbier's two treatments of the Joan story, and having resigned himself to accepting that the sketches of his suite's first three movements might now be irretrievably lost in the post, he bade farewell to Kotek and left Paris on 9 January. After an enforced delay in Dijon through appalling weather, he and Alexey were in Clarens at their much-loved Pension Richelieu on 11 January. The next day he set about *The Maid of Orléans* in earnest.

The early compositional process of Tchaikovsky's fifth surviving

[18] *TPM*1, p. 608; *TPR*, p. 496. This extract is excised in *TLP*7, p. 567.

[19] *TPR*, p. 494. In fact Kotek had contracted syphilis from his earlier escapades; it was probably this which caused Nadezhda von Meck to replace him as her resident violinist.

[20] *TPM*1, p. 560; *TLP*7, p. 566.

opera is far more precisely charted than is the case with its prede-
cessors. 'Today . . . I composed the first chorus of Act 1,' he informed
Mrs von Meck on 12 January. 'The composition of this opera will be
very laborious for me because I have no ready libretto, and have not yet
even worked out fully the plan of the scenario. Meanwhile I have put
together a detailed scheme for the first act, and I am writing the text a
bit at a time, borrowing it mostly, of course, from Zhukovsky, but also
using other sources, and especially Barbier, whose tragedy on the
subject of Joan has many good points.'[21] His method, as he told Anatoly
the next day, was to round off one day's work by preparing the text for
the morrow's music. As usual when deep in composition, he had a
precise daily routine. 'I drink morning coffee with a light breakfast. A
walk while my room is being cleaned. Composing the opera until lunch
[at 1 p.m.]. After lunch a long walk. On returning, reading and writing
the libretto. . . . At 8 p.m. supper with tea. Then letter-writing and
reading. At 11 I go to bed.'[22] His rate of progress fortified his confident
prediction that when he returned to Russia a significant portion of
the opera would be complete. Within two days he had reached the
Peasants' Chorus (No. 4) with which he was very well pleased. The
next day he sat down to Joan's arioso (No. 5); 'at first for some reason it
went slowly – subsequently, by contrast, it really got going . . . and I
didn't notice the passing of time until lunch,' he told Anatoly.[23] Equal
success attended the next day's labours, and the Hymn (No. 6) was
sketched.

The libretto was a very different matter. Although he believed that
the text he was producing was satisfactory, even good, he often had to
wrestle with it. 'This labour will certainly take several days at least off
my life,' he lamented to his patroness. 'It is difficult to convey to you
how tired I get. How many pens do I gnaw to bits before extracting
from myself a few lines! How often do I get up in utter despair because
the rhymes or a certain number of feet will not come out, or because I
am uncertain whether this or that person should be speaking at a
particular moment!'[24] But composition still proceeded swiftly, and on
21 January Act 1 was done. It had taken ten days. Tchaikovsky wasted
no time in launching into Act 2. During the next two days the duet for
Dunois and the King was ready; Tchaikovsky was particularly pleased
with the passage in F major beginning at bar 86. Since the scene of
Joan's recognition had, of course, already been composed in Florence,

[21] *TPM*1, p. 564; *TLP*7, p. 578; *TZC*2, p. 250.
[22] *TLP*8, pp. 15–16; *TZC*2, p. 251; *TPR*, p. 502; *TPB*, p. 199.
[23] *TLP*8, p. 25; *TPR*, p. 504; *TPB*, p. 201; *YDGC*, p. 200 (partial).
[24] *TPM*2, p. 19; *TLP*8, p. 32; *TZC*2, p. 252; *DTC*, p. 101.

Tchaikovsky only required three more days to complete the whole second act. By 26 January half the opera was sketched. That evening he sat down to play through all he had written. He was well satisfied with the total impression. 'If this opera won't be a masterpiece by universal standards, it will certainly be *mine*,' he judged it proudly to Modest. 'It has undoubted simplicity of style. The structures are lucid. In a word, it will be at the very opposite extreme to *Vakula*.'[25]

During all this intensive work Tchaikovsky had several times felt an urgent need for some diversion. He had been reading *Little Dorrit* with enormous enjoyment. 'Dickens and Thackeray are about the only people I forgive for being English. One must add Shakespeare, but he lived at a time when that vile nation was less ignoble,' he told Anatoly,[26] still remembering with bitter rancour Britain's role in the Russo-Turkish war. Reading, however, used mental energy; what he needed was some real respite. Accordingly for two days he did no more to the opera than devise the text for the first scene of Act 3. Then on 29 January he set off to Geneva for twenty-four hours, where he purchased a piano reduction of some quartets by Mozart and Beethoven, the daily playing of one of which was to afford him much delight in the days just ahead. But nothing could distract him from the opera for long. Back in Clarens, he set about Act 3 on 31 January, and completed the first scene on 4 February. Since he wanted to deal with the 'two fundamental and most difficult love scenes'[27] in immediate succession, he plunged the next day into the love duet in Act 4. It did not come easily. 'In general I'm pleased with myself,' he reported to Modest, 'but I'm a bit tired.'[28] It was a full week before he could return to Act 2.

It is clear that Tchaikovsky's rate of composition was slowing. Before going to Geneva he had confessed to fatigue, and now his creative energies were faltering. This is hardly surprising; after all, in little more than three weeks he had sketched music which would occupy some three hundred pages of vocal score. He had been occupied with other things, too. Letter-writing had consumed much time, and he wrote an especially carefully worded letter to Stasov asking him to intercede with Suvorin, the editor/proprietor of *New Time*, to ensure that the violent press attacks which were currently being mounted by this newspaper against Nikolay Rubinstein and his administration of the Conservatoire should be moderated. Tchaikovsky himself would have come out

[25] *TLP*8, p. 48; *TPM*2, p. 597; *TPR*, p. 512; *TPB*, p. 208; *DTC*, p. 103; *YDGC*, p. 202 (partial).
[26] *TLP*8, p. 31; *TPM*2, p. 596; *TPR*, p. 507; *TPB*, pp. 203–4; *YDGC*, p. 201.
[27] *TPM*2, p. 31; *TLP*8, p. 52; *TZC*2, p. 256.
[28] *TLP*8, p. 68; *TZC*2, p. 259; *TPR*, p. 521; *TPB*, p. 213.

publicly against Rubinstein's tormentors, but he feared that they might fall upon him in return with insinuations about his marriage. He felt much mortified when Stasov excused himself from action on Rubinstein's behalf on the grounds that he felt the charges to be justified. Tchaikovsky's lengthy rejoinder, an imposing mixture of uncompromising frankness with dignified tact, is a reminder of that continuing balance and lucidity with which he could observe the personal affairs and problems of others, if not always of himself. To set against such strains and the sheer labour of composition there was the absolute quiet of the Pension Richelieu, the impeccably solicitous hospitality of the family Mayor who ran the hotel, and the enchantment of Lake Geneva with its winter scenery. If it had not been for these blessings his work would not have advanced so far.

His agreement with Nadezhda von Meck was that he should be in Paris on 13 February, but lack of money made a punctual departure impossible, and he had to send an urgent message to his provider for funds. Even before this he had reported that the overture of the opera was now drafted, as well as the whole of Acts 1 and 2, and the first scenes of Acts 3 and 4 respectively; now he used his enforced delay in Clarens to compile the libretto for the second scene of Act 3, and to compose the coronation march which opens it. On 15 February the necessary financial instalment arrived. Two days later the Mayor family, with very visible marks of regret, said goodbye to their sole guest, himself tearful at leaving them. Next day, as he settled himself into the accommodation Mrs von Meck had arranged for him in Paris, he summarized for her his feelings about leaving the place in which he had just passed some five weeks. 'It is very nice to know that there is a corner of Western Europe where I shall always be received with joy, care and friendliness, where my habits and requirements are well known, where they always know how to arrange it so that, while I am there, I feel as though I were at home.'[29]

The stages by which the last quarter of *The Maid of Orléans* came to completion are not clear. Overcoming his initial disinclination to work in the French capital, and having transferred himself to a less luxurious apartment out of earshot of the traffic, Tchaikovsky had, by 22 February, immersed himself in the finale of Act 3. His response to Paris was ambivalent. During his first week there he hungrily dipped into the cultural riches of the city, rejoicing this time not only in the

[29] *TPM2*, p. 45; *TLP8*, p. 91. What Tchaikovsky did not know was that his servant Alexey had made the servant, Marie Savion, pregnant. When later in the year Tchaikovsky heard of this, he promptly sent Marie 100 roubles, and subsequently offered to take her under his protection, an offer which was declined.

Comédie-Française but in musical delights, for two of his favourite works were on immediate offer: Weber's *Der Freischütz* at the Opéra, and Berlioz's *La Damnation de Faust* which Colonne was to conduct at the Théâtre du Châtelet, and which in parts moved Tchaikovsky to tears. But at the same time he was yearning for the peace and quiet he had savoured at Clarens, and after a week he felt little inclination to go out, preferring to remain in his room to read. Dostoyevsky's *The Brothers Karamazov* had just begun to appear in the *Russian Herald*, and Tchaikovsky, deeply moved by the first instalment, enthused about it to Mrs von Meck. 'Why, my friend, are you reading Dostoyevsky – this is not for one with your nerves!' was her alarmed rejoinder.[30] He came across another book, Rousseau's *Confessions*, which he, in his turn, felt would be unsuitable reading for her – 'since,' as he explained mysteriously, 'along with continual flashes of genius, it contains an abundance of very cynical declarations which render this book almost unapproachable for women'[31] (as he later revealed, it was Rousseau's descriptions of his amorous escapades which made his *Confessions* 'almost unapproachable' for genteel femininity). He was deeply impressed by Rousseau's understanding of certain of those very traits he found in his own personality. Above all, the Frenchman offered an explanation of why he, an intelligent man, always appeared so gauche when in company. 'Apropos of this,' Tchaikovsky continued to his confidante, 'he enlarges upon the unsociability of his own nature, and on *the intolerable difficulty of maintaining a conversation as a matter of duty* when, for the sake of keeping the conversation going, you have to speak empty words which you do not really mean and which express no true train of thought or feeling.'[32]

This was an experience familiar to Tchaikovsky, as he pointed out most emphatically to Mrs von Meck when she asked him whether he would call upon Turgenev, who was now resident in Paris. He remembered only too well the problems he had had in talking to another author – Tolstoy. There was something, too, in his patroness's attitude towards Tchaikovsky himself which puzzled him. Though her letters were as ardent as ever, she pleaded headaches and eye-strain as reasons for writing to him only once a week instead of every day, as in Florence; moreover, the wish she had constantly displayed in that city to glimpse him daily if possible seemed to have gone. Only occasionally did they observe each other in a theatre or concert hall. Having to write to her

---

[30] *TPM*2, p. 61.
[31] *TPM*2, p. 73; *TLP*8, p. 142; *TZC*2, p. 276.
[32] *TPM*2, p. 73; *TLP*8, p. 143; *TZC*2, p. 276.

less frequently was, however, some relief. For Pachulski he resumed his twice-weekly lessons begun in Florence. All in all, his mood was unsettled, and this did nothing to facilitate composition. Nevertheless, he persisted with his dogged labour and on 1 March he signed the end of Act 4. What exactly remained to be done is uncertain, but even an optimistic Tchaikovsky reckoned there was a full week's work left. In fact, through unusually intensive application, it took only four days. After this he spent a further two days in ordering the sketches of both the opera and the First Suite, and on 8 March he could report *The Maid of Orléans* drafted to the last detail.

Tchaikovsky remained four more days in Paris. The joy he felt at labour brought to a happy conclusion was fortified by seeing that *The Tempest*, already heard under Rubinstein's direction at the Paris Exhibition in the summer, was to be conducted by Colonne in a morning concert at the Théâtre du Châtelet. Yet even here he felt some gloom. 'I know already both that it'll be badly played and that the audience will hiss as has always happened up to now when my works have been given abroad – and therefore it would have been better if they'd played it after I'd left,' he concluded to Modest.[33] During his time in Paris he had remained obdurately incognito, and no one knew of the composer's presence in the audience when *The Tempest* was performed. The discomforts he endured, despite not having to come forward publicly, were vividly recounted to the same brother the day after the concert.

> The evening before I had begun to have nausea and diarrhoea. Right up to the very first chords my agony all morning went *crescendo*, and when they were playing I thought I would that very moment expire, my heart ached so much. And my agitation did not arise at all because I was anticipating a failure but because for some time every fresh hearing of any of my works has been attended by the strongest disenchantment with myself. . . . *The Tempest* was given a very tolerable if not first-rate performance. The tempi were absolutely right. It seemed to me that the players were performing diligently, but without love and enthusiasm. . . . When the last chords finished, rather feeble applause was heard; then, as it were, there was a new burst, and then three or four very loud whistles were heard – but then there resounded through the hall cries of Oh! Oh! signifying protest against the whistling, and then everything fell silent.[34]

[33] *TLP8*, p. 129; *TZC2*, p. 270; *TPR*, p. 543; *TPB*, p. 225; *DTC*, p. 358.
[34] *TLP8*, p. 138; *TPM2*, p. 604; *TZC2*, pp. 271–2; *TPR*, pp. 547–8; *TPB*, pp. 227–8; *DTC*, p. 358.

When he had become calmer Tchaikovsky wrote to Colonne an open letter of thanks which was published in *Revue et Gazette Musicale* a week later. *The Tempest* received at least one favourable press notice and, on reflection, Tchaikovsky decided it had not been a disaster.

Except for this very mixed experience Tchaikovsky's days in Paris after completing *The Maid of Orléans* were the pleasantest of his three-week stay, and he completely recaptured his youthful delight in the city, describing for Anatoly's benefit the modish outfit he was now sporting in this most fashion-conscious of metropolises. 'I walk along the streets in a new grey coat (demi-saison) with a most elegant top hat, showing off a silk shirt front with coral studs, and lilac-coloured gloves. Passing the mirrored piers in the Rue de la Paix or on the boulevards, I invariably stop and admire myself. In shop windows I also observe the reflection of my elegant person.'[35] That liking for fine clothes which he had displayed many years before on entering government service had now resurged, but such expenditure drained his exchequer, and when he left Paris on 12 March his funds would take him only as far as Berlin. Here he would have to wait until Jurgenson came to the rescue. He relieved his boredom a little by twice going to hear Bilse's orchestra; on the first occasion the Andante cantabile from Tchaikovsky's own First String Quartet was in the programme, splendidly played by the entire string band. Otherwise the days he had to endure waiting in hope of help from his publisher gave him much cause to regret his earlier extravagance, and the situation became so desperate that Kotek, with whom he was staying, had to pawn his watch. Finally, in desperation at Jurgenson's apparent silence, Tchaikovsky telegraphed his benefactress in Paris for an advance against his next instalment from her. She responded by return, and on 19 March he could at last escape from Berlin.

Tchaikovsky stayed only six days in St Petersburg before, on 27 March, setting out for Moscow and the first public performance two days later of *Eugene Onegin* by students of the Conservatoire. As we have seen, he returned to St Petersburg early the following morning. Coming straight from the relative freedom – and sometimes positive joys – of Western Europe, he found his antipathy to St Petersburg at its most extreme. Yet again his arrival coincided with a bereavement: the five-year-old son of Vera Butakova – who, as Vera Davïdova, had some twelve years earlier occasioned him so much distress through her passion for him – died, and the grief of the mother deeply affected the former unwilling lover, Tchaikovsky. That persistent social problem,

---

[35] *TLP8*, p. 133; *TPM2*, p. 605; *TPR*, p. 546.

the nature of which Rousseau had so clearly revealed to him, was one he had to contend with much on his return to the Russian capital, but he had to endure as patiently as he could these meetings with relatives, for his father, now growing daily more enfeebled, begged him to stay until Easter, and Tchaikovsky could hardly refuse what he realized would perhaps be the last request his parent would ever make of him. 'When I look at his wan appearance and thin face my heart contracts at the thought that his end is near,' he confided sadly to Nadezhda von Meck.[36]

But worse torture was to come. Antonina suddenly surfaced and forced a meeting upon him. It was the first time he had seen her since he had fled from her and Moscow eighteen months before, and she ensured that the reunion was as distressing as possible for him. First she watched the house where Tchaikovsky was lodging with Anatoly; the next day, 5 April, she knocked and demanded to see her husband. After she had left, Tchaikovsky recounted all that had happened to Mrs von Meck. Antonina had been asked to wait in Anatoly's study.

Hardly had I appeared than she threw herself on my neck and started to repeat endlessly that she loved only me in the whole world, that she could not live without me, that she agreed to any conditions I wanted so long as I would live with her, and so on. Probably she wanted to work upon me and, through an outpouring of tenderness, to obtain what she had been unable to get through her refusal of a divorce. I cannot tell you in detail the whole succession of scenes with which she tormented me for at least two hours. My brother Anatoly, who heard our conversation from another room, says that I behaved with tact. I tried with as much composure as I could to explain to her that, however blameworthy I might be in respect of her and however much I might wish her every happiness – yet under no circumstances would I ever agree to live with her. I confess it cost me an incredible effort of self-control not to tell her of the feelings of loathing she instils in me. Of course during this she, as always, suddenly digressed and began now to enlarge upon the craftiness of my relatives who had such a pernicious influence upon me in this matter, now to speak of my music to *Onegin* which she finds superb. Then again tears, protestations of love, and so on. I simply did not know how to break off this intolerable scene, and finally seeing that, despite my firm declaration of emphatic unwillingness to live with her, she was still trying to move me with her displays of affection, I asked her to cut

---

[36] *TPM*2, p. 83; *TLP*8, p. 155; *TZC*2, p. 277.

short her declaration and to think over for several days all I had said to her, after which she would receive from me either a letter or else a personal interview in Moscow. Meanwhile I handed her the extraordinary sum of one hundred roubles for the return journey to Moscow. At this she suddenly became as happy as a child, recounted to me several instances of men who had been in love with her during the winter, and expressed a wish to see my [twin] brothers, who appeared, and whom she showered with expressions of affection and protestations of love despite the fact that for half an hour before she had been calling them her enemies. During all this she behaved as though we were all glad to see her. Finally she left, and as she said goodbye, she asked me where we would see each other today and tomorrow as though she supposed that I was longing for meetings with her. I had to tell her that I could not see her here, and I asked her to go off to Moscow today, which she has promised to do.[37]

Much upset by this meeting, Tchaikovsky reflected that there could be no prospect of negotiating a divorce with a woman so disturbed and irrational (Antonina had declared that the stranger who had sought out Anatoly to open negotiations for divorce was a vile intriguer who was in love with her and was acting against her wishes). But Antonina's campaign was only beginning, and a week later Tchaikovsky was recounting the next skirmish to his confidante.

A certain person, having received from me the wherewithal for her return journey to Moscow, nevertheless thought fit to remain in St Petersburg, and one fine morning I met her walking near our house. It appears that she is living in the very same house as we are. I repeated to her my wish that she should go off to Moscow. . . . She replied that she could not now live far away from me, and that she would go off to Moscow at the same time as I. Then I received from her a long letter with a declaration of her passionate love for me. I did not reply. I shall simply have to flee from this unforeseen persecution of hers, and with this aim I have decided to leave here sooner than I had proposed – namely, on Easter Sunday. I shall remain in Moscow three days; on the Thursday Modest and his Kolya will arrive, along with my niece, Anna, after which we shall continue our journey to Kamenka together.[38]

[37] *TPM*2, pp. 86–7; *TLP*8, pp. 159–60.
[38] *TPM*2, p. 88; *TLP*8, p. 163.

Tchaikovsky would have held to this schedule, had not an indisposition of Kolya necessitated an extra day in Moscow, in consequence of which he had another painful encounter with his wife. Besieging him with her sister, she announced that she wished to commute Tchaikovsky's allowance to her into a lump sum of 15,000 roubles since, she said, she could not work in Russia because of the way people looked upon her, and so had decided to go abroad and devote herself to music. Tchaikovsky, of course, refused; he did not possess the necessary funds, and he knew only too well that Antonina would later return for more. Promising to write her a final reply, he left Moscow on 18 April. These meetings with his wife had made him ill, and it was in a tense, nervous condition that he arrived in Kamenka. There he wrote to Antonina the promised letter, declining her request and adding that he would return to her unopened any communication she sent him. This done, he tried to turn his attention to the pleasures and peace of Kamenka, and to scoring his First Suite.

Tchaikovsky spent the spring and summer of 1879 on estates in the Russian countryside, just as he had done in 1878. Brailov or nearby Simaki, Nizy – above all, Kamenka – all claimed a part of his time. His musical occupations included no composition except for the movement he added to the First Suite in August. Instead he devoted himself entirely to orchestrating and making a piano duet transcription of the suite, and to the far larger labour of scoring *The Maid of Orléans*. All work on the suite was quickly finished, and two days later, on 8 May, he set about the opera. It was an occupation in which he found the greatest pleasure. 'It is difficult to convey the delight you experience when an abstract musical idea takes on a real form as the result of its assignment to this or that instrument or group of instruments. If not the most pleasant, it is one of the pleasantest moments in the compositional process,' he divulged to Nadezhda von Meck while engrossed in *The Maid*.[39] The very appearance of one of his scores gave him pleasure, and corrections and alterations were offensive disfigurations of the page, he told her. Orchestration was tending to become a more extended process with him. Just as his views on what constituted good operatic writing had changed much since *Vakula* in 1874, so his conception of the special requirements of operatic scoring had clarified. At an early stage in his summer's work on *The Maid* he read through Wagner's *Lohengrin* not, as he hastened to make clear, in order to filch certain orchestral combinations, but to see what he might learn of Wagner's methods in general from the opera which he considered the peak of that composer's output.

[39] *TPM2*, p. 139; *TLP8*, p. 254; *TZC2*, p. 293; *YDGC*, p. 214; *DTC*, p. 105.

'The older I get, the more convinced I become that these two branches, i.e. *symphony* and *opera*, are in all respects the extreme opposites,' he told Nadezhda von Meck.[40] The scoring was finally completed on 2 September. Compared to the three or so weeks he had taken to score *Vakula*, the nearly four months of actual labour spent on *The Maid* was surprising, even allowing for the fact that there had been none of the urgent conditions in which the earlier work had been created. It is a measure of the careful thought he gave to matters of balance, colour and contrast that he took so long. 'If it should prove that *The Maid* still does not conform to the requirements of operatic style, then it will be clear to me that those who assert that I am by nature exclusively a symphonist, that I ought to leave the stage alone, are right,' he declared to his patroness as he returned to survey the finished score the following December.[41]

The Maid of Orléans was first produced on 25 February 1881 at the Maryinsky Theatre in St Petersburg. Despite the reputation Tchaikovsky was now beginning to enjoy in Russia, the production left much to be desired. The cast was good and the singers were generally delighted with their music. Nápravník, who was the opera's dedicatee as well as its first conductor, had required some cuts and some revisions in the part of Joan because Mariya Kamenskaya, the singer who was to create the part, was a mezzo-soprano; where Tchaikovsky had to transpose he had to do some rescoring. Some of these revisions pained him, but as he had realized when the same Nápravník had introduced *The Oprichnik* seven years before, this conductor knew his job thoroughly, and he prepared the new opera to the composer's entire satisfaction. The problems lay with the theatre management and with the provision for production. The Imperial Theatres' head of repertoire, Nikolay Lukashevich, attempted to be an autocrat in musical decisions, even on one occasion informing Tchaikovsky that he could not revise his own music without permission. Worst of all, because a vast sum had recently been spent on a new ballet, funds were very low and there was a ruling in force that no new scenery was to be made for new operas, nor was any singer permitted two costumes in one opera. Thus Lionel turned up for the coronation in the garb he had worn on the battlefield, while the set for the square outside the Gothic cathedral of Reims had already served to represent two other locations in earlier operas, having started life as a square in Warsaw. Nearly everything on stage was second-hand, and some of the costumes were threadbare.

[40] *TPM2*, p. 111; *TLP8*, p. 198; *TZC2*, p. 287; *YDGC*, p. 213.
[41] *TPM2*, p. 269; *TLP8*, pp. 445–6; *TZC2*, p. 341; *DTC*, p. 106.

The success of the opera with the first-night audience therefore
stemmed entirely from the quality of the performance, which
Tchaikovsky agreed was in general very good. 'Kamenskaya sang the
whole scene with the angels magnificently and I took eight bows after
Act 1,' he reported to Mrs von Meck three days after the première.

> Act 2 also pleased very much. Scene 1 of the third act drew a storm of
> applause. The second scene [outside Reims Cathedral] was far less
> successful; the march and the whole scene in general was mounted so
> wretchedly, grubbily and pitifully that nothing else could be ex-
> pected. On the other hand Act 4 again pleased very much. Altogether
> I took twenty-four bows. *Kamenskaya* was superb; she even acted
> extremely well, which she had never done before. Of the rest the best
> of all was *Pryanishnikov* who sang Lionel.[42]

Modest remembered that his brother had also singled out for praise
Fyodor Stravinsky as Dunois.

The critics were far more doubtful than the first-night audience
about the work's merits, and from Cui it drew blistering condemnation
(though Tchaikovsky must have been a little consoled to find that his
scoring was unreservedly praised by this universal savager).
Tchaikovsky must have foreseen this; what probably disturbed him
more was the blunt pronouncement of one critic who reaffirmed what
Tchaikovsky had heard before, but which he hoped his latest opera
would convincingly refute. 'In *The Maid of Orléans* Tchaikovsky has
again shown that he is by nature a symphonist and in no way an opera
composer,' wrote Pavel Makarov in the *Exchange Gazette*.[43]

The opera did not maintain its apparent initial success. Early next
season it had to be dropped because of a persistent throat ailment
suffered by Kamenskaya. For the revival in the 1882–3 season
Tchaikovsky made some further transpositions in Joan's part to
accommodate Kamenskaya and made new cuts, but the opera was soon
dropped and was never heard again in Russia in Tchaikovsky's lifetime. Nevertheless it was the first of his operas ever to be given abroad
(in Prague in July 1882).

Except for the early, ill-fated *Undine*, which Tchaikovsky had destroyed after it had failed to secure production, *The Maid of Orléans* was
Tchaikovsky's first opera from a non-Russian literary source. The basic
text was Schiller's play, *Die Jungfrau von Orleans*, translated (as had been

---

[42] *TPM2*, p. 478; *TLP10*, pp. 32–3; *TZC2*, pp. 453–4; *DTC*, p. 110.
[43] *DTC*, p. 110; *YDGC*, p. 252.

de la Motte Fouqué's *Undine*) by Zhukovsky. In the following summary of the plot the major excisions made by Tchaikovsky after completing the music are enclosed in square brackets:

ACT I. *A country setting, on one side a chapel with an ikon of the Virgin, on the other a tall leafy oak on the bank of a stream.*
Some girls are singing as they decorate the oak with garlands (No. 1). Thibaut, Raimond and Joan enter (No. 2). Thibaut reproves the girls for singing in such circumstances; Paris has fallen to the English, the King is a fugitive, and their own future has an imminent uncertainty. He counsels his daughter, Joan, in such circumstances to seek a protector; he wishes her to marry Raimond. When Joan remains silent, Raimond, despite his love for her, urges her father not to press her into marriage. 'Let her young life blossom freely as before,' he declares (bar 51). 'If it is not the Lord's will, my longed-for hour will not come!' There develops a terzetto, Raimond professing further his readiness to forgo his joy, while Thibaut continues reproachfully to remonstrate with his daughter, the chorus now supporting his plea. But Joan herself struggles with her inner feelings, and in the following scene (No. 3), she discloses timidly that she has been given a different destiny. Thibaut is furious, and alleges that Joan's pact is not with heaven but with the devil, and he asks her angrily why she repairs at night to the crossroads to listen to the mountain wind, and why she is constantly beneath this oak tree which has long been a haunt of evil. As Thibaut warns Joan of the punishment God will mete out to her, Raimond remains incredulous.

Suddenly the glow of a fire is seen backstage (No. 4), and the tocsin is heard. An off-stage chorus of peasants cries out in terror at the approach of the enemy who is bringing fire and destruction. The chorus rushes in and prays for deliverance. To Thibaut's plea for information Bertrand, one of the peasants, reports that two big battles have been lost, and that the enemy has reached the Loire and laid siege to Orléans, with the treacherous Duke of Burgundy and Isabelle, the King's own mother, participating in the assault. All join in cursing her. Bertrand further reports that Orléans is nervously awaiting the assault, but he adds that the enemy, including the unvanquished Salisbury, will perish. The crowd is less sure, but Joan steps forward (No. 5) and tells them to dry their tears; a saviour is at hand and, she prophesies, an armed maid will lead the defeat of the enemy at Orléans. The crowd is bewildered. When Thibaut tells his daughter to be silent, the crowd adds its disbelief in miracles. 'There are miracles!' Joan retorts (bar 28), and she declares Salisbury to be already dead. As the crowd reaffirms its disbelief, a soldier rushes in to report that Joan's prophecy is indeed correct. Even Thibaut is awestruck by his daughter's prescience, and leaves the stage. Joan exhorts the people to pray and, abetted by Raimond and Bertrand, she leads a hymn (No. 6) of supplication for victory and peace, after which all leave except Joan. She now realizes her time for departure has come (No. 7), and with great sadness she begins (bar 39) her farewell to the hills, meadows, and companions of her childhood. 'You will never again see Joan; she is bidding farewell for ever (bar

47) . . . for it is my lot to tend another flock on the fields of murderous war' (bar 95).

During Joan's farewell the light has been fading. As the finale (No. 8) begins she laments further her destiny. 'O God, leave me in my humble station!' she begs (bar 8). The chapel bell begins to toll, and Joan is suddenly bathed in bright moonlight as an offstage women's chorus of heavenly voices addresses her. 'You must don the armour of battle and encase your young breast in iron. Beware of hopes, shun earthly love! (bar 37) . . . God will place you above all earthly maidens,' the celestial chorus concludes. Joan, still in great distress of spirit, continues to beg fervently that 'the bitter cup may pass' from her, but the choir resumes its exhortation to hasten to the field of battle, where she will lead the French to victory. 'You will bring honour to the warrior, lustre and power to the throne, and you will bring Charles to Reims to take the crown' (bar 105). Joan perceives that her destiny is inescapable, and with the choir assuring her of God's support, she pledges herself to her mission. 'Everywhere I shall be victorious!' are her last confidently repeated words.

ACT 2. *A hall in the palace at Chinon.*
King Charles VII and his mistress, Agnès Sorel, are listening to a choir of minstrels (No. 10). The King finds their melancholy singing does nothing to raise his or Agnès's spirits, and he summons his gypsies, dwarfs and tumblers to restore their morale. After an extensive ballet (No. 11), he orders (No. 12) the dancers to be entertained and each to be rewarded with a golden chain. However, Dunois, a knight, contends that such gifts are impossible because the exchequer is empty and the King's own soldiers, having received no pay, are threatening to desert. The King would mortgage some of his land to raise money, but Dunois points out that the siege of Orléans threatens this land. Agnès pledges all her possessions to the King's cause, and leaves to collect them. As for the King, he declares that he would give up everything, including his kingdom, for the love of Agnès. Dunois reproves him sharply; this is no time for love, he insists, and launches (bar 62) into a vigorous exhortation to the King to remember his God-appointed role. At first (bar 88) Charles remains lost in his love for Agnès, but Dunois finally prevails, and the two men join (bar 148) in declaring their resolve to lift the siege of Orléans. A mortally wounded soldier, Lauret, enters to report a further defeat; the King should either flee or hurry to his troops, for hope yet remained. Having delivered his message, Lauret dies. Charles is in despair, and despite Dunois' exhortation to fight, he feels too much blood has already been shed, and he decides to withdraw across the Loire. In angry dismay Dunois upbraids him. 'We have no King!' he shouts (bar 221), declaring that he at least will go to perish in the ruins of Orléans. After Dunois' abrupt exit, Charles sinks exhausted on to his chair. His expressions of despair (No. 13) are interrupted by the entry of Agnès carrying her jewels. Charles turns to her for comfort, and she offers her wealth to him, including her lands and castles, to finance his campaign. But nothing can lift him from his despair, and he finally breaks down. Tenderly she tries to console him, and in an arioso (bar 70) she promises to go with him, come what may; as for Charles, he continues to find his only consolation in her. Finally they join (lento con anima) in a rapt expression of love.

As they embrace, off-stage trumpets and chorus greet the 'saviour-maid' (No. 14). Dunois and a crowd of knights and ladies rush in to tell a perplexed Charles and Agnès that fate has changed sides, and that the French have scored a great victory. Then the Archbishop [44] enters to confirm Dunois' tidings to an incredulous King: the army was on the verge of defeat when a miracle had happened. A maid had emerged from an oak grove and rallied the army, who had fallen anew upon the enemy and routed them. The Archbishop adds (bar 78) that Joan calls herself a prophetess and has promised to lift the siege of Orléans before the new moon.

Further off-stage praise of the 'saviour-maid' signals the arrival of Joan herself. To test her divine insights, the King instructs Dunois to take his place. When Joan enters (No. 15) with a body of knights and people, she quickly picks Charles out from the throng, though she has never before been in his presence. He asks her how she recognized him. 'I have seen you – but only where you were seen by no one but God,' she replies enigmatically (bar 27), and she offers to recount to him the three prayers he had secretly made one night (she tells him he may send away the crowd, but Charles says they may stay). 'First you prayed the Almighty to choose you as the sacrifice of reconciliation, and to pour for us upon your submissive head the whole cup of punishments' (bar 53). All are yet more astonished, and Joan goes on to disclose the King's second prayer – that if he should lose his throne, he should yet keep his spiritual peace, his friends, and his faithful Agnès. The crowd are again amazed. Asked by Joan (bar 85) whether she should recount the third prayer, Charles cuts her short. 'I believe!' he affirms (bar 91). 'No mortal by himself could do this. God is with you!' The crowd agree. The Archbishop asks her to tell them who she is, and Joan begins her narration (bar 130). She had been born in Domrémy, the daughter of a simple shepherd. Often she had heard how the English had tried to enslave her people, and she had prayed to the Virgin to protect them. Then once (bar 151), after she had prayed all night at the oak tree, a figure dressed like a shepherdess had appeared before her bearing a sword and banner, and had told her of her divine mission to free France and crown the King in Reims. [When Joan had questioned her own ability to do this, the figure had replied that everything was possible to a maid who rejected earthly love. The figure had touched her eyes, and the whole sky had been filled with winged cherubims bearing beautiful lilies, and a sweet voice was heard.] Three nights in a row the vision had appeared, but on the third night the figure had addressed her angrily (bar 196): 'Take up your cross, be obedient to heaven! In suffering lies purification on earth. Here you are lowly; there you will be raised up.' At this the figure had cast off her shepherdess's garb and had revealed herself to be the Virgin, had looked comfortingly upon Joan, and had then slowly disappeared upwards into heaven.

As the finale (No. 16) begins the Archbishop leads off an ensemble in which everyone accepts that Joan is divinely led, and they glorify God. After a further

---

[44] In fact the censor objected to this designation and changed 'Archbishop' to 'Pilgrim'. Tchaikovsky countered by suggesting that 'Cardinal' ought to be acceptable, since the Orthodox Church did not have cardinals.

assurance from Joan (bar 36) that she will return France to the King, Charles entrusts his army to her (bar 48) and offers her his sword. But she will not take it; the sword predestined for her is at the grave of St Catherine at Fierbois – and she wishes to bear a white banner with a purple stripe. The King orders Dunois to fetch the sword. Joan asks (bar 67) the Archbishop for his blessing and kneels before him as everyone reaffirms their faith in victory and urges Joan to lead the army to battle. Finally all go out in the wake of the King and Joan.

ACT 3, SCENE 1. *A place near the battlefield. On the heights the English camp is burning.* Lionel, a Burgundian knight, rushes in. He is followed by Joan, who challenges him. In a heated exchange she discovers his identity as a follower of the treacherous Duke of Burgundy. Joan falls upon Lionel (bar 93), and in the struggle she tears his helmet from his head. Lionel is vanquished, but as Joan is about to despatch him, a shaft of moonlight falls upon his face. Struck by his appearance, Joan stays her hand. Lionel tells her (bar 113) not to delay; he asks no mercy. But she signals him (bar 119) to flee. He scorns thus to escape. Nevertheless, Joan cannot bring herself to kill him, despite his defiant rejection of her mercy. 'Kill me, and go!' she suddenly declares (bar 137). Lionel is utterly perplexed. For a second time Joan raises her sword, but again she is unable to strike. 'Holy Virgin!' she cries out in despair (bar 152). Startled by this invocation, and moved by Joan's evident distress, Lionel feels a welling sympathy for her. He asks her gently (bar 176) who she is. 'Come with me,' he finally pleads (bar 196). 'Leave your fatal sword!' 'Alas, I am unworthy to bear it!' she cries (bar 201). Her inner struggle gives rise to an impassioned outburst. 'O God, why, ah why did I give up my shepherd's crook for a warrior's sword?' she laments (allegro moderato). Lionel's feelings grow warmer still. 'Is it pity or love which suddenly creeps into my soul?' he asks in bewilderment (bar 265). This impassioned duet proceeds until, as Lionel takes Joan's hand (bar 300), Dunois is seen approaching. Again Joan tells Lionel to flee, but he refuses. Finally, to Joan's even greater distress, he declares (bar 418) he has fallen in love with her. Dunois enters hurriedly with a small detachment. Lionel picks up his sword, kneels before Dunois and offers it to him. Dunois returns it to him (andante), accepts Lionel's return to the French side, and then turns to Joan to report that victory is theirs, and that Reims has opened its gates to them. Suddenly Joan collapses exhausted into Lionel's arms, and it is seen that she is wounded in the shoulder. 'She is bleeding!' exclaims Lionel. 'Would that my life might flow away with my blood!' Joan replies in despair. Supported by Lionel and Dunois, she goes out slowly.

ACT 3, SCENE 2. *The square in front of Reims cathedral.*
A crowd is awaiting a procession. To a grand march (No. 18) a splendid coronation cavalcade appears, with Joan preceding the King, and enters the cathedral to the sound of the crowd's loud praise of the King and the 'saviour-maid'. When the procession has disappeared into the building, Thibaut and Raimond detach themselves from the crowd (No. 19). Raimond tries to persuade Thibaut to leave, but the latter refuses. He has seen Joan's pale, distressed face. 'The hour has come to save her!' he declares (bar 39) '. . . I want to make her return to the God from whom she has turned aside!' (bar

50). Raimond remonstrates desperately with him, but Thibaut is adamant; it is his duty to save his daughter, even if her body must be reduced to ashes.

As the finale (No. 20) begins, Thibaut and Raimond once again retreat into the crowd, which begs God's blessing, and praises Him. The King, Joan and the whole procession emerge from the cathedral. The King proceeds to a throne set on a dais, and Joan takes her place near him. The crowd praises Charles, who replies with thanks, extends pardon to his enemies, and ascribes victory to God's mercy. The crowd responds with praise. The King speaks of Joan as the agent of France's victory, and decrees that an altar shall be raised to her. Again the crowd gives praise, this time to Joan. The King addresses Joan as though she were divine, and begs her to reveal her 'immortal image' so that 'we may worship thee on earth' (bar 112). But as Joan stands silent, Thibaut steps forward. Joan cries out as she recognizes her father, and Thibaut straightway denounces her as an agent of the devil. The crowd declares him mad (bar 146), but he vigorously rejects their diagnosis. Then he challenges Joan to her face: 'In the name of the Trinity, do you hold yourself to be pure and holy?' (bar 168). But because of guilt at her love for Lionel, Joan remains silent, and the crowd is horror-struck. In their bewilderment the King and people join in a gigantic ensemble, ending with a plea to God to reveal the truth. Suddenly Dunois rises to Joan's defence. 'I challenge anyone here who dares accuse her!' he shouts (bar 256), but he is answered by a great clap of thunder. All recoil from Joan in horror. Thibaut again challenges Joan, but he too is answered by a great roll of thunder. Finally when the Archbishop confronts her, a third peal of thunder confirms the fears of everyone that Thibaut's accusation is indeed true. [Another vast ensemble unfolds in which all end by turning upon Joan for having deceived them as to the source of her powers; they tell her to flee from them. The King reinforces their demand, but assures her nevertheless of a safe conduct out of Reims. The people repeat their order.[45]] The King and his followers leave hurriedly; the crowd disperses in anger and dismay. Joan remains alone, her head still bowed. Then Lionel approaches her, offering his hand and protection. When Joan raises her head and recognizes him, she recoils in revulsion, crying out: 'Away! You are my hated enemy! You have destroyed my soul!' She rushes out, followed by Lionel.

ACT 4, SCENE 1. *A wood.*
Joan is seated deep in thought. She remains torn between her God-given mission and her love for Lionel. But it is the latter feeling which now triumphs. 'O Lionel!' she cries (bar 93). 'My dear beloved, I love you more than life. Where are you? Come to me!' Lionel enters precipitately and they embrace. An extensive love duet follows (No. 22). Their rapture is broken by an off-stage chorus of angels' voices. 'Heaven's decree is broken. You are a sinner!' they begin. Joan tears herself from Lionel's embrace, to his bewilderment. She listens transfixed to the choir. The sound of advancing English soldiers is heard. [Suddenly Joan awakes as from a reverie. 'Captivity and death! Yes,

---

[45] This cut involved the removal of some 140 bars and their replacement by thirty bars of new music.

yes, but for me, not for you!' she cries to Lionel (bar 244). She urges him to flee, declaring that she will remain. 'Fate has shown me my road, and I must submit to fate,' she affirms (bar 263), but Lionel still presses her not to forgo their love. Their desperate dialogue is interrupted when[46]] a group of English soldiers suddenly rushes in. Lionel draws his sword and attempts to defend Joan, but is mortally wounded. The soldiers try to bind Joan, but she tears herself away and rushes to Lionel as he dies. 'Receive my last kiss, and wait for me. Our meeting is at hand,' she announces quietly (andante). Then she turns and stretches out her hands to her captors to receive their chains. They rush out, dragging her with them.

ACT 4, SCENE 2. *A square in Rouen.*
A crowd is waiting for the procession to arrive with Joan. 'They're bringing her! There's the witch!' the people cry, looking off-stage towards the approaching cortège. Joan enters, a priest beside her, with soldiers and monks following. 'Holy father, support me! I'm afraid!' she gasps (bar 68). The crowd presses forward in pity, but is pushed back. 'Give me a cross,' begs Joan (bar 89), and one of the soldiers breaks a stick in two, ties the pieces together, and gives them to the priest.[47] Joan is bound to the stake. The executioner sets the pyre alight, and soldiers and monks throw on more wood. The priest blesses Joan and holds the cross high before her. As the flames mount Joan cries, 'O Lord, take me to your abode!' (bar 117). The off-stage chorus of angels joins its sounds to those of the crowd. Finally Joan, 'with an expression of joy on her face' [sic], declares 'The heavens have opened! My suffering is at an end!'[48]

Though, as we have already noted, Schiller afforded the main sub-stance of Tchaikovsky's scenario, and Zhukovsky's translation a good many lines of the libretto, suggestions from other sources Tchaikovsky consulted also found their way into *The Maid of Orléans*; thus the idea for the opening chorus came from Mermet's libretto for his own opera, *Jeanne d'Arc*. The rest of Act 1 was drawn largely from Schiller, though Tchaikovsky transferred to this scene Joan's prescient announcement of Salisbury's death which, in *Die Jungfrau*, had been delivered to the King at Chinon. Significantly, most of the chorus's contributions, both here and elsewhere in the opera, were Tchaikovsky's inventions (as was the introduction of the mortally wounded Lauret in Act 2). The chorus of terrified peasants was his idea; so, too, were the angel voices which

---

[46] This section had accounted for some 100 bars.

[47] The censor objected to the representation of the cross on the stage, and this incident had to be excised in St Petersburg with the loss of some thirteen bars.

[48] In addition to the cuts indicated in this résumé of the plot of *The Maid*, Tchaikovsky made some other revisions. The final section (in F minor) of the Act 2 duet for the King and Dunois was rewritten and reduced from some fifty-odd bars to twenty, and a dozen bars in the first part of Joan's narration later in the same act were replaced by four bars of orchestral writing (bars 147–50). Finally the orchestral introduction (andante con moto) to the duet in the first scene of Act 4 was halved in length.

use part of God's command as Joan recalls it in her farewell soliloquy at the end of Schiller's prologue. In Act 2 the brief mention which Schiller made of the King's preoccupations with troubadours and entertainments for Agnès Sorel was the slender excuse for the minstrels' chorus and the ballet. Though most of what follows in this act observes the course of events as set out by Schiller, the libretto itself is almost entirely by Tchaikovsky up to the moment when the first tidings of victory are brought; after this it is drawn almost entirely from Zhukovsky's translation.

Whereas in these two acts Tchaikovsky had mostly been savagely truncating *Die Jungfrau von Orleans*, he had to supplement Schiller liberally in the first scene of Act 3, for Schiller had made the Joan/Lionel conflict very brief. Once the confessions of love begin no help was to be found in *Die Jungfrau*, though part of the final exchange between Joan and Lionel is from that play. It is in this scene that Tchaikovsky introduced the first substantial modification of plot, for Lionel, in Schiller an English officer, is now transformed into a Burgundian knight. This made it easier for him to change allegiance and thus figure in the coronation scene, and also more freely pursue his relationship with Joan in the last act. The end of this first scene of Act 3, where Lionel offers his sword to Dunois, was, of course, Tchaikovsky's invention, though Joan's wound and her last despairing utterance were not.

Schiller's real gift to Tchaikovsky was the coronation scene. The grand march, with its attendant tumult as the royal procession enters the cathedral of Reims, was all specified in *Die Jungfrau* and Tchaikovsky complied with Schiller's stage directions as closely as possible. Though he felt compelled to extend the Thibaut/Raimond dialogue and create a full triumphal chorus for the procession's re-entry from the cathedral, almost everything until Thibaut makes his first direct challenge to his daughter sets a virtually unabridged chunk from Schiller's fourth act. Tchaikovsky did, however, transfer some individual exclamations to the chorus, as well as inventing the texts in the huge ensemble which follows (and also in the second ensemble which he subsequently cut). By contrast, however, both the text and the basic idea of the scene's end, where Lionel approaches Joan to take her to safety, were Tchaikovsky's own. And with this scene Tchaikovsky's debt to Schiller virtually ceased. The first scene of the last act was entirely Tchaikovsky's conception, though Joan's opening words are drawn from her soliloquy at the beginning of Schiller's Act 4, and Schiller provided the suggestion for Joan's voluntary surrender at the end. As for the last scene, the idea for this came from Jules Barbier's tragedy, *Jeanne d'Arc*; in Schiller Joan had received a mortal wound on the field of battle.

Schiller described *Die Jungfrau von Orleans* as a 'romantic tragedy', a clear sign that he had not been concerned simply to filter through his personal vision of the human condition those historical events which had, in 1429, taken a young French peasant girl from her home to the royal court to become the instrument of victory against the invading English, and finally, in 1431, to a brutal end at the stake. For Schiller Joan was a figure of innocence, the reality of whose historical existence might be reshaped into a drama of sin and guilt ending in expiation and redemption. Thus he invented the romantic episode of Joan's love for the English knight, Lionel – an attachment which deflects her from the mission assigned to her by heaven. To be redeemed requires of Joan not merely a resumption of her mission but an act of atonement as emphatic as had been her sin. Had Schiller allowed her to perish through the sentence of an earthly court, as had the historical Joan, she might have appeared merely the helpless victim of events; hence in *Die Jungfrau* she received the mortal blow on the battlefield again actively struggling for her God-assigned cause.

This interpretation of Schiller's drama will scarcely cancel the offence many will feel at his violation of the real Joan, but for Tchaikovsky such distortions did not matter. What drew him to Joan was the image he could conjure of a young, sensitive girl, possessed by divine visions yet vulnerable to her own emotions, who is finally destroyed by circumstances from which she cannot escape. Tchaikovsky saw Joan, like Tatyana before her, as a victim of fate, and it was this, not historical scruples, which moved him to replace Schiller's allegorical end with something closer to chronicled fact. There is an element of fate in *Die Jungfrau*, yet when Schiller's Joan rushes to the field of battle she carries with her the possibility of survival; when Tchaikovsky's Joan enters the square at Rouen, the certainty of her end is absolute.

In the opera there is therefore nothing like Schiller's consistency of dramatic vision. But Tchaikovsky went further, not merely weakening the character of Joan, but debasing it. Schiller had presented her love for Lionel as a sudden involuntary response, scarcely to be condemned as a sin since no act of will was involved, yet sufficient to impair her singlemindedness. Nor was there any question of her yielding to temptation. On the contrary, she strove to master her feelings, begged for death rather than be confronted by Lionel again, and only saw him in captivity where she again unequivocally rejected his propositions. But Tchaikovsky's Joan fully indulges her emotions in a way which makes the attempt in the final scene to transform this languishing girl into an heroic martyr to whom is granted a place in the kingdom of heaven about as credible as turning Juliet into the Virgin herself.

As a piece of coherent, serious drama Tchaikovsky's scenario is therefore irredeemably flawed. Yet given the same basic stimulus as *Onegin* – that is, a central character who is a young girl caught up in a train of events which leads to misfortune – it might have been hoped that Tchaikovsky's inspiration would have been awakened. It was not. Tatyana and her fate had touched the sources of Tchaikovsky's creativity at their very deepest level, where had been born ideas of eloquent directness which embodied some of the central emotions and predicaments of the story; there, too, all-mastering fate had converted itself into pregnant thematic forms which could become generating forces within the musical tissue, or which could infiltrate a variety of musico-dramatic situations, thus ubiquitously signalling the active workings of that ineluctable power. But Joan's plight never really gripped Tchaikovsky, and in *The Maid* there is nothing like the abundance of thematic significances to be found in *Onegin*. True, there is a kind of 'fate' theme associated with Joan's calling, this time embodied in a rising scale since her destiny is heaven-inspired. The words to which Tchaikovsky first devised this protoshape occur in the recognition scene in Act 2 (Ex. 153a), and it infiltrated some of the other music he subsequently wrote for contexts which allude to her calling in the earlier parts of the opera.[49] When Thibaut turns to Joan at the opera's opening, exhorting her to take an earthly protector in such perilous times, the oboe quietly enunciates a similar rising phrase (Ex. 153b) as an intimation of that factor which must override all considerations of earthly security. The idea haunts the following pages, even with a gentle irony affording Raimond his opening in the terzetto where he declares his readiness to forgo Joan's love if such be the will of God (later this same phrase explicitly dresses Joan's confession of her 'other calling' (Ex. 153c)). The protoshape is prominent in Joan's oblique disclosure to the people of Domrémy of her mission (Ex. 153d), and in her farewell aria later in the scene it may again be discerned (Ex. 153e) though, curiously, this seems to be an even more explicit, if inexplicable, quotation from Chopin's famous A major Polonaise (Gerald Abraham has drawn attention to Tchaikovsky's unconscious recollection of Mozart's Jupiter Symphony during the first duet of the second

---

[49] In Acts 3 and 4 this protoshape seems to have no part – except, that is, for one curious moment when Joan, during her first stormy encounter with Lionel, questions whether he had been sent by some infernal power.

act). For a moment, too, just before Joan's entry in Act 2, a hint of this same phrase is slipped in by the oboe as Charles changes place with Dunois, the King observing that Joan will be able to discover him if she truly possesses insight from heaven (Ex. 153f).

Ex. 153

[That is the one to whom heaven has sent me!]

[For a woman in such calamitous times]

[Ah, another calling has been decided for this humble maid!]

d. Moderato [voice part only]

Joan

Spa - si - tel zhiv, grya - det, grya - det on v si - le, mo - gu - chy vrag pa -

[The Saviour lives, he approaches in strength; the mighty foe will fall near Orleans]

- det pod Or - le - a - nom, no

e. [Andantino] L'istesso tempo [voice part only]

Joan

Tak vïsh - ne - ye na - zna - chi - lo iz - bran - nye; me -

[Thus the Almighty makes his choice; it is not a desire for empty things which draws me!]

- nya vle - chet ne - su - yet - nïkh zhe - la - nye!

f. Ben sostenuto il tempo

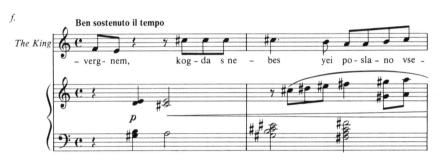

The King

- verg- nem, kog - da s ne - bes yei po - sla - no vse -

[when omniscience is sent her from heaven]

- zna - nye,

g. [Allegro vivo] Poco meno mosso [voice part only]

Joan

Kto tï? te - bya po - slal ne - do - bry an - gel!

[Who are you? A wicked angel sent you!]

Tchaikovsky set about *The Maid of Orléans* with the avowed intention of purging his operatic style of what he felt were inappropriate 'symphonic' features. 'Opera should be the most popular of all musical forms,' he had declared to Nadezhda von Meck while deep in composing *The Maid*. 'Thus operatic style must relate to those of symphonic and chamber music as decorative painting relates to academic.'[50] Patently one consequence of this conviction was the suppression of any thematic working whose effect might be musical rather than overtly dramatic. Certainly there is a very reduced number of thematic cross-references in *The Maid* compared with *Onegin*, and when such repetitions do occur they are so explicit that their dramatic point is unmistakable; indeed, their bluntness often makes them seem trite. The most obvious of these labels is the 'heavenly voices' music which has its origins in Joan's Act 2 narration, and which Tchaikovsky simply slotted in at the two points where these angelic mentors address Joan. Exactly the same passage is quoted in the orchestra earlier in Act 2 to accompany the Archbishop's report of Joan's divinely ordained arrival on the field of battle. The stately music to which the saviour-maid had appeared before the King in Act 2, and which had loudly rounded off the scene, is likewise cited orchestrally in the coronation scene when the King reminds the people how Joan had saved his throne. Later, as Dunois comes forward to defend Joan, and the Archbishop to inquisition her, music associated with each in Act 2 is recalled. Perhaps the Archbishop's self-quotation was intended to be ironic; yet in neither case does the recollection sound like anything more than a formal stamp of identity of the most obvious kind. Nor is there any very compelling dramatic justification for repeating orchestrally the first half of the Hymn of Act I as the entr'acte to Act 2. Recall is used more subtly in the Act 4 entr'acte where faint thematic allusions to the end of the previous scene shadow Joan's thoughts as she broods upon her rejection by King and people, and on Lionel's final bid to persuade her to go with him. But this entr'acte is weakened by excessive use of diminished sevenths, as is the entr'acte to Act 3, where tritely explosive imagery does no more than forewarn of a tense situation when the curtain rises.

This dearth of thematic allusiveness is especially evident in the last stages of the opera where there is no accumulation of familiar material to draw together and finally focus major elements within the drama and music; similarly, at the opposite end of the opera, the overture provides less compendious forewarning of drama to come than some earlier

---

[50] *TLP8*, p. 67; *TPM2*, p. 37; *TZC2*, p. 259; *YDGC*, p. 205.

specimens. In the allegro vivo are represented only the French peasantry (the alarm music preceding their first chorus in Act 1, followed by a derivative from this same chorus) and Joan (her theme of dedication from the end of Act 1, where she had signified her assent to her celestial instructors by briefly echoing their music). As for the attractive tune which provides the substance for the flanking sections, this has no direct connection with anything that follows. This overture's ternary structure, with its patent use of the solo flute as the symbol of innocence, must raise some suspicion that Tchaikovsky's contempt for Verdi's *Giovanna d'Arco* did not leave him unwilling to take suggestions from the earlier opera. Likewise that 'universal symbol, the descending semitone of grief', as Julian Budden calls it,[51] which occurs prominently in the opening of Verdi's opera, is a tiny melodic idea featuring occasionally but significantly in *The Maid*, presenting itself first in the overture's allegro vivo (in the middle of the peasants' alarm music), appearing in the orchestral preliminaries to Joan's farewell aria in Act 1, recurring in the orchestra during the first scene of Act 3 to embody something of Joan's anguish as love for Lionel begins to undermine her zeal for her divine mission (No. 17, bars 125ff.), and similarly disclosing the torment Thibaut experiences in the coronation scene as he braces himself to denounce his daughter for the sake of her immortal soul (No. 19, bars 38ff.).

But such connections with *Giovanna d'Arco* are superficial, and Tchaikovsky showed none of Verdi's crisply dramatic approach, and little of his psychological insight. All too often the music of *The Maid* seems little more than a step-by-step setting of a libretto. Tchaikovsky's avowed strivings for greater lucidity are evident above all in the ariosi of the dialogues, which are sometimes so functional melodically and so sparingly accompanied that they become virtually recitatives. Certainly the dialogue is efficiently despatched, but there is a cumulative impression of melodic parsimony. Only rarely in this flow of musical prose does some memorable phrase raise itself above the general level of the stream as a lyrical or dramatic landmark to give point to the listener's journey. This paucity of inner drama and lack of thematic distinctiveness are by no means compensated by positive qualities in the opera's numerous ensembles. And it is in Tchaikovsky's widespread use of the chorus, mostly in dramatic dialogue with the soloists but at other times united with them in more formal ensemble, that we find the strongest clue to his motivation in this opera. As Gerald Abraham has observed, there can be little doubt that with *The Maid of*

[51] Julian Budden, *The Operas of Verdi*, vol. 1 (London, 1973), p. 209.

Orléans Tchaikovsky was hoping to break into the international operatic scene. The subject of Joan was likely to have a far greater appeal to a non-Russian audience than any he had previously treated; likewise, Tchaikovsky had so shaped the scenario as to afford the sort of situations where he could achieve strong effects which might score ready success. For if Schiller was the source of Tchaikovsky's subject, the French grand opera tradition in general, and Meyerbeer in particular, were the begetters of the musical manners in this opera. Having, in *The Voyevoda* of 1868, succeeded in smothering much of the dramatic life under the sheer weight of the formal ensembles, Tchaikovsky had drastically reduced the use of such movements in the operas immediately following, using them only sparingly in *The Oprichnik* and abandoning them altogether in the original *Vakula*. There is a resurgence of such ensemble writing in *Onegin*, but in *The Maid* Tchaikovsky rehabilitated the solo/choral movement with a vengeance, at any excuse congealing the flow of events into a more formal ensemble, the greater part of the structure being spread across a frame built from a single melody, with the participants simply slotting themselves into the melodic/harmonic fabric. The expressive consistency which results from such a procedure inevitably renders such ensembles statuesque, consensus movements aiming to convey a single weighty emotion, not to demonstrate a diversity of dramatic stances. There is justification for such an approach in the Hymn (No. 6) of Act 1, though the theme with which Joan leads off this corporate prayer is too bland by far. The less extensive ensemble of acknowledgment which the King initiates in Act 2 after Joan has recounted to him his recent dreams is better, partly because it is kept within bounds, partly because the theme on which it is founded, though far from one of Tchaikovsky's best, is stronger. Much the same might be said of the balancing ensemble which follows Joan's narration, though the endeavour of the participants to assume more independent roles begins to expose the crippling constrictions within Tchaikovsky's ensemble technique. The largest of the formal ensemble movements occurs towards the end of the coronation scene as all stand stunned at Joan's refusal to deny her father's charge of impurity. Here Tchaikovsky's method could only spell disaster, for the essential diversity of viewpoint among the participants is engulfed in tumid textures. Drama has been replaced by emotional swell.

Even more disastrous, though for quite different reasons, is the final scene of the opera, which provides one of the two formal tableaux of the piece. The first of these had occupied the opening of the coronation scene which had unfolded against the background of a grand choral/orchestral march, brilliant in manner (the scoring of this caused

Tchaikovsky many problems) but thematically unremarkable, even stodgy, with a particularly gross coda. The second tableau fills the whole last scene, the musical model for which was patently the slow movement of Mendelssohn's Italian Symphony, said to have been inspired by a religious procession seen in Naples. This symphony had long been one of Tchaikovsky's favourites, and he clearly decided that music using the same sort of measured pizzicato bass supporting a leisurely tune – and set, like Mendelssohn's slow movement, in D minor (one of Tchaikovsky's special keys of misfortune, even tragedy) – would make an apt background for the procession leading Joan to the stake. But background it remains. As for the deep emotion which had possessed Tchaikovsky on reading Wallon's account of Joan's end, this had by now been perverted, and the scene becomes a rosy sublimation of Joan's appalling sufferings. The hideous distastefulness of the end, where Joan, supported by angel chorus and thudding drum, ecstatically declares that the sufferings she has patently not endured are over and that heaven is opened to her, makes this one of Tchaikovsky's worst indiscretions. According to Modest, who had perceived the vulgarity of this ending, his brother came to share this view, and in the last weeks of his life was planning to substitute an ending based on Schiller.

Of course there are some positive things in *The Maid of Orléans* – even some fine ones. All Tchaikovsky's earlier operas had contained purely decorative choral movements, and one launches each of the first two acts of *The Maid*. That which opens the opera, it may be objected, places the locale not in France but Russia; nevertheless, one forgives this geographical ineptitude when offered such an enchanting example of that species of female chorus whose origins lay deep in Glinka's art. By contrast the chorus of minstrels at the beginning of Act 2 attempts self-consciously to confirm its location by employing the French song, *Mes belles amourettes*, which Tchaikovsky had used the previous year in his *Mélodie antique française*, No. 16 of his Children's Album, Op. 39. Yet even here Tchaikovsky could not completely silence his national voice, for this chorus's mild languor and melancholy oboe refrain draws it gently eastwards. The following ballet includes some worthwhile music, the dance for pages and dwarfs marking a sudden retreat towards the eighteenth century for another of Tchaikovsky's rococo stylizations, while the final tumblers' dance, vigorous and characterful, provides by far the best instrumental movement in the whole opera. Even the recitative sometimes flickers into life for an instant: for example, at the opening of the finale to Act 1 when Joan, having bade her decisive formal farewell to the familiar places and persons she must now leave, suddenly falters in her resolve as the pain of departure floods

in upon her (Ex. 154), the orchestra sympathetically echoing her cry.
The music to which Agnès offers the King her possessions in Act 2 has
some genuine expressive substance; even more affecting is Joan's
despairing entreaty at the end of her first fateful encounter with Lionel
when, wounded, she pleads for death to escape the new torment
brought into her life by the awakening of earthly love. Her phrase is
taken up by the orchestra and brooded upon before sinking into silence
in a final slow arpeggio. But the loveliest moment in all these wide acres
of undernourished recitative is Joan's first direct address to Charles in
the recognition scene. What man would not fall beneath the spell of a
young girl who addressed him in such meltingly lyrical terms! (Ex.
155).

Ex. 154

[O God, leave me to my humble lot! You, my native home]

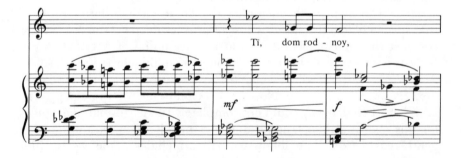

There are few formal solos in *The Maid*. The first is Joan's farewell
aria at the end of Act 1, a piece of some musical substance employing
that descending-chromaticism-over-a-pedal which was such a favoured and characteristic device with Russian composers ever since
Glinka had discovered its potential. This time Tchaikovsky does not
embed the chromaticism in the accompaniment but draws it out into
full prominence by making it fundamental to the opening melody (Ex.

Ex. 155

156). Its pathos is unfailing, while the firmness of melodic outline, already clearly displayed in Joan's first phrase and well maintained throughout the succeeding pages, ensures that pain is matched by resolve. Agnès, too, is favoured with an arioso in Act 2. Though the opening harmonic formula (see Ex. 158a) is perhaps the only readily recognizable Tchaikovskyan mark on this music, the King's devoted mistress roused Tchaikovsky's sympathy sufficiently for her to draw from him some touching music. The brief G flat duet in which she joins with Charles shows Tchaikovsky once again drawing his inspiration from the famous G flat 'Tu l'as dit' in *Les Huguenots*, but this rapt expression of mutual love becomes very much Tchaikovsky's own with its characteristic chromaticism and ravishing emphasis upon the Neapolitan region. By comparison the earlier duet for Dunois and Charles is faceless, though conventionally effective, a compliment which cannot be paid to the duettino between Thibaut and Raimond in the coronation scene. This and the preceding scena, where the need to write music which might credibly be coming from the organ in the cathedral found Tchaikovsky at a loss how to maintain any musical focus, is one of the dreariest stretches in the whole opera.

Ex. 156

[Farewell, hills, my native fields, peacefully sheltering, serene dale, farewell!]

Fortunately the two duets for Joan and Lionel cannot be charged with dullness. As in *Onegin* Tchaikovsky employed two types of scene in *The Maid*: those using large forces, and those which centre exclusively (or almost so) on only two characters — and it is the more intimate scenes which draw the more consistent music from him. The second of these lovers' encounters contains the more formal duet, for here Joan ceases to struggle with her feelings, and both lovers surrender to their impulses with quiet rapture (Ex. 157). The C flat/C natural ambivalence of the motif which concludes Joan's answering phrase is subsequently exploited by Tchaikovsky to broaden the tonal field until the climax is reached in a shift to E major (Tchaikovsky's special key of ecstatic love)[52] for a new phrase (Ex. 158b) in which any lingering hesitancy is set aside for full commitment to mutual passion. That same progression with which Tchaikovsky had favoured Agnès in her Act 2 arioso (Ex. 158a) recurs as this key of joy is reached, and the

[52] That this key possessed special qualities for Tchaikovsky is clearly revealed in a letter he wrote to Nápravník before the first production of *The Maid*, in which, while agreeing to make a transposition of the duet, he added that he would prefer to rewrite the vocal part in the E major section rather than sacrifice the key. In the end, however, Tchaikovsky made a straightforward transposition of the whole duet.

Ex. 157

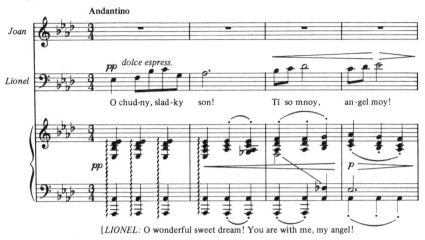

[*LIONEL:* O wonderful sweet dream! You are with me, my angel!

JOAN: O wonderful, sweet dream! You are with me, my dear!]

Ex. 158

a.

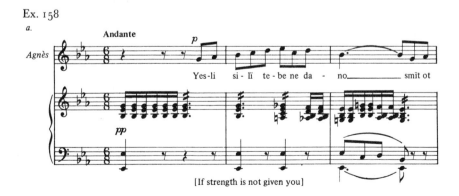

[If strength is not given you]

b.

[*JOAN:* Wondrous gift of love! Unforgettable hour — joyous, blissful — O, if only you

could last for ever. *LIONEL:* Wondrous gift of love!]

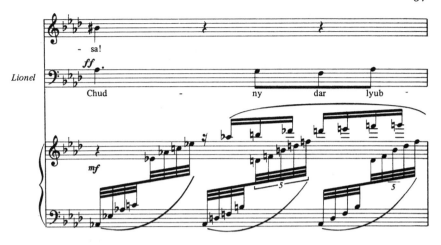

unobtrusive but all-pervading chromaticism, especially when set above a pedal, pronounces these lovers more Slav than Gallic. Yet, characteristic as it is, this duet lacks the melodic expansiveness of Tchaikovsky at his best. Taken as a whole, the earlier Joan/Lionel scene is the more notable achievement, for here Tchaikovsky had to confront the problem of how to effect the transition from extreme antagonism to mutual – if, on one side, undeclared – love. Though patchy, there is much worthy of admiration in his handling of this evolving dialogue, from the plangent C minor music to which Joan first admits the weakening of her lethal intent towards Lionel to that gentle, wondering phrase in which

Lionel confesses the spell Joan's femininity is weaving for him, opening out, as he begs her to come with him, into that same radiant E major in which they are to seal their passion in the next love scene (Ex. 159). There is also a quiet blend of warmth with pain in the phrase with which Joan begins the more formal duet which soon ensues.

Ex. 159

[I feel pity for your radiant beauty, pity for your youth; your sweet image impresses itself

on my soul, and I would wish to save you. But where is salvation? Follow me, abandon your terrible

alliance.]

- di za mnoy, o-stav so - yuz svoy strash-ny,

But all these various moments and movements must yield place to Joan's narration in Act 2. The recognition scene, if inconsistent in quality, is by far the finest stretch in the whole opera: silver rather than gold, perhaps, but certainly more precious than the baser metals from which much of the rest of *The Maid* is cast. And in this silver setting Joan's narration is the jewel. It opens with simple dignity in A flat (Ex. 160a), shifting from its quietly firm diatonicism to a more mysterious chromaticism when Joan begins to describe her visions (Ex. 160b), and ending in the full brightness of E major, the key in which she is also to confess her greatest earthly happiness. It is the most spontaneous

Ex. 160

a.

Moderato e semplice

p simply and calmly

Joan

Svya-toy o - tets, me - nya zo-vut Io - an - na; ya doch prosto-vo pa-stu-

[Holy father, I'm called Joan; I'm the daughter of a simple shepherd.]

- kha.

b.

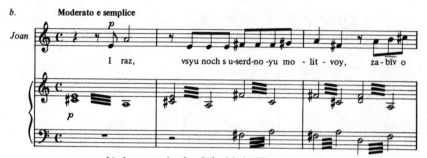

I raz,   vsyu noch s u-serd-no-yu mo - lit - voy,   za-bïv o

[And once, passing the whole night in diligent prayer with no thought of sleep,

sne   si - de - la ya pod   dre - vom,   pre - chi - sta-ya pred-sta - la mne;

I was sitting beneath a tree, when a beautiful figure appeared to me; in her hands were a sword and

v ru-kakh   ye-yo bïl   mech   i znam - ya,   no o-de-ta o-

banner, though she was dressed as a shepherdess like me.]

- na bï-la kak ya, · pa - stush-koy,   i ska-

movement in the whole opera, the declaration of a simple soul who can speak of earthly things and heavenly visions with unaffected eloquence and visionary rapture in a manner so natural, so untainted by rhetoric, that for a moment the stage is occupied by a young girl as real as Tatyana.

In January 1878, less than a year before setting about *The Maid of Orléans*, Tchaikovsky had written to Taneyev from Sanremo defending his earlier choice of *Onegin* in the face of Taneyev's reservations.

I worked [on *Onegin*] with indescribable enthusiasm and delight, caring little whether there were effects, movement, and so on. . . . If you find such things in something like *Aida*, for instance, then I'll assure you that not for all the riches in the world could I now write an opera with such a subject, for I need people, not dolls. I will willingly compose any opera where, even though there are no strong and startling effects, beings like myself experience feelings which I have experienced and understood. I don't know, I don't understand the feelings of an Egyptian princess, of a pharaoh, of some crazy Nubian woman. Some instinct suggests to me that these people must have moved, spoken, felt, but they must have expressed their feelings in some completely individual way, not as we do. . . . You ask me what I need. Let me tell you. I need [a subject] without kings, queens, tumultuous crowd effects, battles, marches – in a word, all those things which are the attributes of grand opera.[53]

And in describing what he did *not* need, Tchaikovsky could have been talking about *The Maid of Orléans*. Beguiled by the figure of Joan as a victim of fate, and prompted, perhaps, by less admirable commercial considerations, he had produced a work which ironically confirmed all too well the wisdom in his letter to Taneyev. Tchaikovsky simply had not been touched by his characters, had not felt with them, and in consequence he had been driven to dramatic formulae. *The Maid* is a work of effects without causes – or, at least, without causes offering adequate justification for the noisy sound edifices which Tchaikovsky so readily fabricated. Any listener who searches for deeper resonances, for those vastly varied, subtler sounds which reflect with truth the variety and richness within human emotion and behaviour – that is, any listener who comes to *The Maid* from *Onegin* – must quickly sense how hollow so much of it is.

[53] *TLP*7, pp. 21–2; *TZC*2, pp. 79–80; *TTP*, pp. 23–4.

A Note on the First Suite, and on
Certain Persons and Places

In Volume I of this study it was suggested that Tchaikovsky secretly embodied
a personal relationship from his own life in his symphonic poem, *Fatum*, and his
First Piano Concerto by the use of material cipher-generated from names. It is
possible that similar procedures may have produced some of the thematic
material of the First Suite. Again, however, the evidence cannot be considered
conclusive; thus I have excluded it from the main text of this last chapter.

The two main themes of the first movement, *Introduzione e Fuga*, of the
First Suite are scarcely characteristic of Tchaikovsky and, moreover, are dull.
This makes it difficult to believe they were really free conceptions. However, in
view of the deliberate mystery with which Tchaikovsky shrouded the identity
of the suite's dedicatee, it seems quite plausible that he should in some covert
way inscribe the dedication within the work itself. In fact, the fugue subject
could well be an abbreviated, but quite strict cipher derivative from one of
Tchaikovsky's forms of address to his patroness: 'Nadejda Filaretoffna, mily
drug' ('Nadezhda Filaretovna, dear friend') (Ex. 161a):

Ex. 161

That this fugue subject had fundamental significance in this suite is
confirmed by its influence upon thematic material elsewhere in the work. Its
conditioning of the main theme of the Gavotte is made explicit when, at the end
of the whole suite, this theme converts itself back into the fugue subject; less
obvious is the way the first theme of the Intermezzo (Ex. 161b) is built upon
the same contour which rises through a tenth from D to F and then sinks back
towards its initial note. The outline of the opening of the fugue subject is
reproduced at the beginning of the *Marche miniature*, and it recurs in the
gentle oboe theme in the middle of the Scherzo (since this movement was
sketched before the *Introduzione e Fuga*, this similarity could be coincidental;
otherwise it signifies that Tchaikovsky had already synthesized this thematic
tribute to his patroness before embarking on composition). The prominent
stepwise mediant-tonic descent at the apex of the fugue subject is reproduced
prominently in the second theme of the Intermezzo and towards the end of the
first section of the Divertimento.

The theme of the *Introduzione* is also a stiff invention. In view of Tchaikovsky's delight in the three main locations in which he spent the summer of 1878, and the joy and comfort he derived above all from the company of his sister, brother-in-law, and twin brothers, it seems equally plausible that he might wish these precious associations also to be secretly incorporated into this work which he began as the summer moved towards its close. It is a fact that if one takes the initial interval(s) which can be generated from the names of these places and persons (in two instances using inversions), every note of the initial theme of the work is neatly accounted for (though one minor modification is required for tonal reasons near the end) (Ex. 162).

Ex. 162

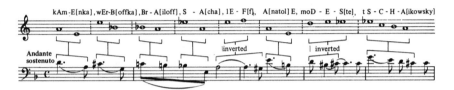

2

A NEW HOME:

SECOND PIANO CONCERTO

STRAVINSKY, ONCE ASKED what he loved most about his native Russia, replied: 'The violent Russian spring that seemed to begin in an hour and was like the whole earth cracking.'[1] As one reads the letters Tchaikovsky wrote from Kamenka in April 1879 it becomes obvious that he, too, responded sharply to this abrupt eruption of long-dormant nature – to (as he wrote) the sudden budding of the trees, the flowering of violet and lilac, the awakening of the nightingales, the splendour of the sunrises and the enchanting moonlit nights. Normally Tchaikovsky found little delight in the situation of his sister's home: the one thing which could reconcile him to the place, he told Anatoly, was a daily walk with Shibka, the Kamenka dog, through the neighbouring Trostyanka woods. But during that time when nature was being so magically transformed all Kamenka's shortcomings became tolerable. 'Spring's beauties are so bewitching that I forget the Yids, the smell of the factory, and so on,' he wrote cheerfully to Anatoly on 28 April, a week after his arrival for the summer of 1879.[2]

The arrangement on which Tchaikovsky returned to Kamenka this time was new. Reckoning that with his allowance from Mrs von Meck and receipts from his own compositions he had an annual income of some 7,000 to 8,000 roubles, he had insisted he should pay his own way – though whether this actually happened seems to have been a different matter. By so doing he could reasonably ask for accommodation more ideal for his requirements, he could install his personal belongings which had been sent from Moscow, and he could be free from some of the social constraints which had hedged round his visits as a family guest. If he had a home at all, then Kamenka was now that home. When he arrived there with Modest and Kolya he wasted no time in settling himself into a daily routine. A month earlier he had asked his benefac-

---

[1] I. Stravinsky: *Memories and Commentaries* (London, 1960), p. 30.
[2] *TLP*8, p. 176; *TPR*, p. 554.

tress whether he might spend some time in the peace of Brailov ahead of her own visit, but he had no intention of leaving Kamenka before Modest's departure in the middle of May; nor for the moment did he want anything to interrupt work on his First Suite. The fortunes of the Fourth Symphony had taught him how important it was to get a new work into print. If the preparation of the piano-duet version was entrusted to another, work might be delayed, and if a single manuscript score was all that was available, this severely restricted the number of performances which might be given. Tchaikovsky had already agreed with Jurgenson that the latter would begin engraving the score, parts and piano-duet transcription of his suite forthwith so that materials might be readily available to meet all demands, and he had determined to finish the orchestration and make the piano-duet version himself before leaving Kamenka. His faith in the successful future of his suite was fortified by the experience of playing it to a Kamenka audience. 'Everybody with me here is crazy about the Andante, and after my brother and I had played it as a piano duet, one girl had hysterics (that's a fact!!!)! To reduce the fair sex to hysterics is surely the height of artistic triumph!' he wrote jubilantly to Jurgenson.[3]

The first three weeks Tchaikovsky spent at Kamenka were marred only by universal concern for Sasha. There is no doubt that, though Lev ran the estate with admirable efficiency, the dominating personality in the Kamenka household was his wife. A few days after her brother's arrival Sasha heard that the French governess she had been trying to engage for her children was in Kiev. Not trusting anyone else to deal with this matter, she had rushed off to Kiev, where she had fallen ill. A telegram had arrived at Kamenka summoning Lev to bring her home, and leaving the rest of the family for two days in a state of alarm. The cares of being a mother and mistress of the estate, coupled with a congenital inability to relax, had reduced Sasha to a nervous state which was to afford much anxiety to the family during this summer, and which proved the harbinger of worse to come. Fortunately his sister's ailments did not impede Tchaikovsky's enjoyment of his own thirty-ninth birthday, celebrated by a day-long picnic in the Trostyanka woods. There was a similar event for Modest's birthday on 13 May; the next day Tchaikovsky left for Brailov.

Here, as intended, he rested entirely from work. Yet for all the peacefulness of his surroundings, Marcel's solicitude, the natural beauty of the place, he was restless. It was not simply that everything about the house was *too* new, that last year he had already exhausted his

[3] *TLP*8, p. 183; *TZC*2, pp. 285–6; *TPM*2, p. 610; *TPJ*1, p. 93.

subjects of conversation with Marcel – nor was it only that he soon became bored with inactivity and was killing time. Haunting him all the while was Antonina. Through Anatoly he had heard that she was again talking of divorce, but in the light of all her past behaviour Tchaikovsky responded very cautiously. He was ready to accept the blame, he wrote, and to pay up to 5,000 roubles of the costs, but he would only agree to begin proceedings if he was convinced that this time she was in earnest. As for the 10,000 roubles she would have received under an earlier settlement, she must understand that these were no longer available, though privately he instructed Anatoly to use his discretion about offering extra money payments if Anatoly thought these would advance his cause. A further reason for unease, even alarm, was to hear that Vladimir Shilovsky had been spreading rumours about Tchaikovsky's financial indebtedness to him. An angry Tchaikovsky wasted no time in denying the alleged debt of 28,000 roubles, claiming that it amounted to no more than 7,550 over the last ten years. Be that as it may, the details as set out by Tchaikovsky in his letter of repudiation indicate that between 1869 and 1876 he had received sums of an order which confirms a particularly close relationship between him and Shilovsky. Yet one suspects that Tchaikovsky was disquieted not by the facts of the relationship as known to himself, but only by the way they might appear to others. His condition for forgiving Shilovsky was unexpected. He began by arguing that if he did indeed owe 28,000 roubles, then 20,450 were still unpaid by Shilovsky. 'Now when I live solely by those casual sums which my morceaux malingres et rachitiques give me,' Tchaikovsky went on mendaciously, 'I cannot give Bochechkarov that firm and lasting support which I did before. And so the idea occurred to me to ask you to assign him a life pension of 300 roubles a year (that is, twenty-five a month). Nik[olay] Lvov[ich] is truly a pitiful, poor and sick old man. But to you this would be a negligible sum. As for my gratitude for this, it will be so great that I agree not to be in the least offended if I should hear that you are continuing to spread gossip about the 28,000 and about the blackness of my soul.'[4] The circumstances which could occasion Tchaikovsky's bursts of generosity could sometimes be strange indeed.

Tchaikovsky left Brailov on 25 May. During a prolonged delay at Kazatin he saw another train pull into the station drawing Nadezhda von Meck's personal coach. The curtains were drawn, so his patroness could know nothing of his presence, but for twenty minutes he pondered their proximity. It was a subject which would occupy him a good

[4] *TLP*8, p. 214.

deal over the next few months. If in Paris his patroness had seemed to be growing indifferent to their closeness, her old longing had now fully resurged. She had just heard of an estate near Kamenka which the owners might be persuaded to sell: if she moved there she would be nearer Tchaikovsky. She asked him to make enquiries and discover what would be the price, while in Brailov itself she was already revelling in the knowledge of his recent stay. 'Here, more than anywhere, I feel our spiritual closeness and I take unspeakable pleasure in it,' she wrote ecstatically. 'Already the rooms you occupied have been accorded the name of *Pyotr Ilich's bedroom* and *Pyotr Ilich's sitting room*. The trees in the Tartaksky and Vladimirsky woods beneath which both of us have drunk [tea], the benches on the crag where we have both sat, those same nightingales we have both heard, all, all *belong to both of us*, all bring us together, all make us still closer to each other. My God! what happiness there is in this!'[5] Even before this she had been planning an idyll of close residence such as they had experienced in Florence, but this time in Brailov itself. 'Near Brailov I have a cottage, Simaki,' she had explained on 17 May.

> . . . This cottage is very pretty, lying in a shady garden with a river at its end. Nightingales sing in the garden. . . . There are six rooms. This cottage stands about three miles from Brailov . . . I am sure you will like it. It is such a solitary, poetic spot that if you would agree to come to it for a whole month or even more during the time I am in Brailov, then I should be unspeakably happy. For me there would be a partial repetition of the most delightful time of my life at the Viale dei Colli [in Florence]. Although, of course, at Brailov I would not be able to walk near your apartment each day, yet each day I would feel you were near me, and from that thought I should likewise be calm and happy. I would also feel that with you close to me no evil could come near me.[6]

Tchaikovsky's response to this proposal was thoroughly ambivalent. In fact, he was clearly reluctant to visit Simaki, but equally he feared to upset his patroness, particularly when he might be needing more money from her to pay off Antonina. Ultimately he was to go there during the last half of August. Meanwhile in Kamenka, as we have seen, he settled down to scoring *The Maid of Orléans* and stepped up his daily work schedule on this, the largest score he had yet composed. His

---

[5] *TPM2*, p. 123.
[6] *TPM2*, p. 109.

brother Ippolit, who was now working for a steamship company on the
Black Sea, had recently made a good speculation and had turned up to
consult with Lev about the 50,000 roubles he had gained. The gap
between Tchaikovsky and his brother had now much widened, and
when Ippolit wanted to accompany him on his woodland walks
Tchaikovsky was irritated. Then, after Ippolit's departure, Vera Butakova arrived. Despite the pretensions she had acquired to high society
manners and acquaintances, Tchaikovsky still warmed to her personality, though he was a little troubled by a suspicion that her old
attachment to him was not completely dead. As for his current and
perpetual torment, Antonina, he had Anatoly acting as his agent in
dealings with her, and at such a distance she seemed only half real.

Tchaikovsky always found solace at Kamenka, yet it is clear that
these weeks with his sister's family were the most enjoyable he had
spent for some years. He found himself becoming far more reconciled to
Kamenka as a place, tried his hand at haymaking, grew poppies, read
more of Dostoyevsky's *Brothers Karamazov* ('every single one of the
characters is mad,' he observed to Modest. 'Usually only one instalment of a Dostoyevsky novel is tolerable; after this, confusion always
comes'[7]); above all, he could enjoy the family life to as great (or as
small) a degree as he chose. He watched with amused detachment the
personality clashes between certain female members of the Kamenka
company, especially the turmoil created among the incumbent gov-
ernesses by the arrival of the new French teacher, Mlle Gautier. 'She's
forty and a bit, her appearance is plain but not unpleasant: to wit, she
has a good complexion, a slightly snub nose, and very kind eyes,' he
wrote to Modest.

> She dresses well. *She eats with her knife!!!* . . . She behaves very
> decorously and very simply. From the beginning she has tried to
> display her talents, which are numerous. Amongst these she models
> in clay *and does it very well*. The day before yesterday we went to
> Verbovka. Lev brought her a piece of clay from which they make
> bricks there, and she modelled a very nice head with uncommon
> speed. *Tasya* [Tchaikovsky's niece Nataliya] has conceived a most
> ferocious hatred for her, and has suddenly been smitten with a very
> touching love for Miss Eastwood [the English governess at
> Kamenka]. The latter also received the Frenchwoman very grimly,
> and in her turn is suddenly manifesting a passionate partiality for
> Tasya. Yesterday there was quite a dramatic scene. Poor *Tasya*, who

[7] *TLP8*, p. 226; *TPM2*, p. 603; *TPR*, p. 571; *YDGC*, p. 215.

is now all miserable, tearful, won't eat, won't smile, wanted to go to Trostyanka with her brothers and Miss Eastwood. The English-woman expressed a willingness to take her. Sasha told Tasya she should ask for *Mlle Gautier's* permission. But Tasya ran to complain to Miss Eastwood, and a minute later the latter flew into the drawing-room looking white and grim, and let forth a stream of reproaches at Sasha. 'What! I've looked after Tasya for five years, I love her, she loves me, yet you won't let her go to the woods with me! You see how miserable she is, how awful she looks, yet you won't let her have a break!' and so on, and so on. Sasha calmed her down and explained that the Frenchwoman had been engaged *for Tasya*, and that Tasya had to be under her control . . . *Persephone* [Pelageya Kostetskaya, another governess] is triumphant. For some reason she looks upon Mlle Gautier as an ally, and received her with open arms. There now fly from her lips streams of such refined French words that it's getting awful. She's even stopped speaking Russian with us, and it's reached a point where yesterday, after supper, when Lev and I were finishing our tea and having a smoke, she started talking Lev's head off in French, and delivered at him the following memorable phrase: 'Je vois tout en beau je ne vois pas les! défections que de près!' Lev fled from her on to the balcony.[8]

But if this sharply observed, well relished account evidences the degree to which the Kamenka world could distract Tchaikovsky from his own inner cares, there was one deep-seated ache from which there was still no refuge. 'On this day exactly twenty-five years ago my mother died,' he wrote to Nadezhda von Meck on 25 June. '. . . I remember every moment of that terrible day as though it were yesterday.'[9]

On 2 July Tchaikovsky set out for Kondratyev's estate at Nizy. He had intended to delay this trip until late in the summer, but news of the precarious health of Bochechkarov, whom Kondratyev had taken from Moscow to his own home, persuaded Tchaikovsky to hasten his visit. He found Bochechkarov in a pitiful state, and during the next twelve days he took his share in keeping company with the old man, in enjoying as much as he could of this estate where, five years before, he had composed *Vakula* so quickly, and in waiting impatiently for Anatoly to join him in the middle of the month. Inactivity was again fretting him, and with the score of *The Maid of Orléans* awaiting his further attention, his impatience to resume work mounted irrepressibly. On 17

[8] *TLP*8, p. 250; *TPR*, pp. 581–2.
[9] *TLP*8, p. 255; *TPM*2, p. 140; *TZC*2, p. 294.

July, after Anatoly's arrival, he bade what he well knew would be his last farewell to Bochechkarov, and then set out for Kamenka.

Before leaving for Nizy Tchaikovsky had received cheering news from abroad of his ever-growing reputation as a composer. Bülow had played the First Piano Concerto in London and Wiesbaden, while also from Wiesbaden Fitzenhagen reported the great success of the Rococo Variations when he had played them at the festival. From Paris Colonne wrote declaring his intention of furthering the cause of Tchaikovsky's music. Nearer home Tchaikovsky was particularly pleased to hear that his Liturgy of St John Chrysostom had been sung several times in the University Church at Kiev (Jurgenson's lawsuit with Bakhmetyev, the director of the Imperial Chapel Choir, over the publication rights of this was, of course, in full swing). In addition, the Grand Duke Konstantin Nikolayevich had requested Rubinstein to mount for him a special performance of *Onegin* at the Moscow Conservatoire.

Fortified by these encouragements, Tchaikovsky pressed on with *The Maid of Orléans* as soon as he was back in Kamenka. As he observed to Jurgenson, if his divorce action was to begin in the autumn and he was condemned to spend a considerable time in Moscow engaged in most unpalatable proceedings, how would he then be able to work? 'Quite apart from this, I always hurry my labour,' he added. 'This always tells unfavourably upon my creations – but such is my nature. I'm always afraid I *shan't finish*. And how many further plans I have! I must make radical improvements to some of my earlier pieces; I must write a thousand more opuses! A hundred lives wouldn't suffice to accomplish all my plans.'[10] With such an inescapable sense of urgency, the scoring progressed steadily. He had lost his enthusiasm for hunting, and so was not tempted out on to those expeditions which claimed so much of Anatoly's time on this visit. He was thoroughly happy, however, to resume his role as prompter in the domestic theatricals which were planned for shortly before Anatoly's departure, mainly to divert Sasha, who was suffering violent fluctuations between a kind of euphoria and intense depression (it was, Tchaikovsky wrote to Nadezhda von Meck, a condition with which he was all too familiar himself). Tchaikovsky had asked to be allowed to invite Kotek for the last part of his stay, since it was intended that his violinist friend should prepare the vocal score of Act 3 of *The Maid*. Thus the pleasures of the dramatic entertainment were enhanced by Kotek playing his violin in the interval between the two plays, and the evening was rounded off with a dance. While all such

[10] *TLP*8, p. 287.

things and the music-making he could engage in with Kotek brought Tchaikovsky the greatest pleasure, he felt some alarm at the news that his father had been seriously ill. Sasha had decided it was time to enrol Nataliya in a boarding school in St Petersburg, and news of Ilya Petrovich's ailment made her the more anxious to speed thither. As soon as Anatoly's leave was up Tchaikovsky looked to his own departure for Simaki. Though he confided to his brother that he still had no wish to go there, it is quite certain that he was longing for a period of solitude. In any case his patroness had made clear her displeasure at the visit he had paid to Kondratyev at Nizy, and Tchaikovsky wanted to pacify her. On 20 August he was at Nadezhda von Meck's estate.

Immediately the problem of proximity again raised its disquieting head. Tchaikovsky was genuinely enraptured with Simaki itself.

A house as old as the hills, a well-stocked garden with ancient oaks and limes, very neglected and thus for some reason delightful, a river at the end of the garden, a wonderful view from the balcony on to the village and a distant wood, the remoteness from the factory, the village, and from all noise and bustle, the absolute quiet, the accommodation arranged with uncommon comfort, consisting of a hall, a large study, dining-room, bedroom and a room for Alyosha – all this couldn't correspond more with my tastes and inclinations. Around the cottage there are fields and copses where you can wander without meeting anyone, which I forthwith did with inexpressible pleasure. Finally, to cap it all, Léon, the old servant with whom I never feel constraint, has been assigned to me, as has a cook whom I don't see, and a coachman with a phaeton and four which I can use, though I would prefer not to have it, for this, as it were, compels me to ride, whereas I'd prefer to walk.

There were facilities for bathing in the river, and an abundance of mushrooms to pick in the woods. His hostess had furnished him with a pile of books but he quickly exhausted these, even though he only read in the evenings and at mealtimes (his special pleasure, he confessed). He asked her whether she had complete editions of Tolstoy and Dostoyevsky, and any volume of Dickens in Russian or French translation which she could lend him. The beauty – above all, the peacefulness – of Simaki, with rabbits in the fields and a family of cats in the roof to banish rats and mice, all conspired to relax him in a way not possible at Sasha's unpicturesque and hectic Kamenka.

But then the contented tone of this letter penned to Modest a day after his arrival changes abruptly. 'The nearness of N[adezhda]

F[ilaretovna] makes me feel uncomfortable – although, at bottom, this is silly, for I know that no one will disturb me. It's simply that I'm used to regarding N[adezhda] F[ilaretovna] as some distant and unseen good angel, and this consciousness that she's living a couple of miles off like an ordinary mortal disturbs me. Yesterday Pachulski met me and spent part of the evening with me, but I've forewarned him bluntly that I want to be completely alone for several days.'[11]

In fairness to his patroness, she had promised to furnish him with a daily schedule of her proposed movements to forestall any chance encounter between them, but Pachulski had proposed to bring Milochka to see Tchaikovsky, and even this, Tchaikovsky felt, was endangering that very special, idealized quality in his relationship with his 'good but unseen angel'. The letter in which he forestalled this suggestion is perhaps the most explicit confession of how he viewed Nadezhda von Meck's role in his existence.

My relations with you *as they are now* are for me the greatest joy and a necessary condition for my happiness. I would not wish them to be changed even one iota. As it is, I am accustomed to regard you as my good but unseen angel. All the inestimable charm and poetry of my friendship with you lies in the fact that you are so close, so infinitely dear to me – but, at the same time, we are *not acquainted* in the ordinary sense of the word – and this *non-acquaintance* must extend to those persons closest to you. I want to love Milochka as I have loved her up to this moment. If she were to appear before me – *la charme serait rompue.* All members of your family are close and dear to me, Milochka in particular – but for God's sake let everything stay as it has been. And how would I reply to Milochka who would start asking *why I did not visit hèr mama?* I would have to begin my acquaintance with a lie – very innocent, of course – but still a lie. That would be very distressing to me.[12]

Though Tchaikovsky's patroness acceded quickly to his appeal, the very worst disaster they had both feared was about to happen. One afternoon he miscalculated the time and set out for his walk too early, she inadvertently delayed her usual return to Brailov at four o'clock, and for the first time ever they suddenly confronted each other on a road through the woods. 'It was *frightfully* embarrassing,' Tchaikovsky wrote to Anatoly on the day following the mishap.

[11] *TLP8*, p. 309; *TZC2*, pp. 298–9; *YDGC*, p. 216 (partial).
[12] *TLP8*, p. 312; *TPM2*, p. 169; *TZC2*, p. 300.

Although we were face to face for only an instant, I was still terribly confused. Nevertheless I raised my hat politely. But she, so it seemed to me, was utterly disconcerted and didn't know what to do. It wasn't enough that she was riding in a barouche with Milochka, for behind were two more carriages with all her family. I wandered for a long time in the wood looking for mushrooms, and when I returned to the [picnic] table where tea had been prepared, letters and newspapers were lying on it. It seems she had sent a rider to look for me in the wood and to give me the post before tea. Altogether there are no bounds to her attentions. What a wonderful person she is for me![13]

The contretemps was quickly forgiven, and once again glimpses of each other became their closest intimacy. As she was boating on the river at Brailov a companion caught sight of Tchaikovsky crossing a bridge, and she strained shortsightedly to discern him. When she organized fancy-dress festivities on the lake at Brailov in celebration of her son Alexandr's nameday, she urged Tchaikovsky to watch them and the ensuing firework display from the opposite bank. He did as she asked, sitting in the darkness close enough to be able to report back to her snatches of conversation he had overheard as they passed close to him. She had earlier requested that Tchaikovsky should come to Brailov to see her recent acquisitions. Now, after both of them had taken stringent precautions to avoid a further collision, he visited Brailov itself, saw her pictures, played her pianos, and rewarded her with the rhapsody of delight for which she craved. All was as before.

Tchaikovsky's main mission at Simaki was to complete the score of *The Maid*. If he had earlier felt some reluctance to stay at his patroness's estate, this was fully dispelled by the conditions in which he lived. The one thing which really marred his stay was receiving the expected, yet still deeply distressing news of Bochechkarov's death. To Modest he summarized simply yet very humanly what this old man had meant to him.

I shall never be able to reconcile myself to the thought that N[ikolay] L[vovich] is no longer in this world. Moscow has become hateful to me. The memory of that huge share he had in the whole course of my Moscow life is like a knife in my heart. I can state unreservedly that he alone made my life in Moscow tolerable and possible. He possessed an astonishing capacity for reconciling himself with life; his presence and his company afforded diversion, calm and comfort

[13] *TLP8*, p. 320; *TPR*, pp. 613–14; *TZC2*, p. 301 (without the last two sentences).

which nothing can replace. What does one care that he was *insigni-ficant* as regards moral and mental power? *He was agreeable always and to everybody*, and this took the place in him of a great mind and great gifts.[14]

Delight in his own comforts at Simaki had not made Tchaikovsky insensible to the needs of others. Suddenly filled with an awareness of his own mortality, he had turned his thoughts to Alexey's predicament if he should find himself masterless, and he had begged Nadezhda von Meck to take Alexey into her service if he, Tchaikovsky, should predecease her. Again while at Simaki he had acted as intermediary for the Polish Roman Catholic priest who lived on the estate. On his previous visit to Brailov Tchaikovsky had interceded with his patroness on behalf of the Catholic community, who wanted to enlarge their church, but who were prevented by one of Mrs von Meck's estate buildings which they wished to move to a new site. 'In my heart I have always been a most firm supporter of absolute freedom of conscience,' Tchaikovsky had explained. 'People must not be hindered from wor-shipping according to whatever rite they wish.'[15] Now Marcel had again approached Tchaikovsky on the priest's behalf, this time to gain Mrs von Meck's agreement to turning the slaughterhouse by the church into accommodation for the church's caretaker. Tchaikovsky's deep innate capacity for sympathy could also be recognized even by those with whom his contact was relatively slight. Marcel had obviously perceived it, despite all Tchaikovsky's insistence on a large measure of seclusion at Simaki, and his petition to Tchaikovsky proved fruitful in every way. An appeal to that same sympathy now came suddenly from Anatoly: a telegram arrived, begging Tchaikovsky to come straight from Simaki to St Petersburg where the twin, having had trouble at work, had resigned precipitately and wished to consult with his composer-brother. In the face of Anatoly's desperate entreaty it was to the Russian capital that he directed himself when he left Simaki on 13 September.

St Petersburg he found even more hateful than ever, and his depress-ion was exacerbated by having to witness the tearful parting of Sasha and her daughter Nataliya when the former left for Kamenka. He went to the opera but met friends there, and had to endure their questions about his affairs, and parry their invitations to visit. Discovering that Anatoly's work crisis was a storm in a teacup only increased his

[14] *TLP8*, p. 322; *TZC2*, p. 302; *TPR*, p. 612; *YDGC*, p. 217 (partial).
[15] *TLP8*, p. 204; *TPM2*, p. 115; *TZC2*, p. 289.

irritation, and he would have left forthwith but for the deep obligation he felt to some of his family, above all to his distraught niece Nataliya and his enfeebled father. While in the Russian capital he took the opportunity of paving the way with Nápravník for a production of *The Maid*; then on 30 September he set off for Moscow. More and more of his time was being absorbed by matters relating to the publication of his works – by making or supervising various arrangements of his pieces, and by proof-reading – and direct discussions on these and financial matters with his publisher and staff were now imperative. He had hoped to stop in Moscow only one day, but he was quickly caught up in Rubinstein's and Jurgenson's drinking habits, and it took three days to complete the various business affairs requiring his attention. By now he seems to have drifted from these friends, and one suspects that this lubricated socializing was less a pleasure than a way of concealing the gap which divided them. 'My friends from the musical world of Moscow always receive me with expressions of great joy, and at first I myself am glad to see them. But as soon as the first moments have passed, and on both sides we have begun to enquire about one another's health and what we are doing, boredom and a certain awkwardness set in. Between us there has formed a gulf which is getting still deeper and deeper,' he confided to his benefactress.[16] Moscow without Bochechkarov was as unpalatable as St Petersburg, and it was with heartfelt relief that he left the city on 4 October. After a night in Kharkov he arrived in Grankino on 6 October.

In Moscow Jurgenson had omitted to tell Tchaikovsky that the piano-duet version of the Fourth Symphony was now issued, and the news reached the composer in a letter from Nadezhda von Meck. She had received a copy, and playing the work over and over again impelled her suddenly to pour out a naked confession of feelings which she had dammed up for over two years. 'I do not know whether you can understand the jealousy I feel regarding you in the absence of personal relations between us,' she began.

> Do you know that I am jealous of you in the same inexcusable way as a woman is jealous of the man she loves? Do you know that when you married I was *terribly* distressed; it was as though something had been torn from my heart. It hurt me, I became bitter; the thought of your nearness to that woman was unbearable to me – and, do you know, I am such a vile person that I rejoiced when things between you were bad. I reproached myself for this feeling, I believe I never in any way

[16] *TLP8*, p. 369; *TPM2*, p. 218.

let you notice it, but all the same I could not stifle it: a person cannot help her feelings. I hated that woman because you were *unhappy* with her, but I would have hated her a hundred times more if you had been *happy* with her. It seemed that she had taken from me what was *mine* alone, that to which I *alone* had a right because *I love you* as no one does, I value you more than anything in the world. If it is distasteful for you to know all this, forgive my involuntary confession. Your symphony is the reason for me pouring out all this. However, I think (and I know better than you) that I am not such an ideal person as you believe. Moreover, this cannot in any way change our relations. I do not want *any* change in them: I just want to be sure that *nothing* will change to the end of my life, that no one . . . but that is something I have no right to declare. Forgive me, and forget what I have said.[17]

Whether, despite her disclaimer, Tchaikovsky suspected she might be seeking a closer relationship cannot be said. He replied warmly, appreciatively, declared that he had always been convinced that she would understand the symphony better than anyone because it was *their* symphony, detailed for the hundredth time his debt to her, yet indicated frankly that she must place no hopes on receiving his love within some confining personal bond. 'I am indebted to you for everything: for life, for the possibility of going forward to a distant goal, for freedom, and for a degree of happiness such as previously I would have considered impossible,' he replied on 7 October. 'I read your letters with feelings of boundless gratitude and love such as I can express only in music, and for which there are no words.'[18] In any case, a direct link between them might in time prove superfluous, for during Tchaikovsky's stay at Simaki he had hatched with his benefactress the idea of engineering a marriage between one of her sons and one of his nieces; thus their relationship would be consummated in a vicarious union. Five years later, in 1884, their desires were to be fulfilled when Nikolay von Meck married Anna Davïdova.

Tchaikovsky's stay at Grankino was only brief, and on 11 October he, Modest and Kolya were in Kamenka. Feeling that the plans he had been conceiving with Nadezhda von Meck might give pleasure to Sasha, he broached the possibility of a von Meck–Davïdova union to Lev and Sasha, and (so he told Mrs von Meck) received their enthusiastic assent. At this stage it was Nataliya, whom Sasha had just installed in boarding school in St Petersburg, whom Tchaikovsky had nominated

[17] *TPM*2, pp. 212–13.
[18] *TLP*8, p. 371; *TPM*2, p. 220; *TZC*2, p. 322.

as the future bride, and the correspondence with his fellow conspirator was much filled over the next weeks with various schemes (in which Tchaikovsky showed the far greater understanding of human nature) for nurturing a developing relationship between the unsuspecting juveniles.

He was delighted to hear from his patroness that her immeasurable enthusiasm for the Fourth Symphony had consolidated into a scheme for subsidizing a Paris performance by Colonne, though the composer gloomily predicted that the work would fail with a French audience. Despite such a cheerless prospect, and notwithstanding the departure of Modest and Kolya for St Petersburg after only four days, Tchaikovsky's spirits rose at Kamenka. For three days he had toiled over the proofs of his First Suite, but then suddenly found himself for the first time in many months with no obligatory musical occupations. For some days he gave himself up to inactivity, idle occupations like hemming and marking towels, and to self-enjoyment. But quickly the charms of such an existence faded. 'These last days I've begun to observe in myself things which at first I didn't understand,' he admitted to Modest on 22 October. 'I experienced a certain vague dissatisfaction with myself, an over-frequent and almost irresistible desire to sleep, a certain emptiness, and finally *boredom*. There were times when I didn't know what to do with myself. Finally yesterday it became fully apparent to me what was the matter. I had to get on with something: I find myself absolutely incapable of living long without work. Today I began to create something, and the *boredom* vanished as if by magic.'[19] He had set about his Second Piano Concerto.

Tchaikovsky had a further fortnight in Kamenka and he determined that this time he would not rush to finish the piece. A week after starting upon the concerto he informed Anatoly of his progress. 'I work only in the morning before lunch – and, strange to say, I'm finding it some effort to compose. I don't feel a great inclination to composition – but, on the other hand, experience has taught me I can't live without work.'[20] Yet only three days later, on 1 November, he could report the sketches of the first movement complete. This done, he devoted the remaining time he felt he could spend at Kamenka to walking and reading. On his last day he discovered that Sasha had kept the letters which he had written to his parents from St Petersburg when he had been a schoolboy. 'It is difficult to convey to you what an agitating impression was made upon me by reading these letters carrying me

[19] *TLP8*, p. 388; *TPR*, p. 629; *TPB*, pp. 232–3.
[20] *TLP8*, p. 394; *TPR*, p. 631; *DTC*, pp. 452–3; *YDGC*, p. 219.

back nearly thirty years, reminding me vividly of my childhood sufferings which arose from a longing for my mother whom I loved with a certain morbid, passionate love,' he revealed to Nadezhda von Meck, knowing that this relationship would cause her no distress. '. . . Already twenty-five years have passed since the day of her death.'[21] That night he scarcely slept. It was a very tired Tchaikovsky who set out for Moscow on 5 November.

Here he paused less than two days during which he toiled over proof-reading, and was lost in admiration at Rubinstein's playing of his Piano Sonata, which that pianist had first introduced to the public a week earlier. He decided immediately that his new concerto should be dedicated to Rubinstein. Arriving in St Petersburg on 10 November, he felt again all his old antipathy for the place. He visited a circus and found himself sitting close to two of Nadezhda von Meck's sons. One of them was the sixteen-year-old Nikolay, now at the School of Jurisprudence where Tchaikovsky himself had once been a pupil. He recognized the lad from photographs his mother had sent him, but since the two boys were ignorant of Tchaikovsky's identity he was able to scrutinize them unobserved, taking special interest in the elected bridegroom. 'I cannot express to you in words what a pleasant sensation I felt seeing two beings so close to you in front of me. Each of them is, in his own way, very nice. Kolya took a very lively interest in the show and talked a lot with his neighbours . . . I observed Kolya's habit of twitching his facial muscles slightly, exactly as my brother Anatoly does. It will seem odd to you, but even these nervous movements appealed to me,' he wrote to their mother, as usual finding every feature and idiosyncrasy of her family 'nice'.[22] She had now abandoned her proposed visit to Naples; instead she had gone to Paris, where she had reserved accommodation for Tchaikovsky. Thus France was his destination when he left St Petersburg on 21 November. In Berlin he saw Kotek, was fascinated by a microscope museum, and was delighted by a tolerable performance of Thomas's opera, *Hamlet*. On 25 November he was in Paris.

Tchaikovsky discovered that his enthusiasm for the French capital remained as strong as ever. Kondratyev was there recovering from a bout of serious illness, and Tchaikovsky visited him, experiencing none of the social strains he confessed to enduring from Kotek's eternal chatter in Berlin. Nadezhda von Meck arranged that a fine Erard piano should be delivered to Tchaikovsky's quarters, and on 29 November he

[21] *TLP*8, p. 402; *TPM*2, p. 239; *TZC*2, p. 328.
[22] *TLP*8, p. 407; *TPM*2, p. 244.

resumed work on the concerto, applying himself first to the finale. As with the first movement he found little enthusiasm within himself during the early stages of composition, but after some six days his creative faculties began to move more freely, and the sketches of the finale were swiftly completed, while the second movement, so he said, was already in his head. This went far better. 'My concerto is ready in rough, and I am very pleased with it, especially with the second movement, the *Andante*,' he could tell Mrs von Meck on 15 December.[23] When he resumed work on the concerto in Rome during February 1880 it was to make the transcription for two pianos so that Jurgenson might have this readily available for publication. The scoring was begun before the end of February, but was not completed until 10 May.

Although Tchaikovsky had determined to offer the dedication of the Second Piano Concerto to Rubinstein, memories of that artist's initial reception of its predecessor made him apprehensive. 'Yet though he [Rubinstein] may this time also be severely critical, this still won't matter if he plays it as splendidly as he does the first concerto,' he observed to Jurgenson on 3 March 1880. 'However, it's desirable that in this instance the gap between the denunciation and the performance should be shorter,' he added sardonically.[24] But it seems that Tchaikovsky's former assailant had decided to keep his peace. 'In the spring,' Tchaikovsky again wrote to Jurgenson on 24 August, 'I sent the concerto to Rub[instein] and asked him to comment upon it when he'd played it through, and to entrust Taneyev with changing as many details as he wished in the piano part, but not touching the essence [of the piece], of which *whatever advice I may receive, I will not change a single bar.* Taneyev has replied that *there's absolutely nothing to change.* This means that was Rubinstein's opinion.'[25] In fact Rubinstein did have reservations and communicated them to Tchaikovsky direct, who then transmitted them, and his own response, to Nadezhda von Meck on 10 October. 'N[ikolay] Gr[igoryevich] tells me in his opinion the piano part appears to be too episodic, and does not stand out sufficiently from the orchestra. . . . If he is right [which he was not] this will be very galling because I took pains precisely on this, to make the solo instrument stand out in as much relief as possible against the orchestral background.'[26]

It has usually been accepted that the première of the Second Piano Concerto took place in Moscow on 30 May 1882 with Taneyev playing

[23] *TLP*8, p. 457; *TPM*2, p. 276; *TZC*2, p. 345; *DTC*, p. 453; *YDGC*, p. 222 (partial).
[24] *TLP*9, p. 59; *TZC*2, p. 379; *TPJ*1, p. 140; *DTC*, p. 453.
[25] *TLP*9, p. 236; *TZC*2, p. 414; *TPJ*1, p. 165; *DTC*, p. 454.
[26] *TLP*9, p. 287; *TPM*2, p. 423; *TZC*2, p. 424; *DTC*, p. 454.

the solo part, but in fact the concerto was first heard in New York on 12
November 1881, when it was played by Madeleine Schiller with
Theodore Thomas conducting.[27] In the Russian performance the
conductor was Tchaikovsky's old teacher, Anton Rubinstein. By this
time Taneyev had developed his own reservations about the piano
writing, and exactly a month after giving the first Russian performance
(at which the composer had not been present), he provided also a brief
and frank digest of critical reaction to the work. 'Opinions about it are
pretty varied, but they all agree on this – that the first and second
movements are too long. . . . Few people approve the violin and cello
solos in the second movement; they say the piano has nothing to do in it,
with which I think one has to agree: there's an excessive preponderance
of the other two instruments.'[28]

Tchaikovsky's reply, written from Grankino on 23 July, was tartly
grateful. 'I'm extremely obliged to you for performing the concerto. I
freely admit that it suffers from its length, and I regret that those
persons to whom it was entrusted two years ago for critical scrutiny
didn't indicate this failing at the proper time. In this they would have
been doing me a great service – one perhaps even greater than the
superb performance of the concerto in its present, so imperfect form. All
the same – merci, merci, merci!'[29]

Among Tchaikovsky's major instrumental works the Second Piano
Concerto was one about whose structure his own uncertainties seem to
have persisted most obstinately. In November 1888 Tchaikovsky
himself conducted the concerto in St Petersburg with the young Vasily
Sapelnikov as the soloist, repeating the performance shortly afterwards
in Prague and Moscow. At the very same time Alexandr Ziloti,
Tchaikovsky's former pupil and now his friend, was preparing a revised
edition of his own. It is apparent that Tchaikovsky himself had already
made modifications for the performances with Sapelnikov,[30] but when
Ziloti offered his more radical changes the composer rejected them
flatly. 'I'm extremely grateful to you for your concern and interest, for
your desire that my pieces should be made easier and more rewarding –
but *emphatically* I can't agree with your cuts and especially with your
re-ordering of the first movement,' he wrote on 8 January 1889.
'Perhaps I'm wrong and you're right – but my feelings as a composer
rebel strongly against your transferences and changes. . . . The version

[27] I am grateful to John Warrack for drawing my attention to this.

[28] *TTP*, p. 80; *TZC*2, p. 536; *DTC*, p. 455.

[29] *TLP*11, p. 162; *TTP*, p. 81; *TZC*2, p. 538; *DTC*, p. 455.

[30] Probably the cut in the central ritornello of the first movement (bars 319–42), and
the two in the Andante non troppo (bars 247–81 and 310–26; in orchestra bar 327).

of the Second Concerto I want is the one I made *Sapelnikov* play. . . . With my changes the consistency and logical sequence of the parts is not destroyed. My . . . hair stood on end at your idea of transferring the cadenza to the end.'[31]

Ziloti did not let the matter rest there, and only three months before his death Tchaikovsky was again having to resist his young friend's persuasions to revise. When Jurgenson heard of this prolonged tussle, he wrote to the composer urging him to hold his ground. 'I agree to some of Ziloti's changes, but to others I emphatically can't,' Tchaikovsky wrote in reply on 1 September. '. . . Those concessions I've made and those cuts he and I have both thought up are quite sufficient.'[32] Yet when Jurgenson printed a second edition four years after Tchaikovsky's death the concerto appeared in a version heavily revised by Ziloti, and it is in this mutilated form that it is still often performed.

In writing to his patroness in July 1878 about his earlier compositions, Tchaikovsky had identified two clear categories: those which he had set about from inner compulsion, and those which he had composed in a spirit of duty (i.e., commissions). That a work belonged to one or other category was, he added, no sure pointer to its quality, for inspiration might fade in works undertaken out of choice, while the contracted task might suddenly fire his imagination. He might have added that a commission was not without its incitements, for there was the expression of faith in Tchaikovsky himself implicit in the very act of commission, and there was the incentive of a fee in prospect. In fact, except perhaps for the Piano Sonata, the Second Piano Concerto seems to have been the first work Tchaikovsky undertook purely as an act of will with no external stimulus except boredom at creative inactivity. And in saying this, we have perhaps pointed straight at the source of the work's weakness. The new piano concerto lacked any vital promptings, and the melodic material reflects this. Nearly all of it is second-rate – and with Tchaikovsky this meant that the work was irredeemably handicapped. The material's identity, too, is sometimes questionable, and the very opening theme suggests Schumann rather than Tchaikovsky (Ex. 163a). The shade of the German master haunting a work by Tchaikovsky rarely boded well, and this chunky beginning collapses into impotence in its fourth two-bar phrase, its rigid symmetries prompting an equally mechanical phrase construction in the ensuing pages. The second subject recalls the second fate motif of

[31] *TLP*14, p. 614; *DTC*, pp. 455–6 (partial).
[32] *TPJ*2, p. 271; *TZC*3, p. 63; *DTC*, p. 456.

Ex. 163

Onegin, and the imitative dialogue of clarinet and horn raises the melodic quality sharply (Ex. 164). Yet the portal which this opens upon richer thematic prospects is not passed, and the gentle, quasi-canonic invention to which this gives way has charm, but little else. Nor is this thematically unremarkable exposition strengthened by anything resembling the First Concerto's thoughtful deployment of materials. Here, from a reshuffling of themes in the recapitulation, had emerged a completely new balance of tonal tensions; in the Second Concerto the recapitulation is little more than an abbreviated review of the three thematic events of the exposition. Nor is there much significant development of exposition ideas beyond their prime form; the matrix of the concerto's opening is stamped upon the end of the second subject to round off the exposition, the work's opening phrase is seen in a new light by being made the rejoinder to a new melodic fragment at the E flat opening of the second of the central ritornelli (Ex. 163b), and there are some hints of developmental possibilities in the end of this, but that is about all. Indeed, since much of the material recurs in cadenza situations, its treatment tends to be loosely rhapsodic, combined with rhetorical flourishes and free interpolations.

Ex. 164

However, though these basic melodic deficiencies are sufficient to deny the Second Piano Concerto a place among Tchaikovsky's best works, it remains a piece of considerable significance, and of not negligible virtues. In the Violin Concerto Tchaikovsky's complete and well-founded confidence in the strength of his melodic invention to sustain the work had enabled him to remain within the well-tried sequence of events of the most traditional concerto structure. But in the Second Piano Concerto, with a solo instrument far less well adapted to melodic delivery, yet admirably suited to tumultuous rhetoric, and utterly self-sufficient, he was both driven and encouraged to essay a new synthesis of events. The result is a first movement with some very original structural features (Ex. 165). Its outlines are clear, even stark,

Ex. 165

SECOND PIANO CONCERTO: FIRST MOVEMENT

Horizontal block indicates that a section centres upon one key (note), sloping block that tonal shifts occur.

Passage for orchestra

Passage for soloist

Passage for soloist and orchestra

and there can be no doubt that the striving after clarity which Tchaikovsky had avowedly pursued in *The Maid*, and which was about to impel him to revise the Second Symphony, was also a powerful force in shaping this Allegro brillante. The harmonic structures, too, are remarkably forthright, with much use of sustained chords (there are some especially prolonged dominants), and the thematic workings are never involved. Thus, for instance, the ritornello which marks the beginning of the development has none of the briskly changing thematic engagements and equally swift tonal changes which mark the corresponding section of the First Concerto. Instead there is a dying rumination upon the melodic dialogue introduced in Ex. 164, all set within a magisterial, almost lapidary harmonic progress which is itself firmly embedded in C major/minor. Thus harmonic tension comes not from key shifts but from modal ambivalence and from the strong Neapolitan harmonies which engage implacably with the almost unbroken tonic pedal which underpins the whole section. Yet elsewhere in this movement it is tonal shifts that are of major importance, as the listener becomes acutely aware when, at the end of the G major-centred first subject, the second subject enters abruptly in E flat (see Ex. 164). As a piece of shock treatment this is, of course, thoroughly effective, but this move is also prophetic, for it is the harbinger of key behaviour in the whole movement. Rejecting any quasi-classical balance of keys, Tchaikovsky follows a procedure similar to that used by Schumann in his great C major Fantasia for piano, Op. 17, and operates almost exclusively on the flat side of the tonic, thus availing himself of that dark, potentially dramatic colouring which may be gained from a consistent probing towards flat regions. This early shift to E flat, by establishing the tonal antipodes to the tonic G major, defines the tonal territory of what follows: only in the second piano cadenza, the most overtly brilliant stretch of the whole movement, is there any significant probing of slightly sharper regions.

The striving for lucidity in this first movement also encourages the segregation of the solo instrument from the main body of sound, drama springing less from the direct and sometimes complex interaction of soloist and orchestra characteristic of the First Concerto than from a grandly spaced alternation of robust orchestral ritornello, grandiloquent cadenza, and even some contrasting passages of almost chamber-like intimacy. And if the exposition's structure is fairly orthodox, that of the development is not. Here Tchaikovsky completely abandons the traditional pattern of opening orchestral ritornello followed by close solo/orchestral collaboration used in the First Piano Concerto. Instead this central section is expanded to become the largest major division of

the whole movement, and is boldly constructed from two ritornello/
cadenza sections, in the first of which the orchestra and then the soloist
each hold rigidly to one tonality (C and B flat minor respectively),
concentrating exclusively upon second subject ingredients, while in the
far longer second section there is a contrasting tonal instability, with
much greater emphasis upon first subject material with the addition of
some new thematic matter. Such fitful, rhetorical discursiveness cannot
match the closely argued course followed in this stretch of the First
Concerto; what it does demonstrate most cheeringly is that the structural resourcefulness which Tchaikovsky had shown in so many of
his finest instrumental works before his marriage, and which had
appeared so paralyzed in the Piano Sonata, is again alive.

If this first movement is the most important Tchaikovsky had
composed since that of the Fourth Symphony of 1877, the slow
movement is the most ambitious since the Andante funèbre of the Third
String Quartet of 1876. Yet its spiritual predecessor is far more the
haunting Andante elegiaco of the Third Symphony. The opening
theme (Ex. 166) is wholly admirable, starting almost naïvely like a
recollection of Gounod's 'Ave Maria' on Bach's C major prelude,
expanding its second phrase adroitly from four to six bars, adding
sudden strength of profile in the abruptly shortened, twice-heard third

Ex. 166

phrase, relaxing briefly in a further two-bar phrase before resuming
and reinforcing this new-found ardour in the following three-bar
phrases, and finally retreating to end in the gentler realm in which the
theme had begun. When it is repeated, starting from bar 11 of Ex. 166,
with cello joining violin in amorous duet, the revised, much-expanded
conclusion confirms the high fertility of Tchaikovsky's melodic inspiration in the first portion of this movement. His employment here of violin
and cello soli on equal terms with the official soloist was patently
determined by their ability to handle such a long-spun thread of lyrical
melody superlatively well. But if this also occasions the first problem of
the movement – that the piano simply cannot compete – there is a
second flaw more fundamental to the music itself – that the melodic
invention falters badly in the central section, which soon resorts to

mounting sequences upon a constricted melodic morsel, and culmin-
ates in pointless cadenzas after the interloping string soloists have
re-entered. Ziloti recognized this impoverishment, and his savagely
truncated version dispensed entirely with this central section. Nevertheless, Tchaikovsky's objections to the young pianist's mutilations
were fully justified, for Ziloti's reduction left nothing but a double
statement of the main theme, followed by a disproportionately long
coda. It is, in fact, still far better to perform the whole movement in its
original form without even Tchaikovsky's excisions of 1888.

The one movement to escape revision was the finale. This is not
surprising, for it is the most neatly packaged portion of the whole
concerto, affording impressive proof of how proficiently Tchaikovsky
could frame a movement which is largely compiled from virtually
discrete sections, ordered in a manner so mechanically balanced and
clear cut that criticism of their organization is silenced, yet which
manages to be less mechanical than it might appear to be at first
hearing. Though its melodic material is not as distinctive as that of the
parallel movement of the First Piano Concerto, this finale is in certain
respects more individual, for it is impossible to assign it confidently to a
particular structural category. The character of the first two themes
and their presentation in the tonic and relative minor respectively
promises the most routine of rondos, but the sudden intrusion, as the
tonic is regained, of a third theme proves this structural assumption
mistaken. A bird's eye view of the movement's thematic organization
might suggest another of Tchaikovsky's three-subject sonata patterns
with minimal development, but the tonal organization seems to exclude
this possibility. Yet, in fact, one way of viewing this movement is to see
it as an approach to sonata structure of the sort Tchaikovsky was to use
with far more pregnant results in the first movement of the Piano Trio –
that is, the reinterpretation of an apparently traditional thematic
scheme by irregular tonal organization. In this Allegro con fuoco
exposition and recapitulation are reversed; the exposition, instead of
concluding in a key other than the tonic, ends firmly back in G major.
After such a tonally enclosed section a full-scale development would
hardly be a natural consequence; yet to have merely prolonged the
tonic into a restatement of the first subject would have made this
recurrence a tonal non-event. Some tonal divergence is necessary, and
Tchaikovsky constructs a link made as a quasi-developmental extension of his third idea, thus enhancing a little the expressive world of the
movement, before passing to the recapitulation. This follows exactly
the thematic course of the exposition, but by setting the second theme in
the dominant minor (D minor), the third theme recurs in F. Thus the

greatest tonal tension is located towards the end of the movement, and the finality of the coda is reinforced by delaying the restatement of the tonic until this last stage. If such a view seems too sophisticated for a movement whose manner of address is so direct and uncomplicated, it at least warns us not to be too dismissive about this finale, even though it clearly makes no attempt to emulate the grander, more ambitious aspirations of the two large-scale organisms which have preceded it.

Tchaikovsky stayed nearly a month in Paris. His aversion to contacts with persons other than those very close to him remained as strong as ever. On the journey he had encountered Józef Wieniawski, pianist-brother of the famous Henryk, and to escape his companionship had pretended he was travelling with a lady – at which Wieniawski had winked and departed. In Paris he saw Kondratyev daily, but had insisted that his friend should introduce him as Mr Petrovsky to mask his identity. Tchaikovsky found most of his pleasures in walking, visits to the Louvre and the Palais de Justice, where the histrionics displayed by some of the participants caused him much amusement, and in the theatrical and musical life of the city. He saw Mozart's *Die Zauberflöte*, but the most momentous musical event of his stay was a con-cert performance by Colonne of Berlioz's entire *La Prise de Troie* in the presence of the French president. Berlioz fever was at its height in Paris, and only a week earlier, at a rival concert conducted by Pasdeloup, Tchaikovsky had heard extracts from this same opera. Thus he was afforded an opportunity for direct comparison between the merits of these two dominating conductors in the Parisian scene. 'The first's [Pasdeloup's] performance was less than middling, the second's [Colonne's] *very good*,' he declared to Mrs von Meck the next day, clearly relieved that the introduction of his Fourth Symphony to French ears had been placed in the latter's hands. 'The work itself, as always happens on closer acquaintance and in a better performance, pleased me considerably more, though I still consider the opera to be weak – even very weak if compared with Berlioz's masterpieces, i.e. *Faust* and *Romeo*.'[33]

A week before, he had passed judgement on a very different musical work to his patroness, who had just heard of the *Paraphrases* which Borodin, Cui, Lyadov and Rimsky-Korsakov had composed the pre-vious year on that best-known of all juvenile, two-fingered piano pieces, *Chopsticks*. Liszt had published a complimentary letter on this collection and he was to substantiate his praise by supplying a mazurka upon the

[33] *TLP8*, p. 440; *TPM2*, p. 265; *TZC2*, p. 338.

piece which was to be added to a later edition. In judging this set of pieces Tchaikovsky's critical aim found the bull's eye; his verdict on these trifles is a timely reminder of how sensible his musical judgements remained. As for his view on Liszt's role, it shows an equally shrewd, yet not ungenerous perception of part of that complex figure's character.

> This composition is, of course, an original piece of its kind, and it reveals in its composers remarkable talents for harmonization – but I find it unattractive. As a *joke* it is too ponderous, too bulky and indigestible because the endless repetitions of the theme are tiresome. As a work of art it is nothing. That several talented people should, for their own pleasure, set themselves the task of devising all kinds of variations upon a trivial, commonplace phrase is not surprising: what is surprising is that these dilettantish trifles should be printed and given currency. Only dilettantes can believe that every piquantly invented chord is worthy of being made public. As for Liszt, this old Jesuit responds with exaggeratedly enthusiastic compliments to every piece submitted to his most august scrutiny. He is a kind-hearted being, and one of the few outstanding artists in whose soul there has never been petty envy, a disposition to hinder the successes of his neighbour (Wagner and, in part, A[nton] Rubinstein are beholden to him for their successes; he also rendered many services to Berlioz) – but he is also too much a Jesuit to be truthful and honest. Returning to the variations, I will say that it is nevertheless a piquant musical curiosity, revealing in its composers great talents – but sadly onesided, i.e., directed solely towards *harmony*. If you should come by the piece, pay particular attention to *Requiem* by Borodin; this is a remarkably successful conceit.[34]

That same positive ability to see clearly the balance between virtues and inadequacies in music which had no great attraction to him led him to rise to Cui's defence when Mrs von Meck delivered herself unsympathetically upon a recently published set of that composer's songs which Tchaikovsky had sent her to look over. 'I am not in complete agreement, my dear friend, with your opinion of Cui,' he replied on 8 December.

> I do not perceive a great creative strength in him, but he has elegance, a pretty harmonic manner, and taste, in which respect he

---

[34] *TLP*8, pp. 421–2; *TPM*2, p. 253; *TZC*2, p. 331.

differs from the other representatives of that circle of musicians. . . .
Do you know *Cui's* opera *[William] Ratcliff?* There are delightful
things in it, though unfortunately they suffer from a certain sugari-
ness and *sleekness* in the harmony. It is obvious that the composer sat
a long while over each bar lovingly polishing it, as a result of which
the design is insufficiently free, the strokes too artificial, too contrived. . . . He took ten years writing *Ratcliff!* The opera was obviously written in bits very carefully finished off, but in consequence of
this one feels a lack of unity, and inconsistency of style.[35]

Though repeating in essentials the assessment he had made to Mrs von
Meck two years earlier of this journalistic tormentor and the other
members of Balakirev's group, the terms are now more balanced, and
the smouldering ferocity in the earlier judgement has died.

While in Paris Tchaikovsky was approached by the Berlin publisher,
Adolph Fürstner, with an offer to market his works in Germany. Much
flattered, Tchaikovsky had nevertheless replied that his relations with
Jurgenson made it impossible for him to accept (what he did not know
was that Fürstner had already issued pirated editions of his pieces).
Though he continued to feel that the good prospects which he believed
such an offer foretold for his music outside Russia did not apply to the
forthcoming performance of the Fourth Symphony in Paris, he was
afforded one other clear sign that his music was making considerable
headway in France; in January there would take place in Paris a concert
devoted entirely to his Third String Quartet and *Sérénade mélancolique*
(the latter with piano accompaniment). It was a somewhat more
self-assured Tchaikovsky who left for Rome on 17 December, the day
after his benefactress had also departed for Russia. Pausing for only a
day in Turin, he joined Modest and Kolya in the Italian capital on 20
December. On that same day in Moscow the First Suite was receiving
its première under Nikolay Rubinstein.

Much postal debate had preceded the decision that Rome should
become the base in which Tchaikovsky would spend the remainder of
the winter with Modest and Kolya. Modest had been the Italian
capital's most emphatic advocate, for he was attracted by the artistic
treasures of the place. Tchaikovsky had raised constant objections
to Modest's choice, but the latter had taken the matter into his own
hands and journeyed quietly to Rome, whence he wrote informing his
brother that he was awaiting his arrival. Tchaikovsky therefore had no

[35] *TLP8*, pp. 439–40; *TPM2*, p. 265; *TZC2*, pp. 337–8.

alternative but to proceed thither, but when he arrived he was surprised at the delight he discovered in it. The weather was wonderful, and there were none of those unpleasant reactions he had experienced two years before, when everything had been coloured by his post-marital gloom. With his Baedeker Modest had explored the city thoroughly, and he now acted as a well-informed guide to his brother. Tchaikovsky felt that the mists which had so obstinately clouded his appreciation of the visual arts had dispersed yet further. 'Michelangelo's frescos in the Sistine Chapel have ceased to be double Dutch to me, and I'm beginning to be filled with wonder at his powerful and original beauty,' he reported to Anatoly on 12 January 1880.[36] But reservations remained, and four days earlier he had given Nadezhda von Meck a clear glimpse of how he found himself affected by what he saw. Like Goethe before him, he found the superabundance of Rome's creative riches quite indigestible. In any case, his range of response was limited. Michelangelo's 'gloomy grandeur' and his muscular figures could impress him, but they could not delight or move him. An old parallel again rose in his mind. 'Is it not true that Beethoven and Michelangelo have very kindred natures?' he suggested to Nadezhda von Meck,[37] feeling that same discomfort at his own inability to respond to the Italian artist's majesty as he did at his antipathy to the rugged strength of the German composer. During this Roman interlude he was to return dutifully to long contemplations of Michelangelo's *Moses* and his Sistine Chapel frescos in the hope of some kind of inner illumination, and by the time of his departure he believed that the dawn of appreciation had truly broken (though one suspects this was more wish-fulfilment than true insight). But on another Italian master Tchaikovsky felt he could confer the highest compliment of which he was capable. 'My favourite is still Raphael, that Mozart of painting,' he had confessed to the same correspondent. Raphael's noble yet sweet lyricism, his poise, his elegant yet strong perfection, all addressed that side of Tchaikovsky which identified so readily with the musical world Mozart conjured for him. 'Paintings by Guercino still appeal to me in the highest degree,' he went on.

His *Florentine Endymion* [and] some of his Madonnas are of such angelic beauty that they fill my whole soul with a certain quiet rapture. However, I have to confess that in general I am by nature devoid of sensitivity to the plastic arts, and only a very few paintings and statues make a real impression on me. . . . Only today I experi-

[36] *TLP8*, p. 488; *TPR*, p. 655; *TPB*, p. 239; *YDGC*, p. 224.
[37] *TLP9*, p. 29; *TPM2*, p. 301; *TZC2*, p. 369.

enced just how important it is to gaze long and hard at a painting. I sat in front of Raphael's *Transfiguration*, and at first it seemed to me that there was nothing particular in this picture; but little by little I began to understand the facial expressions of each of the Apostles and other figures, and the more I peered, the more I was filled with fascination at the whole and the details.[38]

Here we may perceive the very essence of Tchaikovsky's response. Objective appraisal of the mastery in design or the magnificence of the craft had no real part in his reaction, nor were his sensibilities stirred by the pattern of contrasting tones and colours. Just as he felt drawn into the sound world of Mozart, so he needed to *absorb* himself in the world depicted by Raphael. But whereas the ultimate relish of Mozart's creations could be savoured by re-creating them, he had no power to do this with Raphael's. All he could do was sit before a picture until it ceased to be canvas covered with representations, and became a living world peopled by real beings with whom he could identify. When he had thus possessed it, then an emotional response could follow.

Tchaikovsky's new-found delight in Rome saturates the letters he wrote during his first days in the city. There was no music worth hearing, he said, but he used his spare time to begin systematically learning English, and he played Bach and duets with Modest on the piano he had imported into his hotel room. All will to compose had vanished. Then, predictably, his mood began to change, and the urge to work returned. Ten days after his arrival he set about the revision of the Second Symphony, completed the sketches in three days, and then wrote to Bessel (who had years before extracted from him the publication rights to this symphony), making it clear that he had no intention of letting him have the new version without an adequate fee. When abroad Tchaikovsky relied very much upon the good offices of his friends to keep him informed about the fortunes of his works. Ever since arriving in Rome he had been awaiting news of the First Suite, and he was much hurt that none of his friends in Moscow had thought to telegraph him of its success at its première. His dismay at Rubinstein's comments on the alleged difficulties in the piece have already been noted. He consoled himself by reflecting on the history of that same Rubinstein's reactions to the First Piano Concerto; 'what was impossible in 1875 became thoroughly possible in 1878,' he observed drily to Taneyev.[39] He gained no joy whatsoever from Mrs von Meck's adverse

---

[38] *TLP*8, p. 486; *TPM*2, p. 288; *TZC*2, p. 355.
[39] *TLP*9, p. 15; *TZC*2, p. 361; *TTP*, p. 47; *YDGC*, p. 224.

account of a performance of *Swan Lake* she had attended in Moscow, but at least she could report a full house.

However, the other news Tchaikovsky was really awaiting concerned the Paris performance of the Fourth Symphony. It was entirely his own fault that his secret hope of hearing the work was not fulfilled. 'He [Colonne] informs me that my symphony is to be given *tomorrow*, 25, at the Châtelet. This grieved me in the extreme. If he had written to me only one day earlier then I would still have been able to set out and arrive in Paris in time,' he lamented to the work's dedicatee. 'Of course I cannot blame *Colonne* for, wishing to ensure that I remained incognito, I wrote to him that my health prevented me from attending the performance of my symphony, and that he need not trouble to see that his letter arrived in time. But it is so disappointing that the one opportunity of hearing my symphony has eluded me. I was so rejoicing in this opportunity, I had promised myself such delight in being present at the performance of it unknown to and unnoticed by anyone!'[40] In his letter Colonne had confessed that the rehearsals had been long and hard, and he predicted that the Andantino and scherzo would score the greatest success. The event proved him right, and he declared that he would try to repeat these middle movements before the season was over, but there was no such proposal for the remaining two. The symphony's reception, as Tchaikovsky himself had prophesied, had not been brilliant. Despite this he was reluctant to allow his patroness to campaign for further performances of his works in Paris, and when he heard that she had returned to the attack on Colonne with a suggestion that he should conduct the First Suite and promote *The Maid of Orléans* he was firm in restraining her. 'It will be *embarrassing and distasteful* to me in the extreme if you again thank him [Colonne] in a material way for giving attention to my compositions,' he cautioned her on 28 February.[41]

Quite apart from fears that such a repeated arrangement might threaten the secrecy of his relationship with his patroness (Colonne had, in fact, had to be told something of it), Tchaikovsky must now have realized, though he might not have confessed it openly, that the international tide was beginning to run strongly in his favour, rendering such subsidized performances less necessary. From New York a little later he was to hear of the success of the First Suite under Leopold Damrosch and of a performance of the First Piano Concerto, while from Berlin came news of three performances of the concerto; the work was also heard in Budapest. All these performances were, according to

---

[40] *TLP*9, p. 26; *TPM*2, pp. 296–7; *TZC*2, p. 365.
[41] *TLP*9, p. 55; *TPM*2, p. 316; *TZC*2, p. 378.

Modest, highly successful. Indeed, Modest later declared that this period saw the beginning of his brother's international reputation.

Yet the most affecting news received by Tchaikovsky during his stay in Rome was of his father's end. On 20 January he heard from Anatoly of their parent's serious illness. Tchaikovsky would have sped dutifully to St Petersburg if this had been deemed necessary, the more so since the noise and bustle of Rome and the sheer volume of its cultural heritage were now weighing very heavily upon him. But such a journey quickly became pointless, for on 21 January Ilya Petrovich died. The loss did not strike Tchaikovsky very deeply. His father had never occupied that place at the very heart of his affections which his mother always had possessed, and always would. Anatoly wrote him a full account of their father's end, and Tchaikovsky recorded his own reaction to Nadezhda von Meck. 'I wept a lot as I read it, and I think these tears which I shed at the disappearance from this world of an upright man endowed with an angelic spirit had a beneficial effect on me. I feel enlightened and reconciled in spirit.'[42] Over the years Ilya Petrovich had become like a dear ornament to him, treasured because of its age and many associations, and wept over when broken with sentimental, not grief-stricken, tears. This melancholy event certainly had no effect upon the new work he was composing.

The first declaration of intent to compose the Italian Capriccio (or Italian Suite on folk melodies, as Tchaikovsky then envisaged it) was given in a letter to Taneyev of 16 January. In Rome Tchaikovsky had encountered the same propensity of Italians to sing everywhere which had been such a mixed joy during his stay in Florence in 1878, and the idea that such native melodies might be of use to him personally took a swift hold of him. 'Yesterday I heard a delightful folksong which I shall certainly use,' he had written to Nadezhda von Meck as early as 27 December 1879.[43] By 28 January 1880, when he had begun composition, his models had become specific; 'I want to compose something like the Spanish fantasias of *Glinka*,' he announced to his benefactress.[44] A week later he could report to her cheerfully that the basic work was done. 'I have already completed the sketches for an Italian fantasia on folk tunes for which I believe a good future may be predicted. It will be effective, thanks to the delightful tunes which I have succeeded in assembling partly from anthologies, partly through my own ears on the streets.'[45] The scoring was deferred until May, and it was only when

[42] *TLP*9, p. 33; *TPM*2, p. 303.
[43] *TLP*8, p. 466; *TPM*2, p. 281.
[44] *TLP*9, p. 29; *TPM*2, p. 301; *YDGC*, p. 225; *DTC*, p. 393.
[45] *TLP*9, p. 35; *TPM*2, p. 306; *DTC*, p. 393; *YDGC*, p. 226 (partial).

this was finally completed on 27 May that the title was changed to
Italian Capriccio. By now Tchaikovsky had developed doubts about
the musical substance of the piece, but for its orchestral effectiveness he
had no fears. On 18 December 1880 Nikolay Rubinstein conducted the
first performance at an RMS concert in Moscow so successfully that it
was repeated at the next RMS concert a fortnight later. Such now was
the Russian interest in a new work by Tchaikovsky that within a further
fortnight it had been twice heard in St Petersburg.

Here apparently it scored less success, and some critics were already
sharing the composer's own well-founded doubts about its musical
substance. The opening fanfare, according to Modest, was a trumpet
call his brother had heard daily from the barracks which lay alongside
his hotel in Rome. Of the remaining four tunes, the only one to have
been identified is that of the final tarantella, which was known in Italy
as 'Ciccuzza'. The Italian Capriccio unfolds as a loose series of
self-contained sections which grow by thematic repetition against
changing backgrounds in the tradition of Glinka, or by simple developmental extension employing a good deal of sequence. It must remain
uncertain whether the broader tonal planning was prompted by the
highly appropriate Neapolitan chord which Tchaikovsky uses prominently in the coda to engineer a strong inflection of flat keys; certainly it
relates perfectly to the placing, in the preceding music, of deep flat keys
(E flat, D flat, and B flat major/minor itself) against the tonic A
minor/major. This leaning towards the flat side of the tonic recalls the
first movement of the Second Piano Concerto, the immediate predecessor of the Capriccio. But whereas the G major/E flat confrontation early
in the concerto's first movement had defined the field of tonal operation
for the following music, the even more extreme tritonal opposition (A
major/E flat major) exhibited early in the Capriccio heralded a series
of key contrasts used for purely colouristic purposes. In fact, the
projection of bright, warm, contrasting colours through any means at
Tchaikovsky's disposal is patently the main aim in the Capriccio.

Glinka's Spanish Overtures, which Tchaikovsky openly identified as
the prototypes of the Italian Capriccio, were evocative pieces composed
in response to the impressions made upon Glinka by Spain and its
people during his visit there between 1845 and 1847. While the two
pieces had been prompted by a common impulse and had been grown
entirely from Spanish melodies, they had turned out very differently as
designs, the first (*Capriccio brillante on the Jota aragonese*) being an essay in
the free treatment of folk melody within a sonata pattern, while the
second (*Recollection of a summer night in Madrid*) had abandoned any such
formal mould in favour of a free scheme; in fact, Glinka described it as a

pot-pourri, having based it on four themes instead of a single one, as in its predecessor. It was this Second Spanish Overture which was the true model for the Italian Capriccio. But whereas Glinka's vivid imagination and his flair for fantasy, with abrupt contrasts and unexpected juxtapositions, had enabled him to produce a colourful, highly inventive panorama of Mediterranean life, the Italian Capriccio, for all its arguable superiority as a well-made piece, shows Tchaikovsky thin in real inventiveness, and decidedly the inferior in power of suggestion. When the gregarious Glinka had lived in Spain he had soaked himself in the indigenous culture, and *Summer Night in Madrid* is Spain seen and felt from within; the Italian Capriccio is like Italy projected through the pages of a guide-book, evocative yet not real, and without the sheer allure of that technicolor gloss which Rimsky-Korsakov was to exhibit with such dazzling variety in his Spanish Capriccio.

In a letter inscribed to his patroness at the turn of the year, Tchaikovsky summarized what 1879 had meant to him.

As I look back on the passing year I must sing a hymn of thanksgiving to fate for the great number of good days I have spent both in Russia and abroad. I can say that for this whole year I have enjoyed undisturbed security, and have been happy as far as happiness is possible. Of course there have also been bitter moments – but only moments. What is more, these only arose from the misfortunes of people close to me while I, strictly speaking, have personally enjoyed unqualified happiness and contentment. This was the first year of my life during which I was the whole time a free man.[46]

The Italian Capriccio evidences forcefully the price of that freedom. In seeking the insulated conditions which he knew would be most favourable to his day-to-day contentment, Tchaikovsky had protected himself against those assaults on his nerve ends which alone could fully re-animate his creative powers, and had guarded himself from tensions which could broaden his experience and stretch his emotional awareness. The superficiality, even emptiness, of the Italian Capriccio suggests, perhaps more than any other work of this phase, the degree to which Tchaikovsky could not only retreat from the people around him (except for the chosen few), but also – paradoxically – detach himself from his environment. His capacity to withdraw into himself was now complete.

---

[46] *TLP*8, p. 491; *TPM*2, p. 291; *TZC*2, p. 363.

3

UKRAINIAN SUMMER:
TOTAL ISOLATION

When a creative artist becomes as recluse as Tchaikovsky had grown over the last two years, his biographer becomes painfully aware of a deadening monotony invading his narrative. Just as his subject has shrunk from contacts with all but a very few dear and trusted persons, so the events of that subject's life have inevitably contracted towards the trivia of day-to-day existence. 1879 had established what was to be the pattern of Tchaikovsky's existence for several years to come, and it would be otiose to continue particularizing all the minutiae of his by now well-established routines. We may take it for granted that he instituted carefully regulated working practices wherever he was, that he went for daily walks, enjoyed the cultural or scenic fare offered by whatsoever location he found himself in, and read a great deal. Only when, in such matters, something of some significance occurred need it be sifted out for the record.

As for the further compositional activities of Tchaikovsky's present three months in Rome, no sooner were the sketches of the Italian Capriccio complete than he received from Karl Davïdov, the director of the St Petersburg Conservatoire, a commission to compose music for an event celebrating the silver jubilee of Alexandr II as Tsar. This was to take place in the Bolshoy Theatre in St Petersburg on 2 March, barely three weeks away in the future, and would consist of a series of tableaux vivants depicting major events in Alexandr's reign. 'These tableaux will be accompanied by appropriate music,' Davïdov informed Tchaikovsky.

> The music is being composed by Rubinstein (Anton), Rimsky-Korsakov, Cui, Solovyev, Nápravník, Borodin, etc. We must have your name (an album with pictures and the music will subsequently be published). Each of the above-named composers has taken one tableau; because there's little time, and it's impossible to have long consultations between St Petersburg and Rome, I'm sending straight

on to you the content of that tableau which is awaiting musical illustration from you. Bear in mind that there must not be more than seven minutes of music. In view of the facility with which you compose, I'm hoping that your score will be in St Petersburg ahead of many from the local composers.

TABLEAU 10[1]

Montenegro. The moment at which news is received in Montenegro of Russia's declaration of war on Turkey (the leader is reading the manifesto to the Montenegrins).

From 5–7 minutes of music.[2]

Tchaikovsky viewed this scheme balefully, and he suspected that the other composers had taken their pick of the various tableaux, leaving him with the least attractive. He countered by suggesting that his Slavonic March might prove a ready-made background for his tableau, and to encourage Davïdov's favour towards this idea, he promptly offered him the dedication of the new Italian Capriccio. Nevertheless, because there was no time to see whether Davïdov would bite at this suggestion, and feeling he simply could not be left out, Tchaikovsky set himself to discharge the formal request, and in four days had completed his offering. 'It goes without saying that I couldn't think up anything except the most filthy noise and crashes,' he confided gloomily to Anatoly on 12 February, the day after completing the work.[3] We have no way of judging the truth of Tchaikovsky's verdict, for the festal event never took place. In the growing political and social turmoil of the last years of Alexandr's reign the authorities had become increasingly nervous. Tchaikovsky had himself only recently felt the consequences of this when *The Oprichnik*, which was being rehearsed for a revival in Moscow, was suddenly withdrawn after the dress rehearsal, the authorities feeling that its subject matter was too subversive for the times. Then, only a fortnight before the tableaux vivants were to be exhibited, an attempt was made on the Tsar's life in his own Winter Palace in St Petersburg, and the presentation was cancelled. Tchaikovsky was as relieved at this as at the veto on *The Oprichnik*; the Montenegrin tableau music was never performed or published, and the score has disappeared.

Having completed this unwelcome chore, Tchaikovsky rested from active creation for some four months. After all, he had in little more than three months composed the Second Piano Concerto, the Italian

---

[1] In referring to this tableau in his letters, Tchaikovsky numbered it as 7.

[2] *TZC*2, pp. 372–3.

[3] *TLP*9, p. 41; *TPB*, p. 241; *YDGC*, p. 226.

Capriccio, the Montenegrin tableau, and had virtually written anew the first movement of the Second Symphony; now both the concerto and the capriccio were waiting to be brought to their finished forms. Scoring and making transcriptions of these pieces occupied him until the end of May, and in the meanwhile proofs of the vocal score of *The Maid* had begun to arrive and turned out to be so inaccurate that the labour of correction absorbed him until the end of July. As in Paris, he avoided meeting people as far as he could. Twice as a tourist he visited the Villa d'Este, but declined to call on Liszt, though he suspected he was in residence. Being in Rome encouraged him to turn his attention to an author from that city's greatest days, and he read Tacitus in a French translation which revealed to him what a 'great and powerful artist'[4] this ancient stylist was. He also recommended his patroness to read Metternich's memoirs. Certainly he found these books more congenial than the recent Violin Concerto by Brahms, a copy of which Nadezhda von Meck had sent him for his appraisal. This merely consolidated what was to be his lifelong reaction to Brahms's music. Tchaikovsky sensed clearly the inhibition in such music, the iron discipline which held the full emotional force in check. 'There are many preparations for something, many hints of something which must appear forthwith and must charm – yet nothing but tedium comes out of this. His music is not warmed by true feeling, there is no poetry in it, though it has great pretension to *depth*. Yet there is nothing in this depth. . . . For instance, let us take the opening of the concerto; as an introduction to something it is beautiful, it is an excellent pedestal for a column – but the column itself does not exist, and immediately after one pedestal there comes another. I do not know whether I am expressing well the thought – or, rather, the feeling which Brahms's music instils in me.' As so often happened when Tchaikovsky was faced with music he fundamentally disliked, he could display a degree of clear, even penetrating insight until the moment at which that music had to be submitted to the idiosyncrasies of his own most personal receptive faculties; then, if the subject was one he had to recognize as a major figure, the best he could do was to confess to incomprehension, as he freely did when ending this assessment of the Violin Concerto. 'As a musical personality Brahms is simply *antipathetic* to me, I cannot digest him. However hard I try [to respond to his music], I remain cold and hostile. It is a purely instinctive feeling.'[5]

While in Rome Tchaikovsky witnessed the noisy pre-Lenten revels,

[4] *TLP*9, p. 46; *TPM*2, p. 312; *TZC*2, p. 376.
[5] *TLP*9, p. 56; *TPM*2, p. 318; *TZC*2, pp. 378–9.

and concluded that Berlioz's overture, *Le Carnaval romain*, had caught their unrestrained ebullience perfectly. But while he was impressed by the unadulterated good nature of the carnival, and the complete absence of the drunkenness which so often marred similar Russian festivities, the sheer din and chaos weighed on his nerves. He was deeply worried, too, by the impending separation between Kolya's parents. The mother was the guilty party, and Kolya idolized her; now the idol would be seen to be flawed, and Tchaikovsky realized all too well the pain which would attend Kolya's disenchantment. As so often happened when Tchaikovsky was abroad, the identity of his next destination kept changing until the moment of final decision arrived. Modest and Kolya were to remain in Italy, and Tchaikovsky determined to leave Alexey with them to reduce Modest's burden as Kolya's custodian. Since Tchaikovsky would now have to return to Russia alone, he felt that only by a wide detour to his beloved Paris could he find some joy on this lonely journey. There, too, he could see Kondratyev, who had already visited him in Rome, had exasperated him with his drunkenness and general debauchery, but who still commanded a firm hold on his affections. Then he would spend a night in Berlin which was at that time enjoying a high place in his favours. On 9 March, his finances rejuvenated by the 300 roubles he had received from the Moscow branch of the RMS for the First Suite, Tchaikovsky left Rome. Using *Pendennis* on the train as a refuge into which he could retreat to escape the endless conversation of a certain Belgian count (Tchaikovsky decided that Thackeray's novel was as delightful as *David Copperfield*), he arrived in Paris two days later. Here he relished performances of Corneille's *Polyeucte* and Molière's *Les Femmes savantes* at the Comédie-Française, and derived equal delight from a brand new play, *La Petite Mère*, by Henri Meilhac and Ludovic Halévy. 'The play's enchanting,' he enthused to Modest. 'The hero's a young *composer-symphonist* with long hair and a nervous sensibility. I never saw anything funnier in my life – nor, despite some caricaturing, more true to life. In one scene, where he's sitting at the piano in his dressing-room composing the second movement of his symphony, I almost split my sides with laughter.'[6] Patently Tchaikovsky was not in the least solemn about his own profession. But in Berlin, where he arrived on 15 March, disappointment awaited him when, for the first time, he saw Wagner's *Die fliegende Holländer* ('terribly noisy and boring,' he judged it to Modest[7]); he found far more genuine pleasure in the chimpanzee and dog who

[6] *TLP9*, pp. 66–7; *TPB*, p. 242; *YDGC*, p. 228.
[7] *TLP9*, p. 72; *TZC2*, p. 382; *TPB*, p. 245.

shared a cage in the menagerie of the Aquarium. A visit to the Kaiser Friedrich Museum confirmed his feeling that the spell in Rome had advanced significantly his appreciation of the visual arts, especially when he was able to recognize a Correggio without consulting the catalogue.

On 19 March he arrived in St Petersburg. 'I have already begun my periodic *martyrdom*,' he wrote to Nadezhda von Meck the following day,[8] referring to the beginning of yet another spell of bolstering up a depressed brother Anatoly. He had been well prepared for this by the torrents of woe and self-doubtings which had poured from Anatoly's letters to him in Paris and Rome; now, faced with Anatoly himself, with the uncongenial ambience of the northern capital, and with the gap left by the death of his father, whose grave he hastened to visit, his own spirits plummeted. News of the mortal illness of the composer-violinist, Henryk Wieniawski, whom Nadezhda von Meck had taken into her Moscow home to nurse through his last days, depressed him yet further. He spent a good deal of time with the Konradis, trying to understand their domestic plight and to ensure that the blow to their son would be lessened when, at last, he would have to be told of their impending divorce. Tchaikovsky could not complain of boredom, for there were far too many invitations from family and friends, far too many business matters to attend to. But any sort of creative work was impossible. Then, suddenly, the Grand Duke Konstantin Nikolayevich, brother of the Tsar, president of the RMS, and for long an admirer of Tchaikovsky's music, was insisting upon meeting him. Dreading the prospect of this social contact with so elevated a personage, Tchaikovsky nevertheless accepted Nápravník's remorseless insistence that he must endure such trials for the sake of his music, for Tchaikovsky's main preoccupation in St Petersburg was to promote the production of *The Maid of Orléans*, and the Grand Duke's support in this matter could prove critical. Meanwhile, to aggravate his already frayed nerves, the manuscript copy of the vocal score of *The Maid* submitted to the theatre turned out to be grossly inaccurate, and much time had to be devoted to correcting this. Not only did Tchaikovsky have to fulfil his obligation to dine with the Grand Duke; the Grand Duke's son, the Grand Duke Konstantin Konstantinovich, who was a friend of Vera Butakova, and who was not only a great devotee of music but himself an amateur composer and poet, also wanted to meet Tchaikovsky. Knowing, however, of Tchaikovsky's aversion to formal social events, he asked Vera Butakova to arrange an intimate evening at her own home.

[8] *TLP*9, p. 73; *TPM*2, p. 325.

Tchaikovsky could not escape. Yet when it came to the event, he found himself thoroughly disarmed by this twenty-two-year-old, and from nine until two in the morning they talked about music. For his part the Grand Duke was sufficiently taken by Tchaikovsky as a person to propose that the latter should accompany him on a three-year round-the-world trip upon which he was about to embark as a lieutenant in the Russian navy. Much flattered, Tchaikovsky nevertheless baulked at the thought of such protracted loss of freedom, and he declined the invitation. Nevertheless, this meeting marked the beginning of a friendship which was to last till the composer's death, and which was to result in the composition, upon the Grand Duke's own poems, of the Six Romances, Op. 63, and the male-voice chorus, 'Blessed is he who smiles', all of 1887.

Whatever the stresses of such meetings, they afforded Tchaikovsky yet more evidence from which he could take great heart. He could see he was passing from being simply a highly interesting, even respected composer to becoming an established figure whose music was one of the most admired ornaments of the cultural scene. From Moscow came news that, on 26 March, Nikolay Rubinstein was to perform not only Tchaikovsky's Piano Sonata but also the transcription which Liszt had already made of the Polonaise from *Eugene Onegin*, as well as a concert paraphrase on themes from the same opera by the German pianist and pupil of Liszt, Paul Pabst, now one of the professors at the Moscow Conservatoire. Meanwhile in St Petersburg itself there were, during Tchaikovsky's three-and-a-half-week stay, three concerts in which his own music was performed. On 30 March a quartet led by Auer played the Second String Quartet, Tchaikovsky receiving both an ovation and a wreath. Then five days later Nápravník conducted *Romeo and Juliet* at a musicians' benevolent fund concert, and two days later again directed the piece, this time in an all-Tchaikovsky programme in aid of a fund for establishing a scholarship to the St Petersburg Conservatoire. Besides *Romeo and Juliet*, there was the First Suite, the Andante canta-bile from the First String Quartet arranged for solo violin, some romances, and Alexandra Panayeva, who had caused such romantic torment to Anatoly, singing the letter monologue from *Onegin*. The pleasure of witnessing a concert devoted entirely to his own music was offset only by comments from some of his acquaintances, and even from the press, who had decided that the concert was Tchaikovsky's own idea, and that he was responsible for the inflated ticket prices. The concert itself was well attended, especially by the aristocracy, and Turgenev was in the audience; it was a considerable personal success for Tchaikovsky himself. Even that unpalatable round of industrious

visiting in which he engaged on behalf of *The Maid* furnished further
firm evidence of his rising reputation. From Moscow, where he arrived
on 14 April, he described to his patroness the social soliciting of his last
two days in St Petersburg.

> On Sunday from two to five I was at Mrs Abaza's, where the Grand
> Duchess Ekater[ina] Mikhailovna's family were, to whom I had to
> play extracts from my new opera. Her daughter is a very talented
> singer, and sings my romances very nicely. Thence I directed myself
> to dinner with Isakov, the supreme head of the military schools. The
> beginning of the evening I spent with Count Litke, and from eleven at
> night until three I sat with the engaging and very musical Grand
> Duke Konst[antin] Konst[antinovich]. . . . On Monday I attended
> a grand dinner at Princess Vasilchikova's where I was, as they say,
> the hero of the festivities, and where there was a great gathering of
> titled people of every variety, among whom was the Prince Evg[eny]
> Maximil[ianovich] Leichtenbergsky, whose wife is an outstanding
> singer, and who does me the honour of declaring herself my admirer.
> I repeat: all this serves as very comforting proof to me of my growing
> success.[9]

By now Tchaikovsky was desperately tired, but also deeply reassured; even he could see the affair of his marriage was beginning to
pass into history, and his rehabilitation into Russian society had begun.

So much had this social hurly-burly dominated Tchaikovsky's St
Petersburg existence that he decided he would in Moscow need first to
keep his presence a secret so that he might finish the scoring of the
Second Piano Concerto. Nikolay Rubinstein was mounting a Conservatoire performance of Beethoven's *Fidelio*, but Tchaikovsky chose to
absent himself from the dress rehearsal which he would normally have
felt obliged to attend. His attempt to remain incognito for two days
proved vain, and his truancy was discovered. Filled with alarm at how
Rubinstein would react, he hurried off to make his explanations, and
was immediately engulfed in the social world of his Moscow friends. In
consequence his stay had to be extended to more than a week so that he
might do what was urgently required of him by Jurgenson and others.
Little progress was made on scoring the concerto. On 23 April a very
thankful composer was at last able to slip out of Moscow on the way to
Kamenka.

*

[9] *TLP*9, p. 99; *TPM*2, p. 336; *TZC*2, pp. 389–90.

Tchaikovsky was beginning the longest single period he had so far spent in those special conditions of relaxation and freedom from worldly cares which the Ukraine afforded him. For seven months he was to find comfort in his sister's and patroness's homes, and the insulation this provided from the direct pressures of his wider existence was to be further reflected in some of the works he wrote during the next few months. Kamenka was in some turmoil when he arrived because of an influx of guests for Easter, including brother Ippolit with his wife and four-year-old daughter, as well as Anatoly. The need for the last to take up his new post in Moscow added urgency to Tchaikovsky's intention of finishing the Second Piano Concerto without delay, for he wished Anatoly to be his carrier, and when this brother left Kamenka on 14 May, he bore with him the completed score to pass over to Jurgenson. By now Modest had arrived with Kolya and Alexey. Tchaikovsky's distress at the situation within the Konradi household remained as acute as ever, and his heartfelt sympathy went out to all members of that unhappy clan. To Kolya's mother, now viewing the break from her husband with dread, he wrote one of his most touchingly sympathetic letters. 'Please, Alina Ivanovna,' it ended, 'arm yourself with courage, and bear the painful moment with philosophical calm. Remember that no decent person will ever blame you for anything, and will always understand that you are a victim of fateful circumstances beyond your control.'[10] There were times when a belief in fate had its comforts, it seems, for it could offer absolution from responsibility, and thus freedom from guilt.

Further testimony to Tchaikovsky's growing eminence was afforded soon after he arrived in Kamenka by a request from the Kiev branch of the RMS to become their musical director in charge of both concert and teaching activities. Much flattered, Tchaikovsky nevertheless declined the invitation without hesitation. Then, a fortnight later, came a letter from the St Petersburg Philharmonic Society, one of the oldest and most distinguished of Russia's musical associations, informing Tchaikovsky that the Society was planning to promote two concerts of his works, and asking him to propose what might be included. A delighted Tchaikovsky suggested the Second (revised) and Fourth Symphonies, *Francesca da Rimini* and the First Suite, as well as the still unperformed Violin Concerto and Italian Capriccio. Since the Society had a choir, he also put forward his Liturgy of St John Chrysostom, a clear indication that he viewed this work as far more than a purely functional piece of church music. Unfortunately these concerts did not materialize.

[10] *TLP*9, p. 115.

As for Tchaikovsky's more personal affairs, it is clear that Antonina had now realized nothing was to be gained from harassing her husband, and to confirm in her the wisdom of ignoring him totally, Tchaikovsky had twice sent her donations beyond his normal monthly payments made through Jurgenson. Now it became known that she was following her husband's suggestion that she should seek an appointment teaching music in a girls' school. Though Tchaikovsky would have much preferred her to find such a post in the provinces rather than in Moscow, he asked Jurgenson to give her what aid he could. 'The more she's occupied, the less she'll think of and bother me,' he observed pungently to his publisher on 12 May.[11] He brushed aside a proposal which emanated shortly afterwards from Antonina's mother that immediate divorce should again be discussed, for he did not intend to raise the matter with Antonina until September, when she had had a full year to think over his most recent proposals on this matter. A far more pressing cause for concern was Alexey's obligation to do military service. Though there was no escaping this, the period of conscription could be reduced from six to three years if Alexey passed an examination. For some time Tchaikovsky had been devoting time to coaching his valet, and at Kamenka he enrolled him in the local school, thus for a while losing some of his services.

Then Modest fell ill, and Tchaikovsky had to take over half the instruction of Kolya, who had just been told of his parents' divorce and who, for all Modest's careful preparation, had taken the news as badly as Tchaikovsky had feared he would. Finally, early in June, Sasha left for Western Europe with her elder daughters for a desperately needed rest, and Lev had to make a business trip; the result was that Uncle Pyotr was left in charge of the remaining children. Not only was his own work interrupted for a while; he had also to put off his departure for Simaki, where his patroness had hoped he would stay while she was at the great house of Brailov. Though Tchaikovsky expressed boundless regret at this enforced delay, his protestations were less than sincere. Patently the thought of close residence made him uneasy, especially after the unfortunate confrontation of the last visit. His discomforts at Kamenka were of a different order. However well he got on with children, he was simply not equipped by nature to be left in charge of them, and certainly not to handle the moods of girls approaching adolescence. Besides the twelve-year-old Nataliya, who took it upon herself to queen it over the others the moment their parents were gone, there was still in residence Evgeniya Olkhovskaya, daughter of

11 *TLP*9, p. 117.

Tchaikovsky's half-sister, Zinaida, whom Sasha had taken into her own home after the death of her parents. Both girls attempted to dominate, and Uncly Pyotr was powerless to control the situation. 'Zhenya [Evgeniya], no longer being overshadowed by the other female figures, has emerged from the background very clearly and most offensively,' he unburdened himself to Anatoly on 11 June, three days after his regency had begun. 'God, what an unattractive little creature she is! Sometimes you want to take pity on her, to be nice to her through the friendly tone of your conversation, and in reply you'll unfailingly receive some disgusting nonsense from which it appears there's no way even of taking pity on her. Worst of all is that, in the absence of Tanya, Vera and Sasha, she constantly thrusts herself upon me with her endearments – and, my God, how repulsive this is! The children are charming, especially Bobik. Ah, what a delightful work of nature he is! I'm falling in love with him still more and more!'[12] Already from Sasha's children Tchaikovsky was singling out the nine-year-old Vladimir, the favourite nephew of his later years, the future dedicatee of the Sixth Symphony, and another of Modest's zealous allies in founding the Tchaikovsky Museum at Klin. When Lev returned a week later Tchaikovsky admitted that a 'small anarchy' had reigned during his absence. Relieved of these family responsibilities, yet still unable to go to Simaki even if he had wanted to because Alexey's examination had been put off until early July, he decided to utilize a break which had come in his work on the proofs of *The Maid*, and on 16 June set to work on the Six Duets, Op. 46.

'I've come to the conclusion that I'm writing too much, and I want for a whole year to compose nothing except trifles,' Tchaikovsky had written to Jurgenson at the end of April.[13] These duets and their companion romances, Op. 47, mostly answer this specification exactly. On 30 April, only days after his arrival at Kamenka, Tchaikovsky had told his patroness of his own musical contribution to the Good Friday service.

Today I made my début in the capacity of church precentor. My sister was desperately anxious that we should sing *Comely Joseph* when the shroud is carried out. We got hold of the music, made up a quartet from my sister, Tanya, Anatoly and me, and prepared Bortnyansky's setting of this anthem. At home our singing went well, but in the church Tanya got mixed up, and then we all did. My attempts to restore order were in vain, and we had to stop before the

---

[12] *TLP*9, p. 142.
[13] *TLP*9, p. 110.

end. My sister and Tanya are exceedingly distressed by this episode, but on Sunday an opportunity to redeem ourselves will present itself at mass. I have undertaken to practise with them Bortnyansky's seventh Cherubim's Song and the Lord's Prayer from my own Liturgy [of St John Chrysostom].[14]

It seems more than likely that these homely musical activities prompted Tchaikovsky to compose these six duets. Dedicated to his niece, Tatyana, they would have provided excellent domestic fare for mother and daughter, while in one – the setting of the Scottish ballad, 'Edward' – the second voice is a baritone which would have allowed Anatoly or Tchaikovsky himself to participate also. The first to be composed was 'Passion spent' (No. 5), based on a poem by Alexey Tolstoy ('an inexhaustible source of texts for music; to me he is one of the most attractive poets,' Tchaikovsky told his patroness a day after starting composition[15]). The epithet these duets continually prompt is 'charming'; certainly it aptly characterizes the modest music of the nature picture which opens and closes 'Evening' (No. 1) – music which captivates more strongly than that of the central section, where the singers perversely expend much vocal energy in begging to be allowed to rest. Charming, too, is the prettily sentimental vignette of the maiden weeping as the young man stands over her mockingly in 'In the garden, near the ford' (No. 4).

These last two duets set verse by Ivan Surikov, a dilettante-poet who had died only a few weeks earlier, and to whose work Tchaikovsky was strongly attracted; in both, as in 'Passion spent', Tchaikovsky repeated the opening portion of the poem at the end to permit a ternary structure. So strong was his commitment to this mechanical symmetry that in the languishing 'Tears' (No. 3), because he clearly felt that an already highly repetitive text could not be retraced yet again, he reviewed the material of the work's opening in an unexpectedly large piano postlude. Tchaikovsky declared that this was his own favourite, but by far the best are the remaining two. 'Scottish ballad' (No. 2), Alexey Tolstoy's translation of that remorselessly unfolding duologue of domestic tragedy, 'Edward', is aptly set to lean, even curt phrases, supported by the bleakest of piano accompaniments, the mounting tension heightened by the firm tonal shifts of verses three and four. Unable to break completely with the ternary structure, Tchaikovsky returned to the opening music for verse five, then plunged on to

[14] TLP9, p. 109; TPM2, p. 342; TZC2, p. 391.
[15] TLP9, p. 146; TPM2, p. 360; TZC2, p. 393; YDGC, p. 234; DTC, p. 288.

new invention for the final verse as the mother agonisedly asks her murderer-son what he will leave to her (Ex. 167a). Here for a moment Tchaikovsky echoes, though now with brutal force, that climactic moment of Tatyana's letter monologue in *Onegin* (also in D flat), where the musical embodiment of fate in action had impressed itself upon Tatyana's utterance with most poignant eloquence (see Vol. 2, Ex. 139a). The composer himself looked with much favour on this duet also, though he recognized its distinctive character, and feared it would never be performed as he wished ('it must not be sung but, rather, declaimed – and with the greatest fervour,' he told his patroness[16]). By contrast the final duet, 'Dawn' (No. 6) complements the first, setting Surikov's quietly blissful dawn greeting as a waltz in which Tchaikovsky's lyrical invention rises to a level above that of any of its companions. Whereas the previous songs – 'Scottish ballad', of course, excepted – had merely charmed, this one affords a measure of delight.

That same, seemingly indelible passage from Tatyana's letter monologue is recalled in 'Dusk fell on the earth', a Mickiewicz translation which is the third of the Seven Songs, Op. 47 (Ex. 167b). Here is yet another recrudescence of fate as the cause of sadness and dejection; indeed, the full scalic fate motif appears in the singer's final phrase (Ex. 167c). In some respects these songs are more interesting than the duets, for their treatment of the texts is more responsive, their unfolding of the musical ideas more flexible. Yet that fatal melodic flaw which dooms the Second Piano Concerto to second-rank status among Tchaikovsky's compositions is unremittingly evident in all these songs, whether it is pervasively present as in the limp sentimentality of 'Softly the spirit flew up to heaven' (No. 2, which, Tchaikovsky told Modest, was inspired by the duet between Christ and Mary Magdalene in Massenet's oratorio *Marie-Magdeleine*), or more intermittently as in the piano prelude to 'Dusk fell on the earth', which starts well with a shapely opening phrase strongly propelled by the harmonic anacrusis of three bars of supertonic driving into the dominant, but which by the end has sunk into both harmonic and melodic impotence; Tchaikovsky himself was, however, particularly proud of this song. He began sketching this collection before leaving for Mrs von Meck's estate on 13 July, but the main labour of composition was completed there and, like their companion duets, they were finished at the beginning of

---

[16] *TLP*10, p. 163; *TPM*2, p. 530; *TZC*2, p. 477. Besides resurging in the third of the Op. 47 songs, this crucial moment in Tatyana's letter monologue is also to round off the fifth of the Six Songs, Op. 65, which Tchaikovsky composed and dedicated to Désirée Artôt in 1888; this song also appears – significantly – to incorporate a strong hint of Mendelssohn's wedding march at its opening.

Ex. 167

a.

[But what will you leave to your mother, Edward?]

b.

["Why are you sad today, and all around you cheerless?"]

c.

[I am sad, just as before!]

September. The set contains one of Tchaikovsky's better known songs, 'I bless you, forests' (No. 5), a setting of lines from Alexey Tolstoy's *John of Damascus*. Tolstoy's majestic benediction led Tchaikovsky into dignified melodic territory, with aspirations towards epic heights to match the poet's final shout of longing to gather all nature into his embrace. Though, sadly, the achievement scarcely equals the intention, 'I bless you, forests' impresses more deeply than the melancholy cradle song, 'Sleep, poor friend' (No. 4, another of the four Tolstoy settings in this set), where the hypnotic insistence upon a slender vocal phrase and a two-note piano sigh induces repose less through lulling charm than dulling monotony – though one may wonder whether any child could sleep when the ache within the lyric is projected with such noisy vehemence. Musorgsky managed cradle-side fantasizing with incomparably more moving pathos in 'Eremushka's cradle song'. The equally insistent accumulation of short-breathed phrases works better in 'If only I had known' (No. 1), for here it catches something of the breathless obsessiveness with which the image of the young horseman has infatuated the girl whose monologue this poem is, while the metrical straitjacket into which the various phrase contours are strapped conveys admirably her frustrated longing. Nevertheless, the quality of the melodic invention is again too insubstantial, and the sudden demisemiquaver howl of pain at the end of the second verse is an almost theatrical gesture which seeks to project the sheer force of feeling which the preceding music has lacked the substance to convey in full measure. The gay introduction had lightly sketched the carefree object of the girl's passion, and a touch of wistful irony is provided by ending the song with this same sprightly music which had found no part at all in the girl's utterance, just as the object of her adoration had remained unattainable.

The remaining two songs were later to be orchestrated by Tchaikovsky. According to the literary scholar, Fyodor Malinin, 'Does the day reign?' (No. 6) had been begun in St Petersburg in the spring. The words are by Apukhtin and were handed to Tchaikovsky, so Malinin stated, after the all-Tchaikovsky charity concert. Apukhtin had inscribed his verses to Alexandra Panayeva, who sang Tatyana's letter monologue in the same concert, and within days Tchaikovsky had sketched the music for these verses. Malinin's authority for this assertion is unknown; Tchaikovsky did, however, dedicate not only this song but also the others of Op. 47 to Panayeva. Though 'Does the day reign?' is one of the least distinguished in the set, the composer himself thought well enough of it to score it for performance in a concert he directed of his own works in Paris in 1888. Four years earlier he had similarly treated 'Was I not a little blade of grass' (No. 7). This was a far more worthwhile operation; the varying bar lengths ward off that metrical squareness to which Tchaikovsky was so prone to succumb when composing songs, while its modalism steers his invention into a freshly Russian world and away from the trite melodic particles from which some of its companion romances are built. As Gerald Abraham has pertinently observed, this Surikov translation of the Ukrainian Shevchenko's poem 'moved Tchaikovsky as far as he was capable of being moved in the direction of Musorgsky'.[17] The trouble is that Tchaikovsky now trod very unsurely in this special Russian world. As in 'Dusk fell on the earth', the melodic invention continually falters. Bars three to four of the piano introduction (Ex. 168a) provide the lamest of answers to the opening two; so, too, do the final two bars of Ex. 168b (especially the concluding melisma which is grossly inflated in the final verse) after the characterful first two phrases, the second of which had, with such heartfelt emotion, amplified the contour of the first. Yet for all its unevenness, the sadly resigned music of this young peasant girl, married against her will to an unkind, grey-haired old man, is more affecting than the shallow rhetoric of 'If only I had known' or 'Sleep, poor friend'.

When Tchaikovsky finally arrived at Brailov, Mrs von Meck had departed. Awaiting him was an expensive gold watch which she had ordered in Paris the preceding winter; it was intended, she explained, as a memento of her in case she should die soon. 'On one side is portrayed Joan of Arc, the subject of your great composition,' she added, 'and on the other Apollo and the Muses, the common companions of your inspirations – and in all this, impersonal and unseen, will lurk my spirit, for if a person possesses one, then *mine* will always be with you.'[18] Touched as he was by this gift, the impecunious Tchaikovsky would have infinitely preferred to receive the value of the watch in cash. 'Between ourselves,' he admitted to Anatoly the day after his arrival, 'I had hoped to find here not a *watch*, but some special sum of money. Nad[ezhda] Fil[aretovna] has so spoiled me by anticipating my wants and wishes that I had somehow calculated she would know by instinct what it is I now need. But I was mistaken, and now I see I shan't have a kopeck until the autumn.'[19]

His finances, in fact, were in utter disarray. He had already begged several months' advance on his allowance from his benefactress; now,

[17] Gerald Abraham: chapter on Russian song in Denis Stevens (ed.): *A History of Song* (London, 1960), p. 367.

[18] *TPM*2, p. 361.

[19] *TLP*9, p. 170; *TPM*2, p. 623.

Ex. 168

[Oh, you are my sorrow! Such it seems is my lot!]

with debts still amounting to 4,000 roubles, he turned in desperation to Jurgenson. Whether or not the latter would be able to make some arrangement, Tchaikovsky knew he would have to resign himself to remaining in Russia this summer. Spying on his benefactress's shelves a comprehensive collection of his own scores, he was taken aback by the quantity he had composed and by the shortcomings in its printed form. 'I have decided to write nothing for a while and busy myself solely with correcting and republishing all my former work,' he declared to Modest.[20] Meanwhile, during the month he was to enjoy his hostess's hospitality, he resolved to relax as much as possible. It proved a short-lived intention; as we have seen, both romances and duets were to exercise his creative faculties.

At Brailov, too, he found a collection of dances by Glinka, and this prompted him to survey to his patroness both the strengths and weaknesses of this much-flawed father-figure of Tchaikovsky's own native tradition. Though not quite right about Glinka's impatience of criticism or about which polka roused that composer's enthusiasm, it is an assessment far more balanced and perceptive than that which issues from most Russian musicians.

What an exceptional phenomenon Glinka is! When you read his *Memoirs*, which reveal a nice, amiable, but empty and even commonplace man: when you play his slighter compositions, it is just not possible to believe that all were written by the very same man who created, for instance . . . the Slavsya Chorus! And how many other amazing beauties are there in his operas, his overtures! What a stunningly original piece is *Kamarinskaya*, from which all later Russian composers up to the present time (and I, of course, among them) draw, in the most obvious fashion, contrapuntal and harmonic combinations as soon as they have to treat a Russian dance tune. . . . And suddenly this very same man, now in his full maturity, composes such a flat, shaming banality as the Coronation Polonaise (written a year before his death) or the Children's Polka about which he speaks with such self-satisfaction and such detail in his *Memoirs* as though it were some chef d'oeuvre. . . . Glinka was a talented Russian gentleman of his time, pettily proud, little developed, full of vanity and self-adoration, intolerant and pathologically touchy as soon as it came to the evaluation of his own compositions. All these qualities usually belong to mediocrity, but how they could find their place in a man who, it would seem, ought to have been assured and to have

[20] *TLP*9, p. 174; *TZC*2, p. 397; *TPB*, p. 250; *YDGC*, p. 235.

recognized his own strength with proud modesty – that I emphatically do not understand! . . . But all the same he wrote the Slavsya Chorus!'[21]

Feeling that the seclusion of his hostess's humbler accommodation would be far more to his liking, Tchaikovsky had within a week transferred to Simaki, and his rapturous joy is evident from many of his letters written during the first part of his three-week residence. Here he completed work on the proofs of *The Maid*, revelled yet again in Bizet's *Carmen*, investigated Massenet's *Marie-Magdeleine* ('a piece overflowing with virtues, elegance and charm,' he told Mrs von Meck[22]), but railed against contemporary French writers, castigating Zola and especially Victor Hugo, and confessing to Modest that when he had once read the latter's *Les Travailleurs de la Mer* at Usovo, his irritation had finally driven him to tear the book in pieces and fling it out of the window. It was still contemporary English novelists who particularly attracted him, and he continued his study of the English language in the hope that in six months he would be able to read Dickens and Thackeray as well as Shakespeare fluently. He listened to services not only in the Orthodox monastery but also in the new Catholic church in whose foundation he had himself played some part, deciding that the Orthodox service was vastly preferable to the Catholic mass. On a lower level he derived great amusement from a tiny libretto for an opera, *Sasha and Vanya*, which one of the villagers had concocted and which he now requested Tchaikovsky, as a 'musician of genius', to furnish with music so that they might perform it in their domestic theatre. It was to have piano accompaniment, must not be difficult, and must fall easily on the ear. Excusing himself from composing this ludicrous piece on the grounds of insufficient time, he nevertheless undertook to seek a volunteer from among other Russian composers, and circulated the literary bauble among his Moscow friends for their entertainment.

Even the sudden appearance of letters from Antonina and her mother only briefly ruffled his calm. His wife was incensed at gossip which had evidently been circulating in the Russian capital. 'I agree to your proposal [for settling our marriage affair]; I don't want to be even nominally the wife of a man who so basely slanders a woman who has done him no harm,' she wrote furiously on 7 July.

How could you and your brothers bring yourselves to tell all sorts of cock-and-bull stories to your relative, [Amaliya] Litke? What is

[21] *TLP*9, pp. 176–7; *TPM*2, pp. 369–70; *TZC*2, pp. 400–1.
[22] *TLP*9, p. 197; *TPM*2, p. 383.

more, she confirms her own good breeding by spreading these bits of tittle-tattle in St Petersburg! Why didn't you start with yourself, telling her about your own terrible vice, and then passing judgment on me? After all this you emphasize in your letters your own goodness and honourableness. But where are these qualities – and where is confirmation of them? Please don't trouble to reply. Maman has been so kind as to take upon herself negotiations with your lawyer to make an end of this matter.[23]

Antonina's terms still fell short of divorce, however, and she would sign nothing; in return for freedom of movement and guaranteed security, she would undertake to leave Moscow permanently and trouble him no more. A lightly veiled threat lurked unmistakably within the final assurance of 'maman's' letter. 'You are a man of genius, your good name is dear to you. Believe us, we will not sully it, and we will carry out the honourable undertaking we have given you as befits an honourable, noble family.'[24] But at remote Simaki even such embodiments of his most personal problems seemed almost unreal. For three days he was off his food and slept badly, but his initial agitation soon passed and, it seems, he dismissed Antonina as largely irrelevant.

Yet the truth is that, paradoxically, detachment itself was now becoming a strain. 'I confess I'm leaving here reluctantly; yet on the other hand, perhaps it's even harmful for me to stay too long,' he wrote to Modest on 7 August, four days before his return to Sasha's. 'I notice how the constant ecstasy in which I find myself here gets on my nerves. I have become pathologically susceptible to every kind of impression; often an utter trifle makes me weep, especially apropos some recollection or other from the irrevocable past, and especially its *irrevocability*.'[25] At Kamenka there was at least no danger of complete social isolation. Anatoly was daily expected, and Tchaikovsky's nieces had been waiting impatiently for his return so that they might set about mounting some more domestic theatricals – and for the success of such things Uncle Pyotr's participation was still considered essential. And without him there were no walks in the woods and no music making.

By now Jurgenson had arranged for some money to be made available through a bank in Kiev, and on 16 August, four days after his return to Kamenka, Tchaikovsky arrived in the city for a two-day stay so that he might also enjoy the kind of experience which a rural existence could not offer. For nearly four months he had heard little

[23] *TPM2*, p. 624.
[24] ibid.
[25] *TLP9*, p. 218; *TPM2*, p. 625; *TPB*, p. 256.

music except that which he made for himself, and the effect of encountering an orchestral performance again proved overwhelming. He
went to one of his favourite places in Kiev, the Château des Fleurs, in
which a small orchestra played. 'When, as I entered the garden, I heard
the sounds of the celebrated overture to *Robert* [*le Diable* by Meyerbeer],
the strength of the sensation I experienced almost made me faint,' he
told Mrs von Meck.[26] Proofs of the Italian Capriccio and the Second
Piano Concerto had now arrived, the new duets and romances had to be
worked into their finished forms, and at the beginning of September he
returned to his fantasy overture *Romeo and Juliet*, bringing it to that final
perfection in which we know it today. Yet his determination to scrutinize all his earlier music remained. As his letter to Jurgenson of 13
September makes clear, a few pieces were satisfactory, while others
required not to be reworked as compositions, merely to be corrected in
their published form, and friends could be entrusted with this labour.
'Because I lack the strength to do all this properly by myself, I've asked
Taneyev, Langer and Kashkin to apply their combined efforts to
correcting the First and Third Symphonies, and also *The Tempest*. I
hope they won't refuse. Please be so kind as to give them a copy each of
these three pieces. Meanwhile be so kind as to send me my earlier piano
pieces – i.e., everything except the [First] Concerto, the collection with
the Bülow variations [Op. 19], and my last collection with the twelve
pieces of moderate difficulty [Op. 40]. Please add to this my first six
romances.'[27] The letter continued with a further request. 'I think that
on the occasion of the Pushkin jubilee [the unveiling of a Pushkin
memorial in Moscow], there was issued in Moscow a book in which
were collected all the poems which hymned *Moscow*. I believe it's called
Moscow in the works of Russian poets. I need this book very much, for I hope
to find in it some theme for my exhibition music, to the composition of
which I'm going to proceed shortly – and, to tell the truth, with
indescribable aversion.... Have you told Nik[olay] Gr[igoryevich
Rubinstein] that I want more precise and detailed directions about
what's required of me?'[28] Ironically the work about which Tchaikovsky
was setting with such aversion was to become one of his most famed
compositions.

The first suggestion for the piece which was to emerge as the festival
overture, *The year 1812*, had come from Rubinstein early in June.
'Rubinstein has been appointed by Grieg [the Minister of Finance]
head of the musical section of the Exhibition [of Industry and the Arts]

[26] *TLP*9, p. 228; *TPM*2, p. 292; *TZC*2, pp. 412–13.
[27] *TLP*9, p. 253; *TZC*2, p. 419 (partial).
[28] *TLP*9, p. 253; *TPJ*1, p. 168; *TZC*2, pp. 419–20 (partial); *YDGC*, p. 240 (partial).

of 1881,' Jurgenson had written to Tchaikovsky on 10 June. '. . . He is proposing to ask you to choose and agree to compose one of the following pieces: (1) an overture to open the exhibition, or (2) [an overture] for the Tsar's silver jubilee, or (3) a cantata in whatever form or style you like, but with a hint of church music which must certainly be Orthodox, for the opening of the Cathedral of Christ the Saviour. Of course you'll be paid.'[29]

The freedom of choice left Tchaikovsky unimpressed, and he had no intention of agreeing to anything until he knew the precise conditions. 'It seems you think writing ceremonial pieces for an exhibition is some sort of ultimate bliss of which I shall hasten to avail myself, and that I shall straightway proceed to pour out my inspiration, not knowing properly where, how, what, why, when and so on. I won't lift a finger until something is *ordered* from me,' he replied testily on 5 July. '. . . [For commissioned pieces] I need stimulating, encouraging and galvanizing features in the form of precise indications, prescribed dates, and 100 rouble notes (a lot) coming in the more or less distant future. You give me the choice of this or that festal occasion as though one of these could attract me!'[30] Eleven days later he reinforced this distaste to the same correspondent. 'I wrote to you what I felt concerning the proposal, and I felt extreme repugnance. And it is impossible without repugnance to set about music which is destined for the glorification of what, at bottom, delights me not at all. Neither in the jubilee of the high-ranking person (who has always been fairly antipathetic to me) nor in the *cathedral*, which I don't like at all, is there anything of the sort which could kindle my inspiration.'[31] Having declared his position so unequivocally, Tchaikovsky relegated the proposal to the back of his mind until the organizers responded as he required. Nearly three months passed before, on 30 September, a request arrived from Rubinstein. The latter had not lost his touch in handling Tchaikovsky. 'You will understand without any compliments that your composition would be dearer and more precious to me than all the others,' he wrote. 'It's not an order but a great favour to me – firstly, because of the occasion, secondly, yet again because of me. I shall not prescribe either a subject or a form. I ask that the composition should be from fifteen to twenty-five minutes long, with or without chorus – but, of course, without soloist.'[32]

[29] *TPJ*1, pp. 152–3; *DTC*, p. 396.

[30] *TLP*9, p. 157; *TZC*2, pp. 394–5; *TPJ*1, p. 154; *DTC*, p. 396 (first two sentences only).

[31] *TLP*9, p. 171; *TPJ*1, p. 156; *YDGC*, p. 235 (partial).

[32] *TPM*2, p. 626; also in 'P. I. Chaykovsky i N. G. Rubinstein' in *Istoriya russkoy muzïki* (ed. by K. A. Kuznetsov) (Moscow, 1924), p. 182.

Tchaikovsky was persuaded but not reconciled. 'There is nothing less to my liking than composing for the sake of some *festivities*,' he promptly resumed his lament, this time to his patroness. 'Think, my dear friend! What, for instance, can you write *on the occasion of the opening of an exhibition* except banalities and generally noisy passages.'[33] Anxious to get this detestable chore out of the way, he decided upon an offering to mark the consecration of the cathedral, and on 12 October he set to work, composing the piece in a week. 'The overture will be very loud and noisy,' he further wrote to Nadezhda von Meck on 22 October, while buried in orchestrating the piece, 'but I wrote it with no warm feeling of love, and therefore there will probably be no artistic merits in it.'[34] The orchestration was completed on 19 November.

Despite his doubts about the overture's musical substance, Tchaikovsky did not believe it was necessarily unworthy the attention of the concert-going public, and when the exhibition was delayed for a year, he offered it to Nápravník for performance in St Petersburg. 'Nevertheless,' he wrote cautiously on 29 June 1881, 'I don't think it has any serious merits, and I shan't be at all surprised and offended if you find that it is in a style unsuitable for symphony concerts.'[35] In fact, Tchaikovsky had no business to be soliciting performance ahead of the event for which it had been commissioned, and Nápravník advised him to be patient until this had taken place. On 20 August 1882, in a hall specially constructed for the Exhibition, Ippolit Altani conducted the first performance of *1812*.

Since the Cathedral of Christ the Saviour was being built to commemorate the events of 1812, Tchaikovsky's choice of subject for his overture is easily understood. It was an equally obvious decision that he should take the national hymns of the warring powers as musical symbols, allowing the Marseillaise to range freely but fragmentarily in earlier portions of the work before retreating in the face of the Russian cannon which allies its explosions to the already full battery of percussion in the coda; this coda concludes with a full statement of 'God save the Tsar' as the emblem of Russian supremacy. Russia herself is represented by the Orthodox chant, *Save us, O Lord*, and by the folksong, 'U vorot', which Tchaikovsky had already arranged for piano duet in 1869.[36] From his own first opera, *The Voyevoda*, he appropriated part of the duet for Mariya and Olyona in Act 2, Scene 2, using this as the first eighteen bars of the G flat (written F sharp) second subject, an idea

[33] *TLP9*, p. 287; *TPM2*, p. 423; *TZC2*, p. 424; *YDGC*, p. 241 (partial).
[34] *TLP9*, p. 294; *TPM2*, p. 429; *TZC2*, pp. 425 and 484; *DTC*, p. 397; *YDGC*, p. 242.
[35] *TLP10*, p. 143; *DTC*, p. 397.
[36] *T50RF*, No. 48.

extended to lead into the folksong; this, now back in the tonic, acts as
conclusion for the exposition. But whereas Tchaikovsky had modified
his original harmony in the *Voyevoda* borrowing, he decided that his
earlier folksong arrangement would do perfectly well in the new
context, and the first eight bars of the resumed E flat minor are simply
an orchestral transcription of the 1869 setting with a touch of metrical
spicing from the tambourine. Add to all this that Tchaikovsky, con-
sciously or unconsciously, also filched some thematic character from
material invented for other recent works, and it becomes clear that a
good deal of the basic conceptual labour of this unpalatable chore was
eased.

1812 is therefore a thematic ragbag, yet its contemptuous dismissal
by some critics is a little less than fair. The coda is insufferably tumid
with its ridiculously heavy-handed preparation for the restatement of
the Orthodox chant, followed by the national anthem stentoriously
counterpointed to the jogging cavalry tune of the introduction. Yet the
work's opening, with the chant intoned by solo sextet of two violas and
four cellos, later joined by woodwind in simulation of choral antiphony,
is solemnly impressive; effective, too, is the sudden eruption of the full
orchestra and the beginning of the lament with the gruff interjections
from lower strings (the oboe opening is surely a memory from *The Maid
of Orléans*[37]). The first subject clearly gains its character from the new
first subject of the recently revised first movement of the Second
Symphony, while the descending string line, with its crotchet triplets,
which counterpoints the restatement of the second subject material in
that same movement (see Vol. 1, Ex. 62) is surely the suggestion for the
string line which, at the corresponding point of *1812*, counterpoints the
woodwind restatement of the *Voyevoda* material. This *Voyevoda* material
was well worth rescuing, is nicely amplified in its new context, and pairs
satisfactorily with the following folksong. Yet the development is
inadequate, the recapitulation perfunctory, and the coda inexcusable.
If the final impression left by *1812* is of a meretricious piece of bombast,
Tchaikovsky had only himself to blame.

The Serenade for Strings, composed at the same time, is a very
different matter, as Tchaikovsky himself recognized. 'I composed the
serenade . . . from inner conviction. It is a heartfelt piece and so, I dare
to think, is not lacking in real qualities,' he confessed to his benefactress
in the same letter in which he had voiced such unloving doubts about
1812.[38] Though by early September his various labours of proof-

[37] Act 3, Scene 1 (No. 17, bars 125ff.).
[38] *TLP*9, p. 294; *TPM*2, p. 429; *TZC*2, p. 425; *TPJ*1, p. 249; *DTC*, p. 477; *YDGC*,
p. 242.

reading, copying duets and romances, and revising *Romeo and Juliet* had been brought to an end, he found himself again left in charge of the Kamenka children with all the strains which this entailed. On Sasha and Lev's return he had employed his new-found freedom in long walks, in enjoying the company of Modest and Kolya who had arrived immediately after Anatoly's departure, and in discovering anew some of the riches of Mozart's *Die Zauberflöte*. But as so often happened, within a day or two this freedom began to weigh on him, and on 21 September he began to sketch the Serenade, intending first that it should be either a symphony or a string quintet. By 7 October, with three movements complete, it had become a suite for string orchestra, but well before its completion on 4 November Tchaikovsky had decided it should be designated a serenade.

Full of enthusiasm for his new offspring, he was impatient to have it performed. His wish was to be granted sooner than ever he could have expected. On receiving the score Jurgenson turned to Nikolay Rubinstein, and on 3 December, only three weeks later, Tchaikovsky was greeted with a surprise performance given by Conservatoire forces when he visited his old teaching institution. The first public performance took place on 30 October 1881 in St Petersburg at an RMS concert under Nápravník; it was very successful and the Valse was encored. Moscow heard it the following January, and it was repeated in June with Anton Rubinstein conducting. 'At the first rehearsal Jupiter [Anton Rubinstein] declared to me: "I think this is Tchaikovsky's best piece",' Jurgenson reported to Tchaikovsky on 12 June. 'He praised the piece equally unconditionally to others, and at the final rehearsal said to me: "You can congratulate yourself on the publication of this opus".'[39] At last this St Petersburg pundit, who had growled with such consistent disapproval at Tchaikovsky's successive compositions, had found a work by his former pupil which he could endorse.

The Serenade for Strings provides yet further evidence of that complex interweaving of stylistic strands in Tchaikovsky's music. At the furthest extreme from his own most personal works had been the rococo stylizations of the *Vakula* minuet and the cello variations. Between these had lain the works with neo-classical leanings (notably the first movements of the Second String Quartet and Third Symphony). About the merits of his most recent exemplar of this strain, the Piano Sonata, Tchaikovsky was ambivalent, but he made no effort to provide a successor, and the First Suite was further proof that he felt he had more explorations to make if he were to discover an aspect of his

---

[39] *DTC*, p. 478; *YDGC*, p. 271; *TPJ1*, p.249.

true self within some world other than that of his most personal music. In the Suite, as in the rococo stylizations, he had made no use of sonata principles (except, perhaps, in the Intermezzo), resorting to precedents from the Baroque (including fugue), ternary schemes, or loose rondo-type designs which permitted him to assemble a movement by shuffling a number of attractive, basically melodic units. In the Serenade, however, Tchaikovsky turned back to the four-movement sonata paradigm, though this time simply to fill its formal compartments as far as possible with sparkling or gracious melody. Proportions were schemed to have an elegant poise, while an enthusiastic appreciation was displayed for prolonged dominant pedals. Absolved from the weightier responsibilities which had oppressed him in his earlier neo-classical creations, Tchaikovsky abandoned the formal development altogether in the first movement, compiling this Pezzo in forma di Sonatina from a very neat, unfussy and (except for the key of the second subject) identical exposition and recapitulation, whose exactly balanced symmetry is further reinforced by a return to the stately andante non troppo introduction at the end of the movement. Within the main allegro moderato mechanical transition is avoided in both exposition and recapitulation; the first subject simply runs down on an extended dominant, and the second subject follows forthwith. This, like the first subject, is ternary in design, with a lightly developmental centre which draws in the main motif of the first subject, thus providing a gentle and satisfying engagement between the otherwise separated thematic elements of the movement.

To Mrs von Meck Tchaikovsky admitted that this first movement was a deliberate imitation of Mozart's manner. Yet the only melodic idea in this Serenade which explicitly suggests an eighteenth-century precedent is this second subject, with its bubbling moto perpetuo semiquavers which recall those sparkling inventions which so readily spilled over from Mozart's opera buffa world into that of his instrumental music. In fact, this music displays none of the style adopted by Tchaikovsky in his rococo stylizations. Rather it is a resurgent and far richer vein of neo-classicism, but one which looks to the eighteenth century for its models rather than to the nineteenth. Put simply: whereas the rococo stylizations represent the sort of music Mozart would have written if he had been of Tchaikovsky's generation, the Serenade is a quasi-symphonic piece such as Tchaikovsky imagined he would have composed, had he lived in Mozart's time. Thus Tchaikovsky's own creative personality is never masked in this delightful new creation, and the first subject of the first movement has clear aspirations to become a waltz, while the second movement commits itself expressly to this thematic world in which Tchaikovsky always ranged so happily. The third movement, *Elegia*, picks up the ascending scale which had opened the Valse (Ex. 169a), using it to launch a series of four ruminative phrases which, always starting identically, all end differently (Ex. 169b presents the first of these). When the main theme arrives (Ex. 169c) it, too, proves to be an elaboration of this same four-times-heard opening shape. Tchaikovsky's hand is discernible as surely in every bar of this beautiful movement as it had been in the Valse; meticulously scaled and as impeccably presented as is everything in the Serenade, this *Elegia* must count as one of the most comely pieces he had written.

Ex. 169

A few weeks before setting about this Serenade Tchaikovsky had received from Taneyev an energetic statement of his views on the only way forward for Russian music. 'We must not forget that only that is lasting which has embedded its roots in the people,' his former pupil had preached as the central part of his doctrine. 'Among the Western nations all art was *national* before it merged with the mainstream. This is a general rule from which you don't depart. The Netherlanders wrote their works upon folksongs; the Gregorian chants upon which the works of sixteenth-century Italians were founded were originally folk melodies. Bach created German music from the *chorale*, again a folk melody.'[40] However faulty Taneyev's view of music history, it might seem that Tchaikovsky had designed his Serenade's finale as a demonstration of belief in Taneyev's creed since, for the first time within a single movement, he employed not one but two folksongs, the first for the introduction, the second to act as the first subject. Both had already appeared in his folksong arrangements of 1869, and in both cases Tchaikovsky used these, the introduction up to bar 30 being simply a transcription of his earlier piano duet setting of 'A kak po lugu'.[41] By happy chance the outline of the treble line in the last four bars of this earlier arrangement anticipated the opening of the second folktune, 'Pod yablonyu zelyonoyu',[42] and Tchaikovsky was thus able to effect, *Kamarinskaya*-like, an easy transition to the allegro con spirito.[43] This, unlike the opening movement, has all the appurtenances of sonata structure, including an elaborate development. All is accomplished with deftness and energy, though without that verve and boldness which had made the finale of the Second Symphony so dazzling.

Yet the fact is that Tchaikovsky profoundly disagreed with Taneyev. 'If, thanks to Peter the Great, we have been *fatefully* caught on the tail of Europe, then thus we shall remain for ever,' he had countered on 13 August. 'I value very highly the wealth of material which the *slovenly and suffering people* [this had been Taneyev's expression] produce, but we, i.e., we who use this material, will always elaborate it in forms borrowed from Europe – for, born Russians, we are at the same time even far more Europeans, and we have so resolutely and deeply fostered and assimilated their forms that to tear ourselves from them we would have to strain and do violence to ourselves, and from such straining and violence nothing artistic could come. Where there is violence there is no inspiration, and where there is no inspiration there is no art.'[44] Tchaikovsky's own music is perpetual testimony to how deeply he held this belief, and this finale, far from being a recognition that Russian folksong is necessary, is more a pointed demonstration that such folksong might be absorbed into as complete a display of Western stylistic and structural methods as Tchaikovsky could invent. But the real coup de grâce remained. The whole Serenade had opened with a dignified theme wedded to a solemn, stiff harmonic support (Ex. 170a) – a formal gesture little related, it would seem, to Russian folksong; yet

[40] *TTP*, p. 55.
[41] *T50RF*, No. 28.
[42] *T50RF*, No. 42.
[43] The original piano harmonization appears in bars 60–75.
[44] *TLP*9, p. 223.

in the last movement, as the coda begins, Tchaikovsky suddenly reintroduces this solemn opening, only to go on to demonstrate with a touch of impishness that it is in fact fathered by that very same joyous Russian folksong which had acted as the main theme of the finale (Ex. 170b).

Ex. 170

Tchaikovsky remained at Kamenka until late November. Modest had begun to write a play, *The Benefactor*, and, prodded constantly by his brother, completed it to the admiration of the whole family. Tchaikovsky was convinced it would bring recognition to Modest in Russia's literary world, and was already scheming to have it produced in Moscow that season (it was to be given with little success in St Petersburg in February 1881). Nothing disturbed the even tenor of Tchaikovsky's own life. Antonina remained silent, and Zhenya's brother arrived early in October to remove his sister. Only Sasha's health occasioned anxiety. Finally the family discovered the real cause of the nervous tensions and pains which had afflicted and sometimes prostrated her during this summer; she had been concealing from them symptoms which made her fear she had a mortal illness. Now at last she confessed them, only to receive much reassurance from the doctor. Yet there remained the problem that she had for years been taking morphine for relief from various discomforts, and by now she had become addicted to it. In any case, family anxieties constantly beset her with her eldest children. In particular, Tanya, now nineteen, wanted to marry, but many doubts surrounded the prospects for her intended, and by mid-October the relationship was disintegrating. Uncle Pyotr shared in all these worries and sorrows, just as he did in the misfortunes of the Kamenka estate, which had had a bad year.

Yet his own affairs were prospering quietly. *The Maid* had been accepted by the Imperial Theatres in St Petersburg and would be produced during the winter, while in Moscow in January *Onegin* would be mounted at the Bolshoy. Thus Tchaikovsky would have operas being presented simultaneously in Russia's two greatest cities. He wanted publication of the revised versions of the Second Symphony and *Romeo and Juliet*, but the problem was that rights to these works had been assigned to publishers other than Jurgenson. His aim was to persuade Bote & Bock, the original publishers of *Romeo and Juliet*, to agree to engrave the new version and assign the rights to it within Russia to Jurgenson, even though in March he had already agreed that Bessel should have these rights. As for the Second Symphony, Tchaikovsky's relations with Bessel himself were now at so low an ebb that he had no wish to have any dealings with this publisher. In fact Tchaikovsky had got himself into a thorough mess, and he was only too ready to ask Jurgenson to act as his agent in all dealings with both publishing firms, just as he had been happy to transfer to others as far as possible the labour of correcting his own music, an ambitious scheme which proved abortive.

The one real cause for grief was the imminent departure of Alexey on military service. Tchaikovsky's valet had successfully passed the examination which would reduce his period of conscription, and his master still entertained, to the last, hopes that he might be exempted altogether. But Alexey's liability remained, and on 28 October he had to leave Kamenka. 'It's hard being deprived, perhaps for a long time, of a person with whom one has lived ten years,' Tchaikovsky wrote to Nadezhda von Meck on 26 October, even before Alexey's departure. 'I feel sorry for myself, but chiefly for him; he will have to endure a great deal before he becomes accustomed to his new situation. To alleviate my feeling of sadness I am working intensively.'[45] But promptly on Alexey's departure Tchaikovsky himself fell ill with nervous symptoms which may well have been caused by the loss of his servant. All work was forbidden him during his remaining days at Kamenka. On 23 November he arrived in Moscow.

While Tchaikovsky had been in the Ukraine his patroness had been travelling in Western Europe. Pachulski as usual journeyed with her, but on 22 July Nadezhda von Meck, now in Interlaken, informed Tchaikovsky of a new musical addition to her entourage. 'Two days ago a young pianist from Paris came to me. He has just finished his conservatoire course. . . . I have engaged him to work with the children

---

[45] *TLP*9, p. 298; *TPM*2, p. 431.

during the summer, to accompany Yuliya's singing, and to play piano duets with me. . . . He says he is twenty, but he looks no more than sixteen.'[46] Soon she had him playing Tchaikovsky's compositions, including the Fourth Symphony with her in its piano duet version. 'My partner did not play it well, though he performs magnificently,' she observed from Arcachon on 19 August. '. . . He is enraptured with your music. . . . Yesterday I also played your suite with him, and he was utterly delighted with the fugue, and expressed himself thus: "Dans les fugues modernes je n'ai jamais rien vu de si beau. Monsieur Massenet ne pourrait jamais faire rien de pareil." . . . He [the pianist] composes very nicely, and here he is also a true Frenchman.'[47]

Tchaikovsky was soon required to pronounce upon the creative activities of this young man. On 20 September from Florence his benefactress sent him the vocal score of Ponchielli's *La Giaconda* to look over, adding, 'I'm also sending a little composition for you to judge, one of *many* by my pianist . . . This young man is preparing to be a composer and he writes very nice pieces, but they are all echoes of his teacher, Massenet [in fact there is no evidence that this young man was ever Massenet's pupil]. He is now composing a trio.'[48] A month later Tchaikovsky replied dutifully and without enthusiasm; evidently he did not rate the young man's compositional abilities highly. Perhaps, too, he spied a potential rival for Mrs von Meck's affections, and decided to swat him without delay. 'The *Danse bohémienne is a very nice little piece*, but it is certainly too short. Not one idea is worked out to its conclusion, the form is too shrivelled, and it lacks wholeness.'[49]

Meanwhile the young Frenchman was sending his mistress into ecstasies by playing to her from the newly arrived vocal score of *The Maid*; in addition he was required to play Tchaikovsky's Piano Sonata, a number of the shorter piano pieces, as well as participate in the duet arrangement of the First Symphony. Mrs von Meck also set him to make piano arrangements of the Spanish, Neapolitan and Russian dances from *Swan Lake*, and was soon asking Tchaikovsky whether she might have them published. Tchaikovsky replied that Jurgenson held the Russian copyright of this ballet, and that he (Tchaikovsky) had no power to authorize publication; nevertheless, he was sure that Jurgenson would be only too happy to print these arrangements if they were sent to him (and, indeed, they did appear in 1881, though without the name of the arranger, who feared for some reason that

Massenet would be enraged if he got to hear about them). Early in
October a young cellist, Pyotr Danilchenko, arrived to take the pianist's place, but the latter was persuaded to stay on for an extra month so
that Nadezhda von Meck might be entertained with piano trios. 'Pyotr
Ilich, why have you not written a single trio?' she demanded to know on
30 October. 'I regret this every day because every day they play me a
trio, and I always sigh because you have not composed a single one.'[50]
Little did she realize that she was helping to sow a creative seed in
Tchaikovsky's mind, though it was to germinate only later. She had a
photograph taken of her trio and sent a copy to Tchaikovsky. '*Bussy's*
face and hands have a vague resemblance to Ant[on] Rubinstein's in
his youth,' Tchaikovsky noted. 'God grant that his fate may be as
fortunate as that of the "Tsar of pianists"!'[51] Indeed, the final reputation of the young man was to eclipse completely that of this keyboard
giant, though it was as composer, not as pianist. For 'Bussy' was, of
course, the eighteen-year-old Claude Debussy.

[50] *TPM*2, p. 434.
[51] *TLP*9, p. 298; *TPM*2, p. 431.

4

RESURGENT INDIVIDUALITY:

PIANO TRIO

THERE COULD NOT have been a greater contrast between the peaceful Ukrainian existence Tchaikovsky had enjoyed during the last seven months and the hectic round into which he was about to be caught in Moscow and St Petersburg. Proofs and inescapable social invitations filled his days, while his nights were troubled and sleepless. But to set against such trials was yet more hard evidence of the ever-increasing currency his music was gaining. His Liturgy was performed at the Conservatoire to his unqualified satisfaction. ('I experienced one of the sweetest moments of my composing career,' he confessed to Mrs von Meck[1]), and in the same private concert he heard his new Serenade for the first time. Then on 18 December Nikolay Rubinstein conducted the première of the Italian Capriccio. Tchaikovsky was not present as he had been required to visit St Petersburg for ten days to attend to various matters preparatory to the production of *The Maid*, but when he arrived back in Moscow on 20 December it was to hear of the success the work had enjoyed, a success confirmed when the piece was repeated on 1 January at another RMS concert.[2] Between these two performances the First Quartet had been given with its by now almost ritual encoring of the Andante cantabile, while on the very same evening *The Oprichnik*, from which the ban on presentation had been lifted, was being performed to an enthusiastic audience at the Bolshoy Theatre. Then on 30 December the Liturgy was sung publicly by the same choir which had delighted Tchaikovsky at the Conservatoire. 'The hall was full,' he wrote to Modest, 'and despite the forbidding of applause, there was a tremendous unexpected ovation with the presentation of a sort of lyre made from foliage from an unknown person.'[3] As one critic

[1] *TLP*9, p. 319; *TPM*2, p. 451; *TZC*2, p. 431; *YDGC*, p. 244.
[2] In the same concert was also performed the Second Symphony of Borodin, who visited Moscow for the occasion and who was present at the performance of Tchaikovsky's Liturgy.
[3] *TLP*9, p. 337; *TZC*2, p. 436; *TPB*, p. 261; *YDGC*, p. 246.

summarized it: 'The last week of the 1880 Moscow musical season might truly be called "Tchaikovsky week".'[4]

Yet more significant than all these events was the new production of *Onegin* at the Bolshoy Theatre. Tchaikovsky attended a number of the rehearsals and found himself delighted with the way the opera was being prepared. 'I can't deny Bevignani [who was to conduct the opera] his earnest request that I should attend the orchestral rehearsals and the performance,' he told Modest.[5] Despite this, Tchaikovsky slipped off to Kamenka for a fortnight's rest at the turn of the year. On 23 January 1881, four days after his return to Moscow, *Onegin* was given to the composer's complete satisfaction both with regard to the performance and to the opera's reception, though Modest remembered that scenically the staging was weak. A fortnight later Tchaikovsky left for St Petersburg to attend the final rehearsals and première of *The Maid* on 25 February. Though, as we have seen, the presentation of the opera had many shortcomings, and though he had to suffer the dictatorial interference of the management, he realized that his opera commanded great respect among the performers, and he himself enjoyed a personal audience success. Add to this that the Second Symphony was given in its revised form at an RMS concert on 12 February ('I was not there; they say it pleased,' he observed laconically to his patroness[6]) and it becomes obvious that these last three months had been a veritable Tchaikovsky festival. On his visit to St Petersburg barely a year before, he had been treated as a highly respected composer. Now, from being respected, he was beginning to become popular.

Needless to say, this had little effect upon his personal frame of mind. Some months earlier, when Taneyev had accused him of a modicum of hypocrisy about the success of his music, Tchaikovsky had been quick to distinguish between his pride in his compositions and his wishes for himself. 'I compose, i.e., I give vent to my moods and my feelings by way of musical language, and of course, as with anyone who talks and who has, or has pretensions to having, something to say, I need people to listen to me, and the more they listen to me, the more gratifying it is. In that sense I love *fame*, of course, and I strive after it with my whole heart. . . . But it doesn't follow from this that I love the manifestations of *fame* which are embodied in those dinners, suppers and musical

---

[4] *YDGC*, p. 247.

[5] *TLP9*, p. 331; *TPB*, pp. 260–1; *DTC*, p. 84; *YDGC*, p. 246.

[6] *TLP10*, p. 25; *TPM2*, p. 473; *DTC*, p. 352; *YDGC*, p. 249. Modest asserted that his brother had been present but had chosen to remain incognito, adding that none of the critics seem to have noticed that the symphony had been revised.

soirées at which I suffer as I always suffer in any company alien to me.'[7] As soon as he had arrived in Moscow to receive as warm a greeting to himself personally as to his music, his longing to escape surged up within him. Moscow became curiously unreal. 'My love for this old, dear (despite all its shortcomings) city has in no way diminished – on the contrary, has become keener and stronger – but it has taken on a certain morbid character,' he wrote to Nadezhda von Meck on 9 December from St Petersburg. 'It is as though I am already long dead, as though everything that once was has now sunk into the abyss of oblivion, as though I am some completely different person from another world and another time. It is difficult for me to express in words this extremely morbid and tormenting sensation. I have had to drown this mental pain either by increased work or by increased libations of Bacchus.'[8]

In St Petersburg he had hoped to recover from the strains of Moscow, but he was immediately confronted by a dispute over who should sing the part of Joan, then fell ill, and returned to Moscow no better than when he had left. By now he had to accept that his valet could not evade military service. He visited Alexey in barracks and was appalled at both his crushed appearance and his spartan and rigorous existence. 'And he has to live thus for four years!' he lamented to Modest on 31 December. 'The sergeant-major allowed Alyosha to accompany me to the gate. We were both silent because we both wanted terribly to weep, and Alyosha's voice trembled so much when he said goodbye that I could scarcely endure the agonizing moment. When I got home I wrote to *Fanya* [Tchaikovsky's cousin, Mitrofan] a despairing letter begging him to write to the regiment's commander, with whom he's friendly, so that somehow he might ease Alyosha's predicament. . . . I shall visit him again tomorrow.'[9] That evening, when visiting Hubert, Tchaikovsky had a sudden nervous attack 'such as I've never had before',[10] and which he thought was to be attributed primarily to his distressing encounter with Alexey. The extent to which Tchaikovsky had become dependent upon Alexey came home to him forcefully and repeatedly during these months. As for the protection he solicited for Alexey from his commanding officer, Tchaikovsky was to discover that a price had to be paid, for he found himself compelled to accompany the singing of the colonel's wife for whole evenings.

Nor was the position improved when he returned from Kamenka. It

[7] *TLP*9, p. 222; *TTP*, pp. 56–7.
[8] *TLP*9, p. 319; *TPM*2, pp. 450–1.
[9] *TLP*9, p. 337.
[10] *TLP*9, p. 339; *TZC*2, p. 437; *TPB*, p. 262; *YDGC*, p. 246.

was gratifying to have one's music praised in the press, and though he was sensitive to some reserved comments about *Onegin*, he was still not altogether discouraged either by these or by the still somewhat guarded applause on the first night. 'The success increased as the opera proceeded, and all ended more than happily,' he reported to Nadezhda von Meck. 'Of course an opera's success is not apparent on the first evening but afterwards, when it becomes clear how much drawing power it has.'[11] As he had observed to this same correspondent before the Bolshoy production, this would test whether the opera could become a repertoire piece. A vigorous attack upon his Liturgy by the Metropolitan of Moscow himself did upset him, but he knew perfectly well that this work would provoke a diversity of reactions which did not necessarily reflect upon its musical worth. Yet all this press comment could not but draw attention to Tchaikovsky himself, especially when it was supplemented by a good deal of tittle-tattle; it was like a constant exposure of his very being, and he would have fled from Moscow earlier, had it not been for yet another of Anatoly's turbulent affairs of the heart which called for all the moral support an elder brother could offer. On arriving in St Petersburg Tchaikovsky resolved to decline all invitations, for he had Modest and Kolya with him for company. The former had come for the first (and only) performance of his play, *The Benefactor*, which, through the assiduous efforts of his composer-brother, was produced at the Alexandrinsky Theatre on 21 February (later the play was revised, renamed, and enjoyed a moderate success on the Russian stage). Tchaikovsky himself was much absorbed by rehearsals, but even this could not protect him altogether from the endless unwanted attentions of his numerous relatives and acquaintances. His loathing for St Petersburg became more violent than ever, and on 26 February, the day after the première of *The Maid of Orléans*, he was on his way to Vienna. Though even before going to Kamenka he had spent all but ten of the thousand roubles which the RMS had paid him earlier in December, his finances were now again in good order, for he had just assigned thirty-seven of his shorter pieces to Jurgenson for a fee of 7,000 roubles. He thought that before him stretched a whole spring and summer of calm and freedom, as in 1880. During the next month, however, he was to receive three important pieces of news, one of which would contribute coincidentally to a brief rediscovery of his true individuality as a composer.

Tchaikovsky's response to the first of these, which concerned his patroness, cannot have been other than deeply apprehensive, though he did his utmost to mask this. For the last few weeks his letters had

[11] *TLP*10, p. 16; *TPM*2, p. 466; *TZC*2, p. 445; *DTC*, p. 84.

been marked with expressions of yearning for Italy and especially for Rome, in which he had lived the corresponding portion of the preceding year, and it was to Italy that he was now directing himself. As the train bore him towards Austria the press was already beginning its mainly unfavourable dissection of *The Maid*, and approaching Vienna, Tchaikovsky picked up a copy of *Neue freie Presse* from which he got his first taste of some of the things in store. Seeing the splendid production of *Oberon* in Vienna only pressed home how feebly *The Maid* had been mounted, though Weber's opera, which he had never seen before, impressed him less than its presentation: 'the music's rather tedious, though there are some delightful things,' he judged it to Anatoly the same day.[12] On 3 March he was in Florence, the next day in Rome. Then on 6 March he received the painful intelligence that Mrs von Meck had been compelled, because the affairs of the Brailov estate had been mismanaged, to lease Simaki. Tchaikovsky did his best to sound reassuring; she had been his salvation during the last three years, he affirmed, and a post at either of the Russian conservatoires was always available to him if he should be forced again to earn his own living. He was thoroughly aware that this was the last thing his benefactress wanted, and he knew the point would not be lost on her, but he was still to be beset during the summer by nagging fears that she might be unable to continue his allowance.

His current life in Rome gave little time to brood on this, however. Awaiting him at the station at six in the morning was Kondratyev and, with such a companion, Tchaikovsky was immediately drawn into the social whirl of his compatriots living in the city during his own eight-day visit. Prince Alexey Golitsïn, on whose estate at Trostinets Tchaikovsky had composed his first orchestral work, *The Storm*, nearly seventeen years before, was in residence and the Grand Duke Konstantin Konstantinovich's warship was anchored off Naples. The Grand Duke, with two of the Tsar's sons, the Grand Dukes Sergey and Pavel, had taken a villa in Rome and wanted to see Tchaikovsky, a request he could not refuse. Tchaikovsky felt the usual instinct to recoil violently from all the invitations he received, but for Kondratyev's company he was for the moment grateful. His spirits had risen when he had crossed the frontier and experienced the colour and warmth of the incipient Italian spring. But without Modest and Kolya, let alone Alexey, he became engulfed by his loneliness, and he gladly acceded to Kondratyev's proposal that they should together go to Naples, then to Nice, and finally to Paris.

It is yet another sign of Tchaikovsky's spreading fame that he was

[12] *TLP*10, p. 34; *YDGC*, p. 252.

now so sought after as a guest. Not only the Tsar's sons and the Grand Duke Konstantin, but the Russian ambassador wanted his company, and everywhere he was required to play and talk about his own music. In Naples he had hoped to relax, but on 13 March, the day after his arrival, came the second piece of crucial news. Jurgenson's researches had revealed that Antonina had taken a lover and given birth to a child. Now Tchaikovsky had incontrovertible grounds for divorce. 'I strongly approve of, and heartily thank you for your investigation into that creature of the female sex who has brought into the world an unfortunate being who is perhaps bearing my name,' he immediately wrote with fierce satisfaction to his publisher.

> How, I wonder, may I prevent her from registering it *as my* child? Has your spy thought of coping with this? In principle I *very much* want a divorce, but the question of money troubles me. *I know for certain* that at the present moment Mrs von Meck's affairs are in a far from brilliant condition, and I can't ask her for something over and above the sum I receive. In any case, after what is known to have happened, I consider it quite unnecessary to pay Ant[onina] Iv[anovna] any sort of compensation in the form of capital, such as was discussed earlier. If you wish to be my benefactor to the last in this matter, then try to see some specialist in divorce matters (for instance, the secretary of the consistory) and find out from him what I can do at this present moment. . . . *Of course there is no need to pay her a pension!*[13]

Yet relief was tempered with some apprehension, for dangers remained. Antonina could still make damaging accusations if she were pushed too far, and finally Tchaikovsky was to draw back from divorcing her. He felt the bitch was effectively kennelled and muzzled, and would trouble him no further unless roused.

Tchaikovsky's greatest adventure in Naples was to climb to the crater of Vesuvius; his most pleasant memory was of visiting Sorrento. There was a suggestion that he should abandon his prepared itinerary and instead travel with the Grand Dukes aboard their frigate to Athens and Jerusalem, but the assassination of Alexandr II on 13 March necessitated the immediate presence of all three in St Petersburg. Though Tchaikovsky had only a few months earlier expressed reserved feelings about the Tsar, the slaying of the Russian father brought forth a swell of emotion for the condition of his country. 'At such moments it's unpleasant to be abroad,' he wrote to Anatoly on 15 March, 'and with

[13] *TLP*10, pp. 53–4; *TPJ*1, pp. 185–6.

my whole soul I yearned for Russia so that I might be closer to the source of information, so that I might participate in the demonstrations for the new Tsar, know the details – in a word, share the common life of all my own people.'[14] With the departure of the three Grand Dukes the trip to the eastern Mediterranean was out of the question, and on 21 March Tchaikovsky and Kondratyev were in Nice.

Here the third and most crucial piece of news reached him. When Tchaikovsky had been in Moscow and St Petersburg, Nikolay Rubinstein's health had already been giving cause for concern. Rest had been urgently prescribed by the doctors, but Tchaikovsky knew that Rubinstein was congenitally incapable of staying inactive. Perceiving the seriousness of Rubinstein's condition, he was appalled at the prospect of his death. Then, while Tchaikovsky was in Naples, Anatoly had written that Rubinstein had been ordered abroad and was travelling to Nice. He did not arrive, and on 22 March Jurgenson telegraphed Tchaikovsky to say that Rubinstein was desperately ill in Paris. The next day he died.

No death had struck Tchaikovsky so hard since the passing of his own mother nearly twenty-seven years before. Rubinstein had given him his first professional appointment, had directed him, bullied him, but in his own rough, imperious way had nursed Tchaikovsky's gifts, sometimes criticizing his works unceremoniously, but always with unflagging energy presenting them to the world so that their worth might be assessed and their fame grow. No man had done more for the cause of Tchaikovsky's music than this difficult but true friend. Tchaikovsky was preoccupied with such thoughts as he sped towards Paris. So agitated was he that he dreaded having to view the body lest his self-control should give way. On 26 March a funeral service was held in the crowded Russian church in Paris, with Massenet, Colonne, Lalo, Pauline Viardot-Garcia and Turgenev among the congregation. 'Afterwards the coffin was carried into the lower chapel, and here I saw him for the last time,' Tchaikovsky concluded his account of Rubinstein's end given to Mrs von Meck the next day. 'He had altered beyond recognition. My God, my God, how terrible are such moments in life! Forgive me, my dear, that I write to you in such detail – I am terribly weighed down by grief.'[15]

Such was not the condition of Anton Rubinstein, who had hurried from Spain on hearing of his brother's illness. Jurgenson, who had come to Paris for the funeral, offered a convincing explanation of the

[14] *TLP*10, p. 55.
[15] *TLP*10, p. 68; *TPM*2, p. 491.

behaviour which now so affronted Tchaikovsky. 'It is difficult to convey
the sickening impression he [Anton Rubinstein] has produced on me
during these days,' Tchaikovsky wrote in indignant distress to Anatoly.
'He is not only not crushed by his brother's death but is, *apparently*, very
pleased about it. Jurgenson, with whom I spoke about this, explains
this incomprehensible fact by Anton's *jealousy* of Nikolay. For what?
Why? I don't understand. But if this is so, what could be more offensive
than such jealousy?'[16] To all these solemn, distressing events
Tchaikovsky responded with a sudden access of religious emotion.
'All's dark in my mind – but it could not be otherwise in view of such
questions, insoluble by the frail mind, as *death, the purpose and meaning of
life, its infinity or its finiteness* – but still the light of *faith* penetrates yet more
and more into my soul. Yes, dear friend,' he enthused to his sceptical
patroness.

> I feel that I am inclining more and more towards that only bulwark
> we have against all calamities. I feel I am beginning *to be able to love
> God*, which formerly I could not do. I am still visited by doubts: I still
> sometimes try to comprehend the incomprehensible with my weak
> and pitiful mind – but yet louder and louder the voice of divine truth
> begins to reach me. Already I often find an inexplicable delight in
> bowing before God's inscrutable yet, to me, unquestionable wisdom;
> often with tears I pray to *him* (where *he* is, who *he* is, I know not, but I
> know *he* exists), and I pray him to give me humility and love, I pray
> him to forgive me and enlighten me – but above all I say to him
> sweetly: *Lord, thy will be done*, for I know that his will is *holy*.[17]

All this was less a spiritual rebirth than a sentimental yearning for
something which might give purpose to, or at least numb the pain of
such distressing experiences. It had certainly helped at the Gare du
Nord when Tchaikovsky had watched Rubinstein's remains being
loaded into a luggage van on their way to Moscow. The indignity of this
exit struck him hard. 'But fortunately,' he consoled himself to his
patroness, 'I have seeds of *faith*, and I take comfort from the thought
that such is the *inexplicable* but *holy* will of God.'[18] For a moment it would
seem that fate and Christian destiny were conjoined. As a personal
service to this loyal yet abrasive supporter of his music he compiled a
detailed account of Rubinstein's last days which was printed in both the
Moscow Gazette and the *Russian Gazette*.

[16] *TLP*10, p. 73; *TPM*2, pp. 633–4; *TPB*, pp. 268–9.
[17] *TLP*10, p. 70; *TPM*2, pp. 491–2; *TZC*2, pp. 466–7.
[18] *TLP*10, p. 71; *TPM*2, p. 493.

By now Tchaikovsky's longing to be back in Russia was irresistible. The Tsar's violent end still weighed upon him, Rubinstein's death had caused him great grief and agitation, and Nadezhda von Meck had occasioned further anxiety by disclosing that her personal losses had been far greater than Tchaikovsky had been led to believe. She insisted that there was no risk to his allowance, but he remained unconvinced. 'In all probability there lies before me a sudden radical change in my life,' he predicted to his brother-in-law.[19] Yet such was Tchaikovsky's repugnance at Anton's indifference at his brother's death that he decided to delay in Paris for some days to avoid having to observe this at Nikolay's interment in Moscow. Thus it was 2 April before Tchaikovsky left. Pausing briefly in Berlin, he was four days later again in St Petersburg.

Tchaikovsky had not intended to spend a full month in the Russian capital, but Sasha had arrived with Tanya, had fallen ill, and within days of Tchaikovsky's own advent her condition had taken a turn for the worse. Lev was urgently summoned from the Ukraine, but could not stay indefinitely since the affairs of Kamenka required his presence. The doctors ordered Sasha to Carlsbad (now Karlovy Vary) as the only means of cure, but someone had to accompany her, and Tchaikovsky feared that this responsibility would of necessity fall upon him. His spirits remained black. Composition was out of the question, and he turned down flatly an unalluring request to write nine marches for a Moscow production of Alexey Tolstoy's tragedy, *Tsar Boris*. Finally, early in May, escape became possible. With all but one of her children in the Ukraine, Sasha was pining to a degree which persuaded the doctors that she should return there as soon as possible and travel abroad later; meanwhile, because both mother and father were still confined to St Petersburg, Uncle Pyotr was to hasten to Kamenka to fill the parental gap as best he could. Arriving in Moscow on 7 May, he saw Alexey and fought off an earnest appeal that he should become director of the Conservatoire in succession to Rubinstein.

Next day he was on his way south, still feeling no inclination to compose. The children made heavy demands on his time not only socially but musically, for the visiting music teacher, a certain Stanislav Blumenfeld, had remained absent some three months, and Tchaikovsky felt obliged to teach some of the children himself (had he known the role Blumenfeld was very soon to play in the life of one of Sasha's children, he could well have wished he would never visit Kamenka again). He did, however, give some thought to future

[19] *TLP*10, p. 72.

creative projects. Hearing that other commitments were causing Karl Davïdov to despair of completing an opera he had already begun, Tchaikovsky asked the director of the St Petersburg Conservatoire whether the libretto might be assigned to him. 'I find the subject of [Pushkin's] *Poltava* very tempting,' he wrote to Davïdov on 17 May.[20] Meanwhile, still stirred by the religious thoughts and feelings which had been aroused by Rubinstein's death, he turned his attention again to Russian church music. 'I want to try to compose an *All-night Vigil*,' he wrote to Jurgenson on 20 May, 'and for this I need its complete *text.* . . . I've begun to learn *the rules of church singing*, but to have a full understanding of these I need Razumovsky's book (the history of church music), and so I'm asking you to send me a copy.'[21]

The task he was setting himself this time was very different from that he had faced in his Liturgy, for here he would be far less a creator than an arranger, though one whose aesthetic judgment would need to be fully alert. 'I wish not so much *theoretically* as *through the feeling* of an artist *to sober up* (to a certain degree) church music from excessive Europeanism,' he wrote to Modest on 5 June. 'I shall be an eclectic, i.e. something between Bortnyansky and Potulov. The All-night Vigil will be much less European than my mass; *however*, this will arise partly because here (in the All-night Vigil) there are fewer occasions when one can be carried away and compose. Here I shall be *someone setting the Ordinary* rather than a freely creating artist.'[22]

Unable still to discover all he needed from the work of Razumovsky, his old colleague who had officiated at his wedding, Tchaikovsky sent for a battery of service books from Jurgenson, but still found the path before him lay through a thicket of obstacles and uncertainties. At times he could trace neither text nor the correct chant, at others he found it impossible to understand the arrangements of the Propers. Such problems were also experienced by the Russian clergy, he discovered. 'I went to Father Alex[andr Tarnavich, the Kamenka parish priest] for explanations,' he told Modest on 3 July, by which time he had been struggling for at least a month, 'but he confessed to me that he himself knew nothing, and officiated according to some routine without consulting the Tipicon [the manual containing the order of services] or the [liturgical] rule . . . I asked Father Alex[andr] what his deacon did when performing the canon with canticles, and how he managed to find out what and how he should read and sing. . . . He replied: "I don't know. Before each service he tries to find something suitable for

[20] *TLP*10, p. 96.
[21] *TLP*10, p. 102; *TZC*2, pp. 469–70.
[22] *TLP*10, p. 120; *TPB*, p. 271; *DTC*, p. 283 (partial).

himself." '[23] Evidently stirred by Tchaikovsky's request to discover the correct order of events in the service he had so long celebrated defectively, Father Alexandr finally managed to compile for the composer a proper service order which set his feet on firmer liturgical ground, while correspondence with Razumovsky himself also brought some enlightenment. The sketches of the work were completed during July, though not brought to their final form until the following year.

After completing his All-night Vigil Tchaikovsky gave a brief summary of his work to Taneyev.

> In this instance, as always, I worked obeying my instinct rather than my cogitations or any preconceived theories. I treated the melodies of the Ordinary and the Hirmologion quite freely, a little à la Bortnyansky, i.e. never hesitating to force them into metre, sometimes deviating from, changing and, in places, abandoning them altogether, and giving my own invention its head. There is no, or virtually no, contrapuntal element. *The melody is always in the top voice.* As for the harmony, it's always strict – that is, without chromaticism, without $^6_4$ chords or sevenths. The dominant [seventh] chord appears only in a passing function.[24]

In fact, these restrictions on his harmonic resources are not always as strictly observed as Tchaikovsky asserted. The All-night Vigil consists of seventeen numbers, one containing various responses, the other sixteen setting longer, usually more continuous texts, including the Magnificat with a repeated trope, the Great Doxology, and various psalms. Some stretches of the chant are present unfettered by barlines, even occasionally there is free chanting, but elsewhere, as Tchaikovsky noted to Taneyev, he imposed clear metrical structures on the chant, though often preserving flexibility by the use of variable bar lengths, as at the work's opening (Ex. 171a). Most of the harmonizations are for four voices, but others divide a vocal line to permit simple antiphonal treatment or a fuller textural support, as in *O gladsome light* (No. 5: Ex. 171b), which also contains one of the only two brief passages in the whole Vigil which might claim to be contrapuntal. Another moment when an alien style invades the music is at the 'alleluias' in *Praise the name of the Lord* (No. 8: Ex. 171c) which might easily have escaped from a Western composition. Though no Western listener, ignorant of the traditions and ambience of the Orthodox Church liturgy, can be competent to pronounce on the validity of Tchaikovsky's arrangements, by far the greater part of the All-night Vigil gives the impression

[23] *TLP*10, p. 148; *TZC*2, p. 473.
[24] *TLP*10, p. 186; *TTP*, p. 72.

Ex. 171

[Bless the Lord, O my soul! Blessed be the Lord!]

[O gladsome light of the holy glory]

of being as discreet and tasteful an adornment of the chant melodies as might be devised using a Western harmonic technique. Obviously harmonization, even when as simple as Tchaikovsky's, must alter the whole character of the chant, and thus produce something new; even so, the All-night Vigil, unlike the Liturgy, cannot claim a place in the canon of Tchaikovsky's original compositions.

It was Bortnyansky, identified by Tchaikovsky as one boundary mark to the stylistic world of the All-night Vigil, who provided the other major musical preoccupation of this summer of 1881. His funds being low, and having no impulse to compose, Tchaikovsky had requested from Jurgenson some routine commission which might stimulate him to work, and the publisher had replied with a suggestion that he should edit the complete works of this earlier Russian composer. Jurgenson had, of course, just won his right to publish Tchaikovsky's Liturgy,[25] and he was clearly anxious both to relish his victory and to capitalize on it. However, on receiving from Jurgenson a batch of the Imperial Chapel's editions of Bortnyansky's music, Tchaikovsky found himself very uncertain about the musical wisdom of Jurgenson's new venture, and uneasy about his own proposed part in it. 'I've . . . begun my editorial work which has proved to be pretty laborious and boring, mostly because the bulk of Bortnyansky's works are very commonplace trifles,' he wrote on 3 July. 'Why do you need to publish his complete edition? May I advise you to throw out this plan and instead undertake the following: *Publish an anthology of selected works by Bortn[yansky]*. This would be far better for your pocket and wiser in all respects. . . . I've even begun to waver about giving my name to such an edition with which I can have no sympathy. At this moment I'm composing some pieces of church music which are an attempt (very modest, let us grant) to counter the iniquitous style established by Bortnyansky and *tutti quanti*, and suddenly I'm simultaneously presenting the public with a project, of all of which my own work is a negation.'[26] But within a fortnight, through Jurgenson's persistence, he had capitulated. His task was to go over the musical text, correcting it and, where necessary, supplying a piano accompaniment for rehearsal purposes. Having now nearly completed the sketches for his All-night Vigil, Tchaikovsky was soon able to devote himself exclusively to this formidable labour, the results of which were to be issued in ten volumes. A little later, when deeply immersed in preparing his edition, he gave Jurgenson an assessment of Bortnyansky which shows that his critical values had in

---

[25] Despite the decree, the church authorities continued resolutely to forbid liturgical performance of Tchaikovsky's Liturgy.

[26] *TLP*10, p. 149; *TZC*2, p. 474; *TPJ*1, pp. 196–7; *DTC*, p. 535 (partial).

no way been unbalanced by the sheer tedium he found in the task. 'Bortnyansky was *a talent*, but a very second-class one, incapable of breaking even the smallest bit of new ground,' he wrote on 31 August.

> He was an extremely good musician and an outstandingly accomplished technician, and therefore though you may not be doing art a great service by publishing his complete edition, you are not doing anything shameful. He has become hateful to me not because what he wrote was *bad*, but because he was prolific mediocrity incarnate, in the ocean of whose work there is not a single really live passage: everything's fluent, neat, pleasant, but monotonous and barren as a steppe.[27]

Distaste for this drudgery inflamed his zeal to be rid of it, and by 8 November virtually the entire edition was finished. It is obvious that such tasks as this and the All-night Vigil had crowded out any real opportunities for free composition. But not quite: Davïdov had willingly transferred his *Poltava* project, and on 6 September Tchaikovsky could report to Taneyev that it had sown seeds in his creative faculties, and some of these were beginning to germinate. 'I have a serviceable libretto to hand, and in my leisure hours I've already composed four numbers.'[28] Tchaikovsky had made a small beginning upon his seventh opera, *Mazepa*.

This summer at Kamenka was to be very different from the previous one. The wound inflicted by Alexey's departure remained as raw as ever, and constant memories of events and places associated with his valet kept the nerve ends sore. Though there is nothing to suggest an active homosexual relationship between the two men, Tchaikovsky's heightened tone in some of his letters to Alexey is that of a distraught lover, and the emotional depth to his loss is evidenced in many references to Alexey in his letters to others.[29] He had been assigned a new servant, Boris, while at Kamenka, but despite his recognition of Boris's virtues, no one could replace his old retainer. Though

[27] *TLP*10, p. 200; *TPJ*1, p. 205.

[28] *TLP*10, p. 204; *TZC*2, p. 481; *TTP*, p. 77; *YDGC*, p. 257.

[29] In this respect, Tchaikovsky's response in June 1879 to news of the illegitimate child Alexey was expecting by Marie Savion, a servant at the Pension Richelieu at Clarens, is interesting. 'My first feeling was of pity for poor *Marie*,' he wrote to Modest, 'and secondly, an upsurge of the strongest paternal tenderness towards the *embryo* in her womb. From this feeling I could gauge the strength of my deep-rooted love and affection for Alyosha. *His child!* It seems as though it's mine! I don't know whether this feeling will last, and how I should proceed. Sasha, whom I've consulted, says that I ought not to involve myself, and that I need help *Marie* only financially at this time. But, you know, she doesn't suspect how greatly I love Alyosha!' [*TPR*, p. 587].

Tchaikovsky was now uncomfortably aware of Jurgenson's growing irritation at his constant borrowings, he still periodically sent his Moscow publisher requests to make small allowances to Alexey so that his life might be easier. Tchaikovsky's own financial improvidence was worse than ever. Desperately needing 3,000 roubles, he turned to the Tsar himself, asking through an intermediary that this sum might be advanced to him against future performance royalties on *The Maid* and *Onegin*. He knew that the Tsar already looked favourably upon him as a composer, and within a fortnight an effusively grateful Tchaikovsky was acknowledging the Tsar's generosity.

But news from Moscow, whither Tanya had gone, was bad; she had broken her engagement to the officer, Vasily Trubetskoy, after the latter had appeared drunk in her apartment and had made improper advances to her. In the meantime Sasha had returned to Kamenka from St Petersburg much better if not cured, and all the family realized that her improvement was to be accounted for above all by her separation from her moody eldest daughter. Hearing that his niece had evidently not taken her broken engagement too much to heart, Tchaikovsky joined the rest of the Kamenka establishment in praying that the girl would remain in Moscow, and then accompany a friend to Lipetsk. But suddenly Tanya appeared in Kamenka. The reports of her condition in Moscow proved to be false, and on the way south she had been drinking heavily and dosing herself with morphine and chloroform. Sasha was reduced to hysterics, with consequences for her general condition such as the family had dreaded. 'My sister, who was beginning to get a little better, can already hardly move her legs today,' he reported gloomily to Mrs von Meck on 5 June. 'I assure you, my friend, that despite all my love for this family, I sometimes want to distance myself a little from them. Some evil fate denies them happiness.'[30] Lev being away, Tchaikovsky found himself the recipient of confidences from a completely distraught Tanya; Trubetskoy, it seems, had tried to rape her. Tchaikovsky did his best to divert her by playing duets with her, encouraging her to read, and turning her attention to subjects far removed from her own troubles.

It was to little avail. Then Lev returned, and sank into gloom. By 18 June the atmosphere had become so unbearable that Tchaikovsky was frantically seeking an avenue of escape. Then he remembered the stratagem which had rescued him from Antonina after his marriage. 'I beg you to send me a telegram containing roughly the following: *Your presence is needed in Moscow in connection with such-and-such a matter. Come*

[30] *TLP*10, p. 122; *TPM*2, p. 517.

Mily Balakirev
(1880)

Vladimir Stasov
(*c*.1870)

Alexandra [Sasha] Davïdova and
Nataliya [Nata] Pleskaya

Nikolay and Anna
[née Davïdova] von Meck

Above: Max
Erdmannsdörfer

Right: Eduard
Nápravník

Praskovya [Parasha]
Tchaikovskaya

quickly. I'll show them the telegram and then I shan't have such a conscience about leaving,' he confided to Jurgenson.[31] The latter did as he was bid, but when it came to the point Tchaikovsky stayed. 'There are a great number of places where I would now not only be able *to live* as I do here, but where I could enjoy life,' he unburdened himself to Anatoly on 30 June. 'However, I'm not leaving here because the most important thing for me now is that nothing and no one should disturb my habits. Every new place frightens me, for new conditions and a new situation will compel me to change my ways a little, and this is very painful to me. In another respect, to leave at this moment would be somehow awkward, as though I were casting them off when bad times have come to them. . . . How odd is a man's fate!' he continued, projecting light upon why his attitude to Kamenka was beginning to change, despite his continued attachment to it.

Thanks to N[adezhda] Fil[aretovna] I am a completely free man, always able to live where I wish. But here is proof for you that you don't buy *freedom* even by being provided for. Of all places on this earthly sphere I know none more unattractive (as regards natural beauties) than Kamenka. That which formerly was the single charm of life here, i.e. the contemplation of a family of people close to me living happily, has now turned into something quite the opposite. *However,* I'm doomed *to pass a large portion of my life precisely here.* And I have no right even to complain about this, . . . for no one and nothing hinders me from leaving – but I'm staying here for here I'm *at home,* in a thoroughly familiar spot, no one obstructing me in my habits. It's all very curious![32]

Curious or not, this frame of mind remained with him the whole summer. As for Mrs von Meck's personal affairs, these continued to be in disarray. Brailov was still losing money heavily, and Tchaikovsky tried to arrange that Lev should visit the estate to advise its owner on its efficient administration. Early in July Sasha departed for Carlsbad. Lev accompanied her part of the way, and a meeting was arranged en route between them and Mrs von Meck's sons, Alexandr and Nikolay, who was to become their son-in-law. With the absence of both Lev and Sasha, Tchaikovsky found himself again in loco parentis in a household which seemed to be increasingly overrun by hussars from a regiment stationed nearby. The attraction was, of course, the elder Davïdov daughters. Early in the year the sixteen-year-old Varya had become

---

[31] *TLP*10, p. 135; *TPJ*1, p. 195.
[32] *TLP*10, pp. 145–6.

engaged to Axel Samberg, one of the hussar officers, and was married
to him on 24 July, despite her mother's absence. All Tchaikovsky's
elaborate schemes to escape from Kamenka were finally reduced to a
four-day visit to Kiev at the beginning of August, a stay long enough for
him to buy a weighty supply of reading matter, exhaust his exchequer
yet again, and become convinced that no sooner had he left Kamenka
than he was yearning to be back.

Other blows fell upon him as the year dragged on. The new Tsar had
decided that the period of conscription was too short and had extended
it to six years, though as some compensation there was news that
Alexey was to be granted two months' leave from August. In the middle
of July his patroness had told Tchaikovsky that Brailov was again
securely in her possession, and though he had earlier declined her
invitation to stay at Simaki because it would be intolerable without
Alexey, he had now decided to spend a month of this leave with his valet
in this tranquil place. Mrs von Meck had attempted to persuade Lev to
take over the entire management of the estate – though on condition
that, as with Tchaikovsky, they should never meet face to face. But
though she had disposed of some holdings in a railway line, this had
proved insufficient to restore her financial position, and Brailov was
again placed on the market. Then suddenly, at the beginning of
September, came news that the estate had been sold, and that Simaki
could never again be at Tchaikovsky's disposal.

Meanwhile in Moscow Hubert had been appointed director of
the Conservatoire, but Klindworth had resigned, and the institution
was frantically searching for eminent names to replace his and
Rubinstein's. In response to an appeal from Jurgenson Tchaikovsky
offered to allow himself to be nominated Professor of Theory, provided
he was then given indefinite leave. Obviously, as Tchaikovsky must
have realized, this would have been unprincipled, and Taneyev pressed
home the attack begun by Jurgenson, working upon Tchaikovsky's
conscience in a way which made him wretched. 'He demonstrated it
was my duty [to teach at the Conservatoire],' Tchaikovsky moaned to
Modest on 4 September. 'This got me very worked up, and I didn't
sleep all night – rather, I slept badly, and that with the help of wine. No!
Better to perish in poverty than make a stupid sacrifice,' he added
vehemently,[33] then counter-attacking by suggesting, with complete
sincerity, that it was Taneyev himself who could ultimately fill the gap
left by Rubinstein. To set against such distressing matters were Anatoly's arrival in the middle of August and Modest's brief appearance at

[33] *TLP*10, pp. 201–2; *TPB*, p. 272; *YDGC*, p. 256.

the end. A promise of relief from personal strains was afforded when the planned winter migration of Lev and Sasha's entire family to Kiev began at the same time. Sasha returned in early September but stayed only a few days before going to Yalta to continue her cure for a further month. The next day Tchaikovsky learned that Alexey, whose leave had been reduced to a single month, had been forbidden to go beyond the outskirts of Moscow. His mind was quickly made up. Five days later, on 20 September, he left Kamenka, spent a day with those of the Davïdov family already in Kiev, took his two delighted young nephews, Dmitri and Bob, to see *Robert le Diable* at the opera, and on 22 September was reunited with Alexey.

His three weeks in Moscow did nothing to improve his morale, for he found Anatoly gloomily ruminating on his fate, the Conservatoire staff still demoralized by the death of Rubinstein, and Alexey further downcast by the prospect of a longer period of military service. With difficulty he endeavoured to amuse Alexey, spent a lot of money, gave some coaching to Pachulski, who was with Tchaikovsky's benefactress in Moscow, and on 13 October was on his way back to Kiev. In the train he brooded on *The Maid*'s evident lack of success, decided that *Mazepa* was not a subject which could fire him, and then settled down to plan an opera on that 'old, but eternally new subject, *Romeo and Juliet*. And now it's irrevocably decided: I shall write an opera on that theme,' he announced to Anatoly two days later.[34] It seems he may impetuously have begun work, for after his death there were found among his papers sketches for a love duet using some material from his earlier orchestral masterpiece. But on arriving at Kamenka on 17 October he had once again to engross himself with Bortnyansky, and *Romeo* faded as before. The peace and solitude of Sasha's now deserted house soothed his troubled nerves, and he had secretly to admit that he did not enjoy it as much when Lev returned from Kiev and talked incessantly about his own domestic worries. From Sasha, now in Odessa, came news that a second niece was engaged. The name of the future bridegroom must have made Uncle Pyotr start: on 16 November Vera was to marry Nikolay Rimsky-Korsakov, a naval officer and adjutant to the Grand Duke Konstantin Nikolayevich, but evidently no close relation of the composer. Tchaikovsky met Rimsky-Korsakov when Lev brought Vera to Kamenka to receive her grandmother's blessing, and took an instant liking to him. The unbounded joy of the young man in his bride-to-be touched Tchaikovsky deeply. 'Modya, what unfortunate fellows you and I are!' he exclaimed forlornly to his homosexual

---

[34] *TLP*10, p. 231; *TZC*2, p. 488; *TPB*, pp. 272–3; *YDGC*, p. 257.

brother. 'You know, we'll live a whole lifetime thus without experiencing for a single second the fullness of happiness in love!'[35]

There was reassurance in Mrs von Meck's response to his admission that he had been unwillingly devoting much time to editing Bortnyansky. Reproaching him roundly for not having applied to her for funds which would have made this labour unnecessary, she sent him an extra sum of money, thus tacitly confirming that her financial plight did not currently endanger her allowance. But there was a further, more uncomfortable confession he had to make; it was no longer Nataliya, but Vera whom they both were scheming should become the wife of one of her sons, but now this niece also was no longer available. Determined their matrimonial schemes should not be thwarted, Tchaikovsky offered an unsuspecting Anna as the new bridal candidate.

Modest identified three reasons for his brother's creative inertia during 1881: the death of Rubinstein, his increasing sensitivity to the family at Kamenka, and the loss of Alexey's company and services. There is no doubt that the stunning blow of Rubinstein's end did have an immediate effect upon Tchaikovsky's creative life, even if only to make him declare that he found no attraction in composing symphonic works now that the most perceptive advocate of his music was gone. Equally Alexey's absence, by denying him the close society of a loved companion and regulator of his day-to-day existence, deeply affected him, and made him more vulnerable to the discomforts of life. But when Modest defined the cause of his brother's changing relation to the Kamenka world as being his increasing love for that world, he was being disingenuous. 'From this time,' wrote Modest, 'Kamenka, which had so long served him as a refuge from all life's alarms and commotions, began to become the place where he found them most of all, because all his growing attachment to the members of Alexandra Ilinishna's family made him still more sensitive to their sorrows and joys.'[36] In his biography Modest quoted very little from the copious letters his composer-brother wrote to him and Anatoly during the summer of 1881, and the reason is plain to see, for the picture they draw of Kamenka is a very sorry one. It was not Tchaikovsky who was changing so much as the Kamenka family, as Tchaikovsky's own letter of 30 June to Anatoly confirms (see above, p. 145). Sasha was not only physically afflicted but in a dreadful mental condition. Tanya was even more emotionally disturbed, behaved with wild irresponsibility, smoked and drank heavily, and was already following her mother down

[35] *TLP*10, p. 244.
[36] *TZC*2, pp. 486–7.

the road to morphia addiction. Some of the other girls, though far less disordered than their eldest sister, were moody and contentious, while their father, weighed down by a situation which he plainly felt unable to handle, had lapsed into a helpless despondency which aroused more sympathy in Tchaikovsky than did the condition of anyone else. If Modest had been more frank he would, in fact, have been providing even stronger evidence to support his conclusion that Kamenka was a contributory factor in his brother's creative torpor.

Yet in the long term the absence of Alexey, the sad state of Kamenka affairs, and the loss of his havens at Brailov and Simaki were blessings in disguise. An existence such as Tchaikovsky had enjoyed in 1880 was dangerously protected, even cosy. Had this become the regular pattern of his living he would have been insulated too much from those sometimes painful experiences which were essential if his creative powers were again to be stimulated into full activity, once the stupefying emotional effect of his marital catastrophe had passed. Such experiences had been afforded in abundance by 1881; above all the death of Rubinstein was to liberate, if only briefly, something which had been imprisoned in him for four years. And the final factor in this year of 1881 was, of course, the birth of Antonina's child, for now she would be far less inclined to act in ways which would keep the paralyzing memory of the 1877 disaster alive. By now the shackles of that crippling event were beginning to slide from him, and when Tchaikovsky left Kamenka on 9 November with his ultimate destination Rome, his creative individuality was flexing itself to shape a work in which it would stand revealed more clearly and powerfully than in any piece since those two masterworks of 1877.

First, however, Tchaikovsky had to attend Vera's wedding in Kiev. At the theatre he saw *Vanka the steward*, a dramatization by Luka Antropov of a story by Dmitri Averkiev, and immediately decided that this, and not *Mazepa* or *Romeo and Juliet*, should be the subject of his next opera. After a whole year he felt his inclination to compose was again really stirring. All summer he had declared that his next work would be an opera, and in Rome he proposed to apply all his energies to this. He stayed nearly a fortnight in Kiev; on 25 November he was in Vienna, where he paused two nights, evidently in complete ignorance that a week later Brodsky was to give the première of the Violin Concerto with the Vienna Philharmonic Orchestra under Hans Richter. On 27 November he was in Venice, three days later in Florence. Here Nadezhda von Meck was in residence and, as in 1878, he made a special excursion to gaze at the villa in which she was living. On 2 December he settled in Rome where Modest, Kolya and Kondratyev had been awaiting him, together with a young lad, Grisha Sangursky, son of the chief bookkeeper at the Kamenka sugar refinery, who had been brought along as company for Kolya.

Arriving in time for the celebration of Liszt's seventieth birthday, Tchaikovsky attended a special concert of Liszt's works. 'It was impossible not to feel some emotion at the sight of this old man of genius, overwhelmingly moved by the ovations of wildly enthusiastic Italians,' he wrote to Nadezhda von Meck on 8 December, two days later. 'But Liszt's compositions themselves leave me cold; they have in them more of poetic intentions than of real creative power, colours rather than draughtmanship.'[37] But other things in Rome's musical life did give him satisfaction. He found especial interest in the church music sung on important occasions, whether it was Palestrina performed in St Peter's at a papal mass for four newly canonized saints, or the singing in St John Lateran of a castrato, whose physical predicament drew both pity and a degree of revulsion from Tchaikovsky. At orchestral and chamber concerts he found the level of performance good.

The situation in Russia, however, gave him no encouragement to turn his own attention to orchestral composition. Nápravník, rated by Tchaikovsky the only remaining conductor to whom he could safely entrust his work, had been hounded by a press campaign from the conductorship of the St Petersburg RMS, while in Moscow Taneyev, whom Tchaikovsky was supporting as the man who could best occupy the rostrum left vacant by Rubinstein, would need to gain experience before his full capabilities could reveal themselves. Having already received a copy of *Vanka the steward*, Tchaikovsky decided he could not himself fashion a satisfactory libretto, and he requested Jurgenson to arrange that Averkiev or some other competent person should undertake this task. By now, however, Tchaikovsky was raring to compose, and *Mazepa* again claimed his attention as soon as he could find suitable accommodation in which he could both work and successfully defend himself from the barrage of social invitations with which he was continually pestered. What had attracted him to *Romeo and Juliet* a few weeks earlier had been the love scene, and a similar nocturnal episode in *Vanka the steward* had particularly drawn him to that subject. It was the same now with *Mazepa*. 'I have begun composing,' he informed his patroness on 13 December. 'I do not know what will come of it, but I have begun with music for the scene of *Mazepa and Mariya*. . . . If I am fired, then perhaps I shall write a whole opera on this subject.'[38] After this *Vanka the steward* sank from sight.

[37] *TLP*10, p. 277; *TPM*2, p. 578; *TZC*2, pp. 494–5.
[38] *TLP*10, p. 283; *TPM*2, p. 581; *TZC*2, p. 496; *DTC*, p. 119; *YDGC*, p. 260 (partial).

Yet, as Tchaikovsky's final sentence shows, his commitment to *Mazepa* was still not absolute, and within a fortnight his efforts were being directed into a very different project. 'Do you remember that you once counselled me to write a trio for piano, violin and cello, and do you remember my reply in which I openly declared to you my antipathy for this combination of instruments?' he asked Nadezhda von Meck on 27 December. 'And now suddenly, despite this antipathy, I have conceived the idea of testing myself in this sort of music which so far I have not touched. I have already written the beginning of *a trio*. Whether I shall finish it, whether it will come out successfully I do not know, but I would very much wish to bring what I have begun to a successful conclusion.'[39] He made no bones about the act of will which was still demanded of him in composing this piece, but he declared that joy in the pleasure the work would give her reconciled him to this.

Such was not the whole truth. Ever since Rubinstein's death Tchaikovsky had wished to enshrine his memory in a composition containing a substantial piano part in tribute to his friend's keyboard mastery, and this was the main prompting for the Trio. As for Tchaikovsky's doubts about his ability to complete the work, these were quickly resolved. Even picking up by chance a copy of the *Neue freie Presse* and reading in it Hanslick's blistering review of the Violin Concerto did not stun his now rampant creativity, and within three weeks, on 18 January 1882, the sketches for the Trio were complete. Though he felt increasing reassurance about the work's qualities as he brought it towards its final form, he feared that he might have handled the medium ineptly. 'Before you engrave it,' he wrote to Jurgenson on 11 February, two days after completing the piece, 'it's essential that Taneyev, Hřímalý, and Fitzenhagen should play it through. . . . I very much want *Karlusha* [Albrecht], *Kashkin, Hubert* and his wife, and our *whole circle* in general to be at this run-through. *It's absolutely essential* that Karlusha or another stringed instrument expert should give his attention to *my bow* markings and correct what is unsuitable.'[40] On 23 March, the first anniversary of Rubinstein's death, these three players performed the Trio privately at the Moscow Conservatoire. Tchaikovsky was still abroad, but on hearing the work played through a little later, he introduced substantial revisions. Especially anxious that this work, 'dedicated to the memory of a great artist', should be handsomely produced, he found himself well satisfied with Jurgenson's edition when it appeared in the early autumn. So, too, Taneyev's reactions gave him profound pleasure. 'I studied it for three and a half weeks,

[39] *TLP*10, p. 292; *TPM*2, p. 586; *DTC*, p. 499.
[40] *TLP*11, p. 47; *TZC*2, pp. 515–16; *DTC*, p. 500 (partial); *TPJ*1, p. 233.

playing it six hours each day,' Taneyev recorded on 5 November 1882, six days after the first public performance of the work at an RMS concert in Moscow. 'I've been going to write you a letter in which I wanted to express my delight in respect of your wonderful composition. I can't remember ever having experienced more pleasure when learning a new piece than in these three [and a half] weeks. . . . Most musicians are delighted with the Trio. It has also pleased the public. Nikolay Albertovich [Hubert] has received many letters asking for the Trio to be repeated.'[41] Tchaikovsky was the more appreciative of Taneyev's tribute because some of the reviews had been less favourable. 'My self-esteem as a composer is as gratified by your praise as it is indifferent to the press notices, to which experience has taught me to respond with philosophical indifference,' he replied five days later. 'I've read *Flerov's* article. I don't believe that anyone (among the musicians) informed him that the Trio's variations represent episodes from the life of Nik[olay] Grig[oryevich]. I think this brilliant idea must be his very own. But isn't it funny! You write music without any pretensions to represent anything, and suddenly you learn that it represents this or that!'[42] The Piano Trio achieved much popularity in Tchaikovsky's lifetime, and this tribute to a departed friend became an elegy to its own creator in November 1893 when, together with the Third Quartet, it was played in both Moscow and St Petersburg in memorial concerts for Tchaikovsky himself.

Such a purpose it fulfilled admirably, for if the Piano Trio cannot be placed in the very front rank of Tchaikovsky's compositions, it is an ambitious piece with many qualities. Its unusual planning recalls that of Beethoven's last piano sonata: two movements, the second of which is a set of variations. Kashkin related that the theme of these variations was inspired by memories of an enchanting day passed in a beauty spot near Moscow in 1873 when a company, including Tchaikovsky and Rubinstein, had dined al fresco with peasants singing and dancing for them. Kashkin also believed, despite Tchaikovsky's own written testimony, that the variations were some sort of composite character study of their dedicatee. Whatever the role of Rubinstein's personality in forming the piece, there is no doubt about that of Tchaikovsky's own; in no work of the last four years had his own self declared itself with such power and consistency. The first movement of the Second Piano Concerto had displayed admirable structural enterprise, but it had been handicapped by lack of characteristic melody of real quality, a deficiency which in any work of Tchaikovsky was fatal. Not so in the

---

[41] *TZC2*, p. 557; *DTC*, p. 502; *TTP*, p. 88.
[42] *TLP11*, p. 266; *TZC2*, p. 558; *TTP*, p. 89; *DTC*, pp. 502–3.

Piano Trio. True, little of it might claim a place among Tchaikovsky's finest thematic inventions, but from the very beginning there is a freely flowing stream of personal (if, at times, slightly Schumannesque) melody in which one fervent idea passes to the next in most natural succession. The theme of the 'introduction' (Ex. 172a) is made to grow into the 'first subject', while the 'transition to the second subject' (Ex. 172b) harks back to the characteristic rhythmic mould of the 'introduction', supported by a bass which spills over from the end of the preceding section. Such thematic overlaps occur elsewhere; thus the return of the opening key and theme (Ex. 172d) is accompanied by a four-note cello phrase which lingers from a shape prominent in the last stage of the development (see *x* in Ex. 172c and d; in the coda, yet

Ex. 172

d. **Adagio con duolo e ben sostenuto**

another derivative of this cello phrase generates an accompaniment motif to partner the concluding heavy-hearted, vastly stretched enunciation of the opening theme).

The structure of this first movement is equally striking. Heard against the background of a traditional first movement in which a slow introduction passes to an exposition set at a faster tempo, the function of the main thematic elements would seem to be those specified in raised commas in the preceding paragraph. And if one diagnoses the 'transition to the second subject' as the second subject itself, and construes the violin/cello dolce espressivo duet as a third subject, one perceives a pattern very close to the introduction and three-subject exposition of the Fourth Symphony's first movement. Yet the tonally more aware listener will have his suspicions aroused when, after the A minor opening, the first theme of the allegro giusto enters in the dominant. In fact Tchaikovsky had devised a radical tonal reinterpretation of the traditional functions of an apparently conventional thematic pattern. (Ex. 173) There is no introduction; the moderato assai opening theme *is* the true first subject, while the more chunky allegro giusto melody begins the second subject which goes on to spread itself generously and with wholehearted commitment to the dominant. The development, introduced by Ex. 172b, uses a principle of thematic evolution a little similar to that of the First Piano Concerto. But whereas, in the earlier work, themes had shown a protean ability to change into one another, in this development the single four-note cell which opens it (see Ex. 172b, bars five to six) displays a lively fertility in generating a swift succession of new thematic particles which finally arrive in E flat minor, a key which has exactly the same tritonal relationship to A minor as the E major central portion of the concerto's development had to the tonic of that work (B flat minor). What follows is the most memorable moment of the whole Trio: the harmonic movement settles into complete rest on a chord of E flat minor, the music's hectic progress is checked, and the two stringed instruments enter into an eloquent duet (Ex. 174) which inevitably brings to mind the slow movement of the Second Piano Concerto, but which has a more consistent strength of contour, a more muscular and closely argued contrapuntalism and greater harmonic richness than the violin/cello dialoguing of that earlier movement. This extensive, deeply expressive colloquy, at first tonally shifting, finally prepares the key of the recapitulation, which opens adagio con duolo e ben sostenuto (see Ex. 172d), thus wringing from the first subject every drop of its latent sorrow. Yet this recapitulation only emphasizes the structural ambiguities in what has gone before, for not only is the second subject

Ex. 173

PIANO TRIO: FIRST MOVEMENT

Sloping block indicates tonally unstable section
L = Link
Subjects are indicated by ① and ②

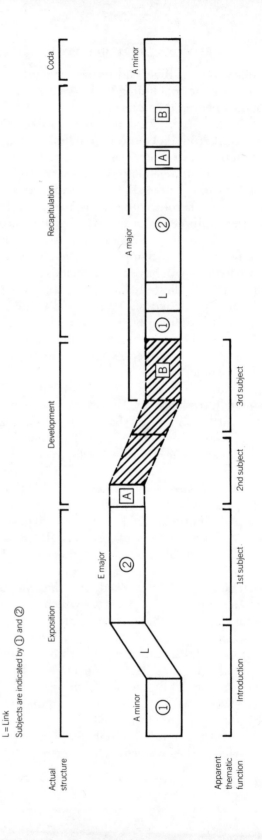

Ex. 174

recapitulated in toto; there follows the theme which had begun the development, as well as the dominant-supported conclusion to the violin/cello duet. Yet nowhere in all this is the tonic seriously challenged, and the movement ends with the first phrase of the first subject, vastly stretched by augmentation and internal repetitions, wearily drawing the movement to rest.

This Pezzo elegiaco, as Tchaikovsky expressly labelled it, is the most impressive piece he had composed since 1877. The following set of variations is matchingly large scale, though the theme upon which the variations are based makes it clear that the issues they are concerned with will be, at least initially, less weighty, for this neatly presented melody has much of the poise, even elegance, of that from which the Rococo Variations had sprung over five years earlier. Yet this ternary theme (Ex. 175a), built from modest two-bar phrases, already has a mild asymmetry which suggests its structure may not remain completely stable in what is to follow, and though the first variation is no more than this theme with its original harmony texturally elaborated, subsequent variations show an increasing readiness to modify the proportions of the theme's constituent parts (Ex. 175), stretching or compressing them until, by variation 5, the original ternary structure has been dissolved, the relationship with the theme asserting itself only in the characteristic contour which begins each half of this charming musical box confection (Ex. 175b). Variation 2 had already turned in the direction of the waltz, but in variation 6 this dance takes entire possession of the field. The Act 2 opening of *Onegin*, which this variation mysteriously – but, surely, significantly – quotes, had incorporated the 'fate embraced' motif; now converted into a waltz, it counterpoints with the first phrase of these variations' own theme in both the central section and the coda.

So far all has been admirable. The theme has been subjected to a number of inventive transformations, the definition of its new identities being further sharpened by a succession of matching key shifts (E major for the theme and first three variations, then a variation each in C sharp minor, C sharp major and A major). But successful as all this is, it has been a fatal miscalculation. Tchaikovsky has gone too far too fast; by removing the waltz from the orbit of the original theme, he has lost his thematic bearings. All he can do is turn back helplessly to the original theme, aping it in a graceless manner which betrays the influence of Schumann at its least beneficent, while the following fugue is an arid attempt to resume that masterly appropriation of new expressive territories so confidently pursued in the earlier part of this movement. These last two variations are the weakest portion of the whole Trio. Fortunately the following andante flebile recaptures something of the

Ex. 175

PIANO TRIO: SECOND MOVEMENT:

earlier quality, and looks forward to the expressive realm in which the whole piece is to end. Taking the familiar opening contour of the theme, though now rhythmically tautened with nervous pairs of semiquavers, Tchaikovsky here spins an affecting cantilena from a series of broadly arching phrases against an almost static harmonic background. A chirpy mazurka precedes the final variation, which leads back to the key and uncomplicated world of the original theme. There follows what Tchaikovsky described as a Variazione Finale e Coda, the finale being a full blown sonata structure with a derivative of the theme as first subject, and with the semiquaver motif from the transition of the first movement's exposition figuring prominently in the second subject and development. Finally in the coda the opening theme of the whole Trio is heard again. By means of the Variazione Finale Tchaikovsky aimed to give weight to the later stages of this essentially episodic movement, and also to build a substantial stretch of vigorous music as a strong foil to the return of that theme which had first established the elegiac purpose of the whole work. Now it bursts in, monumentally presented and extended before collapsing into a brief funeral march which quickly passes into silence.

Tchaikovsky's fatal misjudgment in the direction taken by the earlier variations produces the most serious flaw in the whole Trio. Later he was to sanction the omission of the fugue and the reduction of the breezy but rather tiresome Variazione Finale to the recapitulation only, but this merely diminishes the quantity of second-rate music. The certainty of course charted in the Rococo Variations in their authentic version appears the more impressive when set beside the disorientation of this Trio's variations. Nor can one but compare the textural refinement of the earlier work with the thickness of sound in so much of the Trio, an unattractive aspect of which Tchaikovsky was painfully aware. Yet in the nearly eight years separating the Fourth Symphony and *Onegin* from the Manfred Symphony the Piano Trio remained unique, for that very personal vein of invention which had suddenly been reopened in it by the emotional shock of Rubinstein's death became largely resealed until, three years later, the plight of Byron's hero fully exposed it yet again. In 1882 it was still beyond Tchaikovsky to express explicitly the full force of his own most intimate feelings, but a large measure of his very self could slip out when shielded within the formal grief-laden trappings of a public tribute, and it does so here. Almost inevitably there will be an element of posturing in such a self-consciously elegiac piece, nowhere more clearly heard in the Trio than in the final andante con moto with its monstrous piano textures, exaggeratedly delayed conclusion, and conventional marcia funebre postlude; another eleven years had to pass before Tchaikovsky could summon the confidence to offer a tragic conclusion so honest, so free of factitious attitudinizing as to be emotionally disconcerting. Yet elsewhere in the Trio there escaped inventions which are innocent of affectation – above all, that deeply touching dolce espressivo dialogue of the first movement. Uneven as it is, the Piano Trio is an imposing achievement. Rubinstein, who had served Tchaikovsky so well in life, had rendered a final service in his death.

5

FURTHER UNCERTAINTIES:

MAZEPA

JUST AS IT was the basic instinct of Tchaikovsky's nature for him to turn in upon himself, whether in the act of composition, or in the companionless walks, prolonged reading sessions, or more basic periods of solitary drinking which were regular elements in his daily existence, so in that portion of his life where he had to engage with his environment, he tended to confine as closely as possible his world, living entirely in the present, and responding solely to his immediate surroundings and to the happenings with which he was unavoidably faced. In consequence his reactions could be as limited in vision as they could be intense. In this, for instance, is the clue to his lifelong mishandling of his financial affairs. His current resources could always be drained by the impulses in day-to-day living, or by a sudden appeal from some outside source to his liberal, unthinking generosity. Tchaikovsky was simply incapable of a long-term financial strategy, and when such was required, as in his dealings with Antonina, it was better for someone else to administer the matter.

It was this propensity to live intensely but exclusively within the narrow orbit of the situation in which he found himself which also accounts for some of the apparent paradoxes, even contradictions, so prominent in Tchaikovsky's personality and pattern of existence. It explains, at least in part, the ambivalence in his relationship with his native land. Russia was as dear to him as to any of his musical contemporaries, yet it was also the scene of his greatest pains, both personal and musical. Despite the growing international currency of his music, his homeland was still the place where his works flourished most, where he most wished to be appreciated, and where failure was therefore the more keenly felt. This was just one reason why he would periodically experience the need to flee the land he loved (one notices how such rapid exits could follow hard upon the première of a new composition). But once he had removed himself from the scene of real or imagined failures, the fierce agony might abate to such a degree that he could, as now, lament such misfortunes, yet view them with some detachment. And here is yet another paradox: when he felt that the current fortunes of his music were at a low ebb and when discouragements abounded, his creativity did not necessarily falter. On 16 January, at the very moment when his most intensive work on the Piano Trio was drawing to a fruitful close, he noted bitterly to Jurgenson the setbacks which were besetting various of his pieces.

> They're not giving *The Maid of Orléans*. . . they're not giving *Onegin*,[1] Auer is making mischief against the Violin Concerto, no one plays the Piano Concerto (the Second): in a word, it's bad. But what hurts, pains and vexes me terribly is that the theatres' directorate, not giving a kopeck to *The Maid of Orléans*, gives 30,000 to mount *The Snow Maiden* [by Rimsky-Korsakov]. Isn't it a fact – and isn't it disagreeable to you – that our *subject* has been taken from us, that *Lel* sings the very same words to different music; [it's] as though they've taken from me by force something that is mine, something native to me, close to me, and are presenting it to the public in new, brilliant attire. The pain of this reduces me to tears.[2]

Yet all these unpalatable, even distressing events (even Hanslick's diatribe against the Violin Concerto) had happened far from Rome. Distance lent detachment; such mortifications no more dammed his creative stream than they impeded his pleasure in his surroundings or in his day-to-day living with Modest and his charges.

It was the same with the situation in Sasha's family. Living in the middle of the Kamenka ferment the previous summer had deeply affected him in his work and his mode of living, but now, a thousand or so miles away, he could simply detail in letters the reports of turmoil in his sister's household, and then, it seems, brush them from his mind. In fact, news from Kiev was bad. Tanya was as intractable and disordered as ever, and this intensified the ambivalence in Tchaikovsky's attitude towards those people who afforded him some of the closest and most precious relationships of his whole life. For a moment he did ponder the prospect of returning there with alarm. 'I can't imagine anything more cheerless than life amidst this family,' he lamented to Anatoly on 14 January. '. . . Yet where, except at Kamenka, can I find a similar residence for myself?'[3] Indeed, Kamenka was irreplaceable, and he was to be drawn back there for the summer to risk the same miseries as

---

[1] In fact, this proved untrue, for only six days later *Onegin* was revived in Moscow.
[2] *TLP*11, p. 18; *TZC*2, p. 509; *TPJ*1, p. 226.
[3] *TLP*11, p. 17.

during 1881. Another piece of intelligence, however, brought both pleasure and relief: Anatoly had become engaged at last, and Tchaikovsky thankfully viewed the prospect this brought of an end to his own long-suffering role as comforter of a love-lorn brother. But here again, at this news of his brother's forthcoming nuptials, he looked in upon himself, reflecting upon his own attitude to the opposite sex – an attitude which had been gently challenged during the preceding weeks when he had become aware that Emma Genton, the governess to Kondratyev's sixteen-year-old daughter, Nadezhda, was exhibiting tender feelings ('more passionate than I would wish'[4]) towards him. Her departure from Rome with the Kondratyevs was a considerable relief. 'I'm terribly glad you feel you are happy,' he wrote to Anatoly on 20 February, 'and though I have never experienced anything of the sort, yet I think that I can understand perfectly everything you are going through. It's a certain kind of need for the care and caresses which only a woman can satisfy. Sometimes there comes over me an intense desire to be fondled by a woman's hand. Sometimes I see nice ladies (not, however, young ones) into whose lap I simply want to place my head and kiss their hands.'[5] The image of his mother (the lady with 'hands which, though not small, were unusually beautiful'[6]) remained as ineluctable as ever.

Though the Piano Trio and the need to copy out the All-night Vigil ensured that Tchaikovsky had work enough to occupy him fully, his dwindling funds heightened the attractiveness of a request for six piano pieces to be published in the *Nouvelliste*, the periodical which had already carried his *Seasons* in 1876. It was an easy way of making 600 roubles, but Tchaikovsky felt a moral obligation to consult Jurgenson before undertaking work for another publisher. Jurgenson had, it seems, already heard of this invitation, and his reaction was blunt. 'It would appear to me that you don't need this [commission]. I'm always your willing client,' he wrote brusquely on 26 January, thus smartly nipping Tchaikovsky's plan in the bud.[7] Attending a concert at which he heard for the second time a new quartet by Liszt's protégé, Giovanni Sgambati, he again judged the work worthless, and observed with distaste Liszt's ostentatious display of approbation. 'How I dislike this trait of Liszt!' he exploded to his patroness.

---

[4] *TLP*11, p. 37.
[5] *TLP*11, pp. 55–6; *TPM*3, p. 616; *YDGC*, p. 266 (partial); *TZC*2, p. 519 (with the words in parentheses omitted).
[6] See Vol. 1, p. 21.
[7] *TLP*11, p. 26; *TPJ*1, p. 230.

He never tells the truth, and always approves of everything unreservedly. People keep telling me and writing to me that I'm wrong
not to visit Liszt while living in the same city. But I will not call on
him for nothing, for to his sugary compliments I shall also have to
reply with flattery and falsehood, and that is very repugnant to me.
In addition, he holds an eternal open house, and all the Russian
ladies here are constantly in attendance – and I am avoiding these
ladies, for last year I suffered not a little from their pressing
invitations.[8]

By now it seems that Tchaikovsky's various compatriots in Rome had
accepted that he was not to be drawn into either making or receiving
visits. Bringing the Piano Trio to a successful conclusion was immensely beneficial to his morale, and his good spirits were heightened
by news that Alexey had passed an examination which would reduce
his army service to three years. There had been some discussion with
Modest about visiting Algiers to which a maternal aunt of Kolya had
invited them. But Kolya's father would not hear of such close contact
with a sister of his by now divorced wife, and Naples was chosen instead
as their next place of residence. Certainly it was imperative that they
should leave Rome, partly because of the high cost of living, partly
because Sergey Flerov, the Moscow music critic, had descended upon
Tchaikovsky and was making heavy demands upon his time. On 21
February he left Rome alone, found a six-room flat with splendid views
of Naples and Vesuvius, and on the 25th was joined by Modest and the
two boys.

The new accommodation quickly revealed less attractive features.
First there were mice – one of Tchaikovsky's life-long phobias: a whole
army of them carried out manoeuvres in the attic above his room, he
alleged. Secondly, when the bill was presented at the end of the first
week's stay, it proved to be twice as much as expected. An enraged
Tchaikovsky and brother promptly packed their bags and moved closer
to the centre of Naples into lodgings more convenient for enjoying what
the city could offer, but less attractive in themselves and, worst of all,
intolerably noisy. Street singers and hurdy-gurdies – sometimes as
many as three at a time – made impossible almost all work other than
proof-reading or copying. Nevertheless, on 19 March he could
announce that he had that day brought his All-night Vigil to its final
form. Nor was casual strolling in the streets enjoyable because of
the persistent badgering from hordes of beggars. Despite all this

---

[8] *TLP*11, p. 44; *TPM*3, p. 23; *TZC*2, p. 517.

Tchaikovsky was induced by the beauty of the scenery and the opportunities of visiting the places of interest around Naples itself to stay a full month in this southern city. The secularization of some of the Neapolitan monasteries saddened him. 'As a place where a man distances himself from the world's bustle for the sake of an ascetic life of contemplation, a monastery attracts me,' he wrote to Nadezhda von Meck,[9] further confirming that it was the poetic refuge religion could offer which was the basis of the church's appeal to him. Sarah Bernhardt was in Naples, and Tchaikovsky saw her both in *La Dame aux camélias* and in *Sphinx*, a play by that great favourite of his youth, Octave Feuillet. He also heard Verdi's *Il Trovatore* at the Teatro San Carlo, but this was the only music which gave him any pleasure in Naples.

For some time after receiving news of Anatoly's impending marriage he had been debating whether to return to Moscow for the event or wait in Italy for the arrival of Anatoly and his bride. His finances finally decided the matter. Realizing that his money would not hold out till then, and knowing, too, that business affairs also required his presence in Russia, he resolved to return. Leaving Naples on 23 March, he spent three days in Sorrento, a town whose peace so captivated him that he declared he would return thither for several weeks during next spring. Thence he returned to Naples for two nights, and on the 28th was in Florence, stayed four days, and then left for Vienna alone. Pausing here one night, he arrived in Moscow on 7 April.

It was here that Anatoly had done his courting, and Tchaikovsky was immediately drawn into the social life of the very numerous family into which his brother was to marry. Kondratyev, too, was in town, and his company proved inescapable. But these social distractions did not prevent Tchaikovsky from beginning negotiations with the impresario and producer, Mikhail Lentovsky, who had built a theatre in Moscow, and who wanted a new opera from Tchaikovsky for the next winter season. 'The subject will be either *Sadko*, or *The Tower of Koromïslov* (a legend), or Potekhin's [four-act folk drama] *A Measure of sorrow*,' he wrote to Modest on 13 April.[10] Lentovsky seems to have had something in common with Emanuel Schikaneder, Mozart's partner in *Die Zauberflöte*, in that his theatrical enterprises were aimed at a wide audience; certainly the choice of either a legend or a drama of a popular nature, rather than a literary classic or a subject attractive especially to an upper-class society, was determined by the breadth of appeal such themes might have. A week later the selection had fastened upon *Sadko*; after this the project was never mentioned again.

[9] *TLP*11, p. 79; *TPM*3, p. 38; *TZC*2, p. 524.
[10] *TLP*11, p. 98; *TZC*2, p. 528; *TPB*, p. 280; *YDGC*, p. 269.

The Tchaikovsky clan mustered in force in Moscow for the wedding. Nikolay and his wife appeared, as well as Lev and Sasha with the ungovernable Tanya. Vera and her new husband were also in attendance; they had left Paris hurriedly when rumours had begun to circulate that the Grand Duke Konstantin Nikolayevich, who was openly living with another woman, had married off his adjutant to a girl who had attracted him so that he might have her near him in Paris. After talking with Lev and Sasha, Tchaikovsky was able to report to his patroness upon the highly favourable impression made by her sons, Nikolay and Alexandr, when they had paid a four-day visit to the Davïdovs in Kiev during February. Uncle Pyotr had not been able to restrain himself from discovering Anna's reaction to Kolya. 'I asked Anna how she liked Kolya, and whether she would like him subsequently to become her husband,' he admitted to his fellow-conspirator. 'She replied without the slightest hesitation that she would like it very much, and was prepared to wait patiently until he had finished his studies, though she would have preferred this to have happened earlier. Now Anna is getting ready to go to St Petersburg and stay with my cousin, the Countess Litke. Would you allow Kolya to go to my cousin's house and see Anna? I know in advance, my dear, that you will agree to this,' he went on, but added a qualification: 'my only fear is that, if there should be kindled in Kolya a spark of serious feeling towards Anna, then how might these visits impair his studies?'[11]

The mother's order of priorities was clear. 'You were very right to remind me of his studies, my dear friend,' she replied forthwith. 'The main thing is that now he has examinations, and I fear anything which distracts him from diligent work. . . . And so I shall not hurry to tell him of Anna Lvovna's arrival in St Petersburg. I beg you, my dear, to write me . . . when Anna Lvovna will be in St Petersburg – secondly, the Countess Litke's address, and thirdly: will Anna Lvovna have returned to Kamenka by 13 June, because then both my boys, or perhaps Kolya alone . . . will come to Kamenka. What pleasure all these dreams afford me!' she added reassuringly, lest he should construe her restrictions upon her son's activities as future lover as a sign of indifference to the aim they both cherished.[12]

With Anatoly's wedding on 16 April some of the social pressures fell away a little. Tchaikovsky remained nearly three more weeks in Moscow, hearing for the first time his Piano Trio, an experience which led him to make some revisions of substance. Sasha and her family soon returned to the Ukraine, and life in Moscow was made more

[11] *TLP*11, p. 99; *TPM*3, p. 48.
[12] *TPM*3, pp. 50–1.

uncongenial by Alexey's confinement to barracks because of further examinations he had to pass. On 1 May Tchaikovsky received a simple telegram from a niece at Kamenka: 'The lilies of the valley are in flower. Vera.'[13] It was a summons he could not resist. Two days later he hastened from Moscow, spent his forty-second birthday in Kiev with Sasha and some of her family, and on 8 May was in Kamenka.

Once again Tchaikovsky's return to his homeland had been accompanied by very reserved feelings. 'The Russian porters seemed to me insolent Kalmucks, the gendarmes like bears, the snub-nosed officials who balefully examined my luggage and who subsequently appeared in the restaurant – and who with ostentatious slovenliness snatched what had fallen off the counter – all these aroused in me a wish to do them a mischief,' he had written to Modest from Warsaw on 5 April. 'Perhaps when I reach Russia proper this will pass.'[14] But these feelings had persisted. Moscow itself still had some charms, but the churlish behaviour of some of its inhabitants repelled him, making the attractions of Kamenka seem the greater, despite the prospect of what might confront him when he arrived. However, his first few days there proved pleasant, for Tanya had remained with Sasha in Kiev, while Modest and Kolya had joined Lev, Vera and her husband in Kamenka to make up a congenial ménage in which Tchaikovsky felt he could again turn his attention to *Mazepa*. His contentment was short-lived. Ten days after his arrival came news of the sudden death of Kolya's father, and Modest had to leave hastily for Grankino. Tchaikovsky realized, too, that Kamenka, whose noisy children were already making work difficult, would be overflowing when all Sasha's family with appendages collected there, and accommodation had to be found for the new tutor who was to teach the younger children. Tchaikovsky himself would be in the way, and he even made a half-hearted and unsuccessful expedition to find lodgings elsewhere in the Kamenka estate.

Nor was his restless mood eased by much progress on the opera. Constantly his thoughts turned longingly towards Italy. 'And yet I feel that in the summer it's only at Kamenka that I'm *at home*, and that if I had to go, I should *miss* even that *ennui* which torments me,' he concluded to Modest on 27 May. 'I'm working conscientiously – but I'm not inflamed; for the child I'm bringing forth I'm not experiencing a twentieth part of that inspiration and love which I have experienced before, especially in regard to some of my offspring.'[15] It would be best,

---

[13] *TLP*11, p. 107; *TPM*3, p. 53.

[14] *TLP*11, p. 94; *TZC*2, p. 528; *TPB*, p. 280; *YDGC*, p. 268 (partial).

[15] *TLP*11, p. 120; *DTC*, p. 119 (partial).

he decided, if he joined Modest after Anatoly and Parasha had left Kamenka; at Grankino he would also be able to work in far greater quiet and seclusion than was possible in his present situation. His presence would be especially welcomed by Modest, for Kolya was heir to the estate, and Modest had been entrusted by Kolya's father with his son's entire education. This responsibility, with its accompanying powers, had made Modest the target of pressures from other interested parties, including Kolya's mother, towards whom Tchaikovsky's feelings now became very different from what they had been at the time of her separation from her husband. Nor had the legacy of 10,000 roubles to Modest endeared him to the family. Meanwhile Tchaikovsky occupied some of his time by reading *Bleak House*. He had begun it on leaving Florence and, from the time he took to finish it, it would appear possible he read at least a part of it in English. 'I cried somewhat,' he confided to Modest, 'in the first place, because I pity Lady Dedlock, secondly, because it grieves me to part with all these people with whom I've lived exactly two months . . . thirdly, from tenderness and gratitude to such a great writer as Dickens.'[16] When Sasha finally arrived with Tanya she also brought with her Stanislav Blumenfeld, a circumstance which caused Tchaikovsky much disquiet, for he could see from the long tête-à-têtes his niece and the music teacher engaged in that there was some sort of liaison between them. Meanwhile from Grankino came news of ever-increasing pressures upon Modest; Konradi's will was being contested. On 12 June Anatoly and his wife arrived at last. Four days later Tchaikovsky left Kamenka to be at Modest's side.

Tchaikovsky had expected to spend at least two weeks at Grankino; he ended by staying nearly seven. He discovered with relief that Kolya's mother had departed, though in the matter of the will the advantage at present lay with her. If Modest were to press his case, it was clear that a visit to St Petersburg would be necessary, but his morale was much bedraggled from skirmishes with his rival, and his physical condition was low. For some time he had been suffering from a fistula, and it was apparent that an operation was essential. The local doctor performed this, but further abscesses erupted, leaving Modest almost prostrate. Realizing that his brother would need all his moral support when he was at last well enough to journey to the Russian capital, Tchaikovsky resolved to wait and travel with him. Meanwhile the enforced delay proved thoroughly acceptable, for in the calm of Grankino, with its pleasant bathing, he could work freely, and his rate of progress on *Mazepa* began to accelerate. But as the end of July

[16] *TLP*11, p. 126; *TZC*2, p. 532; *TPB*, p. 281; *YDGC*, p. 270.

approached he became restless, partly because of Grankino itself, partly because of anxiety over his brother's continuing ill-health. Kolya's mother had discovered a simple stratagem for obstructing Modest: she deprived him of money. Thus not only did Modest receive no part of the bequest he believed was due to him from his late employer; Kolya's mother made no move to pay Modest his arrears of salary and, in consequence, travelling to St Petersburg would have been impossible without funds from another source. Since there were no signs of the mother attempting to wrest control of Kolya from Modest, Tchaikovsky decided it would be better to delay the confrontation in St Petersburg until after his brother had recovered properly. And so, on leaving Grankino on 5 August, it was for Kamenka that they headed.

Here news awaited Tchaikovsky of the Czech production of *The Maid of Orléans*, first presented on 28 July. Sasha had taken another cure in Carlsbad, and on her return journey had delayed in Prague to attend a performance which, according to her, was well-meaning rather than meritorious – though Jurgenson reported that the opera had had a great success. For Tchaikovsky the most momentous event of his short stay in Kamenka was the visit of the von Meck boys. As soon as Kolya's examinations had finished, Tchaikovsky and Mrs von Meck had ensured that he should meet Anna in St Petersburg, and even while Tchaikovsky had been at Grankino the brothers had visited Kamenka. Nadezhda von Meck's enthusiasm for their marital scheme had now spilled over into a second project; perhaps her Alexandr could marry Nataliya Davïdova? Tchaikovsky had doubts, however, about Nataliya's compatibility with his patroness's other son, and did his best to extinguish the mother's hopes by painting an unflattering portrait of this niece. But on their original project he remained as committed as ever, and when the von Meck brothers returned, he wrote fulsomely to his confederate of the favourable impression they had created with the whole family. Their joint campaign to foster romance was thriving.

So, too, were the fortunes of Tchaikovsky's music at the Exhibition of Industry and the Arts. This had opened in Moscow two months earlier with attendant concerts in which Tchaikovsky's works were well represented. In the opening concert Taneyev had given the first Russian performance of the Second Piano Concerto with Anton Rubinstein conducting, nine days later the latter also directed the Serenade for Strings, and in other concerts the Hymn from Act 1 of *The Maid* and the Liturgy of St John Chrysostom were given. But most momentous of all from Tchaikovsky's point of view was the programme of 20 August devoted entirely to his own works, and on 17 August he left Kamenka to

attend this. Even before the Exhibition opened he had learned of the
Violin Concerto's great success in London when, on 8 May, Brodsky
had played it with Hans Richter conducting. Now, with Ippolit Altani,
the same soloist introduced it to Russia in a concert which included *The
Tempest*, the Italian Capriccio, some vocal items, and the first performance of *1812*. The concerto enjoyed a particular success. But despite
this, and the warm, welcome signs of esteem which were accorded him,
the inevitable Moscow gloom descended, further deepened by discovering Alexey in hospital and having to visit him daily. Rimsky-Korsakov
was in Moscow to conduct another of the Exhibition concerts, and
Tchaikovsky encountered him and his wife on two occasions. It was a
long time since the two men had met, and the Rimsky-Korsakovs
displayed much warmth towards Tchaikovsky to which he responded
with a good deal of reserve. 'I avoided their advances very decisively,
and neither visited them nor dined with them at the Huberts', and I'm
very glad I did so,' he wrote to Modest. 'This "mighty handful" is very
strange; they always thrust themselves upon me with sickly displays of
affection, and this is completely at odds with their actions towards
me.'[17] Obviously the matter of *The Snow Maiden* still rankled. Meanwhile, though Modest and Kolya had gone on to St Petersburg,
Tchaikovsky now decided he need not follow his brother thither, for
some of the rancour seemed to have gone out of the dispute over
Konradi's will, and Tchaikovsky clearly hoped that Modest would
reach some accommodation with Kolya's mother without his support.
He was also afraid the momentum achieved in composing *Mazepa* at
Grankino would be lost if he did not quickly resume work, and on 30
August he left Moscow for Kamenka, halting for two nights in Kiev,
and revelling in the solitude he could now enjoy after the distractions of
Moscow. He reached Kamenka on 2 September. The simultaneous
arrival of Blumenfeld, who was installed in the room next to his and
whose proximity inhibited Tchaikovsky in his habit of playing and
singing when composing, greatly irritated him. But otherwise
Kamenka was almost deserted. Sasha was in Sevastopol with Vera and
some of the younger children, Lev and Tanya were in St Petersburg,
and other members of the family were scattered in Moscow and Kiev.
Soon came news that Vera had been safely delivered of a daughter, and
that Modest and Kolya's mother had reached a compromise: he was to
be free to live where he chose with Kolya, and was to receive 6,000
roubles a year. In relative contentment Tchaikovsky set about bringing
his opera to a conclusion.

[17] *TLP*11, p. 193; *TPB*, pp. 283–4; *YDGC*, p. 274 (partial).

It is impossible to ascertain exactly what Tchaikovsky had by now composed of *Mazepa*. It was more than a year since Davïdov had sent him Viktor Burenin's libretto and, as we have seen, soon after this Tchaikovsky had begun tinkering with bits of it, composing 'four numbers' during the summer of 1881. In Rome in December he had begun the scene between Mazepa and Mariya in Act 2, reporting this to Mrs von Meck in terms suggesting that this was his first step in setting this libretto, i.e. that those pieces already composed were fairly insignificant in quantity, or only lightly sketched. The editors of the complete edition of Tchaikovsky's letters, having access to his sketchbooks, state that these indicate his efforts during May were directed primarily towards Act 3: to Andrey's aria and the finale, though he also gave some thought to the overture and the women's chorus which opens Act 1. His last work before leaving for Grankino was done on the following scene between Mariya and Andrey, and on the Act 1 finale. At Grankino, in conditions free from the bustle and distractions of Naples, Moscow and Kamenka, he disciplined himself to work more consistently, and after some three weeks of residence he could reveal that his enthusiasm for the subject had grown by degrees. 'I am working very diligently and methodically,' he wrote to Nadezhda von Meck on 12 July. 'Little by little there has come over me, if not a passionate enthusiasm for my subject, then at least a warm feeling for the dramatis personae. Like a mother who, the more her child occasions her worries, anxieties and alarms, the more she loves him, so I am already feeling a fatherly tenderness towards my new musical progeny who has so many times caused me painful moments of disillusionment with myself, almost of despair, but which now, despite all this, is already growing respectably and healthily.'[18] This new mood held, and on 25 July he could further disclose to his benefactress that he had that day finished 'a second third of the opera, i.e. one of the three acts'.[19]

Tchaikovsky clearly did little work after his return to Kamenka in early August, and certainly none during his Moscow visit in the latter half of the month, but in settling back into his sister's home at the beginning of September he picked up the threads of the piece again, and on 4 September, within two days of his arrival, he reported he had finished 'very successfully'[20] the entr'acte to Act 2. Work was interrupted for about a fortnight while he directed his attention to the set of Six Piano Pieces, Op. 51, for the Jurgenson brothers. These were

---

[18] *TLP*11, pp. 158–9; *TPM*3, pp. 70–1; *TZC*2, pp. 541–2; *DTC*, p. 120; *YDGC*, p. 272 (partial).
[19] *TLP*11, p. 165; *TPM*3, p. 74; *YDGC*, p. 272; *DTC*, p. 120.
[20] *TLP*11, p. 193; *TPB*, p. 283; *YDGC*, p. 276; *DTC*, p. 120.

delivered by Tchaikovsky for financial reasons, so he told Modest (paying 100 roubles for each piece, Pyotr Jurgenson had obviously proposed these pieces to compensate Tchaikovsky for having obstructed his *Nouvelliste* commission offered some months earlier). The return of Lev and Tanya from St Petersburg on 16 September brought a resumption of all those vexations now perpetually occasioned by his eldest niece's behaviour. Tchaikovsky's views on the proprieties in the relationship between members of the opposite sex were prim in the extreme, and the spectacle of his niece and Blumenfeld sitting opposite each other in a carriage and rubbing knees under a blanket so shocked him that, as he told Modest, he would have quit Kamenka there and then if he had had money for the journey. However, such constant affronts from Tanya made it easier for him resolutely to shut himself up in his own room, coming out only to eat and go for walks. The result was that by 22 September the piano pieces had been composed, and within a few days the sketches for *Mazepa* were finished. Tchaikovsky had worked on it for a year, and it had cost him much effort. 'I have never yet experienced such difficulty in composing any large piece as with this opera,' he reflected to Nadezhda von Meck on 26 September. 'I just do not know whether it is a decline in my talents or whether, perhaps, I have become more severe with myself – but remembering how formerly I worked without the slightest effort so that I did not know even the tiniest, transitory moments of self-doubt, or ever despaired of my own powers – I cannot fail to notice that I have become a different person. . . . Now I am like a man carrying a weighty, though dear burden which must at all costs be borne to the end.'[21] To Jurgenson the next day, however, he spoke more cheerfully of the result of his labours. '*I think* it'll be a good opera, *I think* that this time I'll not cause you to be out of pocket, *I think* that the public, and the singers, and I, and Jurgenson will be satisfied – but, yet, the devil only knows!'[22]

Without delay Tchaikovsky launched into orchestrating the opera. He viewed this operation with pleasure, and at first all went speedily. His hopes of finishing it by the spring so that it might be produced the next season were high. But just as scoring *The Maid* had proved more difficult than expected, so now he found his work on this new opera proceeding only slowly, for that increased self-criticism he had already perceived in the act of composition was equally evident when selecting the combination of timbres through which the sound would be projected. '*Mazepa* is coming along at a snail's pace, even though each

[21] *TLP*11, p. 216; *TPM*3, p. 102; *TZC*2, pp. 550–1; *TPB*, p. 595; *DTC*, p. 120; *YDGC*, p. 276 (partial).
[22] *TLP*11, p. 218; *TPJ*1, p. 259; *DTC*, pp. 120–1.

day I'm working several hours on it,' he lamented to Taneyev on 10 November.

> I can no longer explain to you why I've so changed in my attitudes. At first I thought it was that general decline of powers which goes with old age, but now I'm beginning to console myself with the thought that I've become more severe with myself, less self-confident, and perhaps it's from this that a bit I could once have orchestrated in a single day I now orchestrate in three or four. I'm very much against leaving Kamenka before I've finished the instrumentation of the first act. I'd thought I would manage to complete this by the middle of November, but it seems I have still at least fifteen days' work before me. But as soon as I finish I shall go to Moscow.[23]

In the event even more time was needed, and it was 24 December before he could report from Moscow that this labour was completed. Because it was only after this that he discovered the sketches for much of the rest of *Mazepa* had not been packed into his luggage when he had left Kamenka, he was unable to proceed further until the middle of January.

Meanwhile he had had some doubts about the dramatic structure of the piece, and on 9 January, now briefly in St Petersburg, he turned to Nápravník for advice. 'Please read the enclosed libretto and tell me whether you find any changes or cuts necessary. I particularly ask you, my dear chap, to direct your attention to Act 1. Would it not be better to divide this into two scenes – to finish the first scene with Mazepa's exit? I shall await your reply with the greatest impatience, and will not begin scoring Act 2 until I get your letter.'[24] In his reply Nápravník endorsed the division of Act 1 and also suggested, among other things, that the scene in Act 2 between Mazepa and Mariya might prove too long. Later Tchaikovsky was to concur with this view.

Despite what he had written to Nápravník, on 16 January Tchaikovsky, now in Paris, resumed work on *Mazepa*. He had passed to Act 3, perhaps because he had promised the conductor, Max Erdmannsdörfer, who had taken Nikolay Rubinstein's place in Moscow's orchestral world, that he would let him have for concert performance the entr'acte which depicts the Battle of Poltava – though when Tchaikovsky set to work he felt disenchantment with the piece

---

[23] *TLP*11, pp. 266–7; *TZC*2, p. 558 (partial); *TTP*, p. 89; *DTC*, p. 121 (partial); *YDGC*, p. 281 (partial).
[24] *TLP*11, p. 302.

and decided to set it aside for later revision; meanwhile he sent the
gopak from Act 1 as a substitute, and Erdmannsdörfer conducted it at a
special RMS concert in Moscow on 3 March. But otherwise initial
progress on Act 3 was rapid and in a week, by 23 January, he had
finished nearly half of it. Then, as before, his pace slackened. Fatigue
and his increasing self-criticism intervened (and also problems with his
niece, Tanya), though in the quality of the opera itself his confidence
does no: seem to have faltered. Commissions for a grand march and a
canta: , *Moscow*, to grace the coronation of Alexandr III interrupted
work . iring March, and it was 7 April before he could despatch the
score o 'the third act. But Act 2 went more easily, and by 28 April the
whole was completed. A fortnight later it was on its way to Jurgenson,
together with the libretto in its final form, and the vocal score. 'I've
spent two years on it,' Tchaikovsky wrote to his publisher on 10 May,
'and it's cost me a great many labours. I entrust its future fate to you!'[25]

What followed was something unprecedented in Tchaikovsky's relationship with his publisher. 'You know that I've never argued with you
regarding the fees you have fixed, and indeed there has been no
occasion to argue. . . . At times I have felt you have paid me too
generously,' he wrote on 9 August.

> Now something completely the opposite has happened. The fee you
> propose for *Mazepa* [1,000 roubles] is *too* inequitable, and I can't let
> this remain without protest. Unless I'm mistaken, even for *The Maid
> of Orléans* I received from you more than 1,000 roubles. . . . But since
> then four years have passed. How can it be that my value in all this
> time has not increased one penny? In addition I didn't on that
> occasion make the transcription [for voices and piano]. . . . When
> you began engraving *The Maid* its production was undecided, its fate
> was unknown. Now, when the theatres of both our capitals are
> competing to get the [choral] parts, score and vocal score of *Mazepa*
> from you, you assign 1,000 roubles to me for an opera to which I've
> devoted two years and three months of assiduous labour.[26]

Jurgenson immediately and readily agreed, observing without irony
that he was glad Tchaikovsky rated his own work highly, and
accepting Tchaikovsky's named price of 2,400 roubles (in due course
Tchaikovsky was able to argue the Imperial Theatres into paying him a
royalty of ten per cent of the box office returns instead of the eight per
cent which was the standard rate for three-act operas).

[25] *TLP*12, p. 146; *TZC*2, p. 585; *TPJ*1, p. 303; *DTC*, p. 122.
[26] *TLP*12, p. 200; *TPM*3, p. 624; *TZC*2, p. 593; *TPJ*1, p. 304; *DTC*, p. 122 (partial).

There were no grounds for complaint, however, about the swiftness with which Jurgenson issued the opera, and by August 1883 both the vocal score and the choral parts were already in print. His publisher's expeditiousness was to be expected: what did surprise Tchaikovsky was the response of the Imperial Theatres to his new opera. As his letter to Jurgenson shows, both the Bolshoy in Moscow and the Maryinsky in St Petersburg wanted to produce it. Not only that: both showed a willingness to accommodate Tchaikovsky's wishes and to allocate production resources such as they had never displayed before. It was all the most convincing proof Tchaikovsky had yet had of his now thoroughly established reputation as Russia's most admired composer, though he himself suspected there might be another explanation for this ardour. 'There must be some secret reason, and I cannot think of anything except that, perhaps, the Tsar himself has expressed a wish that my opera should be mounted as well as possible on the stages of both our capital cities,' he confided to Nadezhda von Meck.[27] It was even reported that the designer Bocharov had been sent from St Petersburg to the Ukraine to study the effect of moonlight there so that it might be properly reproduced on the stage. Be that as it may (and Modest attributed this zeal to the recent appointment of Ivan Vsevolozhsky as director of the Imperial Theatres), Tchaikovsky was asked to approve the costumes and observe the dance rehearsals for the Moscow production, as well as accompany the singers and supervise the musical preparations. Once rehearsals did start, the enthusiasm of everybody involved touched him deeply. 'I cannot complain of lack of zeal or sympathy,' he reported to Nadezhda von Meck on 8 February, a week before the première in Moscow. 'Everyone is treating the opera lovingly and with completely sincere delight.'[28] Even the first orchestral rehearsal did not cause him that disenchantment he had always, so he said, experienced with his previous operas.

The initial stages of the St Petersburg production went less smoothly. Though he had delegated to Nápravník the casting of the opera, disagreements arose, especially as to whether Wilhelmina Raab, who had caused Tchaikovsky much dissatisfaction when she had created the parts of Oxana in *Vakula the Smith* and Agnès Sorel in *The Maid*, should sing the role of Mariya, and these led to Tchaikovsky threatening to withdraw the opera until a more satisfactory singer could be found. Nápravník was angry, but Tchaikovsky's prestige, whether Tsar-inspired or personal, now lent his wishes great persuasive force.

---

[27] *TLP*12, p. 208; *TPM*3, p. 209; *TZC*2, pp. 595–6.
[28] *TLP*12, p. 304; *TPM*3, p. 253; *TZC*2, p. 617; *DTC*, pp. 124–5.

'Nápravník (between ourselves) is very offended by my letter and has written a reply which is not lacking in caustic observations,' he admitted to Modest on 24 September, 'but he strongly urges, even implores, that I should not approach the directorate with a request to postpone the production, promises *for the part of Mariya* some new singer who will shortly make her début, and assigns the part of Orlik to Stravinsky in accordance with my wish.'[29] Once this matter had been settled Tchaikovsky felt he could entrust everything to Nápravník. He could not be in two places at once, and despite pleas from St Petersburg, he decided to direct all his attention to what was happening in Moscow.

Mazepa was first heard in Moscow on 15 February 1884, conducted by Ippolit Altani. 'Immediately after the performance there was a dinner given to me by the performers at which, despite my terrible weariness, I had to be present till five o'clock in the morning,' he related to Nadezhda von Meck from Berlin on 19 February.[30] The last days before this had taken an appalling toll of his nerves, and the day after the performance he had hastened towards Western Europe, missing not only the première of his own Second Suite in Moscow that very evening, but also the opening night of the St Petersburg production on 18 February. '*Mazepa* was successful in the sense that both the performers and I received many ovations,' he continued to his patroness. '. . . My brothers, in view of my terrible nervous condition, persuaded me not to go to St Petersburg but to make haste abroad. . . . Here this morning I found a telegram from Modest informing me that yesterday's première of *Mazepa* in St Petersburg was also successful, and that the Tsar had stayed till the end and expressed complete satisfaction.'[31] He also, as Tchaikovsky was later to discover, expressed surprise at the composer's absence. Both Modest and Jurgenson observed that the opera's success would have been greater if Tchaikovsky had been present.

Of the Moscow production Modest remembered that the staging was excellent, the chorus first-rate, but that the solo singers without exception were all deficient in some way – though Tchaikovsky himself was full of praise for Emiliya Pavlovskaya as Mariya. The Moscow press was generally far more favourable than that of St Petersburg, where the staging, though perhaps even better than that of Moscow, was offset by some serious unevenness among the soloists. Cui led the attack with his by now well-known cry about Tchaikovsky's failing powers. Writing in *The Week*, he informed his readers that the libretto of *Mazepa* was

[29] *TLP*12, p. 230; *TZC*2, p. 603; *TPB*, p. 300.
[30] *TLP*12, p. 309; *TPM*3, p. 255.
[31] *TLP*12, p. 309; *TPM*3, p. 255; *TZC*2, p. 624 (partial).

superbly made. . . . Mr Tchaikovsky has, however, succeeded in spoiling it with his music to such a degree that almost all these wonderful scenes make no impression. . . . For ten years there has been noticeable a slow but continuous decline in Tchaikovsky's creative powers. . . . Once Mr Tchaikovsky's cantilenas were broad, melodious; they were not always equal to the situation, frequently fitted the words badly, but they caressed the ear and embodied sincere feeling and tender warmth. Now they have dwindled away, have faded, become impoverished. . . . The harmony in *Mazepa* is acceptable but rather ordinary – it lacks its former originality. . . . The whole opera has a drab colour, and is also persistently doleful because of the unbroken minor.'[32]

To these sentiments other critics added their voices.

Despite Modest's reassuring telegram Tchaikovsky was soon plunged into gloom when he received a reproachful letter and a dour report from Jurgenson, and news reached him of *Mazepa*'s unfavourable press reception in the Russian capital; his misery was exacerbated by an uneasy conscience about having stayed away from the St Petersburg première. But when Nápravník wrote assuring him that the opera had been successful and that it would become a repertoire piece, his spirits began to revive. Early in April he made some revisions, rewriting especially the end of the love scene for Mazepa and Mariya in Act 2 and shedding some sixty-five bars in the process, and also drastically truncating the end of the opera. These revisions were incorporated when *Mazepa* was revived in St Petersburg the next season. On 1 December 1885 the opera was produced in Tiflis. Despite Nápravník's prediction, however, it was not to hold its place in the Russian repertoire.

Whereas Pushkin had taken some seven years to complete *Eugene Onegin*, he wrote the greater part of *Poltava* in a single fortnight of ferocious activity, basing upon fact not only the broader plot of Mazepa's intrigue against Peter the Great to free the Ukraine, and the account of the tragic fates of Kochubey and Iskra, but also the tale of the disastrous relationship of the young Mariya with the elderly hetman (the apocryphal tale, used by Byron, of the young Mazepa's nightmare ride bound to a wild horse by the husband of a Polish noblewoman to whom he had been a lover, has no part in Pushkin's narrative). The last of Pushkin's three cantos is mainly a poetically vivid description of Peter the Great's victory at Poltava in 1709. The plot of the opera is as follows:

[32] *DTC*, p. 127; *TZC2*, pp. 622–3.

ACT I, SCENE I. *The garden of Kochubey's farmstead on the bank of a river.*
A chorus of girls is singing offstage. Throwing wreaths into the river to tell their
fortunes, they enter in boats. Kochubey's daughter, Mariya, comes out of the
house. They greet her, and she them, but she explains she cannot join them as
the elderly hetman, Mazepa, has come to visit their house. Accepting that
Mariya must stay to entertain the guests, the girls resume their song, and
leave. Thoughtfully Mariya watches them as they disappear down the river.
Left alone (No. 2), she reveals that her only pleasure is to see Mazepa and hear
his voice, and she launches into an aria. 'Some incomprehensible power draws
me to the hetman,' she confesses excitedly (bar 20). '. . . I love everything
about him!' (bar 41). Her ecstatic outpouring is interrupted by the arrival of
Andrey. When he tells her that he has long been aware that 'some fateful
passion' has been tormenting her, she is upon the point of confiding her
feelings to him, for she knows the friendship he feels for her. 'Friendship?' he
exclaims (bar 109). 'No! It is not friendship which draws me to you: from my
boyhood I have loved you passionately!' Moved by this revelation, and
distressed by the anguish she has unwittingly caused Andrey, Mariya reveals
her own torn feelings. 'And I, like you, am unhappy. Do not reproach me: I am
borne along eternally by a secret fate' (poco più mosso); her passion for
Mazepa is invincible. An impassioned duet of tormented love follows, at the
end of which Andrey rushes out sobbing, while Mariya, also deeply distressed,
re-enters the house.

For a while the stage remains empty. Then the doors on to the covered
terrace in front of the house open (No. 3), and Kochubey, his wife Lyubov, and
Mariya come out with Mazepa and other guests. Musicians and servants
arrange themselves on the terrace. Mazepa thanks his host and family for their
warm hospitality, and the chorus responds briefly with a burst of praise. When
Mazepa asks to be entertained with singing and dancing, Kochubey gives the
order, and there follows a chorus and gopak (No. 4). Mazepa is delighted with
the diversions (No. 5). Before leaving, however, there is one other matter he
wants to discuss with Kochubey. While the other guests disperse into the
garden, the two men confer quietly. When they return to the forestage
Kochubey is plainly agitated, for Mazepa has asked for Mariya's hand.
Kochubey thinks he must be joking. 'You are a grey-haired old man, but my
daughter is in the spring of youth,' he insists (bar 74). But Mazepa is adamant,
and launches into a defence of his feelings (andante) in which he contrasts the
fickle affections of youth with the constancy of which an older man is capable.
Kochubey is unpersuaded, and a quarrel begins to develop (No. 6). He
reminds Mazepa that Mariya is his god-daughter, to which Mazepa replies
that he will seek from the church a dispensation to marry. What about
Mariya's own feelings, asks Kochubey – but Mazepa answers that he knows
Mariya loves him, for he has asked her and she has agreed to marry him. The
exchanges become rapidly more heated, but Kochubey remains firm. 'I am
severing our ties of friendship,' he finally shouts (bar 60). 'I ask you to leave my
honourable house!' 'What! You throw me out of your house – me! Have you
forgotten who I am?' roars Mazepa. The noise of the quarrel brings the others
back on to the stage, and they now begin to join in, Lyubov supporting her
husband, Andrey incredulous, yet equally determined Mazepa shall not

marry Mariya, while Iskra and the chorus predict that the powerful Mazepa
will get his own way. As for Mariya herself, she agonizes over how she may
soothe her mother's aching heart and appease her father, but concludes there
is no way: she will have to leave her parents' home, for death would be
preferable to life without Mazepa. Finally Mazepa's patience gives way in the
face of Kochubey's intransigence. Drawing his sabre, he calls to his men
(vivacissimo). Kochubey immediately does the same, and the ensemble
resumes. Suddenly Mariya tears herself from her mother's embrace and
interposes herself between her father and Mazepa, begging them to stop
quarrelling. Immediately Mazepa sheathes his sword and orders his men to
stand back. Kochubey and his company do the same. In the brief calm which
follows (andante non troppo) Mazepa turns contemptuously to his opponent.
'Kochubey, I should not have given rein to my anger; it did not befit a lion to
fight against a sheep.' Drawing a pistol, he fires into the air. Immediately a
second detachment of armed men enter and group themselves around him.
Kochubey and the others draw back. In a last effort to justify himself, Mazepa
observes with some restraint that he did not come as a plunderer but simply to
claim what belonged to him. When Kochubey and his supporters still show
themselves unyielding, Mazepa asks Mariya to make a free but final choice.
Terribly divided, Mariya finally tears herself from her mother and rushes into
Mazepa's embrace. 'I am yours!' she cries (bar 208). 'If you are mine, come
with me!' he shouts in return (bar 210). After giving ironic thanks to
Kochubey, he hurries out, taking Mariya with him. Kochubey and his
followers would attempt to detain him, but Mazepa's men confront them.
Lyubov faints.

ACT I, SCENE 2. *A room in Kochubey's house.*
A chorus of women, surrounding Lyubov on one side of the stage, sings a
melancholy song of sympathy to their mistress, who voices her pain and grief at
the eternal sorrow and disgrace her daughter has brought upon her parents. As
this finishes, Lyubov signals the women to leave, and then approaches
Kochubey, who is sitting on the opposite side of the stage with Andrey and
Iskra. She exhorts her husband (No. 8) to direct action against Mazepa in his
castle, but Kochubey refuses, for he has another plan. He prepares to reveal
this, though not before all present, including the servants, have taken an oath
of secrecy. All pledge to join in seeking revenge against Mazepa. Kochubey
then tells them (bar 39) how, in past conversations with Mazepa, the hetman
had darkly hinted at an intention which Kochubey had nevertheless been able
to perceive. 'Fired by malice, Mazepa has conceived the idea of a perilous
plot,' he reveals (bar 53). 'Traitor to the Russian Tsar, he wants to go over to
the Swede, trusting in his victory. But it is time to frustrate the hetman's
intrigues; I will reveal them to the Tsar!' Andrey, Iskra and the chorus warmly
approve this scheme. Iskra affirms confidently that Mazepa's doom is now
sealed, but Kochubey asks who will have the courage to transmit this
information to the Tsar. Immediately Andrey offers himself as messenger.
Kochubey willingly accepts the offer, but asks Andrey whether he is aware of
the mortal danger in which he will place himself. Andrey replies that he is fully
conscious of the risk, but that since Mazepa had dashed his hopes, his only

thought has been of revenging himself upon the hetman. 'Send me to the Tsar!' he cries (allegro moderato). 'I will fly like an arrow to the capital; swifter than a bird I will bring ruin to our enemy Mazepa!' Excitedly Iskra and the chorus echo his hopes. Kochubey thanks Andrey and the others, and then turns to brood upon the wrong done to him, and his longing for revenge. 'When you are in the hands of the Muscovite executioners . . . you will curse the day and hour when you became godfather to our daughter!' (bar 181). His wife takes up his cry, and the scene ends with a vigorous chorus of hate towards Mazepa.

ACT 2, SCENE 1. *A dungeon beneath a tower of Belotserkov Castle.*
Kochubey is sitting on a stone bench; he is chained to the wall. Not believing Kochubey's accusations, the Tsar has delivered him and Iskra into Mazepa's hands. The next day he is to die. What troubles him is not the fear of death, but the ignominy of his predicament – 'to fall silently before the feet of the villain like some dumb creature,' he groans (bar 132), 'to be given by the Tsar into the power of the Tsar's enemy to be abused, to lose one's life together with one's honour, to take one's friends with one to the scaffold, to hear their curses over one's grave, to go, though blameless, to execution, meeting the happy gaze of one's foe. . . .' He hears a key in the lock (bar 147), and believes it to be some holy hermit coming to give him absolution. But it is Mazepa's henchman, Orlik, who enters to interrogate him further. 'But why?' asks Kochubey (bar 180). 'I have confessed to everything you wanted.' But Orlik wants other information. Kochubey's estate will be forfeit to the Cossack treasury; where, however, is his hidden treasure? Indeed, Kochubey replies (bar 214), he did have three treasures. Two have gone: his honour, which he lost under torture, and his daughter, whom Mazepa stole. But the third – a holy vengeance upon Mazepa – still remains to him (bar 234). Orlik responds impatiently, demanding an answer. Still Kochubey refuses to give the information, telling Orlik to ransack his houses and gardens after he is dead, adding bitterly that he should take Mariya with him: she would readily show him all his treasures. 'But, for the Lord's sake, I beg you, beg you now to leave me in peace,' he pleads (bar 268), reminding Orlik that he, too, will on the Day of Judgement stand before God to answer for the blood he has shed and for all his deceit. Orlik, however, remains unimpressed, and when Kochubey still will not answer, he summons the torturer. 'O night of torments!' is Kochubey's final cry.

ACT 2, SCENE 2. *A room in Mazepa's castle, with an open door leading on to a terrace. Night.*
Mazepa is standing near the door, musing on the beauty of the night, and comparing the calm of the outer world with the gloom of his own thoughts. The stars seem to him like accusing eyes, the poplars like judges whispering among themselves. He broods upon the necessity of Kochubey's death. 'There is no way out! The informer and his minion must perish!' he ends in declaring (bar 120). 'God! How will she take the fateful sentence when she hears it?' Orlik enters to report that Kochubey still will not give way, and Mazepa confirms that he should arrange the execution for the next day. Orlik tries to say something to Mazepa, but the latter will hear nothing. Observing his master's mood, he leaves. Left alone, Mazepa turns his thoughts to Mariya, and

launches into an aria in praise of his young wife (No. 10a) 'O Mariya, in my declining years you, like a spring, have revived my spirit.' As he ends with an explicit confession of his love, Mariya herself enters unseen (No. 11), hesitating before approaching him. Though their greetings are affectionate, she immediately reproaches him for his recent coldness towards her, and reminds him (bar 42) of what she has sacrificed for him. She adds, however, that she does not regret this, for he had once sworn to love her: yet why does he not now love her? Quietly and tenderly Mazepa chides her for her accusations (moderato assai, quasi andantino). 'Mariya, believe me, I love you more than power and glory,' he concludes (bar 68). She continues to upbraid him, however, observing with bitterness that he is always engaged in consultations and affairs which leave no time for her. She has even, she believes, heard him toasting the health of another woman. Again Mazepa replies gently, denying that he is now capable of infatuation. 'You are jealous? Am I, at my age, going to seek the haughty compliments of proud beauty?' he replies soothingly (bar 94). 'Am I, a stern old man, to begin sighing like an idle youth?' She demands bluntly to know what is preoccupying him, and he resolves to tell her to allay her anxieties. After checking that no one is listening, he begins (allegro moderato) to reveal his plan: after years under the protection of Warsaw and the despotism of Moscow, the time is ripe to free the Ukraine. Everything is now prepared, and soon, perhaps, Mazepa himself could occupy a throne. Mariya's doubts are instantly dispelled, and she bursts out excitedly at her husband's prospects. But he checks her quickly, for nothing is yet certain. 'A storm is breaking; who can know what may be in store for me?' he cautions (bar 218). But nothing will now contain Mariya's feelings of excitement and devotion; if he fails, she will die with him. There begins a duet (andante non tanto) in which she continues to dwell on her absolute love and devotion, though his thoughts persist in running on the fate he has prepared for her father. 'Tell me, who is dearer to you, your father or your husband?' he asks (animato). 'Tell me, if he or I had to perish, to whom would you give preference?' Perceiving the urgency in his pleading, though ignorant of its cause, she assures him, 'O do not be angry. I am ready to sacrifice everything for you!' (bar 278) 'Then remember your words, Mariya,' he replies ominously. They bid each other farewell. Mazepa embraces Mariya, and she gazes after him as he leaves.

Mariya goes to the doorway into the garden (No. 12) and, as her husband had done at the beginning of the scene, observes how calm all is, contrasting this with the nagging, tormenting vision she has of her parents, and of their lonely future without her. Suddenly her mother is standing before her in the doorway. Mariya cries out in surprise, but Lyubov urges her to silence. She has come with one tearful request. 'Today is the execution!' she cries (bar 52). 'You alone can soften their rage; they want to execute your father!' Mariya is utterly uncomprehending, and her mother mistakes this for a changed allegiance. 'I see we have become strangers to each other,' she declares (bar 131), but nevertheless repeats her plea for Mariya to intercede for her father; the hetman will not refuse her. Gradually (moderato) the terrible truth begins to dawn upon Mariya, and Lyubov perceives that her daughter may indeed be ignorant of what has happened. With desperate urgency she tells Mariya of

Kochubey's approach to the Tsar and of the fearful consequences of this. When she comes to the matter of Kochubey's execution, Mariya cries out in terrible pain that she is responsible for all that has happened. Again Lyubov repeats (bar 220) that Mariya alone can save her father, but under the appalling strain of this revelation and of her own tormented conscience, Mariya faints. As Lyubov bends over her daughter, frantically trying to revive her, the sounds of a military march are heard, and she concludes that the execution is already in progress. On recovering, Mariya realizes quickly that she must act without delay, and the two women rush out.

ACT 2, SCENE 3. *A field with, at the back behind a rampart, a scaffold with two blocks on it.*
The crowd of people thronging the stage is restlessly awaiting the arrival of the execution party, and they reflect (bar 49) how great men may suddenly fall beneath the executioner's axe. As they ponder Mazepa's remorseless execution of his enemies, they pray to God (bar 81) that they may be spared such calamities. A drunken Cossack breaks into a song which causes the crowd to rebuke him for his untimely merriment. 'And should I not dance and sing?' he asks (bar 150). 'Look, they're going to cut off some landowners' heads. What's that to me?' The crowd is affronted, but he defiantly persists in his behaviour, claiming that it is his right as a free Cossack. Further protests from the crowd, and his resumed song, are interrupted by the sounds of an approaching procession (No. 14). Two executioners with axes enter and, as they go across the stage, they make passes at the women in the crowd, who recoil in horror. The procession then enters with Mazepa on a horse. The crowd makes an obeisance. Finally Kochubey and Iskra are led in, surrounded by guards and monks. Kochubey asks Iskra to join with him in a final prayer of confession, and the two men kneel. As the crowd echoes their prayers, the two men rise, embrace each other, and then mount the scaffold. The people crowd on to the rampart, hiding them from view. The drums roll and the axes appear above the heads of the people. Mariya and her mother rush in as the axes fall. Mariya cries out and falls into her mother's arms. A horrified gasp rises from the crowd, which begs for forgiveness for the dead men.

ACT 3. *The same setting as at the opening of the opera, but the garden is now neglected and the terrace half ruined. Night.*
After a symphonic tableau depicting the Battle of Poltava, the curtain rises. Swedish soldiers cross the stage, pursued by Russians. Then Andrey enters. He has been unsuccessfully searching for Mazepa, but concludes (bar 22) his enemy has fled the field of battle. He becomes aware (andante con moto) of his surroundings, and reflects painfully on the past happiness he had enjoyed here in Mariya's company. 'O, where are you, where, my darling?' he cries (bar 91), but there is no answer to his repeated call, and he returns to his former musings, finally (moderato) calling upon death to deliver him. Suddenly (No. 17) he hears two horsemen approaching. Thinking they may be Swedes, he hides. Mazepa and Orlik enter. They believe they have thrown off their pursuers, and Mazepa orders a halt to rest their horses. Orlik leads the animals away. Alone, Mazepa reflects upon the disastrous change in his fortunes; then

suddenly realizing where he is, he finds his agony intensified. 'O fate, fate, how you have punished old Mazepa!' he cries (bar 73). Meanwhile Andrey has recognized a familiar voice, and re-enters to confront Mazepa. He launches into a denunciation of the hetman for what he has done, a denunciation which strikes Mazepa to the heart. He asks Andrey (bar 110) what he wants with him. 'What do I want? I want your death!' Andrey shouts (bar 114). Mazepa asks that his grey hairs and misery should win him some indulgence, but warns Andrey that if he attacks him, he will find he also is armed. At the end of a furious altercation Andrey draws his sabre and hurls himself upon Mazepa (bar 164). The latter fires his pistol and Andrey falls wounded. 'Unfortunate one!' Mazepa exclaims (No. 18). 'God is my witness – I did not want your ruin!' He summons Orlik, but at that moment the moon comes out to reveal Mariya emerging from the trees. Mazepa cries out at the sight of her. At first she does not notice him, but then hurries up to him. 'Ah, quiet, quiet, my friend,' she begins her wild ramblings (bar 30). 'My father and mother have just closed their eyes. Wait! Wait! They can hear us!' A mad scene develops, Mazepa watching his wife in helpless misery. He tries to bring her to her senses. 'I remember a field,' she recalls (andante) 'a noisy occasion, a mob, and dead bodies – my mother took me there . . . but where were you?' With mounting frenzy she asks him to go home with her, but then abruptly changes: this is not Mazepa she sees before her. 'He is handsome,' she bursts out (bar 109), 'love burns in his eyes, there is such comfort in his words, his moustache is whiter than snow – but yours is congealed with blood!' Orlik enters to warn Mazepa that their pursuers are approaching. Mazepa wants to take Mariya with them, but Orlik vigorously opposes this. In terrible indecision Mazepa gazes at Mariya, then quickly leaves with his henchman.

Mariya suddenly perceives the wounded Andrey (No. 19). At first she thinks it is her father's body; then, bending over Andrey (bar 15), she places his head in her lap. Though she sees it is not her father, she does not recognize Andrey. 'It is a child sleeping in the thick grass,' she concludes (bar 22); but when Andrey whispers her name, she knows that the voice is familiar. The dying man tries unsuccessfully to awaken her to reality (andante un poco rubato), but she begins to sing him a lullaby (andante non tanto), rocking him gently. Again he tries to make her understand, but again to no avail, though she recognizes that the voice had once sung songs to her in her parents' garden. As Andrey dies she resumes her lullaby, rocking him and staring blankly before her.

Though the musical conventions of Tchaikovsky's operas had always remained much the same, the characters of the works themselves had shown great variety. *The Maid of Orléans* had been a foray into a West European world, both in its subject and in its aggressive appropriation of the spectacular apparatus of grand opera. *Onegin* and *Vakula*, very different from each other as they were, had been quintessentially Russian, one digging deep into the strata of upper society to lay bare something of the predicaments and disasters which the mores of that society might bring about, the other revelling in a bright, fantastic country world in which pleasure and pain may take simpler forms, but are no less poignant. *The Oprichnik*, like *The Voyevoda* before it, had possessed none of the integrity of these last two; the plot was contrived, the characters too much like puppets manoeuvred into strong situations. *Mazepa*, frankly, turns back towards this operatic type. Like *The Oprichnik* it is set in the Russian past; a tsar hovers unseen in the background, the characters on stage include historical personages, but their role is not necessarily to reproduce veraciously what they may have done in life. For all the quality of the masterpiece from which the plot of *Mazepa* was drawn, the story as offered in Burenin's libretto can lay little claim to literary merit. It was here that Tchaikovsky's problems originated.

From the composer's request to Karl Davïdov, it is evident that it was reading Pushkin's original, and not the libretto, which aroused his interest. It is easy to see why. *Poltava* is a stirring subject, a substantial portion of the poem being written in dialogue which provided some precious, ready-made material to set within the newly constructed lines. The original libretto has disappeared, but Modest recorded that his brother left Burenin's framework essentially intact, though he made some excisions. 'Thus he cut out the scene of the executioners exchanging jokes with the womenfolk and the crowd before Kochubey's execution,' wrote Modest. 'Burenin had introduced this at the insistence of Davïdov, who wanted something "humorous and folky" as a contrast to the tragic element in the situation. Pyotr Ilich himself was keen on this stage situation, and cut it only on the advice of his friends, primarily Nápravník. In addition, instead of a scene for Mazepa and Orlik in the former's headquarters, Pyotr Ilich composed a symphonic tableau, *The Battle of Poltava*.'[33] Exactly how much Tchaikovsky revised the actual wording of the libretto we cannot know, but even without Modest's evidence it is apparent from the markings in Tchaikovsky's personal copies of *Poltava* that he himself went back to Pushkin's original and worked over it. In the final libretto everything which could be incorporated direct or adapted (usually simply by turning reported into direct speech) was used, and the middle two of the six scenes are virtual transcriptions from *Poltava*'s text; only the execution scene seems to owe nothing to Pushkin.[34] Significantly, it was Pushkin's own lines which inspired much of Tchaikovsky's best music in *Mazepa*.

[33] *TZC2*, p. 598.
[34] In the dungeon scene Kochubey's first thirteen and last ten bars (i.e. bars 272–81) have a newly written text. In the following scene words had to be provided for the short exchange between Mazepa and Orlik, for Mazepa's arioso (No. 10a: these were

The doubts Tchaikovsky felt on receiving Burenin's libretto are self-evident. He toyed only intermittently with setting it, more than once considered abandoning it altogether in favour of something else, and only settled to it wholeheartedly during his extensive stay with Modest at Grankino. What had attracted Pushkin to the theme in 1828 had been the figure of Peter the Great, here engaged in a struggle for national survival as momentous as that which Russia had faced only sixteen years earlier when Napoleon had invaded. Peter had faced separatism as well as incursion, for the encroaching Charles XII of Sweden was supported by Mazepa, the Cossack hetman of the Ukraine, who transferred his allegiance to Charles in the hope of securing Ukrainian independence from Russia. Peter's defeat of Charles and Mazepa at Poltava proved to be one of the most important victories in Russian history. As has been noted, the battle itself and Peter, the majestic Tsar, are the main themes of the last of Pushkin's three cantos, while the preceding two tell of Mazepa's treason and, above all, of his liaison with his own proud, calculating goddaughter, Mariya. *Poltava* is thus both a powerful national epic and a tragic romance, providing a splendidly broad setting in which the various traits of the old Cossack's character could emerge. 'Mazepa is one of the most remarkable figures of that epoch,' Pushkin wrote in his preface to the first edition. '. . . History shows him to be a man of ambition, steeped in perfidy and crime . . . the destroyer of his unfortunate mistress's father, traitor to Peter before victory, betrayer of Charles after his defeat.'[35] Pushkin amplified this in *Poltava*, explicitly characterizing Mazepa as a ruthless schemer and unfeeling cynic who holds nothing sacred, remembers no acts of kindness but who never forgets an insult, who loves nothing, is prepared to shed blood like water, who holds freedom in contempt, and whose plot to free the Ukraine is not a crusade to liberate a people but a bid to gain himself a throne.

We can discern little of this from the opera. Peter the Great has no part in it, and the crucial battle of Poltava is represented solely by the orchestral prelude to the last scene – an idea which must be credited to Tchaikovsky, not Burenin. From Pushkin's heroic panorama, with its confrontation of national leaders wheeling and clashing with the

---

specially written by Vasily Kandaurov), for the first part of the Mazepa/Mariya scene (to bar 40), for the first thirteen bars sung by Mariya when she is left alone (No. 12), and for the final stretch from just before Mariya's faint. In the first scene much of Andrey's, and all of Mazepa's declarations of love are from *Poltava* (No. 2, bars 112–32, and No. 5, bars 82–end respectively), as are a good deal of Kochubey's denunciation of Mazepa in Scene 2 and the ensuing finale, and nearly all the first part of the mad scene at the opera's end. Other lines from *Poltava* appear from time to time.

[35] Alexandr Pushkin, *Polnoye sobrany sochineny*, vol. 4 (Moscow, 1963), p. 519.

destinies of whole tribes and nations in the balance, Burenin merely sifted out the emotional entanglement of Mazepa and Mariya, which from the beginning some Pushkin commentators had criticized for marrying unhappily with the grander issues. Other events were brought in primarily because they were essential to the development of that relationship; everything was reduced to romantic melodrama where all was calculated to wring the heart or chill the nerves. The fact that the opera does intermittently make such an indelible impression must be credited solely to the quality of Tchaikovsky's music. Yet there was little he could do to bring to life the epic side of Mazepa, and the grim, wily figure of *Poltava* enters the opera as a bluff, elderly gentleman chatting with a friend, who declares his love in terms suggesting a provincial Gremin, then quarrels with his friend to music which begins well enough but grows into a finale which is one of the most faceless pieces of the entire opera, for all its carefully built vocal tumults and its pointed solo interventions designed to give some semblance of the cut and thrust of true drama.

The *Mazepa/Oprichnik* affinities have already been noted, and a comparison of the two operas is illuminating; nor is it always to the advantage of the later work. Their most clear point of similarity is in their use of folksongs, for in none of Tchaikovsky's intervening operas had he used as many. Five have been identified, the first providing the foundation for the engaging Act 1 chorus preceding the gopak (it recurs in the coda of the latter), a second turning up briefly in the finale of the same scene (vivacissimo),[36] though this time the national character is well smothered by its context. Indeed, there is a substantial resurgence of a national element in *Mazepa*. From Mazepa's entry until the gopak there is a good deal, and a certain amount is to be found in the overture (especially in the F sharp minor cor anglais theme). There is even more in the women's choruses, the first of which opens Act 1 enchantingly in $\frac{5}{4}$, while the second performs the same service more disconsolately for Act 2, with Lyubov supplying a plangently Slavonic centre. The woodwind arabesques of this chorus's final section make explicit its debt to the Persian chorus in *Ruslan and Lyudmila*. Another memory from *Ruslan*, this time of the spiky, lightly malicious music with which the evil enchantress Naina had been characterized, clearly fathered the musical embodiment of Mazepa's henchman, Orlik (Ex. 176). Yet *Mazepa*'s most literal debt to Glinka comes during the love scene when, as the hero reflects upon his homeland's long bondage 'under the protection of Warsaw and the despotism of Moscow', Tchaikovsky slips in respectively the openings of the Act 2 mazurka and of the Slavsya Chorus from

---

[36] Rubets, *216 pesen*, No. 2.

Ex. 176

a.

[Believe me, you are troubling yourself in vain]

b.

[No, it is not a holy hermit; I recognise another guest!]

A Life for the Tsar (Ex. 177). The most extensive of the self-consciously national stretches of *Mazepa* occurs in the execution scene, the first part of which (No. 13) Tchaikovsky actually labelled 'folk scenes', employing one folksong to open, and a second for the intervention of the drunken Cossack.[37] The last of the opera's five known folksongs turns up in the entr'acte to Act 3, where not only did Tchaikovsky import the famous 'Slava', best known from its employment by Beethoven in the second Razumovsky quartet and by Musorgsky in the Coronation Scene in *Boris*, but also the liturgical chant which had already been incorporated in *1812*. Earlier in *Mazepa* the idiom of Orthodox church

[37] Rubets, *216 pesen*, No. 110, and Balakirev collection, No. 11, respectively.

Ex. 177

[Under the protection of Warsaw and the despotism of Moscow]

music had played a significant, if a less pervasive role than in *The Oprichnik*, materializing momentarily in the dungeon scene when Kochubey mistakes Orlik for a holy hermit come to absolve him, and far more extensively towards the end of the execution scene in the prayers of the condemned men and the people.

Yet except in their plentiful use of folksongs, their element of

Ex. 178

a.

b.

[In an instant the young heart bursts into flame, and is extinguished. In it love passes

and comes afresh.]

c.

[*MARIYA:* O how pale you are! Forgive me, my dear, and believe me: I love you!

MAZEPA: Forgive me, Mariya! My lovely darling, forgive me!]

Orthodox church music, and in their unbridled exploitation of strong situations, *Mazepa* and *The Oprichnik* are fundamentally different, and the sources of these differences lie in Tchaikovsky himself. In composing *The Oprichnik* he had still surveyed the drama from without, identifying the factors which were the moving forces of events, and then embodying them in musical materials which recurred and engaged as the tale ran its course. Though in *Mazepa* there is one theme which does range widely, Tchaikovsky now displayed a greatly reduced interest in such referential materials, and his use of thematic recall is more sparing. All but two of these instances are confined to the last scene; the exceptions are the introduction of Lyubov after the Mazepa/Mariya love duet by an orchestral quotation of the women's chorus which had supported her at the beginning of the second scene, and the recurrence of the brisk march, first heard during Mazepa's conspiracy revelation and again offstage at the end of the scene, to support the entry of Mazepa's forces before the execution.[38] Only one character, the second-rank Orlik, has a reminiscence theme (see Ex. 176b). Tchaikovsky, changed by the searing experiences of the intervening ten years (and with the creative achievement of *Onegin* behind him: we should remember he had described that opera as 'lyrical scenes'), now showed more interest in the emotional lives of his characters, probing deeply into their feelings to discover those creative springs which might then rise to the musical surface in a notable variety of embodiments, with a general consistency of melodic style rather than literal recall

---

[38] It must remain uncertain whether Tchaikovsky really intended to recall the gopak's introduction in the bass just before the andantino non troppo introducing the dungeon scene.

giving some expressive focus. This radical change straightway affects the overture which is not, as had been that of *The Oprichnik*, a preview of certain representative materials with incipient dramatic conflicts. Instead much of it seems more like a sketch of Mazepa himself, for though the legendary ride of his youth is the substance of the initial allegro non troppo (we have Tchaikovsky's authority for this), the following andantino con moto seems concerned solely with the hetman's emotional involvement with Mariya, even opening with a tiny prefiguration of his tender declaration of love in the first scene, and of the coda to the Act 2 love duet (Ex. 178).[39]

[39] In the original, longer conclusion to this scene, as Mazepa had pressed Mariya to his breast, the orchestra had presented yet another version of this idea (Ex. 179)

Ex. 179

A price had to be paid for these dramaturgic shifts. A fundamental fault of *Mazepa* is a general lack of real precision, for in opting for a more abundant melodic fund, Tchaikovsky not only undermined the thematic definition of character and of the dramatic issues, but also put at risk that emotional concentration he had sometimes achieved with notable strength in *The Oprichnik*. Cui's observation that 'once Mr Tchaikovsky's cantilenas were broad, melodious . . . now they have dwindled away' contains more than a grain of truth, for though there are melodic passages of great emotional force in *Mazepa*, there is nothing as redblooded as Natalya's G flat arioso in *The Oprichnik*, for instance. Some of the dramatic associations of certain keys, as established in *Onegin* and used with less commitment in *The Maid*, do crop up again in *Mazepa*. E major can still be the key of happy or aspiring love, as when it is used soothingly by Mazepa in his love scene with Mariya, with pathetically faltering strength by the dying Andrey in the final scene. It had marked his entry at the beginning of the opera, though he had swiftly changed to E minor as he unhappily surveyed Mariya's obvious agitation. This key of doom closes both the first scene[40] and the execution scene. And even before composing the passage where, after her love scene with Mazepa, Mariya suddenly directs her thoughts to her distraught parents, Tchaikovsky had decided this should be in D minor; he had equally prescribed this key of despair and disaster for Mazepa's very last exit and what immediately followed.

Yet such tonal associations are looser in *Mazepa* than in *Onegin*. So, too, is much of the musico-dramatic organization when compared with *The Oprichnik*. Though nowhere in *Mazepa* is there anything as messily structured as the first scene of that earlier opera, neither is there anything as taut as the oath scene. The only comparable section is the Lyubov/Mariya duologue after the love scene, where the three statements of the mother's desperate plea for intercession provide structural cornerstones for this stretch of the opera, as well as hammering home the main dramatic point. Yet Tchaikovsky himself clearly felt that it hardly mattered if he paid less heed to such thematic and tonal operations and such structural procedures as the means of dramatic articulation, since there was an overriding force which made the use of these things almost incidental. For *Mazepa*, like *Onegin*, is an opera governed by fate. What finally fired Tchaikovsky to set purposefully

---

[40] In the original version, i.e. when this scene had been joined to that which followed, Tchaikovsky had ended this ensemble in C minor, thus leading up to the key of the following chorus. It is the more significant, therefore, that when he made such continuity inessential by separating the two scenes, he should have chosen to end in E minor instead.

about Burenin's libretto was the highly personal view he could take of
the Mazepa/Mariya relationship. As with Tatyana and Joan, Mariya
was the 'innocent' girl who became a victim of that all-governing force.
But whereas Onegin had been fate's instrument through rejecting
Tatyana, Mazepa had performed the same function through appropriation, becoming the central, ever-present factor in Mariya's existence, and therefore able to act as the direct surrogate of this irresistible
power. This being so, the musical embodiments of fate and Mazepa
could be joined in a single theme (Ex. 180) which leaps up powerfully
and abruptly, only to be caught into that Tchaikovskyan symbol of fate,
a descending scale, the end of which is twice repeated and unceremoniously amputated. As presented in Ex. 180 it launches the whole
opera, demonstrating its absolute power at the end of the overture by
remorselessly crushing out of existence Mazepa's more susceptible
feelings which might have endangered its subsequent operations. It
plays no part in the early stages of the opening scene, but resurges as
Mazepa discloses to Kochubey that Mariya has declared to him her
love – that emotion through which fate will finally claim its victim – and
it plays an increasingly prominent role in the final stages of the action
when Mariya's moment of decision approaches. Yet, aggressive as it is,
this theme displays little of the potency of either fate theme in *Onegin*,[41]
neither infiltrating itself as ubiquitously as had the 'fate in prospect'
motif, nor stamping its shape indelibly upon new melodic conceptions
as had the 'fate embraced' contour. Rarely does it exhibit even the
implacable intrusiveness of the Fourth Symphony's motto theme.
Instead its use is sparing, sometimes perfunctory. It has no part in the
opera's second scene, and is heard only briefly and fragmentarily in the

Ex. 180

[41] Curiously, the second fate theme of *Onegin* does seem to play some part in the Mariya/Andrey encounter at the opening of the opera, haunting the aria in which Mariya feverishly reflects upon the 'unexpected power' which has drawn her to Mazepa (Ex. 181a), then repeatedly conditioning Andrey's vocal line as he begins to exercise himself over Mariya's evident inner agitation, finally appearing explicitly when Mariya replies (Ex. 181b). There are occasional suggestions of it subsequently, above all in Mariya's mad scene. Gerald Abraham has commented on other thematic legacies from *Onegin* (see his study of the operas in *Tchaikovsky: a symposium* (London, 1945), p. 163, and *Slavonic and romantic music* (London, 1968), p. 158).

Ex. 181

a.

[Some incomprehensible force draws me to the hetman]

b.

[If you would know my secret, I will not deny you,]

introduction to the dungeon scene. Even in the love scene it is relatively muted, its opening motif flickering nervously in the orchestral introduction, resonantly confirming Mazepa's sentence of death upon Kochubey, and then disappearing until Lyubov begins to open her daughter's eyes to Mazepa's ruthlessness. As the two women rush out on their fruitless mission to save Kochubey, it is this theme which abruptly brings down the curtain in E minor, just as it had done in the very first scene. And just as it had pronounced Kochubey's doom before the love scene, so it breaks out momentarily as the sentence is carried out. But in the final scene it loses its more portentous role, becoming little more than Mazepa's label, heralding his arrival and marking his ignominious exit in a muffled, expiring presentation.

It is this conjoining of the underlying force of the tale with the personality of Mazepa which is the pointer to Tchaikovsky's failure with his nominal hero, and to his relative success with Kochubey, Mariya and Lyubov – for the opera is by no means the lost cause it might appear to be from what has already been written. It was to these last three characters and, to a much lesser extent, to Andrey that Tchaikovsky really responded, just as he had done to Tatyana and Lensky rather than to Onegin. Mazepa himself, despite all his moments of conventional theatrical projection, is largely a cipher serving something outside himself. His best bits are those where his emotions are most engaged by Mariya – for instance, in the first scene, where he declares his love in a touching arioso in E flat, Tchaikovsky's key of noble pathos (see Ex. 178b). Even more did he stir Tchaikovsky when Mariya's relationship with Mazepa places the Cossack himself under pressure, as when, in the preliminaries to the love scene with Mariya in the second act, he contemplates the beauty of the Ukrainian night in enchanted yet despondent music which grows out of the opening section of the preceding orchestral prelude (one of the loveliest passages in the whole opera, so superior to the Poltava entr'acte), agonizing on an implacable conscience and on the truth which she soon must know, then pouring out his love in an aria of rare tenderness.[42]

But when he engages with Mariya in duet, his soothing rejoinders to her scolding at his neglect are in danger of sounding bland when intersected by her more pointed utterances. This was evidently the first scene of the opera to be composed, and from the beginning it was Mariya who exercised the greater power over Tchaikovsky. Her reproaches are spirited, not whining, and when, after Mazepa has

---

[42] This G flat aria was composed at the end of 1883 at the request of the baritone, Bogomir Korsov, who was to sing the title role.

uncovered his scheme for a free Ukraine, she hails him as a future tsar, a little of the seething ambition of Pushkin's heroine breaks through in the surging of the three-bar phrases from which her melodic line is mostly built (Ex. 182); Mazepa never achieves such vibrant self-projection. In the final scene, now defeated and finding himself in Kochubey's desolate garden, he is an ineffectual shadow who can do no more than lament fate's harshness, confront and reluctantly kill Andrey, then gaze helplessly at the sight of his deranged wife. Whatever dramatic life Mazepa now possesses stems from his tormented impotence at the heart-rending condition to which he has reduced Mariya.

Ex. 182

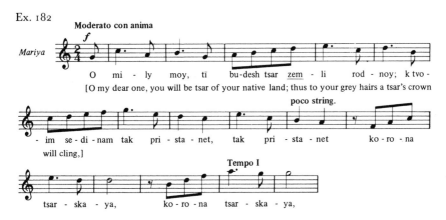

Kochubey makes an altogether more solid impression. If in the opening scene he had never emerged as much more than a costume figure, he does so assertively in what follows. Tchaikovsky's touch with Lyubov is admirably positive, too, for he had followed her lament over her daughter's abduction by furnishing her with a brief but vigorous exhortation to her husband, couched in musical terms which suggest she possesses something of the same spirit in adversity as the Boyarïna in *The Oprichnik*. Indeed, she is the only character in the opera who can match her own daughter in melodic breadth, as is impressively demonstrated by the vast melodic arc of her thrice-heard exhortation to Mariya to save Kochubey (Ex. 183). This whole duet is a brilliantly tense confrontation, Lyubov ever more remorselessly insistent in her determination to break through her daughter's incomprehension, Mariya almost disorientated as the truth dawns on her.

But Kochubey is yet more impressive, and the trenchant strength which begins to gather within his denunciation of Mazepa in the opera's second scene (Ex. 184) – so much richer in substance than the bustling end to the finale – re-emerges battered but indomitable in

Ex. 183

Te - be od - noy, ___ te - be od - noy ___ svi - repstvo ikh ___
[You alone can soften their ferocity; they intend to execute your father, they are cruel and

___ smyag-chit voz - mozh - no; o - ni ot - sa ___ kaz - nit khot - yat, ___
godless. Save your father, I beg you, my daughter, save your father!]

___ o - ni zhe-sto - ki i bez - bozh - nï. Spa - si ot - sa, spa -

- si ot - sa, o doch mo - ya, mol - yu te - bya, spa - si ___ ot - sa!

Ex. 184

Tï ne ist - leyesh sred po - zha - ra, tï ne iz - dokh - nesh ot u - da - ra ka-
[You will not be reduced to ashes in the conflagration, you will not find rest

- zats - koy sab - li; net, ___ zlo - dey, net, ___ zlo - dey, net! Vru-

from the blows of a Cossack sabre; no, evil one, no!]

Ex. 185

[What is death? a longed-for sleep; I am ready to lie in a bloody grave.]

the dungeon scene which follows. Any charge that Tchaikovsky was incapable of treating the grimmer things of life except through conventionally melodramatic musical imagery or rhetoric is powerfully refuted by this imposing monologue. Now alone and imprisoned, Kochubey first ponders his predicament in austerely gloomy terms, then reflects upon death in music where intimations of a more wondrous, blissful prospect are conveyed in chords structured upon a bass which descends in alternating major and minor thirds (Ex. 185);[43] this same mechanical progression had been used to expose Joan's wonderment as she had begun to recall the vision of the Virgin which had inspired her crusade in *The Maid of Orléans* (see Ex. 160b). Racked less by fear of the ordeal before him than by bitterness at the injustice and ignominy of his situation, and sick at heart at the ruin he has innocently brought upon others, Kochubey is able at times to rise to a level of melodic inventiveness which admirably conveys the strength with which he confronts pain, as when he bursts out despairingly at the thought of his own daughter's betrayal of himself, then begs for some relief in the same music to which, a little earlier, he had reflected upon the one treasure which remained to him: vengeance upon Mazepa (Ex. 186). Nevertheless, his end in the execution scene strikes less for

[43] Striking harmonic structures synthesized by mechanically repeated bass shifts occur elsewhere in Kochubey's music (see No. 6, bars 54–59, No. 8, bars 53–58).

Ex. 186

Kochubey

S so - boy____ voz - mi - te doch mo - yu, o -

[Take my daughter with you, she herself will tell you all, will show you all my

- na sa - ma____ vam vsyo ras - ska - zhet, sa - ma vsye [kla - dï vam u -

treasures.

- ka - zhet.   No ra - di go - spo - da mol - yu, mo -

But for God's sake, I beg you, leave me now in peace. I am prepared to submit to Him who [will be]

- lyu te - per o - stav me - nya v po - ko - ye, go - tov - lyus ya pred-

[your terrible [judge]]

- stat to - mu, ___ kto va - shim groz -

anything it uncovers of Kochubey's inner world than for the extremity of his plight. The execution itself is grimly effective, the preceding prayers calculated to elicit a strong, but basically sentimental response, while the vigorous folkchorus and earthy contributions of the drunken Cossack, admirable as they are (though Nápravník disapproved of the latter), afford simply ironic background for the gruesome end.

Yet for all the sympathy with which Tchaikovsky conveys Kochubey's feelings, it was with Mariya that he identified most fully. From the moment when she is left alone on stage to declare her passion for Mazepa, and thus commit herself to the emotion through which fate will claim her for its own, Tchaikovsky invests her with an abundance of emotional life, her declaration of love being substantiated orchestrally by a sudden upward sweep of melody and a surge into appoggiatura-fortified, flat-key regions which suggests a delirious excitement (Ex. 187) found nowhere in *The Oprichnik*. Yet her following aria, with its nervous melody broken into short segments, is highly strung rather than passionate, as is the first part of her following duet with Andrey. Though an altogether weaker creation than Kochubey, Andrey, like Mazepa, takes on extra life when fired by Mariya. Yet even in this duet he cannot match the expressive eloquence of Mariya's finely projected misery at the opening of the G minor section,[44] while in the second scene his response to Kochubey likewise has a cramping stiffness; the short-breathed, repetitive melody of his C minor andante arioso sounds almost prim, certainly small-scale against Kochubey's declarations. His big solo scene opens Act 3, but apart from devising conventionally agitated or broken-hearted music, Tchaikovsky can do

---

[44] The opening sixteen bars of this were one of the first passages in the opera to be composed. Tchaikovsky noted it down in his copy of the Obikhod, using as text his favourite first phrase from the tale of Francesca da Rimini in Dante's *Inferno*; he dated it 25 May 1881.

Ex. 187

[But I have only one pleasure; to hear Mazepa's voice and see his proud face!]

little for him. All, however, is transformed by Mariya's entrance. From this point to the end it is she who dominates the stage. Mazepa soon slips away, and the dying Andrey is little more than a vocal prop necessary for a situation which is to give his demented beloved full scope for a deeply affecting scena. And deeply affecting it certainly is. Our capacity for sentimental compassion is especially vulnerable to the spectacle of a ruined, crazed heroine, and Tchaikovsky was heir to a cultural tradition which had recently bred a healthy crop of such ladies, whose common habitat was ruins or wilderness, and whose characteristic call was maniacal laughter. It is easy to deride such creatures, but

Tchaikovsky took Mariya very seriously, and from the moment when she emerges from the trees into the moonlight, and a solo violin recalls her avowal of love which had opened the final section of the Act 2 love duet, the whole musical level rises and maintains its most consistent height. A melancholy phrase introduced by the oboe obsessively haunts the orchestral background to her plaintive ramblings; faced with this, Mazepa suddenly acquires some true emotional response in his tonally tortuous interjections. In the section in G flat (a key which Tchaikovsky had always associated in his operas with particularly intense emotion) she snatches at memories of her father's execution, then turns on Mazepa with bitter reproach and a confused sense of recognition, and ends the first part of this scena with a frenzied recall of the image of Mazepa as she had once known him, ironically returning to that portion of their love music in which she had hailed him as a future tsar (see Ex. 182), and in which her husband had checked her ambitious dreams of their future together: 'A storm is breaking; who can know what may be in store for me?'

By now Tchaikovsky is again on the threshold of writing great opera, as he had been in Kochubey's prison monologue and the Lyubov/Mariya duet, and his drastic revision of the remaining portion of this fine scene is confirmation that Mariya finally took a grip upon his creative being almost as firm as that which Tatyana had exercised some five years before. For the original production he had written a much longer, elaborate finale. At the moment when Mariya had begun her lullaby for the second and last time (significantly, perhaps, set in D flat, also Tatyana's very special key), the chorus had started to drift back and, perceiving Mariya, had pitied her plight. When she had recognized among the crowd the same girls who had invited her at the beginning of the opera to join them in divining their fortunes by casting garlands on to the river, Mariya had issued the same invitation to them, actually quoting from their $\frac{5}{4}$ chorus; then suddenly leaping up, with demented laughter she had plunged into the river. With more noise than action the chorus had expressed horror at this sudden turn of events, though some of the men had taken to canoes to recover the body, which they had then placed alongside Andrey's on the forestage. After lamentations over this 'unfortunate victim of fate', the crowd had implored God's blessing, while the offstage band had played part of the Petrine march which had ended the Poltava entr'acte. Brutalized orchestral echoes of the first bar of Mariya's lullaby had loudly closed the scene.

This end was irremediably stagy, as Tchaikovsky quickly perceived, and his solution was as simple as it was masterly: cut all this gratuitous tableau, extend Mariya's lullaby, and let her alone sing the opera towards silence, rocking in her arms the body of the man who, if fate had allowed, might have brought her happiness. The momentary resurgence a little earlier of the Ukrainian march and of the G minor portion of her Act 1 love duet (the latter also touchingly recalled during Andrey's earlier scene) had marked the moments when her disordered mind had fleetingly fastened on her father's execution and her days with Andrey. But such memories would remain for ever her only contact with the outside world; the present itself was now shut out for ever. Tatyana had retained a loving husband, and some hope of a future; Mariya is not only crushed and out of her mind, but withdrawn and alone. It is an end of consummate, unashamed pathos – and absolutely right.

A fortnight after finishing the last sketch of *Mazepa*, a letter arrived for Tchaikovsky addressed in a hand he had not seen for eleven years. The writer had been looking over some of Tchaikovsky's scores of the intervening period. 'I have rejoiced to see your talent developing and getting stronger,' he observed. 'Your apogee is your two symphonic poems, *The Tempest* and *Francesca da Rimini*, especially the latter.'[45] These excellent impressions afforded by past achievements had persuaded the writer that he should intervene in Tchaikovsky's creative life. 'I should be happy to see you, and I have a programme for a symphony to impart to you which you should handle superbly.'[46] Such an intention might, in view of Tchaikovsky's reputation, seem impertinent, and the unqualified warmth of his reply to this long-lost correspondent is therefore the more striking.

I can say quite simply that if I should live another ten or twenty years without seeing you, I would still never forget you, nor cease to think of you affectionately as of one of the brightest and undoubtedly most upright and talented artistic personalities whom I have ever met.

I thank you most heartily for your intention of suggesting to me a subject for a symphonic poem, and I rejoice in your sympathy.

If I should be in St Petersburg I will certainly come to see you. My inclination to seclusion and a life outside society cannot, of course, extend so far that I should deny myself the pleasure of seeing you and

---

[45] *BVP*, p. 164.
[46] ibid.

talking with you, and your summoning me is sufficient for me to consider it a pleasant duty to present myself before you.[47]

Balakirev was re-entering Tchaikovsky's life – with momentous consequences, as the last chapter of this volume will show.

[47] *TLP*11, pp. 241–2; *BVP*, p. 164.

6

A TIME OF CHILDREN:

SECOND SUITE

ON 8 OCTOBER 1882, the Sunday after he had completed the sketches for *Mazepa*, Tchaikovsky journeyed to Kiev to collect from a bank the latest instalment of his patroness's allowance. As had been his practice whenever the opportunity had presented itself, he attended mass at the Brothers' Monastery. And as had happened several times before, he fled from the service before the end. For a couple of days he pondered whether to write openly to a newspaper, but finally decided to address himself privately and bluntly to the bishop about what had given him such offence.

The cause is none other than the singing of the Brothers' Monastery choir. It will probably surprise you, your Grace, that their singing, famed throughout Kiev as uncommonly beautiful, should irritate, pain, even horrify me. But the point is that, in my capacity as a Russian musician who is endeavouring to foster the cause of Russian church singing, and who has expended much thought upon the subject, I stand unfortunately (I make bold to say) above the level of general discernment in what I require of singing within the liturgy – and, in any case, am at extreme variance with the tastes not only of the Orthodox public, but also the majority of the clergy. Without going into historical details I will only observe briefly that, because of a fateful conjunction of circumstances, the sickly sweet style of eighteenth-century Italian music has, from the end of the last century, become established with us. This, in my opinion, does not conform with the requirements of church style in general, and in particular has no relationship either in spirit or structure with our Orthodox liturgy . . .
So what is to be done? You cannot alter history, and against my will I have reconciled myself with the established style of church music, even as far as not disdaining to take upon myself the editing of a new printing of the works of Bortnyansky, who is the initiator,

albeit gifted, of this trend which is so false and alien. . . . I repeat, I have reconciled myself with it, but only within certain bounds. . . . Last Sunday . . . I listened reluctantly to that strange, mazurka-like, nauseatingly affected three-fold *Lord have mercy* . . . with rather less patience to the *Unction of grace*. . . . But when they opened the central doors of the iconostasis, and the singers gabbled on one chord *Praise God from the heavens* as though casting aside the heavy burden of praising God in favour of their obligation to entertain the public with concert music, and, summoning up their strength, began performing a long, mindless, shapeless concerto, based on an alien mode, trivial, without talent, overflowing with vocal tricks ill-befitting a place of worship, I experienced a surge of indignation which increased the more they sang. Now a bass solo bawled out in a wild, howling roar, now a solo treble began to squeal, then a snatch of a phrase from some sort of Italian trepak was heard, now an operatic love motif rang out with unnatural sweetness in the most rough, bare, tame harmonization, now the whole choir faded to an exaggeratedly delicate pianissimo, now began to roar, to bellow at the tops of their voices.

O God! And just where, at what moment did this musical orgy occur? Precisely at that moment when the central act of the whole religious ceremony was being enacted, when your Grace and your officiants administered the body and blood of Christ![1]

And so on for many more unsparing lines. Manifestly Tchaikovsky was still capable, when roused, of that flow of blistering invective he had sometimes poured out during his toils as a music critic in the early 1870s. Yet this was but one of the torments which the later months of 1882 held for him. The troubles in his sister's unsettled, sometimes turbulent household seemed to come in waves, and now another broke over Kamenka, for news came that Sasha, who was still in the south after the birth of Vera's child, was suffering from kidney stones, while at Kamenka itself Tanya was becoming anorexic, though her behaviour had improved a good deal ('because there aren't any men about,' her uncle noted tartly[2]). Tchaikovsky, as so often before, observed pityingly the burden these anxieties placed upon his brother-in-law. He was longing to go abroad, but his finances would not yet permit it and, in any case, he would have had to go alone. It is no wonder that in such fraught circumstances he should have envisaged an ultimate

[1] *TLP*11, pp. 233–4.
[2] *TLP*11, p. 220.

withdrawal to another environment. When he wrote to his servant Alexey, conjuring a vision of their future life together, he was not merely attempting to cheer a very low spirited conscript; he was fortifying himself with a vision of escape. 'I dream that, when you've finished your period of military service, if I'm still alive, I shall cease living in other people's homes, and will settle for ever in some pleasant spot somewhere in Moscow. The two of us will make our home in a nice comfortable apartment, and we'll live in clover. . . . I pray God that the two years will pass the more quickly, and that these dreams may be fulfilled.'[3] And so they were to be – almost exactly.

But the wave, having broken, passed, and a calm followed. Sasha returned home, seemingly in good health, and Tanya continued to make an effort to control herself which won her uncle's deep gratitude. Even the new tutor for two of Sasha's sons, whose advent had deprived Tchaikovsky of part of his accommodation, brought a bonus, since the new arrival was also an enthusiast for vint, a card game to which Tchaikovsky himself was addicted. For a while he was again reconciled to Kamenka life, especially since Modest, who was now marooned in St Petersburg because Kolya's education required the services of other teachers also, was chafing at his confinement, while in Moscow Anatoly was endlessly worrying about his own health and the condition of his wife, who was pregnant. Tchaikovsky told both brothers roundly that St Petersburg and Moscow were bad enough in themselves, but with a miserable brother demanding moral support in each they would be intolerable.

But then the next wave rolled over Kamenka. Blumenfeld appeared, and the weather broke. During the music teacher's stay he and Tanya returned to those intimacies which had so shocked Tchaikovsky during an earlier residence. It was this wilful niece who finally roused him to make escape from Kamenka his central obsession. At dinner one day he innocently observed he would be going to Moscow and St Petersburg. 'Suddenly Tanya turns to me and says: "I can go with you, can't I?" I don't know what I muttered in reply,' continued a panic-stricken Tchaikovsky to Modest on 13 November, 'but I know that for a moment the blood rushed to my head, and I must have gone terribly red. . . . The painfulness of the feelings I experience in regard of her is such that no pen can describe it. Not only am I incapable of spending two days travelling with her tête-à-tête, but even here, with a lot of people, I become positively *ill* when she enters a room I'm in.'[4] To

---

[3] *TLP*11, p. 219.
[4] *TLP*11, p. 272; *YDGC*, p. 281 (partial).

outmanoeuvre Tanya, he decided he would have to leave unfinished his scoring of the first act of *Mazepa*, and instead bolt from Kamenka during the three days the family were to be away at a social occasion; he would leave a note that Nápravník had summoned him to St Petersburg in connection with the revival of *The Maid*. But Sasha suddenly suffered a new eruption of kidney stones and the trip was cancelled. So instead Tchaikovsky announced that he would be travelling with Jurgenson to see the Prague revival of the same opera, and that he would have to meet his publisher in Kiev; from there he would write that the performance had been postponed, and that he had instead gone to Moscow. Under this pretext he left Kamenka on 27 November. He was painfully aware of his ever more changing feelings towards his sister's home. 'I've left my *nook* without any regret,' he wrote to Modest three days later. 'Its cosiness vanished once I had become surrounded on all sides by neighbours, and I confess returning to Kamenka is something I shan't want at all – and, you know, that's sad. Having nowhere my own home, incapable of settling down anywhere else in Russia, fearing loneliness when abroad, I'm now at last a sort of nomad – and this thought distresses me.'[5] In Kiev he fell ill, and it was 2 December before he arrived in Moscow. Meanwhile Kamenskaya, who had created Joan in *The Maid* in 1881, had insisted she would only sing in the St Petersburg revival if the entire part were converted into a true mezzo-soprano role. Effecting this, as well as making some cuts suggested by Nápravník, had already cost him ten days of work on *Mazepa*, and the scoring was behind schedule. It is therefore no surprise that the idea he had hatched two months before of drawing a concert suite out of *Swan Lake* slipped into oblivion.

Life in Moscow proved as distracting as he expected. He was dined by his old Conservatoire colleagues, and scrutinized with especially close interest the musical gifts of Max Erdmannsdörfer, for this Leipzig-trained conductor and former musical director at Sondershausen would now be Tchaikovsky's principal advocate in Russia's second city. 'He is a very skilful, very experienced and expert conductor,' he concluded to Nadezhda von Meck after a fortnight.

But I have to admit that the Muscovites overrate his accomplishments. He is now the fashion, but I doubt this will last long. His shortcomings are as follows: 1. He cares too much about external effects, and is inclined to indulge the public's taste for exaggerated nuances. Thus, for instance, his *pp*s are so quiet that sometimes

[5] *TLP*11, p. 285.

neither the harmony nor the melody is at all audible, only a shadow of the sound being heard. This is terribly effective, but hardly artistic. 2. He is too much *a German*. His programmes are too German, and he doesn't play French music at all, for instance – and he is offhanded in his attitude to Russian music (except mine).[6]

Tchaikovsky had been quick to make Erdmannsdörfer's acquaintance, and readily recognized his flair for establishing a good relationship both with his fellow-professionals and the public. But for Tchaikovsky there was a painful side to the enthusiasm with which the RMS audience reciprocated, as he confided to his patroness: 'It is as though it [the audience] is trying to show it rates him much higher than Nik[olay] Grig[oryevich], whom it never received so enthusiastically. Not only has Moscow in general already acclimatized itself, as it were, to the loss of Nik[olay] Grig[oryevich], but it has begun to forget him. That is sad.'[7] The personal poignancy of this circumstance was heightened by attendance at a mass for Rubinstein, followed next day by a further requiem at the graveside.

In Moscow Tchaikovsky put the finishing touches to his All-night Vigil, and was also able to hear extracts from it at a public concert. He was greatly flattered that Pavel Tretyakov, a director of the Moscow RMS, and one of the founders of the picture gallery which still bears his name, should wish to augment the collection with a portrait of him by Vladimir Makovsky, though for this Tchaikovsky had to endure the penance of four long sittings.[8] He saw Alexey and was relieved to find that he was now reconciled to army life for the next two years. He was determined not to leave Moscow until the first act of *Mazepa* was scored, but it was 24 December before this was done. The next day he set out for St Petersburg to join a very impatient Modest. Here he met again Laroche, was deeply impressed by the performance of Lucien Guitry in the name part of Daudet's *Jack*, and revelled in a fine production of *Carmen* at the Maryinsky Theatre. He would have left the capital earlier, but illness enforced a delay. To his relief he saw little of Tanya, who was also in the city but installed with other relatives. On 9 January 1883 he slipped away en route for Berlin.

'I always adore Berlin when I'm travelling from Russia, though I can't bear it when I'm returning home,' he observed buoyantly to Modest. '. . . What a delight to be able to take a walk without being afraid of meeting people I know. . . . I'm enjoying *being abroad* exactly as

[6] *TLP*11, p. 293; *TPM*3, p. 128; *TZC*2, p. 564.
[7] *TLP*11, p. 287; *TPM*3, pp. 123–4; *TZC*2, pp. 562–3.
[8] The portrait subsequently disappeared, and no copy of it is known.

I did twenty-one years ago when I went for the first time.'[9] The one Berlin resident he did intend to see was Kotek, with whom his relations had become strained through the violinist's continued failure to perform the concerto he had inspired five years before. But each day of his stay Tchaikovsky could not bring himself to call, and he ended by promising himself that he would make good this omission on the return journey, a resolution he did not keep. He stayed longer than expected in order to see *Tristan* for the first time in his life. He had heard that 'bad piece',[10] the *Siegfried Idyll*, on the eve of his departure from Moscow, but this performance of *Tristan* was a far more substantial opportunity to check the judgment on Wagner he had delivered so forcefully after the Bayreuth experience of six-and-a-half years earlier. It had not changed. 'I did not like the opera at all,' he began his broadside to Nadezhda von Meck.

> ... To make us listen four hours on end to an interminable symphony, rich in sumptuous orchestral colours but poor in ideas clearly and simply stated: to make singers for four hours on end perform not independent melodies but melodic fragments appended to that symphony (in addition to which, these fragments, though high in tessitura, are not infrequently swallowed up in the orchestra's thunder) – this, surely, is not the ideal towards which contemporary composers ought to be striving. Wagner has transferred the centre of gravity from the stage to the orchestra, and because this is a manifest absurdity, then his celebrated reform of the opera signifies nothing if you discount the above-mentioned negative consequences.[11]

He was convinced the audience was bored throughout, despite their favourable reception of each act, and he offered his patroness his own explanation for this troubling contradiction. 'It was probably a patriotic sympathy towards the composer, who has indeed dedicated his whole life to waxing poetic about Germanism.'[12] Yet, curiously, *Tristan*'s spell still seems to have lingered with Tchaikovsky, for just as *Der Ring* had conditioned *Francesca da Rimini* in 1876, so this other hateful creation of Wagner may well have contributed to the opening of the piece in which, in 1885, Tchaikovsky was to rediscover fully his own individual voice.

Tchaikovsky received more than adequate compensation for this

---

[9] *TLP*11, p. 303; *TZC*2, p. 565; *TPB*, pp. 290–1.
[10] *TLP*11, p. 293; *TPM*3, p. 128; *TZC*2, p. 564; *YDGC*, p. 283.
[11] *TLP*11, p. 304; *TPM*3, p. 131; *TZC*2, pp. 565–6.
[12] ibid.

unpalatable operatic experience when he settled in Paris on 14 January. 'I have just returned from the Opéra Comique, where I have heard *Le Nozze di Figaro* for the second time [since my arrival], and if there are to be more performances, then I shall go again, and again, and again,' he began one of his periodic bursts of Mozart enthusiasm to Nadezhda von Meck on 23 January.

> I know my worship of Mozart surprises you, dear friend. And even I myself am surprised that a man as flawed as I, not completely healthy either mentally or morally, has been able to preserve his ability to delight in Mozart, who possesses neither the depth nor the strength of Beethoven, neither the warmth nor the passion of Schumann, nor the brilliance of Meyerbeer, Berlioz, Wagner, etc. . . . Mozart neither overwhelms nor stuns me – but he captivates me, makes me happy, warms me. When I hear his music it is as though I am doing a good deed . . . and the longer I live, the more I get to know him, the more I love him.'[13]

During the previous performance of the opera Tchaikovsky had encountered the Grand Duke Konstantin Nikolayevich, and fearing this would be the preliminary to a dizzying social round, he was reduced to pretending that he would be leaving Paris in a couple of days. Modest was soon to join him – without Kolya this time – and in the meantime his single aim was to proceed with the scoring of *Mazepa* as expeditiously as possible. In any case, Paris was the one city in which Tchaikovsky knew he could be alone yet content. Quickly he established a routine which included frequent visits to the theatre. His old favourite, Musset's *On ne badine pas avec l'amour*, was but one of the pleasures offered by the Comédie-Française, though the most powerful impression of these first Paris days came from yet another of Sarah Bernhardt's performances, this time in Sardou's *Fédora* at the Vaudeville. Tchaikovsky had planned, after Modest's arrival, to spend some further days in Paris, and then to proceed with his brother to Rome. But Modest's arrival on 28 January brought an utterly unexpected and unpleasant shock. With him was Tanya. The declared purpose of her visit was that she should be placed under the supervision of the distinguished neurologist, Jean-Martin Charcot, in the hope of curing her morphine addiction. Since she would have to stay in Paris at least until the spring, Tchaikovsky accepted gloomily that he and Modest were also condemned to remain.

[13] *TLP*12, p. 27; *TPM*3, p. 139; *TZC*2, pp. 568–9; *YDGC*, p. 285 (partial).

Then work on scoring *Mazepa* was interrupted to complete the first of a batch of three commissions relating to the coronation of Tsar Alexandr III for whom, as Tsarevich, Tchaikovsky had composed his very first occasional piece, the Danish Festival Overture. Even before he had journeyed to Paris, Nikolay Alexeyev, a director of the Moscow branch of the RMS, had asked him to arrange the Slavsya Chorus from Glinka's *A Life for the Tsar* to be sung by a gargantuan choir of 7,500 students on the Red Square while the Tsar was crossing to enter the Kremlin. After four verses sung to the Slavsya tune Tchaikovsky was to devise a link leading to the Russian national anthem. The choir was to sing in unison, and the accompaniment would be for string orchestra. Tchaikovsky rebelled against the first condition, arguing that instinct and custom would cause some choralists to devise supporting lines of their own, and that if the spectators joined in this famous tune, as well they might, some of them would try to sing in parts also. Mindful of the vocal limitations of most of his singers and of the problems posed by the venue, Tchaikovsky completed the piece on 16 February, and promptly despatched it to Jurgenson. His own judgment on his labours is clear from the covering letter.

In all this the only free *composition* is a few bars of transition, and also the third couplet of the text. The amount I should receive from the city of Moscow which, as you put it, is going to fork out a large sum for me, is as follows:

For simplifying the choral parts and orchestrating sixteen bars, repeated three times	– 3 roubles
For composing eight bars of transition to the hymn	– 4 roubles
For composing four lines for the third couplet, at 40 kopecks a line	– 1 rouble 60 kopecks
Total:	8 roubles, 60 kopecks

These eight roubles, sixty kopecks I donate to the city of Moscow. No, but seriously – it's ridiculous even to raise the question of payment for such work, and I'd find it distasteful. Such things are to be done gratis, or not done at all.[14]

The requests for the remaining pieces arrived some three weeks later. 'The city of Moscow has commissioned from me a ceremonial march to

[14] *TLP*12, p. 57; *TZC*2, p. 572; *TPJ*1, p. 280. Only the chorus parts appear to have survived.

be played at the festivities which are to be organized for the Tsar at the
Sokolniky Park, and the coronation commission has sent me the text
written by Maikov for a big cantata which they have pressed me to
compose. . . . My first thought was to refuse,' he confided to Nadezhda
von Meck on 21 March, 'but then I decided I had at all costs to try to
fulfil both commissions on time. I know from reliable sources that the
Tsar is very disposed towards me (that is, to my music), and I would
not want it to reach him that I *had refused.*'[15] The first approach for the
cantata commission had been made to Anton Rubinstein, but he had
declined because of the pressure of other commitments, and had
suggested Tchaikovsky. Anxious to get these interruptions to *Mazepa*
out of the way, Tchaikovsky applied himself to both without delay. The
march was done first; it is, as might be expected, a thoroughly efficient
response to the requirements of the situation, and it was conducted by
Taneyev on 4 June, thirteen days after the Slavsya concoction had
failed to impress because of the noise made by the spectators on the Red
Square.

But the third piece was musically something much more than either
of these works, as Tchaikovsky recognized. 'The march is noisy but bad
. . . but the cantata is not nearly as poor as might be thought,
considering how quickly it was composed,' he wrote to Taneyev.[16] Six
days before, on 7 April, while still in the throes of composition, he had
explained to his patroness what had fired him. 'The text Maikov has
written for the cantata is very beautiful and poetic. There is a bit of
patriotic vapouring, but apart from this the piece is deeply felt and
written with originality. It has freshness and its tone is sincere, which is
making it possible for me, too, somehow not only to stand aside from the
difficulties of the task but, as long as I observe a proper decorum, to put
into my music a measure of the feeling warmed in me by Maikov's
beautiful lines.'[17] He had sufficient confidence in its musical virtues to
hope it might be repeated at one of the RMS concerts in Moscow. Its
première took place in the Kremlin on 27 May during the ceremonial
act which immediately followed the coronation, when the Tsar dined
alone in the presence of the others who had taken part in the main
ceremony; the performers were the chorus and orchestra of the Bolshoy
Theatre, conducted by Nápravník. Tchaikovsky had decided to accept
payment for neither commission, for he remembered how indebted he
had been to the Tsar when, two years before, he had solicited from

[15] *TLP*12, p. 80; *TPM*3, p. 159; *TZC*2, p. 576.
[16] *TLP*12, p. 102; *DTC*, p. 280; *TTP*, p. 97.
[17] *TLP*12, p. 97; *TPM*3, pp. 166–7; *DTC*, p. 280 (partial); *YDGC*, pp. 289–90
(partial).

Alexandr an advance of 3,000 roubles against future royalties for performances of his works in the Imperial Theatres, and had received instead the whole sum as a gift. In any case, if it was the city of Moscow which was commissioning the march, then the sum of 500 roubles being offered was an insult. Nevertheless, Alexandr himself now gave instructions that Tchaikovsky was to receive 1,500 roubles for his coronation offerings, but decided to disburse this in the form of a ring, just as he had for the Danish Festival Overture eighteen years earlier. Being currently insolvent, a dismayed Tchaikovsky promptly pawned the gift for 375 roubles, and on the same day lost both money and redemption ticket. The sole gain he made from his efforts was, as he shamefacedly told Nadezhda von Meck, 'a feeling of having committed some sort of improper act'.[18]

The cantata *Moscow* was the third and last of Tchaikovsky's major essays in the form, and it was by far the best. The first had been his 1865 graduation exercise on Schiller's 'An die Freude', while the second was composed for the opening of an exhibition celebrating the bicentenary of the birth of Peter the Great. Saddled with a poor text, Tchaikovsky had been able to find little to prompt musical inspiration in 1872, but Maikov's lines for *Moscow* were a very different matter. They sketched the history of the ancient capital from its peaceful origins through times of trouble to its peak of glory and its self-appointed role as protector of other Slav peoples. Their structure was simple and economical, their rhythms and images alive, and they unlocked in Tchaikovsky a vein of true, if less than first-rate lyricism, well able to support an extensive text without recourse to the shock treatment of abrupt tonal shifts or the grandiloquence of pedantic counterpoint, through which he had attempted to animate his earlier cantatas. And Tchaikovsky's music has not only much freshness; it is also impregnated with Russian intonations, at times intermittent and veiled, but at others sustained and explicit. Significantly, he had been concerned with Glinka's *A Life for the Tsar* in discharging the first of his coronation commissions, and during the cantata it becomes clear that within its fabric there lurk certain contexts from this opera so beloved by Tchaikovsky – above all, the opening phrase of the noble fourth act monologue in which Susanin greets his last dawn on this earth (Ex. 188b; the protoshape against which this and Tchaikovsky's derivatives are conceived is outlined in Ex. 188a). Yet it is Tchaikovsky's own *1812* overture which seems to have prompted the short andante religioso introduction for divided cellos. At the più mosso the mood becomes credibly arcadian; most

---

[18] *TLP*12, p. 199; *TPM*3, p. 203.

Ex. 188

[c, e, f, g, h and k are transposed]

striking here is the engaging flexibility of the choral phrases (Ex. 189a), and this flexibility is enhanced when the opening music later returns in three- instead of two-beat bars (Ex. 189b). The reduction to men's voices only, together with an increased agitation in the fertile orchestral ornamentation, is sufficient to signal the arrival of the alien hordes rolling wave after wave across Russia, and the voices finally die away as impenetrable night descends on Moscow, their concluding two-pitch phrase being taken up by the horns and hauntingly coupled with the

Ex. 189

[From a tiny freezing spring there flowed a river.]

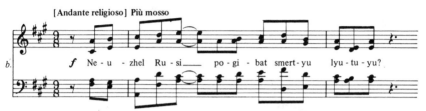

[Is it really possible for Russia to perish in a cruel death?]

[... impenetrable!]

[*In a and b the orchestral part is omitted*]

receding sounds of the chorus's opening theme (Ex. 189c). It is here that the first echo of Susanin is heard, for the horns finally give birth to a cadential phrase (Ex. 188c) whose outline summarizes Glinka's opening; it is surely not coincidence that it also comes close to the initial contour of the Russian national anthem, the other element which had featured in Tchaikovsky's first coronation offering (Ex. 188i). And out of this cadential fragment there flowers, in the most unaffected way, the following mezzo-soprano arioso (Ex. 188d). Quietly Moscow recovers, becoming a beacon to the surrounding peoples, and this rebirth is joyfully celebrated in the rousing chorus of the third movement. But the blessing of security and prosperity should be extended to brothers, and in the baritone monologue of the fourth movement the warrior of Moscow (a lightly masked symbol of Alexandr himself) goes forth to encounter the heavy plight of the Serbs, Montenegrins and Bulgarians. The echoes from *A Life for the Tsar* are now clearer, for not only is the baritone's succinct opening phrase (Ex. 188e) fathered by Susanin's monologue: it is also apparent that the brief imitative passage for strings which precedes this is conceived against the background of the fugal outburst in the opening chorus of Glinka's first opera (Ex. 188j and k record Glinka's and Tchaikovsky's phrases; Glinka's phrase is, in its turn, related to Susanin's opening). As for the baritone solo, Tchaikovsky here builds an arioso of imposing power, capped by the solid intervention of the chorus to echo the final words: 'Truly it is said of Moscow: "Two Romes have fallen – a third stands – there shall not be a fourth!"'. The orchestra celebrates the grandeur of this sentiment in a sonorous coda generated from yet another relative of the Susanin shape (Ex. 188f) and, even more, of the Russian anthem. The mezzo-soprano in the fifth movement also sings with a national accent as she voices the hero's sober reflections upon the responsibilities he must shoulder, shaping her opening (Ex. 188g) against a portion of the Susanin phrase, and then in the brief middle section pointedly borrowing the baritone's beginning when she ponders the possible fateful consequences paralleling those which had so implacably faced Susanin: 'If I am destined to die in battle, I am prepared to meet death face to face.' Then, to the music of her first section, she makes the act of dedication. In his preamble to the finale the baritone picks up thematic fragments from what has gone before, exhorting the people to brotherhood, truth and courage, and the chorus replies, finally rounding off the cantata with a shout of praise built from reiterations of yet another theme generated from the Susanin protoshape (Ex. 188h). Only in the noisy pealings of this finale does Tchaikovsky's response to a patriotic duty begin to sound dutiful; for the rest, *Moscow* is a piece with an attractiveness sufficient to merit it an occasional hearing, especially since, translated, it would be by no means difficult to perform.

The composition of these coronation commissions was not the only matter which slowed Tchaikovsky's progress on scoring *Mazepa*. Tanya's arrival had produced instant despondency, and a whole series of anxieties further distracted him at different times. Anatoly's wife was in the final stages of pregnancy, Sasha was still ailing in Kamenka, then Alexey fell seriously ill in Moscow. The expenses of Tanya's accommodation and treatment had been unforeseen, and the financial situation quickly deteriorated. Fearing, for a reason which will emerge later, to apply to Kamenka for the full cost of Tanya's budget, he looked in desperation to his patroness for a two-month advance on his allowance, to which she responded with customary alacrity. But these funds in due course became exhausted, and Tchaikovsky now turned to Jurgenson, extracting from him two sums of 1,000 roubles each to supplement the modest 600 roubles Tanya's father had despatched. 'I am a victim of fate, against which you can do nothing,' he was finally to reflect in self-justification.[19]

It was not long before Tchaikovsky was tiring of Paris itself, visiting the theatre less frequently and deriving even less pleasure from the local music. The death of Wagner on 13 February meant that the city's concert life was suddenly swamped by his works. 'The French are really funny! While Wagner was alive they didn't want to know him; now all the concerts are full of his works, and the furore is indescribable. You have to die to earn the attention of Paris,' he concluded sourly to Anatoly on 9 March.[20] This was not quite true, for an equal storm was being created by Saint-Saëns' new opera, *Henri VIII*, which had received its première at the Opéra four days before. Yet the French composer's success only deepened Tchaikovsky's pessimism over prospects for his own latest opera. 'I feel, I know that my *Mazepa* is much better than Saint-Saëns', and yet my opera will get no farther than the filthy stage of the Maryinsky, and I shall receive a miserable pittance for it,' he reflected.[21] He left Paris still ignorant of *Henri VIII*, but he did see *Figaro* at least four times, and was reduced to tears by Gounod's *Roméo et Juliette*. The death of Flotow had created a vacancy in the Académie des Beaux Arts for a foreign corresponding member, and Gounod had supported Tchaikovsky as one of five nominees for the place. But it was to be nearly ten more years before he gained election.

Predictably his longing to be back in Russia grew. Then he was troubled by a nagging conscience over Antonina. 'Perhaps I'm not acting completely impeccably in finally casting to the mercy of fate the unhappy being who is joined to me by the bonds of, as it were, matrimony. Now more and more often this thought disturbs me. If this being is in need, if she has been deserted by her lover (which is

[19] *TLP*12, p. 147; *TPJ*1, p. 303.
[20] *TLP*12, p. 70; *TPB*, p. 291; *TPM*3, p. 621; *TZC*2, p. 576.
[21] ibid.

exceedingly likely) and she's nowhere to lay her head, then I must come
to her aid,' he wrote to Jurgenson on 12 March. 'And so I want to ask
you to get hold of that gentleman who has already been employed to
enquire about her, and again entrust him with seeking her out and
discovering whether she needs material help. If so, then she must
certainly be given money. Forgive me that I am imposing on your
friendship.'[22] Nor was Antonina the only one to stir his compassion.
Some weeks earlier he had received a letter from a Mrs Loginova who,
as Mariya Palchikova, had once taught him the piano. She was in
difficulties, and Tchaikovsky requested Jurgenson to send her fifty
roubles against his account, for he remembered it was she who, over
thirty-five years earlier, had begun his musical education.

But the chief preoccupation remained Tanya. She had been installed
in a maison de santé, and Elizaveta Molas, a former governess in the
Konradi household, had been hastily engaged from St Petersburg to act
as nurse and companion. Since Tanya's personal maid, Sasha, was also
in attendance and could give support to Elizaveta, the brothers felt able
to take turns in visiting their niece on alternate days. Each stage of
progressive withdrawal of the morphine caused violent physical and
emotional reaction in the patient, and this was distressing to the
spectators. Yet on other days Tanya would be in good spirits, able to
enjoy the pleasures of Paris and accompany her uncle Modest to the
theatre. Tchaikovsky himself was grateful for the appearance of
Kondratyev for a fortnight at the end of March, though he was
alarmed at the signs of premature age already appearing in this
disorderly but engaging friend. But by now it was becoming imperative
that Modest should return to Kolya in St Petersburg. Reluctant to leave
his elder brother to cope with Tanya alone, he delayed his return until
Tchaikovsky himself insisted he must go. On 18 April Modest finally
left.

No one reading the copious letters which Tchaikovsky had written
during the last eleven weeks could have guessed the event which he
himself knew perfectly well was facing him. There had, in fact, been a
far more compelling reason which had caused Modest to bring Tanya
to Paris. She was pregnant by Blumenfeld. So far the secret had been
guarded with extraordinary efficiency. Even Tanya's parents knew
nothing about it. Modest was one of the first to be told, but he had
withheld the information from his composer-brother while the latter
was still in St Petersburg, and had told him nothing of the plan to bring
their niece to Paris. Since it was imperative that Tanya should receive

[22] *TLP*12, pp. 72–3; *TPJ*1, p. 285.

treatment for her morphine addiction, the search for a cure through consultation with a distinguished – and distant – authority became the convincing excuse for removing her from Russia. Modest had to confide in his elder brother when he arrived in the French capital, but the secret was to remain until much later between them, Tanya's maid, Sasha, and Elizaveta Molas. Thus Tchaikovsky's letters to the family in Russia dealt solely with the cure for addiction, and when these are set beside the generally favourable reports on Tanya's health written to Modest after the latter had returned to Russia, there is some suspicion that the earlier accounts of Tanya's predicament and sufferings had been much heightened for the benefit of the family back home. In addition an operation to treat a condition resulting from the addiction was fabricated, presumably to account for the expense of the confinement, and to cover the possibility of death in childbirth.

Tchaikovsky's composure as the event neared is impressive, but he had every reason to believe that Elizaveta and Sasha could cope with everything more than competently. This they did. Being now without Modest, he found work on *Mazepa* an antidote for the loneliness of his situation, and his progress, both in scoring the opera and in devising the vocal score, accelerated accordingly. He did, however, find time to visit the recently opened exhibition of nineteenth-century portraits at the Académie des Beaux Arts ('very interesting and completely to my taste', he told Modest[23]), and he was also reading much, particularly enjoying Maupassant's recent collection of stories, *Mademoiselle Fifi*, and Zola's *Au bonheur des dames*.

The baby, a boy who was to be baptized Georges-Léon, was born at one o'clock on the morning of 8 May, the day after Tchaikovsky's own forty-third birthday. When he called at the maison de santé later that morning and saw Tanya with her son, he was struck by the strength of his own feelings towards this infant against whose arrival in this world he had seemed so steadfastly to set his thoughts. He had become aware of these emotions the day before: 'now I experienced them tenfold, and I told Tanya that while I had life in me she need have no worry on his [Georges-Léon's] account.'[24] He was the more upset, therefore, by the equanimity with which Tanya viewed the event and its implications, especially the prospect of having to live a lie when she returned to her parents' home. Tchaikovsky himself attended to the formalities of registering the birth and arranging the child's baptism. For the moment he was teased by the idea that he might himself in due course

[23] *TLP*12, p. 132; *TPB*, p. 296; *YDGC*, p. 292.
[24] *TLP*12, p. 140.

assume responsibility for the boy. But within a few days the wet nurse had borne Georges-Léon away to her home south of Paris at Villeneuve. He was to be kept in France for three years until, in 1886, Tchaikovsky's brother Nikolay and his wife adopted him.

The speed with which Georges-Léon had made his entrance and exit left Tchaikovsky suddenly free to plan his own departure from Paris. Tanya was to stay for a further six weeks, but with such sensible supervision as Elizaveta Molas could give, her uncle felt no unease about returning to Russia. Other causes, too, contributed to his much better mood. Anatoly's wife had been safely delivered of a daughter, Alexey had been granted a whole year's leave to recover from his illness, and *Mazepa* was finished. Together with Elizaveta he visited the wet nurse at her home in Villeneuve and returned fully confident that Georges-Léon would be well cared for. Preoccupations with the child's welfare could not prevent him inspecting the cathedral at Sens, where they had to spend a night on the return journey; Tchaikovsky rose at six the next morning to visit 'this vast, wonderful building', as he judged it to Modest.[25] And while in Paris he had heard that Jurgenson had been approached by the publishing house of Hamelle for French rights to the Piano Trio. Jurgenson, whose view of publishing was never timid, set the fee at 1,000 francs; expecting to be beaten down, he heard instead that Hamelle accepted the price, requesting in addition that Tchaikovsky's three works for violin and orchestra should be sold to him.

From the beginning of his time in Paris Nadezhda von Meck had been pressing Tchaikovsky to stay on her new estate at Pleshcheyevo near Moscow, and he had at first been much tempted by the idea, since it would be within easy distance of Anatoly and his wife. But his enthusiasm had progressively diminished, for it would also probably mean that he would be constantly visited by her sons and pestered for tuition by Pachulski. While in Paris he had received a batch of the latter's efforts, and though he had scrutinized them with that exemplary thoroughness and kindly rigour which seems to have marked all his teaching, he felt an increasing despair at Pachulski's lack of any gift for composition. Yet his own desperately straitened circumstances compelled him to think of spending the summer either as a guest or where the expenses would be minimal; the question of whether he should tear up his roots in Kamenka could not, therefore, yet be resolved. Anatoly had rented a villa at Podushkino outside Moscow, and Tchaikovsky excused himself from coming to Pleshcheyevo until the autumn, plead-

²⁵ *TLP*12, p. 157.

ing that his brother had prior claim to his company. Being again nearly penniless, he applied for a loan from brother Nikolay to pay his travel expenses, but this proved insufficient to cover also all Tanya's needs, and yet again his patroness's help had to be sought. On 22 May he left Paris. His parting act was to pen a letter to the newspaper *Gaulois*, clarifying Anton Rubinstein's position in the pre-history of the coronation cantata. Aware that rumours were impugning Rubinstein's patriotism in the matter, he rose strongly to the defence of his former teacher by publicly setting the record straight. His return through Berlin offered him a far more palatable Wagnerian experience than had his previous passage: a performance of that 'best of all *Wagner's* works', *Lohengrin*.[26] But Berlin itself seemed very provincial and barren when compared with Paris. On 27 May, the day his cantata was being offered to the Tsar in Moscow, he arrived in St Petersburg.

The relief felt by Tchaikovsky on leaving Paris was enormous, especially since he had the prospect of extended relaxation before him. The coronation taking place in Moscow had virtually emptied the Russian capital of those people he was always in fear of encountering; to have such freedom was compensation enough for missing the première of his cantata, especially since he was subsequently reassured that both performance and reception had been excellent. The fine weather and the chance of visiting favourite places with Modest and Kolya caused him to delay his departure for Podushkino, and it was 11 June before he was with Anatoly. He found that family life had wrought a vast improvement in this brother. The absence of Anatoly's former excitability and fussiness delighted him; so did his new niece (also called Tanya) and the presence of Alexey, as well as the news that Anna Davïdova and Nikolay von Meck were now officially betrothed. The location chosen by Anatoly for their summer residence proved idyllic. 'I am like a child revelling in all these delights,' he informed his patroness two days after his arrival, 'and literally the whole day yesterday I roamed through the surrounding woods.'[27] Every day, when circumstances permitted, he would collect mushrooms. He paid visits to Moscow to see Kondratyev and Vladimir Shilovsky, with whom his relations had recently been strained, as well as to deal with more weighty matters. Among these was a session with Pachulski, whose new symphony drove Tchaikovsky to the brink of telling him the blunt truth about his lack of talent. He took counsel about this with Nikolay von Meck, who was also in Moscow. 'For God's sake don't say anything;

[26] *TLP*12, p. 164; *TPM*3, p. 185; *TZC*2, p. 587; *YDGC*, p. 294.
[27] *TLP*12, p. 170; *TPM*3, p. 190.

mother will be terribly upset,' was the reply,[28] and Tchaikovsky remained silent not merely out of self-interest, but because his benefactress was already deeply distressed by the death of her youngest son, Mikhail, only days before.

Sympathy for the needs of others also impelled him to intercede with Karl Davïdov, director of the St Petersburg Conservatoire, on behalf of Laroche in the hope that appointment as professor of music history might help draw him out of the lethargy in which he still languished. He was very upset, too, that Nikolay Hubert, having been driven from the directorship of the Moscow Conservatoire by the recent troubles, had severed all connection with the institution. He knew Hubert was no administrator, but he acknowledged his gifts as a teacher, and he was alarmed at the idea that the twenty-two-year-old Anton Arensky should become head of the Conservatoire's theoretical studies, even though he already recognized Arensky's prodigious musical endowments. It was now five years since he himself had resigned from the Conservatoire, but it had been a major factor in his own past, and under Nikolay Rubinstein it had become an indispensable part of the musical life not only of Moscow but of Russia itself. A little earlier, while in Paris, he had been approached through Jurgenson to rejoin the staff, but even the bait of a two-room flat of his own could not entice him. Nevertheless, the surge of concern he felt for his old institution now drove him to devote several days to acting as an intermediary in trying to make possible Hubert's return to the professoriate. The hope proved impracticable, but since his plea to Davïdov on Laroche's behalf had been unfruitful, he was at length able (though with much misgiving) to persuade the Moscow Conservatoire to offer Hubert's vacant place to this long-standing but sadly unstable friend.

Tchaikovsky's period of relative relaxation was finally broken in early July when the proofs of *Mazepa* began to arrive. And once more his creative urges were proving irrepressible. 'I am also beginning to do a little work on a new suite, but I do not intend to hurry,' he confided to Nadezhda von Meck on 9 July[29]. But there would have been little time for this, even if his inspiration had been flowing freely. As has already been recorded, simultaneous productions of *Mazepa* were planned in Moscow and St Petersburg, and the roles were being allocated; thus the printed vocal score was urgently needed. To make matters worse, the engravings were deplorably inaccurate, and Tchaikovsky lamented bitterly that publishers in Russia did not have the excellent professional

[28] *TLP*12, p. 179; *TPM*3, p. 622.
[29] *TLP*12, p. 181; *TPM*3, p. 194; *TZC*2, p. 591; *DTC*, p. 400; *YDGC*, p. 296. In fact the sketches for the piece indicate he had actually started work on 13 June.

proof-readers who lightened the composer's task in Western Europe. Nor could he do anything about the constant procession of guests who visited Podushkino, and he found himself inescapably drawn into return invitations. In such conditions projected activities like resuming his study of the English language and exploring unknown Mozart had to be shelved.

So also, he decided, would he have to abandon his original plan to visit Pleshcheyevo that autumn. For the fact is that, ever since leaving Paris, he had been missing Kamenka badly, and the reproaches he constantly received from that quarter decided him that he should travel to the Ukraine for an extended stay. Pleshcheyevo would have to wait until the next spring, for in November rehearsals for *Mazepa* would demand his presence first in Moscow, then in St Petersburg, after which he planned to end the winter recovering in Italy. Tanya was remaining in Paris longer than expected, and by borrowing from his servant and his sister-in-law he scraped together some 200 roubles to send to her for maintenance of Georges-Léon. But the disaster with the Tsar's ring compelled him yet again to turn for an advance to his benefactress. By mid-August, having read three sets of proofs of *Mazepa*, he was suffering from nervous headaches and a persisting mild fever. Yet even now he could not rest; 'the demon of composition has taken possession of me with invincible power,' he wrote to Nadezhda von Meck,[30] and when he left Podushkino on 13 September, the sketches of the Second Suite were complete. After two days in Moscow, he headed for Kiev where, despite his outburst of the previous year to the bishop, he again attended mass at the Brothers' Monastery. Before leaving the city he bought a copy of Cui's opera, *A Prisoner in the Caucasus*, and of the First String Quartet by the eighteen-year-old Alexandr Glazunov. His judgments upon the two works were very divergent – and, one suspects, hardly impartial, for memories of the critical manglings he had received (and still was receiving) from one of the composers gnawed at him to the end of his life. Glazunov's work pleasantly surprised him. 'Despite its imitation of [Rimsky-]Korsakov, its unbearable way of restricting itself to countless repetitions of an idea in a thousand keys instead of *developing* it, despite its contempt for melody and its exclusive pursuit of harmonic curiosities, a remarkable talent is discernible. The form is so fluent I'm astounded, and I suspect his teacher helped him,' he told Modest. '. . . I also bought *A Prisoner in the Caucasus*. This is trivial in the extreme, weak, childishly naïve – but, most of all, it's odd that a critic who has all his life persecuted *routine* should, in his declining years, produce an

---

[30] *TLP*12, p. 208; *TPM*3, p. 209; *TZC*2, p. 596.

opera so unashamedly *routine*.'[31] On 17 September he was in Kamenka; the next day he transferred to the much more congenial surroundings of Verbovka.

Tchaikovsky remained at Sasha's home for the next two and a half months. His first objective was to score his Second Suite; as he had explained to Nadezhda von Meck at the beginning of September, if it was not ready by the beginning of the winter season, he would not be able to discover how it sounded during his time in Moscow, which he was most anxious to do 'because I have used some new orchestral combinations which interest me greatly'.[32] The fact that he took more than five weeks to complete this operation, despite sometimes devoting six hours a day to it, is proof enough of the care he took. Even when the inevitable fatigue began to weigh on him, he remained convinced that the *Scherzo burlesque* and *Rêves d'enfant* at least would receive approbation. The work was finished on 25 October, and Erdmannsdörfer conducted the first performance on 16 February the next year in Moscow, where it had a success so brilliant that it had to be repeated a week later. But if the composer's eagerness to hear how it would sound was satisfied, then this must have been during rehearsal; at the performance itself he was absent. As already noted, the tensions of the première of *Mazepa* the previous evening had proved too much for him, and he had left for the West to recover.

The Second Suite is not a great piece, but it is a fascinating one, and very different from its predecessor. Why Tchaikovsky conceived it as he did is not as readily apparent as in the case of the First Suite, where the use of specific pre-classical types (Introduction and Fugue, and Gavotte) as the outer movements had defined the model as baroque, despite the expanses of Tchaikovskyan melody in the central movements – and despite his declared intention, when he started work on it, that it should be in the style of Lachner. The liberal doses of contrapuntalism in the Second Suite's opening *Jeu de sons* might suggest a parallel course in prospect, but this time the model is classical, with the allegro molto vivace designed as a sonata structure. For all its contrapuntal labours, the first subject still displays the Tchaikovskyan paradigm of tonic flanks with an extensive quasi-developmental centre. An explicit fugue provides a tonally undramatic substitute for the development, while the recapitulation is telescoped by the two subjects being played simultaneously, showing them to be in invertible counterpoint.

[31] *TLP*12, pp. 230–1; *TZC*2, p. 603; *TPB*, p. 300. In fact, *A Prisoner in the Caucasus* was an early work of Cui, composed in 1857–8, but revised in 1881–2 in anticipation of its première in 1883.
[32] *TLP*12, p. 216; *TPM*3, p. 212.

The anonymous counterpoint which occupies so much of this first movement renders it no more attractive than its counterpart in the First Suite. The remaining movements are not only more alive, but are something of a collective landmark in Tchaikovsky's evolution. His researches into new instrumental combinations, to which he had alluded at an early stage in the work's gestation, went well beyond the devising of brief orchestral piquancies and surprises, for in these four movements he undertook a reassessment of his orchestration some-times as radical (but a good deal more profitable in creative dividends) as that he had conducted four years before when scoring *The Maid of Orléans*. It confirmed the bifurcation in his orchestral technique, for whereas the shift in the opera house had been towards generalization, in these new pieces, designed for the concert hall, it was towards greater particularization. In *The Maid* the sections of the orchestra had been treated more as choirs, the textures being more simply designed and sonorously presented. With this less detailed approach the brush strokes had become broader and simpler, with whole sections of dialogue now proceeding with spare chordal support scored only for strings, perhaps alternating with blocks of wind sound. Except in the more intimate scenes for Joan and Lionel there was much less use of solo wind instruments providing background counterpoints or decorative dialogues.

Similar preoccupations had seemed to condition the plainer approach to the organization and realization of orchestral colour in the First Suite, upon which Tchaikovsky had worked in parallel with *The Maid*, for even in the march each section had exploited a single, not a multiple sound world. Nor did the Italian Capriccio, his next orchestral work, mark any new departure, for its southern tunes were entities as self-contained as the melodic structures which were the main substance of the suite, and they had suggested matchingly broad areas of tone colour. The difference was that the pigments were now far more vivid, the contrasts fiercer, the backgrounds idiomatically designed to make possible strikingly projected accompaniments. But in the new suite Tchaikovsky sought to refine and detail his sound world to a degree which required some reappraisal of whole parameters of his technique. In the Valse there is a pronounced shift in the melodic manner. In earlier examples he had composed melodies mostly in sixteen-bar periods, each normally employing a limited range of rhythmic com-ponents; variety had come from an uncommon resourcefulness in diversifying the triple-time metre with duple-time inflections (see Vol. 2, p. 79, Ex. 115). Such tunes were customarily presented through one colour or divided between, at most, two; to broaden the rhythmic field, contrasting melodic lines or fragments might be counterpointed to the principal line. But Tchaikovsky's intention of introducing brisk and varied colour changes into this new Valse prompted him not only to widen the contrasts in melodic character between the different sixteen-bar periods but, at a more local level, to absorb into the main line the sort of variety formerly provided by subordinate fragments, thus abetting melodically the new extra diversity of colour. And so the agile quavers with which the violas complement the violins' benign opening phrase (Ex. 190, bar 3) are soon transmitted to the principal line (bar 8) which leaps up with new-found energy, while the repetition of these sixteen bars brings modifications both in scoring and substance; the meticulous detail in the directions for performance is striking throughout. The continuation, again of sixteen bars, broadens this melodic world unprecedentedly; the two-beat ostinato-like figure in low clarinet, punctuated by loudly chopped chords, can be accepted as a waltz only by association with what has gone before. In the first section of the First Suite's Divertimento (89 bars), which had many waltz affinities, there had been some fifteen changes of orchestral colour; in this Valse's first section (106 bars) there are nearly fifty, some lasting no more than a single beat. By contrast, the centre of the movement, with its sixteen-bar periods of unchanged scoring, emphasizes the newness in what surrounds it.

Ex. 190

Yet the modification of melodic manner within this Valse is modest compared to the transformation of texture in the first section of the *Scherzo burlesque*; the optional introduction of four accordions later in the piece is only its most startling novelty. Gone are the stolidly functional basses and explicit harmonic supports of the First Suite; gone, too, is contrapuntal stodge in favour of a mercurial polyphony from which is spun a protean variety of textures, sometimes of such fineness that the harmony is only barely sketched. In this opening section everything from a single line, through two-part counterpoint, to tutti chords is used (though the last very sparingly, and never with the full orchestra). Merely to distribute among different permutations of instruments these fleeting lines, chords and other morsels which momentarily appear was to guarantee endless variety of sound; Tchaikovsky's achievement is to have used these resources so discriminatingly. It is no wonder that, with such fine judgements being demanded, the scoring should have taken so long. The first of the two episodes[33] affixes the quaver-two-semiquaver figure of the opening section to a series of pedal points which, being set a major third apart, reinforce the tonal uncertainty also created by the presentations of the new three-crotchet motif. Like the fourth movement of the Third Symphony, this *Scherzo burlesque* crosses into the musical territory of the Russian supernatural.

Nor is this the only context in these four movements which connects with the past, for the second episode suddenly flourishes a national manner redolent of the Second Symphony; it is difficult to believe (though it appears to be true) that the melody lustily sung by the horns is not a genuine folktune. Also of the Second Symphony's world is the last movement, the oddly named *Danse baroque* (i.e. 'quaint' or 'grotesque'). But it has equal affinity with the gopaks in Tchaikovsky's operas, though now possessing a more concentrated brilliance, with stretches in which the harmony is fragmented into a series of brilliant background splashes at different pitch levels. This dance is more helpfully defined by its sub-title: *Wild dance in imitation of Dargomïzhsky*. The specific model is that composer's *Kazachok*, though Tchaikovsky

---

[33] In Tchaikovsky's autograph score three pieces from this suite were considerably longer than when they were published in 1884. The *Scherzo burlesque* had started life as an extended rondo (ABACABA); after bar 333, at the end of the second episode (C) Tchaikovsky had continued for 44 further bars, then picked up the first section at bar 41, and continued to bar 205, concluding with 48 bars of coda which incorporated material from the second episode. The first section of *Rêves d'enfant* was longer by what was essentially a varied but reorganized version of the first 33 bars. In *Danse baroque*, starting from bar 219 (i.e. shortly before the coda), 90 bars were to be cut (these incorporated an exact repetition of bars 41–83). To smooth the gap Tchaikovsky added three new bars (bars 219–21 of the printed score).

takes no suggestion from the slow music in this roughly made but likeable piece. Predictably the model is far outstripped by the tribute; Dargomïzhsky's lively but crude inventiveness is transformed into a heady series of ear-enticing variations and digressions, never more engaging than when, just before the coda explodes, the dance pounds forward with earthy wit through some twenty bars of close two-part canon.

It is the remaining movement, *Rêves d'enfant* (No. 4), which contains both the most conventional and the most original music in the whole suite. The harmonic support to this gently folky berceuse is orthodox enough, and such it remains for over half the piece, though some of the textures have a rare fastidiousness. But the easy fantasies of the waking world give way to the evanescent images of unconsciousness as a series of E flat minor chords suddenly recalls those flutterings into which Miranda's first hesitant phrases of love had dissolved in *The Tempest* some ten years before. This time, however, the progress is not to a surge of physical passion but into a realm of yet more intangible images, conjured in textures so fragmented and chromatically ornamented that their harmonic foundation remains elusive (Ex. 191); only at the end of each does a shimmering harp-washed triad bring a brief stability. The convoluted oboe phrase introduces an image of some substance, but it dissipates within a progression of tonally unrelated triads before the whole impalpable creation sinks into limbo and vanishes. Like the opening of the Second String Quartet, this is a passage quite unprecedented in Tchaikovsky's work, and like that earlier music it seems to leap towards a distant future; the listener coming across it for the first time may momentarily wonder whether there will open before him the world of Bly, that other setting for disturbing childhood dreams and fantasies in Britten's *The Turn of the Screw*. Even within the enchanted music of *The Sleeping Beauty*, which it clearly presages, there is rarely quite the same disquieting sense of shapes indefinable and forces unknown. But in this present piece such things quickly pass; the conscious world returns and the child resumes its musings before falling into dreamless sleep.

Matters of childhood, though now seen very differently, are the whole subject of Tchaikovsky's remaining work of 1883, the Sixteen Songs for Children, Op. 54, upon which he started only a week after finishing the suite. The idea for such a collection was not new. In January 1881 he had set Axakov's 'Child's song' ('My Lizochek'), and five months later he told both Anatoly and Jurgenson that he intended to compose further songs of this kind. In the meantime 'Child's song' had been published as a supplement to the monthly *Recreation for*

Ex. 191

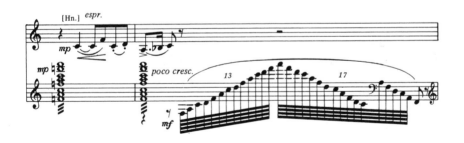

Children, and that autumn this periodical had approached Tchaikovsky for more of the same. He had firmly rejected the proposal, partly because of the unsuitability of the texts proposed, partly because of the inadequate fee. With this he seems to have set aside any idea of such creative work. It cannot have been entirely coincidence that, having just completed a piece in which a vision from the world of childhood had so deeply touched his creativity, he should now be impelled to return to this other project in which everything had been of that world. But it was a very long time since, in his daily existence, children had been such a close and absorbing factor as during the last few months. First Tanya's son, with whose welfare he had been so closely involved; then Anatoly's daughter, who had given him such delight during his weeks at Podushkino. And now, at Sasha's home, there was Irina, Vera's daughter born the previous year, whom he first thought unattractive ('she reminds me very much of a widow, and such children aren't to my taste'[34]), but whom he admitted he very quickly came to adore. It was difficult any longer to look upon Sasha's offspring as a group of children. Two were already mothers, a third about to be married, and only Yury, now seven, remained at home. But suddenly a new generation had begun to spring up, and had become for a while a part of his life – and, it seems, of his creative world. 'I've set about composing children's songs, and I'm writing one regularly each day,' he told Modest on 5 November, three days after beginning work. 'But this is a light and very pleasant labour, for as my text I'm taking Pleshcheyev's *The Snowdrop*, where there are many delightful things.'[35] At this stage it seems he was confining himself to musical sketches, but the compulsion to bring these, and the others he drafted during the next week, to their final form soon turned leisurely recreation into assiduous toil, and by 15 November he could despatch fifteen completed songs to Jurgenson. 'So that this [collection] may serve as a rather special gift for children, it would be desirable to publish them as attractively as possible, and with pictures – but otherwise, as you think fit,' he wrote to his publisher. 'If you want you can add "Lizochek" to it.'[36] This last suggestion appealed to Jurgenson, and the earlier nonsense song was duly appended.

Tchaikovsky had known the minor poet, Alexey Plescheyev, from his first days in Moscow, and had already used two of his lyrics for much earlier romances. It must have been the appearance of 'Child's song' at the beginning of 1881 which had prompted Pleshcheyev to present

---

[34] *TLP*12, p. 232.
[35] *TLP*12, p. 264; *TPB*, p. 599; *YDGC*, p. 300.
[36] *TLP*12, p. 273; *TPJ*1, p. 310.

Tchaikovsky with a copy of his anthology for children, *The Snowdrop*, printed three years earlier. If the poet's hope was that this might lure the composer into setting more of his verses – and the inscription ('. . . as a mark of affection and gratitude for his beautiful music to my poor words') suggests that it was – then he was richly rewarded, for fourteen of the 1883 songs use Pleshcheyev's texts. Nearly all are sentimental; a number are translations, but in Pleshcheyev's jingle they mostly lose any real poetic quality they may once have possessed. There is the expected quota of seasonal ditties, though only the early arrival of autumn brings cheerlessness into any of them (No. 14). Spring gets three (Nos. 3 (a translation from Polish), 9 and 13) since it is the happiest time of all, and thoughts may run freely on budding nature, birds and insects. The two on winter skirt its less pleasant features, for one (No. 12) treats of children's excitement at the first snowfall, the other (No. 7) first paints a cosy domestic scene where mother tells her children a story in front of a blazing fire, then plays the piano for them to sing and dance, after which the poet reminds his young readers of less fortunate mortals ('paupers and orphans') who have to endure the howling blizzard and whom, he says, they ought to 'caress like brothers', should they ever come across any. A storm is also a distant background to a reassuring cradle song (No. 10). There is one other vignette of family life (No. 6, a translation from an English source): a fisherman's family is anxiously awaiting his return because he has been away three days, not two, and is the more excited when he does appear with a particularly good catch. Gardens, flowers and birds are not only liable to crop up anywhere, but have lyrics of their own; a modest patch is held to be much nicer than a grandly designed garden (No. 4), a solitary domestic plant resists the summons of its more fortunate confrères to join them in the garden because it must stay to gladden the sufferer and prisoner (No. 11, a translation from L. Ratisbonn), while God's bird intercedes with the Almighty for the poor ploughman (No. 2, another Polish translation). A swallow is the central figure in a more distinctive lyric (No. 15), bringing an orphan remembrances from her brother in prison: does she still weep for him? Significantly the text of this one is by Ivan Surikov from the Polish of Lenartowicz. But this worthier seriousness is also evident in Pleshcheyev's translation which produced the most famous song of the whole set, the 'Legend' (No. 5; the source is English), where the Christ-child in his garden is crowned with thorns by children who have ransacked all his flowers. Yet the set has humour, too, both in the opening song, which tells how a boy, bored with amusements, finally asks his grandmother to point the way to school, and in No. 8 (a translation from Gellert), in which a cuckoo,

enraged that other singing birds are getting all the attention, deter-
mines to command notice by remorseless repetitions of its two notes.

With texts such as are used in the majority of these, the worst might
be feared. In fact, this set is far from contemptible. Such songs are not
upgraded nursery rhymes, but mostly simple romances, some for
children, some about them. Most are slender in substance, a few are
weak (Nos. 6, 12 and 14), but one or two are, of their kind, quite
first-rate. It may be useful to approach them after reflecting upon the
judgement made by Taneyev, that very perceptive critic of his former
teacher's work. 'In the majority of these songs the required mood is
fully achieved through simple means,' he wrote to Tchaikovsky on 4
July 1884. 'In addition, being harmonically uncomplicated (something
it's impossible not to praise in a composition of the 80s), they are at the
same time unusually interesting in the construction of their musical
sentences and sections. . . . Among the individual numbers the first
place without doubt belongs to "The Cuckoo" [No. 8] . . . "Christ"
[No. 5] is a delight . . . "The Bird" [No. 2], "Spring" [No. 3], the
second "Spring" [No. 9], the "Cradle song" [No. 10], "The Little
Flower" [No. 11], "The Orphan" ["The Swallow": No. 15] are little
masterpieces.'[37]

Taneyev's selection is thoroughly characteristic of a composer for
whom resourceful musicianship rather than inventive brilliance was
the central issue. His 'little masterpieces' are above all the well-made
pieces, whose fluency could have become somniferous, had not
Tchaikovsky incorporated phrases of doubled or halved length, for
instance, or employed overlaps between voice and piano to diversify the
jogtrot monotony which Pleshcheyev's prattle could so naturally have
bred. The listener alert, like Taneyev, to such unobtrusive resourcefulness will find a good deal else to admire in this set. True, it is rare to find
anything quite as sophisticated as the vocal opening of 'The Swallow'
where the piano, having established the prevailing three-bar phrase
structure (Ex. 192a; however, it pointedly dislocates this with a final
phrase of four bars), then settles for a new kind of six-bar unit while the
voice retraces the piano's first thoughts (Ex. 192b), at first out of phase,
then delaying its final phrase to end simultaneously with its partner.
This is certainly one of the best songs in the set, and the shift into the
minor on the last page gently points up the pathos of the end. In the
opening song, 'Granny and grandson', key is used to differentiate
character, the grandmother's music being set in A minor, her grandson's in G or C major (it is surprising that Taneyev's list did not include

[37] *DTC*, pp. 307–8; *YDGC*, p. 321 (partial); *TTP*, p. 106.

Ex. 192

this thoughtful little sketch, which Tchaikovsky treats with charmingly ironic seriousness). Such shifts are between closely related keys, of course, and only very infrequently do any of these songs step outside the most narrow tonal boundaries; the expedition towards the flattened sub-mediant at the end of the first strophe of 'Spring' (No. 9) is quite an adventure. Even more surprising, perhaps, is the infrequency with which Tchaikovsky employs musical onomatopeia in this set: the 'busy bees' in the prelude and postlude of 'My little garden' (No. 4), the children's laughter and the general din at the ends of the first two strophes of 'Winter evening', the stormy left-hand semiquavers in 'Spring' (No. 9) and the obvious bird noises in 'The Cuckoo' are about the only examples.

Whatever debate there may be over the list of 'little masterpieces' among these songs, there can surely be no disagreement with Taneyev about which are the finest two pieces. The 'Legend' quickly became, and has remained, one of Tchaikovsky's best-known short pieces. In April 1884 he transcribed the accompaniment for orchestra at the request of the tenor, Dmitri Usatov, and in 1889 he arranged the piece for unaccompanied chorus, which is the version most people know (usually under the title 'The Crown of Roses', with a first line: 'When Jesus Christ was yet a child'). The re-telling of one of the most pitiful incidents of the Passion story in terms of humanity's most innocent representatives has a poignancy which transcends its unblushing sentimentality, while the solemn procession of symmetrical phrases and the pervasive modalism of Tchaikovsky's setting bestow an almost hieratic quality which enables the piece to be both touching yet dignified. It affords the most substantial experience of the set – yet even among these unaffected pieces its simplicity is striking. There could scarcely be a stronger contrast of character than with 'The Cuckoo'. Humour rarely looms large in Tchaikovsky's music, but it does here, and with a lightness of touch which ensures that no point in this little scene is trampled upon. The cuckoo's disingenuous questions ('What are people saying about the singing of this or that bird?') have an arch simplicity which contrasts pointedly with the starling's chattery and mortifying replies; Taneyev thought Tchaikovsky had here worked bird-song into the accompaniment 'splendidly'. The end is hilarious, the piano petulantly thrashing (or flapping) in all directions until the starling explodes with laughter at the parasite's rage. Tchaikovsky wrote songs of greater substance, but none more delicious.

Tchaikovsky's return to Kamenka was greeted with much warmth from the whole clan. He found a special interest in encountering for the first time in nearly thirty years his cousin, Anastasiya Popova, a third of a century older than he, who had been a member of the Tchaikovsky household in his very earliest years, who had returned to take over the running of Ilya Petrovich's establishment on the death of Pyotr's mother in 1854, and who had now come to end her days in Sasha's care. Tchaikovsky had expected to find himself rather intimidated by Anastasiya, but instead found her to be amiable, grateful, yet hardly of this world, for her thoughts ran entirely on memories of thirty or forty years before. The kindness and attention which his sister was showing to this old lady, whose wits were gently slipping away, deeply touched

Tchaikovsky; whatever his views on Sasha's shortcomings, he freely admitted that responsibilities of this sort brought out the best in her. Tanya had already arrived from Paris with Elizaveta, but plans were being made for them to return, partly so that Tanya might continue her official treatment, partly to remove from her mother a presence which always adversely affected her health. Apart from concern for her child, Tanya had her own reasons for wishing to be back in France. One of the doctors who had attended her before her confinement was a certain Ferré. Tchaikovsky had noted he seemed attracted to Tanya, but the relationship had developed much farther after he had left, and the Frenchman had proposed marriage. In Paris Tanya would finally decide whether to accept his offer. Meanwhile, being in a highly nervous state, she soon removed herself to Kamenka to be nearer the local doctor, as a result of which the Verbovka establishment became far more relaxed.

Though Tchaikovsky believed that marriage to Ferré could be a good step for Tanya, he doubted the seriousness of her love. 'She talks to everyone too much about it for it to be a strong feeling,' he commented to Modest. But he was surprised at his own changed views about this troublesome niece. 'I'm exceedingly glad I've lost completely last year's feeling *of spite* towards Tanya. On the contrary, I feel a great deal of friendliness towards her, but not a trace of tenderness.'[38] For Blumenfeld her emotions were now violently hostile. But Tchaikovsky's judgements on the shallowness of her more recent attraction to Ferré was vindicated when an old aspirant, the merchant Otto Kern, appeared and immediately stimulated her interest. A proposal, swiftly made, that he should accompany her to Paris met with almost desperate opposition from her uncle. 'I have frankly advised her not to rush, but to attempt to visit Italy during the winter so as to try to entice some wealthy Englishman,' was his improbable counsel, as he told Modest. '. . . Lev isn't sending Tanya [to Paris] for the whole winter, but only for two months. Yet she will probably stay longer, and I foresee she's again going to cost me a lot of money. However, I shan't begrudge it, if only she gets married,' he added hopefully.[39] Within a fortnight of his arrival Tanya had left. His own emotions surprised him. 'My heart was wrung when she said goodbye,' he confessed to Anatoly. 'Somehow she's become pitiful and, above all, so distanced from her family that she's just like a stranger, and everyone breathed freely on being released from such a difficult guest. Even her parents, however much

[38] *TLP*12, p. 229.
[39] *TLP*12, pp. 235–6.

they love her, cannot hide that things are better and more carefree for them when she's far away.'[40] Once again with Tchaikovsky humanity had shown itself stronger than reflex. There could have been no greater contrast than the joy he felt at the celebrations of Anna and Nikolay's engagement. Yet even here, within the pleasure of seeing how the lovers 'sit all day in the corner and endlessly kiss each other', there was for him a pain which he knew Modest would understand. 'I look at them with envy, and think all the time that this indeed is real happiness, and that I shall never experience it.'[41]

When Tchaikovsky begins to gossip it is a sure sign that he is at his most relaxed, and the letters he wrote at Sasha's are well laced with small talk about the family. All such trivial matters of human behaviour, both generous and petty (and there was a vast number of the latter among the highly ramified tribe at Kamenka), provided an environment which he could both observe and share in a way not possible elsewhere. Kamenka, he discovered, remained necessary for him. And Kamenka still wanted him also, as he noted when Lev went to considerable trouble to install a fireplace in his room so that he might have more comfort and privacy as winter approached. Apart from spending a few days in Kiev in late October to avoid being left alone with Anastasiya while everyone else had gone to a family baptism, he spent all his time at Kamenka or Verbovka. His pattern of recreation was as before. Matters of geography and the history of Peter the Great featured in his reading, and operas seem to have been the most noteworthy element in his private music-making: Serov's *Judith*, but above all *Carmen*, which he played right through three times in as many days – though he also 'not without pleasure' investigated Rimsky-Korsakov's *May Night*.[42] He now found time to resume the study of English which had been impossible at Podushkino, and he made a start on *David Copperfield* in the original. Ippolit appeared for a few days, and both amused and aggravated everyone with his minor ailments. 'I very much love Ippolit's kindness, but God preserve me not only from living in the same house with him, but in the same town,' he confided to Modest.[43]

In fact, apart from intense irritations at the time-consuming inaccuracy of the Second Suite's proofs, and growing premonitions of the tensions he would have to face in Moscow and St Petersburg during the preparations for *Mazepa*, the only major disturbances during this two

[40] *TLP*12, p. 240.
[41] *TLP*12, p. 243.
[42] *TLP*12, p. 244; *TZC*2, p. 605; *YDGC*, p. 299; *TPB*, p. 599.
[43] *TLP*12, p. 270.

and a half months concerned Tanya. First she wrote from Paris telling him the cost of arrangements she was making for Georges-Léon, though she offered some hope that her uncle would soon be released from this financial burden, since she expected to marry that winter – but whether to Ferré or Kern she did not say. Then came the startling news that the former was no longer eligible, for on meeting Tanya he had told her calmly that he was now engaged to a French girl. Even worse was a sudden suspicion that Sasha had guessed the real truth behind her daughter's earlier stay in Paris. Yet most alarming of all was to be told all the essentials of Tanya's escapade by Alexey, who had picked them up from a former servant who had aided Blumenfeld in his nocturnal visits to Tanya's room. Then the story penetrated the fringes of the family itself, and for a few days Tchaikovsky lived in terror of the truth coming to the parents' ears. But before that could happen it was summarily dismissed as incredible; the very enormity of the scandal finally killed it, and he realized that for the moment at least the secret was safe.

Tchaikovsky left the Ukraine earlier than expected. The First Symphony had not been performed since its première in 1868; now, at Tchaikovsky's own instigation, it was to be played for a second time at an RMS concert on 1 December. On that very day he arrived in Moscow and received an ovation. The day following he attended a recital by the nineteen-year-old Glasgow-born German pianist, Eugen d'Albert, whose prodigious talents he was able to admire further at more private musical events. Within these encounters there began to germinate the seed of a future work for piano and orchestra.

A Note on the Second Suite, and on Certain Persons

It has already been suggested that two themes in the first movement of the First Suite may have been cipher-generated. The opening *Jeu de sons* of the Second Suite resembles that of its predecessor in that it is fugal and its thematic material is uncharacteristic of its composer – indeed, like that of the earlier movement, dull. Moreover, Tchaikovsky's sketches for this first movement indicate that it cost much effort to form it to his satisfaction, and since he had no lack of technical facility, it seems possible that certain constraints within the material were posing special problems. This offers some reinforcement to the suspicion that ciphers may be behind certain of the thematic ideas. The following suggestion concerning the first theme of the second subject cannot be considered any more conclusive than those made about the First Suite, and it is therefore excluded from the main text. It will be noted, however, that it is of a kind similar to that made with regard to the earlier piece.

The cipher system Tchaikovsky would appear to have used was that which both Ravel and Debussy, amongst others, are known to have employed later, and it provided a pitch equivalent for every letter of the alphabet (Ex. 193).

Ex. 193

A	B	C	D	E	F	G
H	I	J	K	L	M	N
O	P	Q	R	S	T	U
V	W	X	Y	Z		

Tchaikovsky composed the Second Suite while staying with his brother Anatoly and his family at Podushkino. The suite was dedicated to his sister-in-law, Praskovya, but her husband and their new daughter, Tanya, had an equal part in the composer's joy and affections during this summer episode. It would not be unreasonable, therefore, for him to incorporate these two as well as the work's dedicatee, though it would also be reasonable to assume that Praskovya would be the major element in any cipher generation. Applying a German transliteration of the three names to the system of Ex. 193 produces the following (Ex. 194):

Ex. 194

P R A S K O W J A   A N A T O L   T A N J A

If we take the first five pitches of 'Praskowja', then the contours produced by the first three pitches each of 'Anatol' and 'Tanja', and finally the contour of the last five pitches of 'Praskowja', but overlapping these shapes, we create the note sequence of Ex. 195a. The overlapping might signify the family bond, the placings of the divided 'Praskowja' contour might symbolize the embracing love of the mother for the family. Be that as it may, if the thirteen-note shape of Ex. 195a is inverted by simply reversing the initial interval but then keeping to the white notes (the system is, of course, concerned only with white notes), we have the exact pitch sequence of the second subject in the exposition (Ex. 195b). If these suggestions are indeed valid, it seems highly probable that other elements in this movement's material are also cipher-generated.

Ex. 195

7

INTIMATE INSIGHTS AND MARKS OF
REHABILITATION: THIRD SUITE

THE BIOGRAPHICAL PORTIONS of this study have been for the most part a chronological charting of the events of Tchaikovsky's life, blended with a selection from such passing evidence as illumines the man himself, his attitudes to life and his art, and his relationships with the people around him. Writing it has involved an increasingly drastic sifting of the data, for what appears in the pages of this present volume represents only a tiny portion of the information afforded by extant materials. But among these abundant documents there are some which, even though they contribute little of importance to the main biographical narrative, do seem to merit extensive attention, simply because of the unique illuminations they cast upon particular aspects of Tchaikovsky and his behaviour patterns. This chapter draws heavily upon two such bodies of material. The first consists of the letters to and about one individual; the other is a personal diary.

THE ODD CASE OF LEONTY TKACHENKO

During his last stay at Kamenka Tchaikovsky had ended a relationship he had been conducting with a young man who, four years earlier, had suddenly solicited his aid. The episode itself is bizarre but unimportant; the interest lies in Tchaikovsky's part in it. It shows him plunging into a deep involvement in the life and welfare of a person previously quite unknown to him, but whose sudden cry for help had been sufficient to engage his complete and sustained attention. It had begun, therefore, in raw innocence, and because there was no conditioning from existing ties of love or friendship, as in so many of his other numerous acts of kindness and support, the whole affair reveals with an engaging artlessness – indeed, perhaps more clearly than any other relationship in his whole life – that mixture of wild impulse and measured sympathy, of clear-headed insight and gullibility, which were such fundamental traits of the real Tchaikovsky.

The beginning of it all had been documented to Nadezhda von Meck on 3 November 1879.

> A fortnight ago from Poltava I received a letter written by a Mr Tkachenko, who is unknown to me, in which he informed me that, nourishing a passion for music and wishing to dedicate himself to the study of it, but having no means, he would like to become my man-servant, promising to carry out with all possible zeal the duties of a servant if only I would give him at least a chance of acquiring some knowledge, albeit small, of the theory of music. Because the letter was written very correctly and was shot through with sincerity, I replied that, although I could not accept his services in the capacity of a man-servant, I could help him to the means of acquiring a musical education if, from his next letter, I saw he was sufficiently gifted and young enough for study to lead to something. Yesterday I received his reply. He is twenty-two, and his musical knowledge is as weak as his wish to become a professional musician is strong. His letter was so written as to breed a great sympathy towards this youth. From all this it is evident that he is intelligent and talented. But what can you do with a person who for twenty-two years has only loved music, and can do nothing except what he has picked up by ear? I had to write in reply my frank opinion that he *had left it too late*, and that the years in which study might bear fruit had passed. I am very sorry for him.[1]

A full year went by. Then on 29 December 1880, Tchaikovsky picked up the tale.

> The day before yesterday I received a letter from him; he is returning my letters to me, lest after his death they should fall into someone else's hands. He bids me farewell, and says he has decided on suicide because his struggle with life's misfortunes and his despair of ever being other than a man labouring solely for a morsel of bread have instilled in him an aversion to life. The letter exuded such sincerity, such a deep despair, that I was very shocked. From the postmark I learned that the letter had been written in Voronezh (formerly he had lived in Poltava), and I immediately decided to telegraph, asking one of the inhabitants of Voronezh to seek out Tkachenko through the police and to tell him, if it was not already too late, to await a letter from me. Fortunately Anatoly has a good friend, a certain

---

[1] *TLP*8, pp. 400–1; *TPM*2, pp. 237–8.

Stoikov, whom I quickly telegraphed. Yesterday evening I received a reply that *Tkachenko* has been found *in time*. He was in a frightful state. Now I have sent him money for the journey, and I am inviting him to come to Moscow by 22 January – i.e. the day on which I myself must return from Kamenka. What will come of all this I do not know, but I am happy that I have saved him from destruction. Judging from his letters he is a strange and wild young man – but intelligent, and very honourable and good.[2]

Tchaikovsky admitted that, on reading Tkachenko's letter, he had wept like a child. The day before writing to Nadezhda von Meck he had addressed himself directly to the unfortunate.

I certainly must become acquainted with you personally – and I want to . . . I have no idea at all in what way I shall be able to show you that moral support you need, but do not doubt that in me you have a firm friend, very disposed to be a support for you in enduring life's misfortunes. In any case, I think that I shall be able to draw you out of that painful moral condition in which you find yourself. But correspondence is not enough for this – I must see you, know you more closely, and then take action. . . . If I were at this moment a completely free person I would come *to Voronezh*, but for various reasons I cannot do this, and therefore it would be more convenient if you came to me here. I am sending you fifty roubles for the journey. . . . I have adequate means, and it costs me nothing to show *a friend*, such as I consider you to be, not only moral but also material support. . . . And so, farewell. Set aside gloomy thoughts, look more kindly on life and the future – and, most of all, do not doubt that, although I do not yet know you personally, I am already your sincere and firm friend.[3]

Within a fortnight this young man, in whose life Tchaikovsky had felt compelled to intervene 'in a fateful manner', had replied, but in terms Tchaikovsky had hardly expected.

His letter did not please me at all, and bred in me fear for the future. I confess I had expected him to say thank you to me for the helping hand I had extended to him. Not in the least. He hastens to assure me that it is useless for me *to take upon myself to assure him of the existence of*

---

[2] *TLP*9, pp. 333–4; *TPM*2, p. 457; *TCZ*2, pp. 434–5.
[3] *TLP*9, p. 335; *TCZ*2, pp. 435–6.

virtue (though I never thought to speak of anything of the sort), *that I shall not be able to prove to him that it is worth living in this world*, that he did not need the money I had sent him and would manage without it – but he promised, all the same, to come to Moscow on 22nd and to hear me out. All this is very strange and incomprehensible.[4]

A badly wounded Tchaikovsky now waited with much uncertainty the arrival of this odd character. But Tkachenko was punctual. 'I have met him,' he continued to Nadezhda von Meck two weeks later.

> ... In general he is a sympathetic person. His sufferings have stemmed from the disparity between his aspirations and the gusts of stern reality. He is intelligent, developed – but nevertheless, for the sake of a morsel of bread he has been forced to serve as a guard on the railways. ... He is very nervous, timid, abnormally shy. ... Poverty, loneliness and circumstances of life have developed in him misanthropy and a hypochondriacal condition of the spirit. His views are rather queer – but, I repeat, he is far from stupid. I am extremely sorry for him, and I have resolved to take him into my care. I have now decided to send him for this half year to the Conservatoire. ... I shall not find it difficult to cure him and turn him into a being both useful and reconciled with life because he inspires me with sincere sympathy.[5]

Fortified with this extraordinary prediction, Tchaikovsky had not long to await results. 'I will tell you, dear friend, a little about Tkachenko,' he began his letter of 8 February.

> He is a very strange person. I arranged everything for him thoroughly in every respect and, to be fair to him, he set about his studies with great zeal. On the eve of my departure he presented himself to me, and forewarned me that he had to have a serious talk with me. I settled myself to listen, and the more he developed his thoughts, the more and more I was convinced that here was a nature sick both morally and mentally. The following is the essence of his speech. The thought had entered his head that I had rendered him help and assistance *not for his good but for my own, in order to earn the reputation of a philanthropist.* He compared me with *those ladies* who occupy themselves with philanthropy because it is fashionable, and so that they

---

[4] *TLP*9, p. 347; *TPM*2, p. 463.
[5] *TLP*10, p. 17; *TPM*2, pp. 466–7; *TCZ*2, pp. 445–6.

will be much talked about. During this he stated that he did not want to be *a victim* of my weakness for making myself popular, that he emphatically refused to consider me his benefactor, and forewarned me I should not count upon gratitude on his part.[6]

Greatly affronted by this outburst, Tchaikovsky defended himself with dignity and reason, then dismissed Tkachenko. 'I told him I was leaving [Moscow], that I would not see him again, and asked him not to think about me at all, but only of his studies.'[7]

But Tkachenko was not to be shed that easily. Tchaikovsky spent the summer at Kamenka; then on 21 August he began a letter to Modest.

This morning I was going, as always, to write to you when suddenly Sila appeared from the station, informing me in confidence that some unknown young man wanted to see me. Because he didn't say who this was, I refused to go. Then Biryukov appeared; he had seen the strange young man, and been filled with pity for him. He had come from somewhere on foot, had spent a full day at the station, had had nothing to eat, had stubbornly refused all offers, and declared the police could take him if they wished. From the description I guessed it was Tkachenko, and ran in great agitation to the station. I thought he was waiting for me so that he could forthwith blow out his brains in front of me. I won't describe the desperate condition I found the unhappy man in. He was *inexpressibly* glad to see me and could not restrain his hysterical sobs. He's a strange person! I calmed him as best I could, told Sila to pour him some tea and let him sit alone in order to calm himself. Then I left, and at evening returned to him again, and sent him via Kharkov to Moscow [from where it seems he had walked all the way]. His object was to come to me to decline my allowance in view of his lack of ability, will, and his worthlessness in general. However, he has promised to send me from Kharkov [where he has a sister] his diary for the whole summer, which contains everything he wanted to say but couldn't *de vive voix*. I'm very exhausted from the upheavals I've suffered today – but Tkachenko has again become sympathetic; he has a good, but broken nature à la Dostoyevsky.[8]

The diary duly arrived – a fat volume with seven months'-worth of entries. It showed some flair with words, was disconcertingly frank ('he

[6] *TLP*10, p. 23; *TPM*2, pp. 471–2; *TZC*2, p. 448.
[7] *TLP*10, p. 24; *TPM*2, p. 472; *TCZ*2, p. 449.
[8] *TLP*10, p. 189; *TZC*2, p. 479.

discloses things such as even Rousseau wouldn't tell'[9]), and convinced
Tchaikovsky he understood the roots of Tkachenko's problems. And in
attempting to turn psychiatrist, his words suddenly take on a personal
resonance which transcends the pathetic absurdity of the relationship
which prompted them. Tkachenko's troubles all originated in the
excessive tribute he had paid to sensuality in his youth, Tchaikovsky
decided. 'As for the moral side of your *excesses*, in the first place I have no
right to cast a stone at you, for I myself am not blameless,' he went on,

> and secondly, in my opinion a man in this regard finds himself in a
> fateful dependence upon his temperament. Very often chastity is no
> more than the lack of an element of sensuality in the temperament.
> The whole point is this: to be able to stand above one's bodily desires
> and to be able to control them – and this comes with training. In your
> case this [training] was bad – or rather, there wasn't any, and so I do
> not label you *a profligate*. A profligate, in the true sense of the word, is
> one who makes physical pleasures *the aim of life*, whose spirit never
> protests against the pleasures of the flesh.[10]

Over the next week Tchaikovsky absorbed himself in Tkachenko's
diary. Whether the lengthy analysis of the writer's problems with which
he continued his letter really fitted the case is impossible to say, but
there is much in it which is plausible. He identified Tkachenko as 'one
of those *artistic natures* often met among Russians, who has a bent to
artistic activity in general, but within his talents no specific inclination
to this or that branch of art. Meanwhile,' he went on, ' "step-mother
fate", as though wilfully, cast you without rhyme or reason now into the
Erivanskaya school, now into the army, now into the Consistory, now
on to the railway – and everywhere. . . . Ah, Leonty Grigoryevich,' he
cried, 'you are a good, nice person, but morally sick, for which of course
you are not to blame, but circumstances.'[11] By now he was preparing
Tkachenko to accept that, though he had managed to pass his Conservatoire examinations, as a musician he was unlikely to become more
than a humble teacher; however, he thought that the diary offered
powerful evidence of talent as a writer. What transpired during their
meetings in Moscow we do not know, but from Rome in early December Tchaikovsky, who had meanwhile asked Modest's opinion of
the diary, reinforced his advice to his protégé that he should turn his

[9] *TLP*10, p. 210.
[10] *TLP*10, p. 215.
[11] *TLP*10, pp. 215–16.

mind to a literary career. Accordingly Tkachenko withdrew from the Conservatoire.

During the next year, 1882, Tchaikovsky continued to subsidize Tkachenko with twenty-five roubles a month to give him time to learn his new craft. The patient understanding which Tchaikovsky had sustained for so long now reaped its fullest reward. For the next year Tkachenko showed a remarkable persistence in trying to shape his talent as a writer, and from June a series of his literary efforts began to arrive for Tchaikovsky's perusal. The latter's judgements on them were frank, but kindly. He recognized that Tkachenko needed to write from within his own experience (he had already observed to Modest that the diary could make the basis of a novel), and he was unsparing in his verdict on the comedy Tkachenko included among these exercises because it attempted to deal with human matters the writer did not understand. But still Tkachenko persevered, though his constant changes of address presented persisting problems to Jurgenson, who had been charged with dispensing the monthly subsidy.

Yet it is apparent that, before the end of the year, a sense of realism had invaded Tchaikovsky's assessment of his protégé's literary abilities. Nor can he have failed to reflect that before him stretched the prospect of indefinite demands on both his moral and financial support. And so that powerful persuasiveness, which had earlier been directed towards encouraging Tkachenko's literary activities, was now applied to edge him towards a second objective. 'Since it is only very recently that you have begun to take your literary talent seriously, and since it will still be a long time before, through your own efforts, you will make up for the inadequacies in your schooling and become a mature writer, you will need to live for several years, despite having a firmly projected aim, without a definite position and, above all, without those *responsibilities* whose fulfilment completes [and] adorns our life,' Tchaikovsky wrote on 20 November. 'What you do need is occupations such as would interest you and make your life useful in the near future before you become a serious writer, while not distracting you from your main aim. And do you know what occupation I find completely suitable for your temperament? *The occupation of a village schoolteacher!* No, in my view there is no more honourable, more *holy* service to society than service as a village schoolteacher.'[12]

How Tkachenko really reacted to this sudden proposal we do not know for certain. He wrote one more hasty letter to Tchaikovsky, then a silence descended. 'How are you? Where are you? Let me know what

[12] *TLP*11, p. 276; *TZC*2, pp. 559–60.

you are up to. It's already more than two months since I had word from you,' Tchaikovsky wrote urgently from Paris on 26 January 1883.[13] But no reply came. It must be assumed that Tkachenko perceived in this new proposal a hidden verdict on his gifts as an author. Certainly that confidence which Tchaikovsky had enabled him to discover within himself had crumpled, and the relationship was to collapse as suddenly as it had arisen. The editors of the complete edition of Tchaikovsky's correspondence state that Tkachenko did indeed become a village schoolteacher with Tchaikovsky's help. But Modest, who must surely have known whether anything further passed between the two men, states that after this his brother's protégé soon vanished for ever. The final act of the relationship was told to Modest in the letter of 1 October 1883 from Verbovka. Everything ended almost as it had begun, except that, by now, Tchaikovsky's view of this strange bird of passage had once again suffered a harsh revision. His last words say it all.

When I arrived here I found awaiting me a parcel from *Tkachenko* who is in Poltava. On being opened it proved to be all my *letters* to him. Because the first time he wanted to kill himself he'd sent me my two letters, I understood this time he was, as it were, informing me of his impending suicide. Nevertheless, it was only for the first instant that I was a little worried; afterwards I somehow decided my Tkachenko was almost certainly alive. And, indeed, today I receive a request from him to send money, with no mention of my letters. His letter is, as always, ironical in tone. A pathetic, but rather unsympathetic person![14]

'The other day I was very touched by the ovation I was given at the Fisher High School for girls,' Tchaikovsky wrote to Nadezhda von Meck on 2 January 1884, a month after his arrival in Moscow to hear his First Symphony for the second time. 'The head of that institution had already several times written to me letters expressing ardent sympathy towards my music. Now she persuaded me to accept an invitation to a musical evening at the school, and the other day I went. I was met by *Miss Fisher*, surrounded by the mistresses and boarders. After this, choral performances of a whole series of my works began. These girls sang delightfully, and though I found it somewhat uncongenial to be the subject of general attention, I could not but be

---

[13] *TLP*12, p. 31.
[14] *TLP*12, p. 237; *TZC*2, p. 604.

touched by the unusually fervent sympathy which those present displayed towards me throughout the whole evening.'[15] Tchaikovsky was now becoming increasingly aware of the price of growing fame. The modesty of this occasion made such attentions easier to face than some he received at the more prestigious events, like the ovation on 1 December for his First Symphony ('both pleasant and flattering, but at the same time excruciatingly painful'[16]), or the prospect he faced on the first night of *Mazepa*. Being famous also made appalling demands on his time. Every would-be composer, however untalented (and most of them were), wanted to show him his work ('without exaggeration . . . not less than two or three each day,' he lamented to his patroness[17]). Not that this ever deterred him from exerting himself on behalf of the truly gifted, such as Arensky, whose abundantly inventive First Symphony had just received its première in Moscow under Erdmannsdörfer; Tchaikovsky interceded with Balakirev in the hope that it might be repeated in St Petersburg at a concert of the Free Music School, of which Balakirev had resumed direction in 1881.

But distractions of all kinds were the more difficult to avoid during these first weeks in Moscow because he could not plead that daily professional commitments were claiming his time. All the promises from Moscow and St Petersburg that *Mazepa* would be mounted before the end of 1883 had shown themselves to be worthless. Hardly had he arrived in Moscow than he was protesting to Vsevolozhsky about the delay, observing that if he had been forewarned he could have organized his winter differently. A flying visit to St Petersburg in mid-December to see Modest at least confirmed that, since he had to kill time, Moscow was the place to do it. He was staying at the same hotel as Laroche, whose indolence had become so extreme that Tchaikovsky decided he must act. 'I proposed that I should come to him each day for a couple of hours so that he could dictate to me an article for *The Russian Messenger*,' he told Nadezhda von Meck. 'This so flattered and touched him that half a big article, which you will probably read in the next number of *The Russian Messenger*, is already prepared and gone to the printers. . . . He needs *a nurse*; I've taken this role upon myself, because I have no business on my hands.'[18]

At the New Year this state of enforced inertia was at last broken. With the Russian Christmas Modest arrived for a fortnight, and both brothers were in St Petersburg for the wedding of Anna and Nikolay

[15] *TLP*12, p. 289; *TPM*3, p. 242; *TZC*2, p. 614.
[16] *TLP*12, p. 282; *TPM*3, p. 236; *TZC*2, p. 611; *YDGC*, p. 302.
[17] *TLP*12, p. 290; *TPM*3, p. 245.
[18] *TLP*12, pp. 288–9; *TPM*3, pp. 241–2; *TZC*2, pp. 613–14.

von Meck on 23 January. Needless to say, since Tchaikovsky was to be present, the bridegroom's mother did not return from Cannes for the event, but three of her daughters did appear and, as their mother had requested, Tchaikovsky recorded his frank and (predictably) favourable impressions of them. The première of *Mazepa* was now scheduled for 8 February. As noted earlier, Tchaikovsky committed the musical destiny of the St Petersburg production entirely into Nápravník's experienced hands, and devoted his personal energies to the Moscow preparations. He had predicted correctly that *Mazepa* would be yet again postponed, but on 15 February the opera was finally presented. His precipitate departure for the West the next day occasioned not only comment from the Tsar when the composer failed to appear at the first night of *Mazepa* in St Petersburg three days later; it also wounded Erdmannsdörfer that Tchaikovsky was not present to excite yet further the enthusiasm with which the Second Suite was greeted at its première, which was taking place at the moment the truant's train was pulling out of Moscow. To make his peace with this conductor he was to offer him the dedication of his next work, the Third Suite.

But for the moment Tchaikovsky's only concern was to put out of his mind everything connected with the strains and harassments of the last weeks. Pausing for two days in Berlin because his overwrought state had made it difficult to decide where to head next, he opted for Paris, and on 21 February settled himself into the same hotel room in which he had lived for five months in the previous year. His prime feeling was loneliness. Alexey had been unable to accompany him, for he had soon to return to the army, and Tchaikovsky confessed himself grateful even for Tanya's presence. He found her and Elizaveta comfortably installed, and noted with resignation that his niece had relapsed into her customary idleness. The Parisian theatre claimed him a few times, though apart from the Comédie-Française performing Molière's *Le Malade imaginaire* and *L'Ecole des femmes*, he seems to have found the plays on offer boring. The main experience of this three-week residence was offered by Massenet's *Manon Lescaut*, which had received its première a month earlier. He did not like it. 'I had expected something more. Very elegant, very individual, but not for one moment capable of touching, captivating, or arresting. . . . Because he [Massenet] cannot bear *dialogues*, everywhere conversation is going on he has fully developed music, and this never lets up for one moment, so that it actually becomes tiresome,' he told Modest.[19] Nor could he again avoid comparing the Parisian presentation ('*superb* performance . . . What a

[19] *TLP*12, pp. 317–18; *TPM*3, p. 626 (partial); *TZC*2, p. 625; *TPB*, p. 304.

production, what a superb musical performance!'[20]) with those his own operas customarily received in Russia. His main concern in France was to visit Georges-Léon. He went twice, giving no warning of his arrival the first time, and he left confident the child was being well cared for. Only two things really troubled him. First, the boy reminded him more of Blumenfeld than of his niece; second, what was to be Georges-Léon's future? 'How am I to place him in Russia? What name will he bear?' he wondered to Modest.[21] Whatever the answers, he knew *he* would have to find them.

Tchaikovsky had intended after Paris to proceed to Rome, where Anna and Nikolay were on honeymoon and had asked him to visit them. He had also been attracted by the idea of returning to Kamenka by boat from Naples to Odessa. But a decline in Tanya's health and an acute shortage of funds decided him he must stay in Paris. *Manon Lescaut* was already an enormous success and its press had been excellent; now Tchaikovsky received tidings about *Mazepa* which showed that Modest's favourable reports had been less than truthful. Yet he remained grateful that his brother had tried to spare him.

> You did well to lie, for indeed *the truth* might have killed me. . . . Only yesterday did I learn the facts from a letter of Jurgenson, who had the brutality not only to tell me the truth outright, but *to reproach* me for not going to St Petersburg. I don't know how I got through yesterday. It acted upon me like a crushing blow, and all day I suffered as terribly as though some colossal, irreparable misfortune had occurred. Of course this is my eternal [tendency to] exaggeration, but indeed at my age, in my position, when it is already difficult to have hope for the future, every even *relative* failure assumes the dimensions of a shameful fiasco.

'And,' he added bitterly – and uncomfortably, 'what is most galling of all is that, if I had been other than what I am and had upped and gone to St Petersburg, I would probably have left crowned with laurels.'[22]

Meanwhile the constant demands on his time which quickly built up from his acquaintances in Paris consolidated the yearning for a place of his own. Nadezhda von Meck had recently purchased a château at Belair in Touraine, and had invited him to spend some time there, but he had declined. His patroness was only one of the persons to whom, while he was in Paris, he confided this ever-strengthening wish.

[20] *TLP*12, p. 316; *TPM*3, p. 258.
[21] *TLP*12, p. 318.
[22] *TLP*12, p. 322; *TPM*3, p. 627; *TZC*2, p. 626; *TPB*, pp. 304–5.

'Nomadic life is beginning to weigh heavily on me. Whether this [home] will be somewhere on the outskirts of Moscow or somewhere a little farther away and a little more isolated I do not yet know. Thousands of plans crowd into my head – but, one way or another, I must finally have a place of my own.'[23] His immediate intention had been to return straight to Sasha's family circle, but a letter from Nápravník now told him of the Tsar's surprise at his truancy, and of his wish to see the composer. Tchaikovsky realized there was no escaping a visit to the Russian capital; to have stayed away would have been even more impolitic, since the Tsar had readily agreed to Nápravník's request to produce *Eugene Onegin* next season, declaring it to be his favourite opera. Because Anna and Nikolay were expected imminently from Italy, Tchaikovsky felt they could take over supervision of Tanya. On 12 March he left Paris, not knowing that the Tsar had decreed that the Order of St Vladimir (fourth class) should be conferred on him.

The investiture took place in the palace at Gatchina, just outside St Petersburg, on 19 March, four days after Tchaikovsky reached the Russian capital, where he learned that the Empress also wished to see him, and that there would be two audiences. She received him first, but though he had already sedated himself with a liberal quantity of bromide, his nerve nearly failed him, and at the very door he gulped down another dose lest he should fall senseless before his sovereign's consort. The kindly attentiveness with which he was treated soothed him, and by the second audience he was more self-possessed, though it was several days before his nerves returned to normal. This meeting certainly confirmed for Alexandr one subject's lifelong loyalty. 'I think that the man who has but once in his life had occasion to see the Tsar close to will be for ever his fervent admirer, for it is impossible to describe how charmingly attractive is his manner and whole way of behaving,' Tchaikovsky told Anatoly.[24] He summarized the especially pleasurable side of the occasion for Nadezhda von Meck. 'I was touched to the depths of my soul by the sympathy which the Tsar showed towards me. . . . [He] talked with me for a very long time, repeating several times that he loved my music very much, and altogether showed me an abundance of kindness.'[25]

This event was of profound importance to Tchaikovsky, not so much for the award itself as for what it signified. Though probably few others saw it as such, for the composer himself it was the visible symbol of full rehabilitation. The stigma which he felt had marked him in the eyes of

[23] *TLP*12, pp. 330–1; *TPM*3, p. 261; *YDGC*, p. 311 (partial).
[24] *TLP*12, p. 335; *TZC*2, pp. 629–30.
[25] *TLP*12, p. 334; *TPM*3, p. 263.

society ever since the scandal of his marriage nearly seven years before was now erased – or, at least, masked – by this public honour from the father of the Russian people. The people themselves might never forget, but at least they would now forgive. It was clearly much time before the full import of this awesome occasion sank in; what Tchaikovsky did immediately perceive, as he reflected on the Tsar's words and on what he could observe in St Petersburg itself, was that, despite Jurgenson's letter and the adverse press, *Mazepa* was no more an initial failure with the public than with their monarch. It was in a buoyant mood that he arrived in Moscow on 31 March.

Here he first devoted much time to making substantial revisions to *Mazepa*. This done, he once again took Laroche in hand, for a second time acting as amanuensis. By now he feared that his friend's oblomov-shchina might force the Conservatoire to dismiss him, for though Laroche had begun the session conscientiously enough, he was now giving no classes. Tchaikovsky's main pleasures were found in Anatoly and his family, and in a Conservatoire performance of *Die Zauberflöte*, with which his acquaintance had been but sketchy, but which now took its place alongside *Figaro* – though a little lower than *Don Giovanni* – as one of his favourite operas. At a supper afterwards Arensky had proposed a toast to him, to which all had enthusiastically responded. He also had a chance at a grand musical soirée at Pavel Tretyakov's to assess the progress of his former student, the twenty-year-old pianist Alexandr Ziloti, who was to become a significant figure in Tchaikovsky's later years. He would have left Moscow sooner, but illness forced a delay, as did his personal endeavours to finalize the arrangements which others had successfully begun on his behalf to free Alexey from the remainder of his military service; he also wished to benefit from the abundance of Easter-tide services being celebrated, sometimes very splendidly, in the churches and cathedrals of Moscow. His three-week stay strengthened his longing for a home of his own to such a degree that for the first time he began inspecting possible properties. His searches were fruitless, but he left instructions with Anatoly to watch for anything which might be suitable near Moscow. Having mistakenly bought a ticket which took him via Kharkov instead of Kiev, he arrived in the city to discover that *Onegin* was being performed that evening. He would dearly have liked to see the performance, for he could have attended incognito, but he had already notified Lev that he would be in Kamenka on the 24th. On that day he began a new diary.

KAMENKA DIARY

Next to his letters, Tchaikovsky's personal diaries are the most important source of information on his outer biography and inner world.

According to Modest, his brother had kept a regular succession of daily diaries from the end of the 1870s to the end of the 1880s (and intermittently after this), but two years before his death had burned the greater number of these. This Kamenka diary was therefore only one from a whole mass of such notebooks of which ten have survived, though one of these perhaps hardly qualifies as a diary since it contains no information on day-to-day affairs, but was a receptacle for Tchaikovsky's views on creative individuals and matters of life, set down in a series of widely spaced entries between 1886 and 1888. Seven of the others relate to the period 1886–91; three are consecutive, covering a twenty-month period from February 1886 to October 1887. Of the remaining six, the longest runs for nearly six months, the shortest for five weeks. The scrappiest is the first, which contains some twenty-five irregular entries made between 23 June and 30 July 1873, from when Tchaikovsky left Russia for a trip through Germany and Switzerland to his arrival in Italy.

The one he was now beginning was to contain fifty-nine consecutive daily entries covering his entire stay at Kamenka. It differs from his first not only in its continuity, but in its content. The 1873 diary had been a record of external events – of places visited or traversed, persons whom Tchaikovsky encountered, trivia of his daily existence. It tells us a little about creative schemes which occurred to him during these weeks, and a good deal about his immediate reactions to the various situations he met, but apart from single entries on his love for his native Russia and on his yearning for solitude, it reveals nothing of his deeper desires and responses. The 1884 diary, on the other hand, exposes to us the pattern of his daily life, his work practices and his recreations amid a group of people with whom he shared the closest ties of family relationship or simple friendship. It records his emotional responses to the passing events and encounters of each day – responses all too often more violent than was warranted, as he himself frequently admitted. But it does much more. Letters, even when the recipient was as intimate and trusted as Modest or his patroness, were for the eyes of others; a diary, being a private repository, could harbour a degree of frankness which no letter could, and this Kamenka diary became a place of confession for the most private of feelings and most personal of secrets in a way that that of 1873 did not. This is what makes it so precious. The intimate letters written in the days after his marriage had mostly indicated what

Tchaikovsky's sexual nature was *not*; this Kamenka diary points to its positive characteristics, for there can be little doubt that the symbols X and Z which recur in it, and about which he writes so openly, denote homosexual drives. Most clearly of all, it vividly records an early stage of what was to be the central sexual attraction of his remaining years: his passion for his nephew, Bob.

Because of the unique insights afforded by this 1884 diary, there follows extensive quotation from it even though, apart from the composition of the Third Suite, the actual events of this two-month period at Kamenka were of no greater importance in themselves than were, for instance, the details of Tchaikovsky's relationship with Tkachenko. It is fortunate that, when these diaries were printed in 1923, they were overseen not by Modest, who had died seven years earlier, but by Ippolit, who was far less squeamish about those elements in his brother's personality which might be considered disfiguring or diminishing. In the following transcription[26] only four entries are given in full (the first, last, and those of 8 and 31 May); about one-third of the total text is reproduced. Because the entries use abbreviations liberally, the following pages would become irritatingly dense with square brackets if every editorial amplification was thus noted. Square brackets are therefore reserved for clarifications of the text, or for where significant matters have been incorporated to fill out the diary's record of these two months.

24 April.
Slept right up to Fundukleyevka. A sharp, cold wind. No one met me, but when I arrived [at Kamenka] I found Levushka was up. Chat, tea (I am in a mad-passion-for-tea phase). Letters. Visit to the old ladies [Lev's mother and her unmarried daughters, Alexandra and Elizaveta]. At the big house a most heartfelt meeting. How nice they are! Sat there a long time. Letters from Tasya [Tchaikovsky's niece, Nataliya]. Lev arrived. With him I visited Nikolay Vasilyevich [Lev's elder brother]. There I saw dear Varya [Nikolay's daughter], who's gone thin, and Axel [Samberg]. Dinner for three: Lev, Sister [the family nickname for Anastasiya Popova] and I. Sister's incredible stories and complaints about Pelageya Osipovna [the Kamenka music teacher] during and after dinner. Walk to *Dubkovyar*. Violets. Cold. At home tea, letters to Modya, Tolya, Nadezhda Filaretovna, Jurgenson, Kondratyev. Supper for two with Lev. Flegont [the Kamenka tutor] arrived, and we played four rubbers of buy-vint. A cold north wind is howling outside.

---

[26] *TD*, pp. 11–29. There are twenty-one extracts from it, mostly very brief, in *TZC*2, pp. 634–45, and numerous even more fragmented ones, in *YDGC* and *TPM*3, pp. 628–9.

25 April.
Got up late. Still cold. After drinking tea, went to Lev who soon left, and I stayed to strum and think up something new. I hit on an idea for a *Concerto* for *piano*, but it turned out too wretched and wasn't new. Walked a little in the garden. Dinner for two: Sister's ill. Played Massenet's *Hérodiade*. Strolled for a bit . . . Drank tea at home . . . Read *Otto Jahn* [on Mozart] . . . After supper real vint. . . .

26 April.
Again got up late. Visit to Father Alexandr [Tarnavich, the Kamenka priest] . . . Sister was at dinner. . . . A terrible, incredible north-east wind continues to blow, but I heroically knocked off my obligatory walk . . . At home wrote letters . . . Read Lopukhin's memoirs. After supper vint for three . . . Terribly unlucky. Continue to do nothing and haven't the slightest inspiration.

27 April. Sunday.
The weather's improved a bit, but it was still with difficulty I completed my morning walk . . . Lunch at home . . . Read English, warmed myself by the fire . . . Dinner at the big house. For some reason it was tedious and heavy going . . . The Englishman frightened me with his proposal for [English] lessons. Vint at home . . . I won. Didn't get to mass today. . . .

28 April.
Rose at 9. The weather's clear . . . Spent all the time until dinner in the Trostyanka woods, gathering violets and deriving deep enjoyment . . . Tried to lay the foundations of a new symphony both in the Trostyanka woods and at home after dinner, but I'm dissatisfied with everything . . . Walked in the garden and conceived *the seed* not of a future symphony, but of a suite . . . Vint for three . . . My bad luck was colossal.

29 April.
In the morning, despite the cruelly cold wind, I went to the Trostyanka woods where I found comparative peace. Noted down some ideas. Dinner for two. Made music. English language. Vint for four . . . I had very bad luck.

30 April.
Trostyanka woods again, and noting down some wretched ideas . . . Visit to the big house . . . After tea English language. A walk to the mills . . . At dinner Nikolay Vasilyevich, Roman Efimovich [Derichenko, the Kamenka doctor] and Flegont. Vint. Lev's departure for Elizavetgrad [now Kirovograd].

1 May.
Woke up off colour . . . Completed a walk . . . Drank tea, played the piano a long time (unprofitably), dined at the big house . . . Read, drank tea, and played vint . . . Very dissatisfied with myself because of the banality of everything that comes into my head. Am I played out? . . .

2 May.

Wonderful weather. All morning in the Trostyanka woods . . . Read English after lunch . . . played the piano and jotted down something in my notebook . . . After dinner conversation about Schopenhauer, Tolstoy, and so on. I'm getting more and more stupid. As soon as there's serious conversation, my head's completely empty . . . Vint for two with Flegont. I lost . . .

3 May.

. . . Walked . . . Lev got back from Elizavetgrad at 7 a.m. and slept till 12 . . . Dined with Lev . . . Worked on English language, and in no time had to go and dine for a second time at the big house . . . Vint for four in the evening . . . Nikolay Vasilyevich came and frayed my nerves terribly with his gossip.

4 May.

. . . Went to the station to meet our people . . . A joyful meeting. Bob . . . Read for a long time . . . Collected *signatures* at home to send to Modya for his birthday . . . Vint for five. My luck was bad and I got terribly cross. Have just read the first Book of Kings.

5 May.

. . . Walked a distance in the field by the Trostyanka woods . . . Dinner with guests . . . Went to the big house . . . Sasha recounted the court news . . . Tea at home, a walk with no enjoyment . . . Two lots of vint. A lot of Z. Ah, what a depraved person I am!

6 May.

11 o'clock. Soon I'll be 44. How long have I lived and, in truth, without false modesty, how little have I done! Even in my regular occupation – for, putting my hand on my heart, there is nothing *perfect, exemplary*. Still I'm searching, wavering, unsteady. And for the rest? I read nothing [significant], I know nothing. Only on vint do I expend an abundance of precious time. But I believe *my health* will *come to no good* from it. Today I was so cross, so irritated, that I believe another moment, and I would have thrown an ugly scene of anger and hatred. My temper today is generally very bad, and my period of calm, quiet life, untroubled by anything, has passed. There's a lot of fuss, a lot of jars, a lot which a madman of my years cannot bear with indifference. No! it is time to live *in my own home* and *in my own way*.

[In his letters Tchaikovsky makes it clear that the return of Sasha and others two days earlier, and the ensuing extra bustle and fuss at Kamenka, accounted for this surge of feeling.]

The whole morning was spent on a pleasant walk . . . I'd hardly managed to get in my evening walk (to the mills) than I was summoned to supper – this is a new arrangement. I suffered from hunger and from *lack of attention* towards me. It's petty – but why hide that even such a trifle can anger me. Then vint and endless anger . . . The Elizavetgrad piano turned out to be a false trail: I'm without a piano [of my own]. I sent Alyosha with Vasily to look for one – as though there was any hope! All day Bob has rejoiced my eyes; how incomparably lovable he is in his white suit . . .

7 May.
Alyosha congratulated me with great affection . . . A very long walk . . .
Judging from yesterday I thought everyone had forgotten my birthday, but I
was wrong. I was congratulated, and we drank champagne . . . Tea at home
. . . English language. Went to the big house . . . A piano from *Mr. Druzhin* . . .
Vint. Irritability, but less than yesterday. . . .

8 May.
I'm a sort of walking malice! Because Sasha enjoyed getting me into difficulties
at cards I was the more enraged because, out of magnanimity in view of her
bad luck in the game today, I had only just previously let her have the bid in
clubs (there were three of us playing). How do you like that? Are these the
feelings of an artist who enjoys fame? Ugh! Pyotr Ilich, it's shameful, my good
fellow! But then, since morning I've not been myself. The abominable state of
my stomach is beginning seriously to poison my life. During the morning
worked with the maximum effort (the scherzo). At dinner I was again in a
rather bad mood. Walked to the Nikolayev field. It was damp, windy and
overcast – but in the end it didn't rain. Drank tea in my room. Afterwards
wrote a bit more. Bob walked about the garden with me, then came to my
room. Ah, what a delight this Bob is! After supper (I was out of temper) vint for
three. Ugh! What a life!

9 May.
. . . After a short walk worked all morning; it was now going better. Was angry
at dinner because of the extreme chaos reigning in the household's arrangements . . . At home drank tea in company (Vera Vasilyevna [Butakova, Lev's
sister]); sat at my window and chatted with Nata [Pleskaya, Lev's cousin]
and Bob (. . . Ah, what a perfect being this Bob is!). . . .

10 May.
This vint for three so irritates me, I'm beginning to fear it will affect my health
. . . But I haven't the strength to give up the game. Meanwhile today has been
exceedingly successful – in the first place, because my work has gone excellently: secondly, because my stomach is in order . . . In the morning strolled in
the garden with Bob (what a darling he is!) . . . *At teatime Sasha was eating her
dinner* . . . It's very nice when they speak English at dinner. I'm beginning to
understand – but Sister always butts in at the most interesting place. Worked
after tea. Went to church for Vespers with Sasha . . . After supper there was
. . . vint . . . Wrote to the directorate regarding *The Oprichnik.*
   [A proposal put to the Imperial Theatres to revive Tchaikovsky's early
opera was firmly resisted by the composer, who loathed the piece. He was able
to thwart the current plans by pleading that he would need first to revise the
work; he confided to Jurgenson, however, that he had no intention whatsoever
of undertaking this operation.]

11 May.
. . . Finished the scherzo. After dinner (Pelageya Osipovna) walked . . . There
was no game. . . .

12 May.
Why do I play vint? The only result is upset and bad temper . . . As regards the weather, an abominable day. Spent all day writing the waltz for the suite, but I'm far from certain it's completely satisfactory. After dinner . . . forced myself to take a walk . . . to the Trostyanka woods.

13 May.
. . . Continued the waltz . . . Fearing the wind, walked about my room for an hour . . . After supper (before which, to his great joy, I played duets with my darling, the incomparable, wonderful, ideal Bob) played vint . . . In the breaks between rubbers, I visited my angel Bob . . . Played vint till 1 a.m. . . .

14 May.
Walked the whole morning . . . The waltz came along with enormous difficulty. No, I'm growing old. After dinner sat in the drawing-room . . . Laboured on the waltz until nearly 7 o'clock, but got nowhere. Walked in the garden . . . After supper vint for four. A miracle – I won! . . .

15 May.
. . . After strolling in the garden a little . . . finished the sketch of the waltz . . . The communal outing didn't take place. Lev went off with Bob. I wandered about the vegetable garden and my room . . . Worked on English diligently. Lev and Bob were away a long time – and, in fact, I got worried . . . We were late sitting down to vint. . . .

16 May.
I decided in the morning . . . to walk to Zrubanets for lilies of the valley . . . Having, with the greatest composure of spirit, sat down to play Mozart's *Zauberflöte* I was, in the middle of the most exquisite pleasure, interrupted by the entrance of *Bob*, with a horrified expression, to tell me of the death of Tusya Bazilevskaya [the daughter of Lev's niece, Sasha (née Peresleny)]. Great sorrow . . . Wrote letters till teatime, then worked . . . After supper . . . I first wandered about aimlessly . . . At last, after all, our vint took place. I am very weary. Darling Tusya! Ah, the poor things, the poor things! And why? But God's will be done!

17 May.
. . . In the morning took a short walk . . . Worked . . . After dinner wandered about with Bob . . . Until 7 o'clock struggled with one spot in the Andante. I was tired. Went to Vespers. Sad thoughts and tears because of Tusya. Was late for supper . . . Vint for two. . . .

18 May.
Wonderful weather . . . Went to mass. Was very susceptible to religious impressions; stood nearly all the time with tears in my eyes. I'm always touched to the depths of my soul by the manifestation of simple, wholesome religious feeling in the common people . . . Was at the big house . . . Went to the market with Bob. Worked very successfully . . . Strolled to the mills at

sunset. After supper played dances for the children . . . No vint at all. I confess vint is almost a necessity for me – it's really disgraceful.

19 May.
A wonderful summer day. It tempted me to walk the whole morning . . . Only managed to work a little . . . Picked lilies of the valley with Bob, drank tea, revelled in the wonderful evening . . . Vint for four. When I was winning I was embarrassed and tried to lose; when my luck changed I was angry. . . .

20 May.
. . . Worked all morning – not without effort, but my Andante is coming along and I think it will come out very nicely. After dinner . . . walked . . . Drank tea with Sasha and Nata. Tragic details of Tusya's death received – so painful, they make you weep. Worked till 7 o'clock . . . English language . . . After supper . . . a fairly quiet game of vint. I was less out-of-temper than usual.

21 May.
Put on my new clothes. Went to church . . . Called in at the big house . . . Worked and finished the Andante, with which I'm very satisfied. Bob's ill. Immediately after dinner . . . a pleasant stroll . . . Bob's well. Supper, Flegont was late. Vint. . . .

22 May.
. . . Slept excellently . . . Strolled all morning . . . After dinner sat in the drawing room, then worked a little . . . After supper vint, at which Flegont and I won. . . .

23 May.
Again cold and windy . . . The first movement of the suite, called *Contrastes*, with the themes –

[Ex. 196]

– is so loathsome to me that, having played about with it all day, I decided to discard it and write something completely different . . . How hard has work become for me! Is it old age at last? . . . English language . . . After supper (by oil lamp) vint . . . In the morning received news from Pachulski about the unsuccessful performance of the [Italian] Capriccio in Paris.

24 May.
At 9 o'clock went for a walk . . . Played Mozart. After tea was on the point of struggling *again* with the loathsome *Contrastes*, but suddenly a new idea flashed into my head, and the matter sorted itself out . . . Bob (in the end he will simply drive me out of my mind with his unspeakable fascination) . . . Was terribly

angry during vint, but not on account of the cards but just generally because of something indefinable which might be called Z. Yes, this Z is less tormenting . . . than X – but all the same, it's unpleasant.

25 May. Sunday.
. . . Mass finished early, and for a long while I didn't know what to do with myself. Finally went to Alexandra Ivanovna [Lev's mother] and sat with her and Sister in the drawing-room. Worked. After dinner sat in my workroom with Bob . . . After tea composed a bit . . . Played [vint] with moderate luck . . . Today Z is especially tormenting me. May God forgive me such foul feelings! . . .

26 May.
. . . During the morning I walked a long time about the garden. Worked successfully until dinner. After dinner read Krïlov with Bob . . . Was at Sister's (at her invitation). She was upset that they're sending her to Verbovka [to make room for Nikolay and Anna and other expected guests], and wanted to go to a monastery. During the morning Sasha came to me to talk about this. At first (in the morning) I wasn't sympathetic towards Sister, but after visiting her I understood her feelings very well . . . Vint. I was incredibly irritable and angry, but not about the game, but because Z was tormenting me, which was the more annoying, seeing that during the morning it had subsided.

27 May.
. . . Strolled in the garden. Composed the final variation (the polonaise-finale). After dinner walked . . . Worked again after tea . . . After supper there was vint . . . As usual I was angry – at what I don't know – but most of all at Nikolay Vasilyevich who was talking loudly about this and that, and how he'd got his feet wet. . . .

28 May.
Walked in the garden in the morning . . . Wrote right up to dinner. Dined en petit-comité; Sister has gone off to a monastery . . . After tea again worked . . . Sat for a long time with Bob and Flegont on a bench in the conservatory . . . Worked at English. My successes in understanding what I read are significant, but I still don't understand anything when Miss Eastwood is talking . . . Vint . . . I won.

29 May. Ascension Day.
. . . Sat down to work without taking a walk and wrote until 12 o'clock. Walked with great pleasure . . . Dined at the big house . . . Tea for two with Nata. Worked with great effort . . . Played Mozart and was in ecstasy. Idea for a suite from Mozart . . . I declined to play vint. . . .

30 May.
I am working too hard, as though I'm being driven on. This straining is unhealthy, and it will probably show in the poor suite. In the morning (the weather was marvellous) I walked . . . Worked very successfully (the

variations before the finale). After this sat with Bob on the roof (I'd only climb up there for this angel!) . . . After this drank tea . . . and then worked furiously so as to be able to begin something new tomorrow. Sister's come back from the monastery. Dropped in on her before supper . . . Vint. I was very "tired and played withaut [Sic!] great pleasure" [Tchaikovsky wrote these words in English]. I lost.

31 May.
Tasya's sixteenth birthday was celebrated. Tolerable weather. In the morning I wrote a variation. Dinner was special, with champagne. Walked to the Trostyanka woods. Drank tea in my own room. Wrote letters. With Bob (the darling!) walked to the cliffs; there joined a boating party, and returned home with him. Dropped in at the conservatory with Bob and sat with Em. Fed. Played [my] children's songs to Bob. At Vespers. An evening with dancing: I was the pianist. Bob was amused beyond words that I played quadrilles on themes he gave me. At the end, when everyone had dispersed, Nata, who'd been very thoughtful, suddenly said to me: "Ah, Petichka, life isn't worth living!" Such words on the lips of so healthy and balanced a person as Nata made a very sad impression on me. In the course of the evening Vera Vasilyevna recalled the past – and apparently with regret. But all that she recalls is personally loathsome to me, and I wouldn't want any of it to return. [Seventeen years earlier, at Hapsal, Vera had been strongly attracted to Tchaikovsky, to his great embarrassment and distress.]

1 June. Sunday.
Was late for church . . . Afterwards walked to the big house . . . Was at Vera Vasilyevna's. Talked with her about Tanya. At home I managed to write a variation. After dinner a trip to Verbovka in the landau with Lev, Sasha and Bob . . . Vint after supper, at which I lost 7½ roubles. . . .

2 June.
. . . I worked well today, for I wrote a whole four variations. In the morning I only made a tour of the garden, and afterwards worked, finishing at 12.30 in expectation of Bob, who'd promised to come to learn singing, but who disappointed my expectations . . . Walked . . . Worked. Walked about vainly searching for Bob . . . Had supper (unusually tasty) at the Pleskys'. On returning home we played vint, and I won a little.

3 June.
Woke in the night because of a pain in my throat and nausea, and was off-colour all day, even though I worked well. Before dinner Bob came, and I played him my [children's] songs. After dinner got to the Trostyanka woods and back with the greatest effort. After tea was sitting down to work, but Bob lured me away . . . As soon as I'm not working or walking . . . I begin to long for Bob, and feel lonely without him. I love him terribly . . . A rehearsal. I accompanied Tasya's couplets. Unsympathetic performance, this. Vint with interruptions from Nikolay Vasilyevich. I won a lot.

4 June.

. . . Worked successfully . . . After dinner walked to the Trostyanka woods . . . *Finished the suite* . . . Wonderful evening . . . A rehearsal – *Les Femmes savantes*?!!? I was very nervy. Everything irritates me, and not without reason! The pain or, rather, the strange feeling in my throat . . . begins to worry me . . . Vint. I won. Despite this I was very out of spirits.

5 June.

A letter from Pachulski telling me of the sale of *Dvoryaninov* [an estate Tchaikovsky had considered buying]. Mixed feelings about this. Wrote a long letter to Nadezhda Filaretovna regarding my plans for purchasing an estate, which I have decided to set to one side. Walked to the big house, and talked a great deal with Vera Vasilyevna. Either I'm very mistaken, or she's not completely changed in her old feelings . . . After supper read Gogol with Bob – and dreams of producing *The Inspector-General* [by Gogol]. Tasya's perform-ance is cancelled. Vint. Nikolay Vasilyevich.

6 June.

All day I was worried and extremely irritated by the persistent *strange* feeling in my throat. Worked during the morning on arranging the variations for piano duet. Walked after dinner . . . Wrote, worked at English, and still worried about my throat . . . Played vint with difficulty . . . Was very tortured not by the actual feeling Z, but by the fact that it's in me. . . .

7 June.

Woke . . . out of spirits and worried about *my throat* . . . What is it? Probably nothing, but it doesn't make my nerves more easy . . . Because of my slight indisposition and the marvellous weather, didn't work, but went to the Trostyanka woods . . . Lunch was late . . . Sat on the balcony steps with Bob and Tasya, who combed my hair . . . Afterwards did a little work at home . . . Wrote two variations . . . It was very nice at Vespers . . . Bob hurt his knee . . . My anxiety. The doctor. Vint. Appalling luck.

8 June. Whitsunday.

Mass . . . After dinner *the feeling* began again . . . I managed to do some work . . . After supper dancing. Vint for five.

9 June.

. . . Completed a splendid walk . . . Did a little work. After supper vint. . . .

10 June.

In the morning took a long walk . . . First I worked at the transcription of the variations, then at selecting my piano pieces for a volume of *Ausgewählte Werke* which Pyotr Ivanovich [Jurgenson] is projecting . . . A trip in the *landau* to Prussy: Sasha, Nata, Tasya, Sister and I. It would have been very pleasant if it hadn't been for *the feeling* which had seemed to be going, but which had returned with renewed strength. . . .

11 June.
Since the morning *the feeling*. Completed a long walk . . . Worked on (1) the variations, (2) proof-reading Mozart [Jurgenson was publishing a vocal score with the translation Tchaikovsky had made in 1875 of the libretto of *Figaro*] . . . After dinner *the feeling* vanished suddenly and completely unexpectedly – but in the evening it returned again. After dinner the proofs. Got Bob ready for his ride on horseback . . . Walked to the mills . . . After supper vint for two with Flegont . . . *The feeling*.

12 June.
. . . In the morning managed to get in my two hours walking . . . Worked and finished *Figaro*. For two hours after dinner was inseparable from my wonderful, incomparable Bob; at first he lounged about on a bench on the balcony, and was enchantingly *relaxed* and chatted about my compositions (*Stone Moscow* [the coronation cantata]). Then he sat in my room and made me play. After tea I worked . . . All day *the feeling*. . . .

13 June.
Marvellous weather. A long walk . . . Wrote the transcription of the finale. After dinner *the feeling* began to pass. Trip to Verbovka . . . At supper heard that Blumenfeld had summoned Vladimir Andreyevich [Plesky, Nata's brother] for some reason. Terrible, insane alarm, especially when Lev instructed that he should be summoned. Could hardly play two rubbers.

14 June.
A walk . . . Wrote the transcription of the finale. After dinner dropped in at the big house . . . Tea at home (for two with Sister . . .) . . . Wrote letters and worked on English. Unsuccessful attempt to get to Vespers at the Pokrov church . . . After supper sat in my study with Bob and talked about school matters. Vint. No luck . . . There was a bit of *the feeling*. . . .

15 June. Sunday.
. . . A trip to the great wood for the whole day . . . Supper and vint with Kern at home. Terribly strong feeling Z. My God! Forgive and calm me! *The feeling* has passed completely . . . A strange thing: I'm *terribly* unwilling to leave here. I think it's because of Bob.

16 June.
Dreamed about M and consequently was all day a little – and even more than a little – in love . . . It's nothing, nothing! Silence!!! In the morning was in the Trostyanka woods . . . At tea, and during the whole day in general, poor Sister irritated me; I am not nearly as affectionate towards her as I ought to be . . . After supper lots of people came to say goodbye to Sasha [who was going to Carlsbad]. Vint. I did very badly. Because of this, and most of all for a thousand other reasons constituting what I call Z, I was as angry as a vicious snake. Arrived home under the distressing, heavy pressure of this Z.

17 June.
Awoke with a severe pain in my throat . . . Made myself go for a walk. Worked at home. After dinner the pain began to get worse . . . so that each time I swallowed it was hellish torture. The night was terribly agonizing.

18 June.
A little better towards morning, thanks to a heavy sweat. How much friendship and sympathy Alyosha shows on such occasions! . . . Slept nearly all day. . . Ate very little . . . All the same, I played vint, and made myself survive two rubbers. Slept intermittently that night. Heard Sasha leave.

19 June.
Stayed indoors all day . . . Much better . . . Dined in my room . . . had supper at the house. Vint with Flegont, Lev and Dima [Lev's nephew]. . . .

20 June.
Walked to the Trostyanka woods. After dinner was at the big house . . . A ride through the fields in a wagonette . . . After supper, vint. At 11 o'clock left for the station with a drunken Alyosha and intolerable, good-for-nothing Mitya. At 1 in Znamenka. . . .

21 June.
Slept a lot. At four in Kharkov. Because of the exhibition I stayed not at the Grand Hotel, but at the Metropole. Idled about. The cathedral. The singers. Dinner at the Grand Hotel, tea at home. With Alyosha in the Tivoli Gardens.

The creative energies whose operations were to produce the Third Suite had begun quietly to collect themselves almost immediately following Tchaikovsky's post-*Mazepa* flight from Russia in February 1884. After only a fortnight in Paris he was thinking of starting upon a symphony when he returned to Kamenka, and in St Petersburg, after his audience with the Tsar, these intentions consolidated themselves. But, as his Kamenka diary reveals, within four days of his arrival in the Ukraine he had abandoned the idea of a symphony in favour of a suite because, as he explained to his patroness on that day (28 April: see above, p. 22), it was the freedom which the latter form offered which attracted him to it. Satisfactory ideas were slow to form themselves, however, and it was a further eleven days before he had decided on its overall shape; it would consist of five movements, and the last would be a set of variations. The ensuing birth process has been recorded in the Kamenka diary, and Tchaikovsky's letters of these same weeks confirm the dogged persistence which was demanded of him; indeed, the intended first movement (*Contrastes*) so dissatisfied him that he scrapped it. But the final stages of composition seem to have gone more easily. Certainly he now had much more confidence in its worth, and after completing the sketches on 4 June he felt it might prove to be the best of the three he had now composed. His faith in it increased during scoring at Grankino. It was finished on 31 July, and first performed at an RMS concert in St Petersburg on 24 January 1885, conducted by Hans von Bülow.

Tchaikovsky had thought the suite might score a success. 'But reality far exceeded my expectations,' he wrote to his patroness six days later. 'I have never before experienced such a triumph. I saw that the entire mass of the audience was moved, and grateful to me. These moments are the finest adornment of the artist's life. Thanks to these it is worth living and labouring.'[27] Modest remembered that his brother had never been more rapturously applauded, even declaring it was the greatest public triumph yet achieved by a Russian symphonic work. Moscow also greeted it with enthusiasm a week later, though Modest reported that its reception here was not so ecstatic as in St Petersburg, attributing this to the fact that Erdmannsdörfer's advocacy was less electrifying than that of Bülow. In both cities the press was unanimously favourable; even Laroche roused himself from his lethargy to claim that some of Tchaikovsky's works of the last three or four years had moved the centre of the musical world from Germany or France to Russia, and that the music of Tchaikovsky was now the true music of the future. Yet this din of public tribute and chorus of praise from the press for this one work had a still sweeter import for Tchaikovsky himself. It was another palpable endorsement by a wider public of what the Tsar's award had already symbolized.

Laroche's judgement was, of course, absurdly wrong, but it is a useful reminder that what may now strike us as merely conventional may have sounded very fresh at the time of its creation. There had certainly been little deep investigation of new expressive territories in Tchaikovsky's recent music, but there had been inventiveness – or, at least, real conviction – in the handling of old expressive issues and forms. Even the fugues of the earlier suites, dull as they had been, were not stale. The Third Suite is most notable for its further exploration of melodic and orchestral possibilities exposed in its immediate predecessor, and for Tchaikovsky's return to the challenge of the large-scale variation form. These matters are of concern in the last three movements; what most commands admiration in the opening Andantino molto cantabile is the skill with which well-tried practices are adapted

[27] *TLP*13, p. 25; *TPM*3, p. 337; *TZC*3, p. 20; *DTC*, p. 405; *YDGC*, p. 335 (partial).

to provide support for a very extensive flow of simple melody. Though it scarcely sounds like it, this *Elégie* is a sonata structure sharing many features with *Romeo and Juliet*. Thus both subjects are large ternary slabs, and while the middle section of the first opens up further the preceding melodic world, the central portion of the E flat paragraph is a new melody which gives this secondary tonal area the thematic dualism of *Romeo*'s second subject. Elements of the two subjects, or natural extensions from their melodic worlds, are set against one another in the development; as in *Romeo* there is a reordering of events in the recapitulation, though this time it is not a switch within the second subject, but a reversal of both subjects, for as G major is re-established the second subject is heard first. Yet when the first subject emerges out of its predecessor, it returns at a point within its middle section, as had the first subject of *Romeo*. As for the extensive rumination for cor anglais in the coda, this takes its departure from the drooping cadential phrase of the first subject, just as the new chorale-like melody in the coda of the Fourth Symphony's first movement had grown, also by augmentation, out of a portion of the fate theme.

Yet there have been none of the tensions or contrasts of true sonata thought in this lyrical movement. As was noted during discussion of the 1875 songs, $\frac{6}{8}$ rarely drew the melodic best from Tchaikovsky, and the narrow bars of the present movement, despite their $\frac{2}{4}$ shifts, foster a rhythmic sameness in both main themes, neither of which (especially the second) has much distinction. They possess charm, but their unvaried fluency becomes bland, whereas the first theme of the following *Valse mélancolique* has such ingenious variety that the stiff rhythmic personalities of its companions in the episodes of this simple rondo become positive assets. In the presentation of both these subsidiary themes running counterpoints have a prominent part; in view of what transpires in the finale, there must be some suspicion that these were incorporated as features which would especially please the German dedicatee. But the initial 22-bar waltz theme (Ex. 197) was even more novel than its counterpart in the Second Suite (see Ex. 190), with the rhythmic fluctuations taking on a yet more fundamental role, conditioning the momentum of the whole tune. Thus the energy released in the opening bar is promptly curbed in a single note B, is restored within three bars and enhanced in the two-bar sequence which builds from a natural extension of the opening configuration; then at bar nine it is fully released into a broad phrase which drives on, then winds down, first to rediscover something of its opening profile, finally to expire in a delayed, long-held E. Like its opposite number in the Second Suite, the repetition of this opening strain takes a new course, and this time

Ex. 197

reaches its harmonic destination in the penultimate phrase, its final
four bars being merely a melodic postlude. A theme such as this, rather
than a more conventional invention like the famous horn tune of
the Fifth Symphony's Andante cantabile, emphasizes the rarity of
Tchaikovsky's melodic gift; if the dancers of the first *Swan Lake* found
the waltzes of that score bewildering, it is difficult to imagine what they
would have made of this one.

This 'obligatory waltz' cost Tchaikovsky much effort, so his diary
tells us, but it was labour well spent. By contrast the Scherzo seems to
have come more easily. It continued the special researches of its
predecessor, the *Scherzo burlesque*, in the spheres of texture and orchestration. The *Valse mélancolique* had especially explored the lower register
of the orchestra, but this Scherzo lives in an altogether brighter world.
The kaleidoscopic variety of colour of the *Scherzo burlesque* is here
displayed with even sharper contrasts, and the central section, with its
procession of piquant four-note phrases on trumpets and trombones,
punctuated with delicate flecks from alternating strings and woodwind
and the lightest of contributions from cymbals and snare drum, is one of
the most ear-enchanting mixtures Tchaikovsky had yet confected. The
incorporation of a pertly chattering phrase for oboes and bassoons
provides the neatest of rhythmic connections with the flanking sections.
Laroche saw in this music a lilliputian army, tiny elfin-soldiers on
parade. One may question Laroche's particular image (and one
certainly would the 'sense of sepulchral cold, of menacing, stony
hopelessness'[28] he had detected in the *Valse mélancolique*), but not his
instinct to discern in this brisk, spicy music suggestions of sprightly

[28] *TZC3*, p. 22.

miniature beings such as were, some seven years hence, to spring to life within the toy and tinsel world of *The Nutcracker*.

The theme and variations of this suite was only the fourth set in the official canon of Tchaikovsky's work; it also proved to be the last. His first, the twelve variations for piano, Op. 19, No. 6, of 1873, is an untidy set, handicapped by a theme of indifferent quality, a concern for enterprise in harmony and dissonance more ingenious than judicious, and textural turgidity. It foretold, however, Tchaikovsky's readiness to remodel, even rebuild his theme, a technique used more boldly in the vastly superior Rococo Variations, but with a control that ensured that the structural coherence and expressive focus of the whole was never impaired – that is, until Fitzenhagen laid his vandal's hands on it. In the finale of the Piano Trio the stylistic constraints of a rococo ideal had been absent, and Tchaikovsky had guaranteed the expressive gamut would be wide by laying a special emphasis on the character variation, as he was to do in this suite's finale, even though the theme of the latter could easily have fathered a second rococo set. As in the Trio there are twelve variations, some of which rigorously preserve, while others reject, the ternary structure of the theme. Similarly, there are numerous changes of metre and key, the one element always preserved being at least a portion of the theme's opening contour, even though the rhythm may be drastically restructured, additional notes may be inserted, or accidentals added to introduce a new key (Ex. 198).

Yet for all the variety of shape and character, and the thematic freedom of individual variations, this set's coherence is impressive for, unlike that of the Trio, it controls the range and pace of its expressive evolution, and it avoids the long-winded fugal labours and gargantuan sonata-patterned finale into which the heavy epicism of the earlier set had tempted Tchaikovsky. Nevertheless, it would appear from the evidence of the music itself that some of these variations, like those of the trio (if we are to believe Kashkin), were conditioned by the person of the dedicatee, and that the first four odd-numbered ones were kindly tributes to Erdmannsdörfer's nationality. Three are studiously contrapuntal; in variation 1, above the theme on pizzicato strings, flutes and clarinets paired in octaves weave unbroken florid counterpoints exactly as they had done in the first episode of the *Valse mélancolique*, while in variation 3, another cantus firmus study (scored only for three flutes, two clarinets and two bassoons), the tune is sustained against up to six supporting parts. Variation 5 is a fugato based on the theme's first four bars (Ex. 198c), the counterpoint having a studied gawkiness which ensures that the sort of thing which in the trio had sounded drily pedantic here sounds tongue-in-cheek, even mildly humorous. Variation

Ex. 198

7 converts the first three bars of the tune into the beginning of a four-line chorale. And if in the intervening variations Tchaikovsky has seemed intent on displaying a verve and capriciousness very much his own, there is in variation 4 a touch which cannot have been lost on Erdmannsdörfer when Tchaikovsky demonstrates impishly that he can surreptitiously turn his theme into the 'Dies irae'. But in the remaining five variations he is entirely himself. Indeed, after the Lutheran tones of variation 7, the theme fathers a plangent cor anglais cantilena, as Russian as could be (Ex. 198e), then for variation 9 generates a two-bar fragment which is repeated, *Kamarinskaya*-like, against a swift series of ever loudening backgrounds. After these variations-within-a-variation the sudden interruption of a violin cadenza signals a soloist's variation – a sort of hesitant waltz (Ex. 198f) which could easily have found a home in one of Tchaikovsky's ballets. The preceding two variations had raised the key a tone (to A minor and major respectively), and the move is repeated in variations 10 and 11, the latter moving back towards the original theme by restoring its rhythmic structure, though not its contours. The key is now B major, thus providing a neat balance to the opposite major third shift (G to E flat major) early in the first

movement. The unbroken tonic B pedal which has contributed so much to this variation's pervasive melancholy becomes finally a pivot upon which a series of G major chords can be swung into this B major context, thus forecasting the final return of the whole work's tonic. After portentous preliminaries G major is restored, and the polonaise-finale bursts in augustly, the opening pitches of the original theme now squeezed into a string of semiquavers which teasingly sounds like both an anacrusis and an opening bar (Ex. 198g). The disappointment in this sonorous finale is the theme of the second episode; otherwise this whole grand importation from the world of opera makes a colourful and bright end, neatly incorporating brief echoes from the scherzo's trio to remind us of but one of the delights that have gone before.

8

A HOME OF HIS OWN

'I WILL TELL you the details concerning my requirements. Land is quite unnecessary to me – i.e., I want only a modest house with a nice garden, *but established. A river* is certainly desirable. If there is a wood nearby, so much the better – but I mean, of course, a wood belonging to someone else – for, I repeat, I want to own only a modest house and garden. This dacha or cottage must be completely detached, and not in a row of other *dachas* and, most of all, it must be not far from a station so that *Moscow* is always at hand. . . . The most important and vital condition is that the location should be sympathetic, beautiful. If the house is situated somewhere low down so that there is no view from the windows, then it does not answer my requirements. A factory nearby is also very undesirable. That, I think, is everything.'[1] Thus, while at Kamenka, Tchaikovsky had set out the specifications for a home of his own so that his patroness could transmit them to Pachulski. This problem pupil had offered to help in the search, but he was only one of the agencies through which the composer had conducted enquiries during his early weeks at Sasha's. Though the disparity between his current resources and the price he would now have to pay brought a sudden sense of realism into his plans so that for the moment the project was shelved, within a year his hopes were to be realized.

After meeting Modest in Kharkov, Tchaikovsky headed for Grankino, where he planned to spend some time with his brother. The activity of the two months passed in the relatively uncongenial setting of Kamenka had wearied him, and in the peacefulness, fresh air and attractive living of the Konradi estate he found both rejuvenation and encouragement to work. Not only did he press ahead with scoring the Third Suite and further correcting the proofs of the vocal score of *Figaro* which contained his Russian version of da Ponte's libretto (an operation during which he decided that sometime he would perform the same translation service to *Don Giovanni*); he was soon making sketches

[1] *TLP*12, p. 372; *TPM*3, p. 279; *TZC*2, p. 643.

for a new piano concerto, a project which he quickly decided should be a two-movement concert piece instead. So contented was he that he delayed joining Anatoly and his family until after he had finished with the suite. The next day, 1 August, he left for Skabeyevo, where this brother had rented a villa and from which Moscow was easily accessible.

Skabeyevo he found yet more attractively situated than Podushkino, where he had passed the previous summer. It had been arranged that Laroche should share the villa, but this produced constant tensions. By now he was in an appalling condition, riddled with syphilis which Anatoly was in constant terror of contracting from him, and deteriorating intellectually, as even Tchaikovsky had to recognize. Once again he acted as scribe for this pathetic friend, but was dismayed at the 'empty-headed chatter'[2] about Mozart which he had to record, for he believed Laroche had once been without equal in Russia as a writer on music. Tchaikovsky's luggage containing the score of the suite and sketches for the new work for piano and orchestra had temporarily gone astray, but he would have been unable to work on it since the Skabeyevo villa owned no piano. Yet his equanimity held. Modest, who had been labouring on a new play at Grankino, was now in despair at his inability to find a satisfactory ending, and Tchaikovsky provided both moral support and a possible conclusion. And while bolstering Modest, he was also attempting to mollify Taneyev. The performance of *Die Zauberflöte* which Tchaikovsky had attended at the Conservatoire in April had been conducted by Karl Albrecht, even though it had been prepared by Taneyev – or so the latter claimed. Furious that Albrecht had plucked the glory from another's labours, Taneyev had turned to Tchaikovsky, who had gently reproached his former pupil for begrudging an older yet less publicly esteemed colleague a rare opportunity to gain some recognition. But Taneyev had remained unpersuaded by Tchaikovsky's balanced and sensitive words, and he now returned to the matter, provoking a substantial reply notable for its clear-headed perception of human character and relationships, and for its persuasive tact in both soothing yet chiding a badly ruffled friend. First he outlined the hard course of Albrecht's early professional career, then dwelt on his integrity, selflessness and conscientiousness, and ended by confronting squarely Taneyev's cause of offence, but with an evenhandedness which is both uncompromising yet disarming.

Even now the circumstance that you didn't conduct doesn't particularly trouble me. Let us suppose you had to do all the *menial work*. But

---

[2] *TLP*12, p. 411; *TZC*2, p. 652; *TPB*, pp. 313 and 601.

with your love of Mozart there cannot be any menial work when the matter concerns the performance of one of Mozart's best pieces. And most important: if Albrecht were a bad conductor, capable only of spoiling what you had prepared excellently, then I would very likely have been angry. But the point is that he directed the opera *superbly*. Whom, therefore, am I to pity? You, because you were deprived of the pleasure of conducting? But I cannot hide that I would have been even more sorry for Albrecht if, in his present position, being capable and worthy of occupying the conductor's rostrum, he had again for the thousandth time hidden in the shadow behind the scenes. Certainly I cannot deplore the fate of Mozart's opera, for though I don't doubt you would have conducted it superbly, Karlusha also conducted superbly.[3]

It was, of course, pure coincidence that Tchaikovsky should find himself in so short a time acting as nursemaid to Laroche and counsellor to both Modest and Taneyev. Yet the fact that he found such abundant reserves of wisdom and patient sympathy to deal so sensibly and amply with these three problem people is surely further confirmation of the increasing inner balance and confidence in himself which the Tsar's recognition and his ever-rising status in the public's eyes were fostering.

Tchaikovsky remained some six weeks at Skabeyevo. The new concert piece continued gently to form itself; his other musical activity was playing duets with Laroche, including items from Mozart's *Idomeneo*, Liszt's Faust Symphony and Borodin's *In Central Asia*. His reading again included Maupassant, in whose stories he found far more enjoyment than in Daudet's *Sapho*, where he suspected the author, under a pretence of offering a moral warning to his sons, of merely titillating French taste with a tale of debauchery. During one of two brief visits to Moscow he was introduced by Taneyev to his new Third Symphony, for which he admitted he could not feel much enthusiasm. The intention had been to return to Kamenka when Anatoly and his family left for the Crimea, but news came that Lev had journeyed to Paris to see Tanya and had brought her back to the family home. Since this would mean that no one would be on hand to guarantee Georges-Léon's continuing welfare, Tchaikovsky was quick to request Jurgenson to despatch a further 750 francs through a trusted agent in Paris to ensure that the child would remain secure until he himself could travel thither. Meanwhile, with Tanya present, Kamenka would be uncongenial, and since Anna and Nikolay were occupying

[3] *TLP*12, p. 407; *TZC*2, pp. 655–6; *TTP*, p. 111.

Tchaikovsky's own quarters there, he knew composition would be impracticable. So instead he turned to his patroness to ask whether he might at least take up her offer of a period at Pleshcheyevo when she left in mid-September. Her assent was immediate. Yet on leaving Skabeyevo on 13 September he headed first for Moscow, since he wanted to acquaint Taneyev with the finished sketch of the Concert Fantasia which he hoped his friend would introduce during the coming season. Tchaikovsky had asked that Laroche might periodically stay with him at Pleshcheyevo, partly so that their duet playing might continue, partly to gain Laroche's help in his study of English, and partly in the hope that he could fan further Laroche's fading literary spark. Otherwise, however, he had arranged that only Alexey and a cook should attend upon him, thus ensuring the maximum peace and privacy.

The house at Pleshcheyevo he found typical of his patroness's taste: overgrand and over-furnished, but well provided with musical instruments, books, music and wine. He would have preferred its situation to have been less enclosed, but the grounds, which ran extensively along the banks of a river, were delightful. Apart from a two-day visit to Moscow, Pleshcheyevo claimed him for a whole month, consolidating his longing for the quiet of a country environment, even though almost his sole visitor was Laroche, who returned with him from Moscow but only for one night, since he was again endeavouring to discipline himself into discharging properly his Conservatoire duties. In Moscow Tchaikovsky had heard Paul Pabst play his new *Grande fantaisie* on themes from *Mazepa*, which he judged 'very effective'.[4] He had much respect for Pabst; earlier at Kamenka, while planning that collection of his own piano works which Jurgenson wished to issue, he had entrusted Pabst with the final decision on what should be selected, giving him licence to edit them as seemed to him appropriate, though he was not to tamper with the substance.

At Pleshcheyevo Tchaikovsky re-read in Russian literature, discovering that as his regard for Tolstoy increased, so his enthusiasm for Turgenev cooled. He continued to work his way through *David Copperfield* in English, and made the acquaintance (in translation) of Goethe's *Wilhelm Meister* ('a complete *révélation* to me; I'd always thought it was terribly boring but, God! – what a delight it is!'[5]). He found among his benefactress's vocal scores Musorgsky's recently published *Khovanshchina* ('I discovered exactly what I had expected: pretension to realism in the peculiar way he understands and applies it, pitiful technique, poverty of invention – from time to time episodes with

[4] *TLP*12, p. 445.
[5] *TLP*12, p. 434; *TZC*2, p. 660; *TPB*, p. 317; *YDGC*, p. 324.

talent'[6]) and Wagner's *Parsifal* ('where, instead of people with characteristics and feelings with which we are familiar, there are fairy-tale beings fit to adorn a ballet but in no way a drama . . . Their sufferings, their feelings, their triumphs or misfortunes are completely alien to us – and what is *alien* to the human heart cannot be the source of musical inspiration'[7] – though he freely admitted that its 'harmonic richness is amazing'[8]). From the Paris journal *Gaulois* he received a request to contribute to an anthology of piano pieces in aid of impoverished musicians, and responded with the *Impromptu-Caprice* which he inscribed to Sofya Jurgenson, and which her husband swiftly reprinted for Russian musicians. Otherwise there was nothing to distract him from completing the scoring of the Concert Fantasia, and this he did on 6 October. He now had no important outstanding commitments; all that remained was to name to Jurgenson the prices for the suite (300 roubles) and the fantasia (200 roubles).

Just as Kotek had fired Tchaikovsky to compose his Violin Concerto, so he had been spurred to write his Concert Fantasia by a particular performer, 'a certain d'Albert', he told Nadezhda von Meck on 26 July, some four weeks after starting upon the piece, 'a young man who arrived in Moscow last winter, and whom I heard a great deal both at concerts there and in a private house. In my opinion he is a pianist *of genius*, and the true successor of the Rubinsteins.'[9] Yet though d'Albert had been the original inspiration for the work, and though, when writing to his patroness in July, Tchaikovsky had compared Taneyev unfavourably with d'Albert, the former was Tchaikovsky's choice of soloist when it received its première at an RMS concert conducted by Erdmannsdörfer in Moscow on 6 March 1885, and he was delighted both with Taneyev's account of the solo part and the audience's response, which was equally enthusiastic when Taneyev introduced it to St Petersburg on 16 April 1886, with Bülow conducting.

The Concert Fantasia enjoyed some popularity in Tchaikovsky's lifetime, but has since sunk into complete neglect. Its crippling weakness is that it contains not one really strong idea, yet its very original structure suffices to show that Tchaikovsky was concerned to fashion something more than a mere showpiece to gratify a virtuoso pianist or inflame a lionizing audience. His confessed dislike for the sound of piano with orchestra had inclined him to segregate the soloist in the Second Piano Concerto, nowhere more rigorously than in the develop-

---

[6] *TLP*12, p. 436; *TPM*3, p. 310; *TZC*2, p. 660; *YDGC*, p. 323 (partial).
[7] *TLP*12, p. 436; *TPM*3, p. 311; *TZC*2, p. 661.
[8] ibid.
[9] *TLP*12, p. 402; *TPM*3, p. 289; *TZC*2, p. 650; *DTC*, p. 457.

ment of the first movement, and the complete exclusion of the orchestra from the central section of this fantasia's first movement was the logical goal towards which this precedent had pointed. Elsewhere in the later work, however, Tchaikovsky seems to have been intent on exploiting that more selective approach to orchestral sound which had preoccupied him in his two recent suites (hence the time occupied in scoring the piece), and a glance through the opening pages of this fantasia's first movement quickly reveals the swiftly changing variety in the orchestral combinations, and the finely judged, yet sometimes highly detailed textures, so different from the Second Concerto's plain and solid slabs. The title of this first movement (*Quasi Rondo*) is unhelpful, since apart from the playfulness of the first two themes, which Tchaikovsky may have felt gave them some affinity with the sparkling ideas of classical rondo finales, there is no connection with rondo practice. Instead it resembles a sonata movement, with an exposition and recapitulation unfolded by soloist and orchestra, the development being replaced by a gigantic cadenza. This sonata view is well supported by the outer sections, for the first is a three-stage exposition much like that of the first movement of the Third Symphony, with the three themes (Ex. 199b, d and e) segregated tonally by being placed in the tonic, relative minor of the dominant, and dominant respectively (G, B minor and D), while the recapitulation simply shifts the last two themes into the relative minor and tonic (E minor and G). Despite the diversity of these themes, some simple protoshape (Ex. 199a) had haunted Tchaikovsky's creativity during their conception, and this same process also conditioned the two seemingly quite new ideas upon which the centre of the movement is based, the first (Ex. 199c) taking its contour from the movement's opening (Ex. 199b), the second (Ex. 199g) more distantly deriving from an inverted form of the 'third' subject (Ex. 199h); it is from this subject also that the extension of the first cadenza theme derives its shape (Ex. 199e and f).[10] The First Piano Concerto had employed thematic transformation, but whereas it had been in that work's development that the themes had progressively converted themselves into new forms, in this *Quasi Rondo*'s centre the two new themes retain their initial identities. And in one fundamental respect this enormous piano rhapsody rejects a developmental role, for instead of pursuing a consistently unstable tonal course, it is bounded by large slabs of G major and D major music. True, its central portion

---

[10] Nor, bearing in mind that, only the day before first hearing d'Albert, Tchaikovsky had once again listened to a performance of his own First Symphony, should we overlook the affinity between this first melody of the cadenza and the thematic world of the symphony's slow movement (see bars 46–9).

does explore flat key regions; but as it approaches its end, the calm cadencing and gentle thematic resolution denies to the orchestral re-entry any strongly marked function of being a tonic-resolving culmination; instead there is a modicum of surprise when the bright wind theme breaks in, its freshness redoubled after the textural ungainliness of much that has preceded it.

If the Andante mosso first movement had exhibited an unobtrusive thematic unity, the second, Andante cantabile, is built upon explicit melodic polarity; it was, in fact, the refugee conception from the Third Suite, and still carried the title *Contrastes*. When he had first had the idea

Ex. 199

for this movement at Kamenka in May, Tchaikovsky had quickly abandoned it, merely noting in his diary its two principal and highly contrasted themes (see Ex. 196). It is not known whether he intended the ramifications of this thematic dualism to be as far-reaching as they ultimately proved to be, but in this fantasia he not only effectively juxtaposes the two themes (first consecutively, then simultaneously), but makes them the initiators of very extensive sections which provide respectively the slow movement and finale elements of a conventional concerto's second and third movements. The mildly folky first theme begins as a pallid eight-bar invention, and comes to life only when a solo cello breaks in to reflect upon its cadence. The ensuing duologue is followed by a wistful string theme (più tranquillo), itself partnered by a rocking two-note horn line. Memories of *Romeo and Juliet* are inescapable, but this time the function of the quasi-ostinato is not to recall a theme just passed, but to provide a link to the future, for after the whole opening theme has been repeated, this oscillation suddenly re-emerges in the violas, foretelling the imminent intrusion of the contrasting theme which it also accompanies; the brief tussle for supremacy between these thematic opposites provides the most arresting passage in the whole fantasia. This second movement now reveals it has sonata-structure affiliations as had the first, for the course initially pursued by the molto vivace suggests that an exposition is being unfolded, though the brillante second subject is swiftly followed by a number of interrelated themes which only re-establish the dominant after an extended excursion through a variety of keys. After the abrupt return of the slow theme in the tonic, soon to be counterpointed by its capricious thematic antithesis (Ex. 200), the whole second subject section of the molto vivace is re-run, now also centring on the tonic. After such extrovert high spirits the repetition of the long-absent più tranquillo string theme is in danger of sounding mawkish. The hectic coda begins by lightly echoing the opening of the whole fantasia.

For all its melodic shortcomings, the Concert Fantasia has some engaging qualities and a structural freshness which should win it the occasional hearing. Tchaikovsky himself clearly had reservations about the second movement, and appended to his autograph score an alternative ending to the first movement for use if it was wished to perform this separately. The conclusion of this corresponds to the final twenty-four bars of *Contrastes*.

With the Concert Fantasia completed, Tchaikovsky steeled himself for his visit to St Petersburg to attend the later rehearsals and first night of the new production of *Onegin* which the Tsar had authorized at the Bolshoy Theatre. Yet in the time which remained to him at Pleshcheyevo he could not remain entirely idle, and before leaving he had composed two of the six romances which were to make up his set, Op. 57. Besides reading copiously, he found much fascination in experimenting with the various stops on the harmonium his patroness had sent for his pleasure. On 15 October he set in order the books and music he had used, and confessed the single mischief he had committed during his stay. 'One night I wanted to wind up the big clock which

Ex. 200

hangs in my bedroom (it had stopped, and I'm terribly fond of the ticking of a clock at night), and I turned the key so vigorously that the weight fell with a crash, and the clock needs a substantial repair.'[11] Two days later he was in the Russian capital.

Even more than when *Mazepa* had been produced at the beginning of the year, Tchaikovsky was aware of the respect and cooperation with which the performers and staff of the Imperial Theatres were preparing *Onegin*. Nápravník had rehearsed the music thoroughly, and both the production and the principals were good, especially Pavlovskaya as Tatyana and Pryanishnikov as Onegin. In fact, the next few weeks were to be one of the most decisive phases in the relationship between Tchaikovsky's music and the public, though the first performance of *Onegin* at the Bolshoy Theatre on 31 October gave little sign of this; despite Modest's disclaimer, there even seems to have been some hissing after the first scene. Nevertheless, the applause strengthened as the evening proceeded; the ball was warmly received, the composer was given repeated ovations, and was presented with a laurel wreath, all of which signified at least a notable personal success, and which brought on an instant attack of nerves from which he took some days to recover. Yet the press produced its customary mixture of reactions. There was some enthusiasm ('all the sympathetic aspects of Mr Tchaikovsky's gift are boldly expressed ... *Eugene Onegin* must be acknowledged ... as Tchaikovsky's operatic masterpiece'[12]), but also incomprehension ('there is no doubt that *Eugene Onegin* was written under the influence of Dargomïzhsky's declamatory style [in *The Stone Guest*]'[13] ... 'there is much, very much music, but in it the symphonist mercilessly crushes the operatic composer'[14] ... 'many melodious bits ... but little scenic movement'[15]). As for the opposition party within the press, it was led by the implacable Cui, whose malevolence reveals more about himself than his subject; the duel scene made 'a comic impression', Lensky's aria was 'a mournful diatonic whimper', the polonaise produced 'only boredom', Gremin's aria was 'banal' and Onegin's arioso 'commonplace'; even Tatyana's letter scene had only 'one or two successful phrases' to redeem the 'monotony, emptiness ... and, in places, the vulgarity of the rest', and the whole opera was judged 'stillborn, absolutely worthless and weak', though Cui did concede it was excellently scored.[16]

[11] *TLP*12, p. 454; *TPM*3, p. 317; *TZC*2, p. 665.
[12] *DTC*, pp. 87–8; *YDGC*, p. 327 (partial); *TPM*3, p. 630 (partial).
[13] *DTC*, p. 87; *YDGC*, p. 326.
[14] *DTC*, p. 88; *TZC*2, p. 670; *YDGC*, p. 327.
[15] *DTC*, p. 88.
[16] *DTC*, pp. 88–9; *TZC*2, p. 669 (partial).

But when Tchaikovsky himself came to reflect upon all this a month later, he felt able to make a confident distinction. 'I hear that *Eugene Onegin* continues to please the public, but not the press. . . . Of the two evils, *dislike from the public* or *dislike from the press*, I, of course, prefer the latter.'[17] By this time events in St Petersburg had more than gratified this preference. Even before he had left the Russian capital on 13 November, the enthusiasm of the public for *Onegin* had powerfully demonstrated that his music was soaring to a quite new level of popularity which he admitted took him completely by surprise. Tickets for the second night had sold out by 1 o'clock on the day booking opened, and subsequent performances were playing to capacity houses. This, so Modest claimed, became the rule for years to come, and the popularity of the opera quickly spread to the rest of Russia, guaranteeing that Tchaikovsky would never lack for material means for the rest of his life. Reviewing this moment of his brother's life some fifteen years later, Modest had no doubts about its importance. Up till then Tchaikovsky's name had been famed only within the limited circles of fellow professionals and music lovers; after this it 'becomes known and appreciated by the masses, and Pyotr Ilich achieves the highest degree of popularity ever attained by a Russian composer within the borders of his native land'.[18] The events of Tchaikovsky's remaining years are incontrovertible proof that this time Modest was not exaggerating.

Tchaikovsky had planned to leave St Petersburg after the first night of *Onegin*, but because a period of court mourning had caused the Tsar to absent himself from the theatre, the composer decided it was prudent to delay his own departure, especially after the Tsar's observations on his non-appearance at the St Petersburg première of *Mazepa* earlier in the year. In the end his Imperial Majesty had his revenge, for it was only after three further performances with the Tsar still absent that Tchaikovsky felt he himself could decently depart. By now his plans were radically altered; news had come from Switzerland that Kotek was seriously ill with tuberculosis, and it was therefore for Berlin that he headed. The obvious success of *Onegin* had put him in an excellent frame of mind. Despite the urgency of his mission, he had no intention of rushing the journey. In any case the unremitting pressure of professional and family commitments during his three and a half weeks in St Petersburg had made it impossible to tackle other obligations, and he used his four days in Berlin to discharge two compositional tasks. Having misinterpreted something said at the audience in the spring,

---

[17] *TLP*12, p. 491; *TPM*3, p. 325; *TZC*2, p. 678; *DTC*, p. 89; *YDGC*, p. 331 (partial).
[18] *TZC*2, p. 671.

the Tsar had become puzzled that Tchaikovsky had written no further music for the church; now Tchaikovsky promptly set about sketching two Cherubim's Songs as a first step towards satisfying his sovereign's implied command.

The other order had arrived only a week before the first performance of *Onegin*. It was for a musical contribution to the celebrations surrounding the golden jubilee of the eminent actor, producer and playwright, Ivan Samarin who, as professor of drama at the Moscow Conservatoire, had been one of Tchaikovsky's former colleagues, and also the man responsible for mounting and producing *Onegin* when it had received its première at the Conservatoire in 1879. Now in Berlin Tchaikovsky could at last sit down to devise a *Grateful greeting* for strings, an elegantly shaped ternary piece of haunting melancholy, with a gently plangent introduction and a wistful coda. This musical tribute was duly performed at the celebrations in the Moscow Bolshoy Theatre on 28 December. Feeling the piece was too slight, Tchaikovsky at first denied it publication, but in 1890 he relented, dedicating it to the memory of Samarin who had died five years previously, but retaining the original designation (the title *Elegy* by which it is now usually known is therefore unauthorized). Tchaikovsky was right to feel that his initial verdict on the musical worth of this piece had been too harsh, and he thought well enough of it in 1891 to re-use it as the entr'acte to Act 4 in the music he provided for a production of *Hamlet* in St Petersburg.

What above all made his stay in Berlin so pleasant was his solitude. Even Alexey was not with him, and when he encountered the Polish violinist, Stanislaw Barcewicz, in one of the beer halls, he was quick to insist that news of his own presence should not reach either Anton Rubinstein or Karl Klindworth, both of whom he knew to be in the German capital. He attended two of Bilse's concerts, at one of which, just as in 1879, he heard his own Andante cantabile, noting that this piece seemed to have enslaved Berlin's ears to the exclusion of all his other music. Most pleasurable of all was hearing again Weber's *Oberon*. He was mistaken in believing it was the first time he had seen it, for he had attended a performance in Vienna in 1881, when he had been mostly unimpressed. This time he reacted rather differently. 'In places the music's delightful,' he told Modest, 'though the subject's nonsense like *Die Zauberflöte*. But it's fun to see, and . . . everywhere that he [Oberon] appears the music is inspired and poetic.'[19] Munich, where he arrived on 19 November, also pleased him; he spent two days in

---

[19] *TLP*12, p. 478; *TZC*2, p. 674; *TPB*, p. 320.

visiting the National Museum and the two main art galleries, then directed himself resolutely towards Davos, where Kotek awaited him.

Resolve was certainly required for the last stage of Tchaikovsky's journey. Further overnight stops at Lindau and Landquart preceded an eight-hour lone trek up into the mountains in a one-horse carriage. On arrival he was amazed at the contrast between the magnificent yet gloomy mountain setting and Davos itself, for he discovered the town to be well, even luxuriously appointed, and certainly self-sufficient, with its own theatre, newspaper, gas lighting, and a tolerable orchestra. But its dedication solely to the cause of curing consumptives depressed him. 'Davos inspires horror and despondency in me,' he confessed to Nadezhda von Meck the next day. '. . . My stay here will be very brief.'[20] He found Kotek outwardly better than he had dared to hope, but soon suspected that his true condition was far worse. Besides keeping his friend company, he added a further Cherubim's Song to the two composed in Berlin and posted all three to Balakirev, who was now reinstated in Russian musical life as director of the Imperial Chapel Choir, with instructions to select whichever he felt to be the best and to perform it with the Chapel Choir, if the Tsar so wished. Earlier in the year Tchaikovsky had asked Jurgenson to send him a score of Balakirev's recently published *Tamara*, and he was now finding much to admire in it. Before leaving Davos on 29 November he agreed in principle to Stasov's highly flattering request that certain manuscripts of his works should be deposited in the St Petersburg Public Library. As Stasov had explained: 'You are such a major Russian composer that your best pieces ought to be preserved in their originals in our national collection, along with the best pieces of Glinka, Dargomïzhsky, and such-like.'[21]

Tchaikovsky spent only six days in Davos. Before departure he secretly visited Kotek's doctor, and received an ambivalent prognosis. But to have remained longer would have been more than he could have borne. Leaving with Kotek some funds for use in an emergency, he passed through Zurich on his way to Paris, where he hoped to find some days of true relaxation, and to visit Georges-Léon. He found that a thriving lad was now resembling much more his mother than his father, and his morale was further improved by the care and attentions of his favourite hotel and the delights of the Parisian theatre, which he judged to be in peak form as regards its performers, if not its repertoire. However, the only opera he attended was Thomas's *Hamlet*, of

[20] *TLP*12, p. 482; *TPM*3, p. 324.
[21] *TLP*12, p. 490; *YDGC*, p. 330.

which, he said, he loved the first three acts. From St Petersburg, through Stasov, he heard that his *Romeo and Juliet* had earned him one of the newly instituted Glinka Awards, which had been anonymously endowed by the wealthy timber merchant and music publisher, Mitrofan Belyayev, for works by contemporary Russian composers. Tchaikovsky, however, seems to have been more pleased by the prospect of acquiring an instant 500 roubles than by the prestige of the award itself, for he had been unable to resist ordering a wardrobe of new clothes while in Paris.

But pleasure and idleness did not claim him completely during this fortnight. With both *Onegin* and *Mazepa* running in St Petersburg, and with the revival of *The Maid of Orléans* imminent, his thoughts returned to *Vakula the Smith*, 'one of my own favourites among my children. But,' he continued to Nadezhda von Meck, 'I am not so blind as not to see the fundamental faults from which it suffers, and which have prevented it from remaining in the repertoire.'[22] Nor was his creative work confined to projecting a whole series of revisions in this work; he also composed four new pieces, one a setting of *We sing to Thee*, a text he had treated once before in the Liturgy of St John Chrysostom, while the other three were romances. Although the Children's Songs had been composed only a year before, it was over four years since Tchaikovsky had produced a set of adult romances, the Seven Songs, Op. 47, and he was quick to group these new creations with the two Pleshcheyevo romances lying in his portfolio and a setting of Sollogub's 'Tell me, of what does the spring nightingale sing?' from earlier in the year, and to issue them as his Op. 57. All six were originally inscribed to singers, for though 'Sleep' (No. 4) was to be dedicated to Vera Butakova, it had first been given to Mariya Slavina, who had been Tchaikovsky's favoured choice for the role of Lyubov in the Moscow première of *Mazepa*. Since the dedicatees of three of the remaining five – Bogomir Korsov (No. 2), Emiliya Pavlovskaya (No. 3) and Dmitri Usatov (No. 5) – had created the roles of Mazepa, Mariya and Andrey respectively, it is no surprise that the musical world of *Mazepa* seems to linger in some of these six songs. Couple this occasional stylistic allegiance with the confined range of the subject-matter of the lyrics (all are monologues or meditations on love or loneliness), and it was to be expected that the music of the set would show less variety, both in style and quality, than had the Op. 47 songs.

Yet it was not Korsov but Fyodor Komissarzhevsky, creator of the role of Vakula eight years earlier, whose song, 'Tell me, of what does the

---

[22] *TLP*12, p. 498; *TPM*3, p. 326; *TZC*2, p. 679; *YDGC*, p. 332.

spring nightingale sing?', has the most explicit relationship with Tchaikovsky's newest opera; singing the opening, Komissarzhevsky must have wondered momentarily whether he was beginning Mazepa's soothing assurance, also in E major, that Mariya need not doubt his love and constancy. But in 'Tell me' passion is not a matter for reaffirmation but for discovery; excitement quickly accumulates, the vastly arching bass line of the opening supporting the singer's swelling fervour as he prepares to disclose that magic word which answers all his questions: 'Love!' Set as a ternary structure, 'Tell me' confirms Tchaikovsky's skill for manufacturing a beautifully turned romance – charmingly affecting, but not troubling our deeper responses. As for Pavlovskaya, who had first sung Mariya, she may well have thought that it was Slavina who had been given a fugitive invention from Mariya's music early in Act 1, when the young girl still rejoiced in her love for Mazepa with no inkling of the disasters it would breed. Though 'Sleep' makes no attempt to gather up the expressive weight its lightly kindred music had borne in *Mazepa*, it serves its text nicely. This time the single word towards which each of the three strophes moves signifies not boundless joy but quiet repose, and in each strophe Tchaikovsky pointedly avoids any cadential resolution until the last imperative: 'Sleep!' Though designed as a plain strophic piece, it moves at the very end on to new material to conclude, not in the relative minor as in the first two strophes, but in the tonic, with a gentle coda to confirm this true resolution.

Pavlovskaya herself was allotted Strugovshchikov's translation of 'Heiss mich nicht reden' from Goethe's *Wilhelm Meister*. It was Tchaikovsky's third attempt at one of Mignon's songs, and his least successful. The worlds of personalities become confused; Tatyana's letter monologue of explicit confession soon threatens to burst in with an uncontained passion which falsifies the suppressed love and longing which are Mignon's predicament. But such a central outburst is seemly in 'On the golden cornfields' (No. 2). The lyric has the widest range of these six romances, for before the main substance of the song, which is a lament of separation, there comes a brief picture of the country at evening (Ex. 201). But this is seen, not with the charmed eyes which had looked so easily upon that earlier pastoral scene in 'Evening' (Op. 27, No. 4; see Vol. 2, pp. 36–7, Ex. 103), but with the sombre gaze of the lover who has failed to confess his love; it is not the bewitching sound of birds and insects but the heavy tolling of a bell which finally marks this dark image of the outer world.

By far the weakest of the set is the fifth. Treating a song entitled 'Death' in a manner not far removed from that of a waltz must seem

Ex. 201

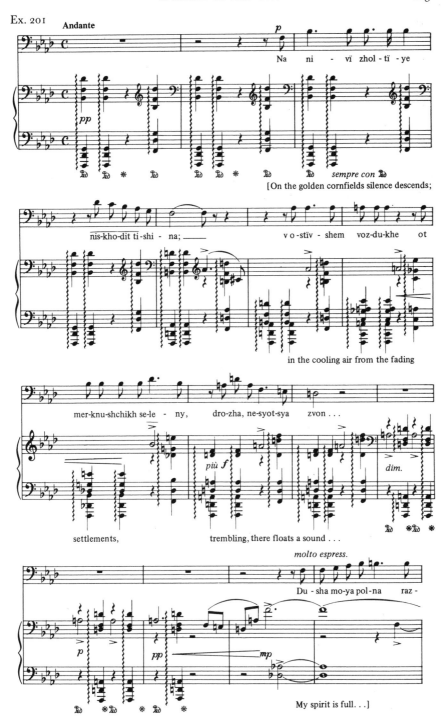

Na ni - vï zhol - tï - ye
[On the golden cornfields silence descends;

nis-kho-dït ti -shi - na; ____   v o -stïv - shem   voz-du-khe   ot
in the cooling air from the fading

mer-knu-shchikh se-le - ny,   dro-zha, ne-syot-sya   zvon . . .
settlements,   trembling, there floats a sound . . .

Du - sha mo-ya pol-na   raz -
My spirit is full. . .]

curious, even though the poet's mission is to persuade us cheerfully that the extinction we daily witness around us in nature should condition us to meet our own end 'submissively, with a gentle and triumphant smile'. 'Only thou alone' (No. 6), Pleshcheyev's translation of a lyric of love withheld, drew a far more pointed response; because sympathy and understanding cannot be transformed into love, the final naked cry of pain is here appropriate. Of the preceding five songs only one, 'Death', had employed Tchaikovsky's well-practised routine of repeating the piano prelude as postlude. In that song it had merely substantiated how perfunctory had been Tchaikovsky's response; in 'Only thou alone' it sets the seal on the piece. Frustration has found its voice, and there has been much restless freedom within the three strophes. But by the end nothing has changed.

The same was certainly not true of Tchaikovsky's mood during this Paris interlude. Suddenly, as had happened more than once before, the enthusiasm for Parisian existence which he had rediscovered on arrival evaporated. He ceased visiting the theatre, and that solitariness which had seemed such a blessing abruptly became an intolerable loneliness. 'I can't describe to you, dear Modest, how bored and depressed I've been during these last days,' he wrote on 15 December. '. . . It's longing for my native land, a wish to be *at home* which cannot find satisfaction in the fact that tomorrow I'm going to Russia, for there is still no *home* for me there. . . . One way or another, I must have a *home.*' But his current longing for the company of others raised a further tormenting dilemma. 'It means that to a certain extent I need *society*. All this confuses me. It means that to live alone in the country won't suit me. So where is my home to be? . . . How I long to talk with you! . . .'[23] The longing proved irresistible. He had intended going straight to Moscow, but on 19 December he was in St Petersburg with Modest.

Tchaikovsky's arrival proved timely, for Modest's play, *Lizaveta Nikolayevna*, which had caused such labour and anxiety at Grankino during the summer, was to receive its first performance at the Alexandrinsky Theatre, and a good deal of care had to be devoted to soothing a brother's nerves ahead of a modestly successful première, and subsequently bolstering that brother's spirits which fell in the face of what he believed was an unco-operative theatre management and a hostile press. But for Tchaikovsky himself this visit, and the next few weeks, were to afford further evidence of his own growing stature in his countrymen's eyes. The grip *Onegin* was taking on the public was confirmed for him when he attended the twelfth performance of the

[23] *TLP*12, pp. 508–9; *TPB*, pp. 324–5; *TZC*2, pp. 680–1 (partial).

season. On a more personal level came inscribed gifts: from Rimsky-Korsakov his new textbook on harmony, and from the young Glazunov a copy of his *Poème lyrique*, about which Tchaikovsky had waxed enthusiastic to Balakirev some weeks earlier, and which he had recommended to Jurgenson for publication. Even more flattering to him personally was to discover that, when Bülow came to Moscow a month later to give an enormously successful performance of the First Piano Concerto in the same concert which was to introduce the Third Suite to that city, he now had the personal authority to persuade the Bolshoy's management to put on *Mazepa* especially so that the German pianist could see the opera. He was also about to be unanimously elected a director of the Moscow branch of the RMS.

Tchaikovsky stayed ten days in St Petersburg, then left for Moscow to take up residence with Nikolay and Anna in Nadezhda von Meck's own house. But sadness abruptly descended upon him, for he found news awaiting him that Kotek had taken a turn for the worse, and within a week a telegram had announced his death. Tchaikovsky was entrusted with the painful task of breaking the news to Kotek's parents, and for three days he could not bring himself to do so. Deeply distressed personally, he found the need to immerse himself in proof-reading a welcome distraction.

The word 'fate' had cropped up in Tchaikovsky's letters more than once over the past weeks. Everything that now followed must have seemed yet further quiet confirmation of the operations of this overriding force; everything, unpleasant and pleasant, conspired to reinforce his need for a home of his own, and finally drove him to act. First there was his residence with Nikolay and Anna, for he discovered the negative side of their characters. He had always admitted that Anna could be acid in her comments on others, but Nikolay was now acquiring this trait, and the atmosphere which built up from their malicious strictures soon became intolerable. 'One story about *Nata* [Pleskaya] is enough to make you hate the lot of them,' he told Modest after enduring this a fortnight. 'Anna and I talked about *Nata*. She [Nata] is now not only a schemer, trying to alienate a mother from her daughters, but dishonourable, malicious, of use to nobody. In Anna's opinion I would do very well if I sent Nata off to Elizavetgrad, for (so she says) Sasha and Lev's only dream is to send her packing, but they can't bring themselves to say this to Nata. What sort of people are these? And your Molas is to go also! Every day Kolya Meck says again and again in every possible way that – 1. Nad[ezhda] Fil[aretovna] is, in essence, an unbalanced and unbearable old woman; that – 2. Vlad[imir von] Meck is a scoundrel and his wife a dissolute old hag;

that – 3. Yuliya [von Meck] is an evil virago; – 4. Sasha Beningsen [née von Meck] a *scandalmonger*; – 5. Sashok [von Meck] is wicked, vindictive, heartless; – 6. [Elizaveta] *Yolshina* [née von Meck] an arrant fool – and for some reason he praises only Sonya [née von Meck] to the skies. Do you remember that good-natured fellow – the Kolya who used to take photos of members of the family? What has Anna made of him! Today I learned from Sasha Bazilevskaya that Anna, Tanya and Liz[aveta] Mikh[ailovna Molas] consider that *Parasha* [Anatoly's wife] is a very unattractive, empty person, and *hangs* on the neck of every man.'[24] And now into this hideously spiteful world Tanya was about to return, bringing her own special brand of moody indolence. It is clear from the Kamenka diary alone that backbiting and malicious gossip were not confined to the newly weds, but were widespread in the family. How could he bear to commit himself to permanent residence with any of these?

Then there were the unremitting pressures of his professional life. What had brought him to Moscow was the urgent need to check the proofs of the Third Suite in readiness for the première which Bülow was imminently to conduct in St Petersburg. They were in a frightful mess, and for days on end Tchaikovsky was condemned to sit fuming over them, in the meantime warding off a deluge of invitations of varying kinds which would have absorbed any free time he might have had. And so the need to have a retreat where he could recover from labour also became more evident still during these three and a half weeks in Moscow. Nor could his home be within Moscow itself. There he would be too accessible; he had to distance himself sufficiently to ensure that his social participations would be at times and on terms of his own choosing.

Finally there were the swiftly mounting pressures of his own enormous success. These were brought home forcefully at the première of his Third Suite on 24 January, two days after his return to St Petersburg. As noted earlier, Tchaikovsky admitted he had never gained such a huge personal triumph, but six days later, having just arrived back in Moscow, he was detailing to Nadezhda von Meck something of the physical and social strains which were the price of such public acclamations. 'The weariness afterwards is enormous. The next day I was just like some sick person . . . I suffer rather than take pleasure in the awareness of my growing success. A wish to hide myself somewhere; a thirst for freedom, quiet, solitude prevailed over the feeling of a satisfied artistic self-esteem.' On the final day of his stay the Emperor had at last

[24] *TLP*13, p. 16; *TPM*3, p. 631 (partial).

attended a performance of *Onegin*, the fifteenth of the season. 'The Tsar wanted to see me, chatted with me for a very long while, was in the highest degree sweet and gracious towards me, with the utmost interest and in the greatest detail enquired about my life and my musical affairs, after which he took me to the Empress, who in her turn showed me the most touching attention.'[25] It all confirmed that his privacy would now be even further diminished, that he would be increasingly sought after, even lionized, and that self-protection was imperative. Before leaving Moscow he had inserted an advertisement in a Moscow paper: 'Single gentleman seeks a country dacha to rent.' The St Petersburg visit gave even stronger urgency to the search.

His first expedition to inspect a property proved disastrous. From the literature it looked ideal; the reality proved so disheartening that he almost determined to abandon everything and go abroad. But the decision, no sooner made, was reversed, and a new strategy evolved. 'A certain indescribable terror in the face of this impending journey enveloped me so strongly, a certain incomprehensible melancholy stifled me so terribly that yesterday I took an heroic decision and sent Alexey to rent a dacha which I had heard stood in a beautiful location and was provided with furniture, crockery and everything that was necessary,' he told Nadezhda von Meck on 15 February. 'Tomorrow I am going to St Petersburg, in a week everything will be ready, and I shall move into my own long-term quarters. . . . The dacha is situated in the village of *Maidanovo* about a mile and a half from *Klin*. The house has a lot of rooms, extremely well furnished; there is a magnificent park alongside the house, the view from the windows is very beautiful. . . . I shall have to live there a year, and if it proves that its upkeep is beyond my means, I shall manage to find something more suitable during the year.'[26] The location was certainly well-chosen, being some fifty miles to the north-west of Moscow on the railway joining the two capitals. The annual rent was to be 1,000 roubles.

Once again Tchaikovsky experienced a degree of disenchantment when he returned from St Petersburg a week later and saw what had been acquired for him. 'What Alyosha thought was luxurious and splendid seemed to me pretentious, tasteless, shabby and dingy. Immediately I decided most emphatically that Maidanovo won't be my continual and everlasting abode.' But then his tone softened as he reflected on its more positive virtues. 'Yet it's possible to live here a year, or at least until the beginning of next winter, and in summer it'll

[25] *TLP*13, p. 25; *TPM*3, p. 337; *TZC*3, pp. 20–1.
[26] *TLP*13, p. 31; *TPM*3, pp. 341–2; *TZC*3, pp. 23–4.

be really splendid . . . the situation's *delightful.* . . . The view from the
windows, the quiet, the awareness that I'm in *my own home* – all this is
so pleasant that I spent the whole day in the most agreeable state of
mind. . . . Despite a certain disenchantment I'm happy, contented,
glad, composed,' he told Modest.[27] His piano had been delivered, and
he now engaged an excellent cook, arranged for a laundress, and within
two days the drawbacks seemed still less serious. What mattered was
not the shortcomings of the house itself, but what it signified. 'What a
joy to be in my own home! What a bliss to know that no one will come
and interfere with my work, my reading, my walks!' he exclaimed to his
benefactress. 'Now I understand once and for all that my dream of
settling for the rest of my days in the Russian countryside is not a
passing whim, but a fundamental requirement of my nature.'[28] Three
more days, and he was ordering his existence still better, he told
Modest. 'I've begun receiving newspapers and journals, and this has
greatly enriched my life here. I read a lot, I'm enjoying getting on with
English, my work's going excellently, I eat, walk and sleep when I want
and as much as I want: in a word, *I'm living!*'[29]

On Maidanovo, or nearby, he would base the rest of his life. His years
of wandering were over.

Modest chose to call the period covered by this volume his brother's
'Kamenka years', partly because Sasha's Ukrainian home had been the
chief haven for the composer during this restless phase of his life, but
also because it was only in Kamenka, so Modest claimed, that his
brother had found conditions which answered his spiritual needs. The
sententiousness of Modest's title is understandable from a man anxious
at all costs, as we have observed, to demonstrate his brother's depen-
dence upon the support of a family whose loyalty and love were
matched by a stability and orderliness which the world might envy and
admire. But such was not, as we have also seen, the condition of Sasha's
household – certainly not during the latter part of this period. Nor,
perhaps, would it have been good for Tchaikovsky if it had been, for this
might have encouraged him to linger further in the cosiness and
comfort of her family circle. Instead he was inexorably driven from it.
Yet the self-esteem fostered by the growing public enthusiasm for his
music, the more than adequate means of livelihood which he now
commanded, the reassurance he felt in his visible social rehabilitation –
all created a confidence which enabled him once again to live indepen-

[27] *TLP*13, pp. 33–4; *TZC*3, p. 25; *TPB*, p. 327.
[28] *TLP*13, p. 35; *TPM*3, p. 344.
[29] *TLP*13, p. 36; *TZC*3, p. 26; *TPB*, p. 328.

dently. Meanwhile, this new self-sufficiency and self-assurance, which Modest rightly identified, seems to have fully and finally unstopped that blockage which, since the appalling events of 1877, had come between the composer's most personal inner world and his music. At last Tchaikovsky the creator could be completely himself again. And since this, rather than Tchaikovsky's enthusiastic words, is surely the most eloquent proof of what his newly begun existence really signified, the final chapter of this volume will leap beyond the natural biographical boundary afforded by this move to Maidanovo, and examine the first major work to be created within this new existence.

9

BALAKIREV RESURGENT:
MANFRED SYMPHONY

IN THE WINTER of 1867–8, on that visit to Russia which had first brought Balakirev into Tchaikovsky's personal life, Berlioz had conducted his own *Harold en Italie*. Both Balakirev and Vladimir Stasov had been hugely impressed, and it was this event, it seems, which prompted Stasov to outline a programme based on Byron's *Manfred* upon which Balakirev might also compose a four-movement symphony.

MANFRED

First movement
Manfred wandering in the Alps. His life is broken, his obsessive, fateful questions remain unanswered; in life nothing remains for him except memories. From time to time *memories of his ideal, Astarte,* creep in upon him. Memories, thoughts – burn, gnaw at him. He seeks and begs for oblivion, but no one can give him this.

Second movement
The way of life of the Alpine hunters, full of simplicity, good-nature, of a naïve patriarchal character, with which Manfred clashes, affording a sharp contrast. This is a quiet, idyllic adagio incorporating Manfred's theme which, like an idée fixe, must infiltrate the whole symphony.

Third movement
The Alpine fairy appearing to Manfred in a rainbow from the waterfall's spray.

Fourth movement
A wild, unbridled Allegro, full of savage audacity. Scene in the subterranean halls of the infernal Arimanes. Further on there follows the arrival of Manfred, arousing a general outburst from the subterranean spirits – and finally the *summons and appearance of Astarte* will

present a lovely contrast to this unbridled orgy: *this must be music light, limpid* as the air, and ideal. Further on the diablerie comes again, finishing Largo – Manfred's death.[1]

But when Stasov had offered this programme to Balakirev, the latter had felt it unsuited to him, and instead had tried to press Berlioz himself into composing it. Yet he, too, had refused. So the matter rested; in little more than a year Berlioz was dead, and by 1872 Balakirev himself was in the grip of that personal crisis which crushed his capacity to compose. The *Manfred* project, it seemed, was extinct.

Then in 1876 Balakirev began to creep back into the musical life of his native land. It was five years since he had made his exit from Tchaikovsky's professional world, and four since his last direct contact with his own former musical associates. The process of rehabilitation was slow, and even by 1881, when the ten-year silence between himself and Tchaikovsky was at last broken, this old campaigner for Russian music had still regained no position in the Russian musical scene of the sort he had once commanded with such energy and power. Yet when the initiative to renew contact was taken, it came not from this faded figure of the 1860s, but from his former willing protégé, now one of the chief ornaments of his country's music. In the summer of the previous year Tchaikovsky had made his second and final revision of that early masterpiece which Balakirev had, with such benevolent authority and stern coaxing, wrung from him a decade before, and the need to republish the score had enabled him to rectify an embarrassing omission.

'In the spring I had already corrected the proofs of my overture *Romeo and Juliet*, which Bock has printed in a new and somewhat improved form,' he wrote to Balakirev on 13 September 1881.

I asked him to send you a copy. Have you received it? I have always been a little tormented by the fact that, through an oversight, the first edition didn't carry the dedication to you on its title page. Now it's there – or, at least, it should be. I'm quite sure you are thoroughly indifferent to this dedication, but I do attach importance to it. I want you to know that I have not forgotten who was responsible for this score's appearance in this world, that I vividly recall the friendly sympathy you showed at the time, which I hope even now is not completely extinguished.[2]

---

[1] *BVP*, pp. 170–1.
[2] *TLP*10, pp. 217–18; *BVP*, p. 163.

Not knowing Balakirev's current address, Tchaikovsky had sent his letter to Bessel for forwarding. The publisher seems to have delayed shamelessly, however, and it was more than a year before a reply was received which proved as warm as Tchaikovsky's own letter had been. It also revealed that Balakirev's instincts to command remained undiminished. 'Your kind letter and dedication to me prove you have not completely struck me out of your heart's memory,' he wrote on 10 October 1882.

And if this is so, then why should you not afford me the pleasure of coming to see me? . . . You will find no superfluous persons at my place – only the company you know, with the addition of its new member, the talented Glazunov. If you wish to meet no one, that's even possible – but give me warning at the above address of such a wish, and of your arrival. And so I shall hope to receive news of you, and that when you arrive in St Petersburg you'll remember also your old friend, who sincerely loves you,

M. Balakirev

P.S. By the way, give your attention to a glaring error in the score of *Francesca*. On p. 92 the horns have been omitted, and the result's terrible.[3]

In this same letter, as we saw earlier (see above, p.204), Balakirev had offered to provide Tchaikovsky with a programme for a symphony which he thought would suit him admirably. Tchaikovsky had just finished sketching *Mazepa*, and though he knew it would be some months before he would complete scoring the opera, he also knew he would be restless for a new creative project, once this was done: Balakirev's proposal might therefore prove timely. Certainly his agreement to compose a piece on this undisclosed creative project was quite unequivocal, though for some reason he thought it was only to be a symphonic poem.

As might have been expected, Balakirev wasted little time, and on 9 November he despatched his plan. It proved to be Stasov's old scheme for a four-movement symphony on *Manfred*. 'I had originally offered the subject to Berlioz,' Balakirev confessed. 'He declined because of age and ill-health, not being disposed to compose anything more. Your *Francesca* suggested to me that you would be able to tackle this subject brilliantly – provided, of course, you *make an effort*, that you apply to your work just a little more criticism, allow your fantasy to mature in

---

[3] *BVP*, pp. 163–4.

your head, and don't hurry to finish at all costs.'[4] Balakirev went on to detail the programme, supplemented it with a number of requirements of his own, added some instructions on setting out the score such as one might offer to a student, and concluded with further commendation of his own proposal. 'Besides being profound, this subject is also contemporary, for the sickness of present-day mankind lies in this: it has not been able to preserve its ideals. They are shattered, nothing remaining to content the soul except bitterness. Every affliction of our time stems from this. How happy I shall be if this subject pleases you!'[5]

But it did not. It was now Tchaikovsky's turn to decline *Manfred*, as he did in his letter of 24 November.

> I haven't a translation of *Manfred* to hand, and I don't want to give you a final reply regarding your programme until I've read through Byron's text. Perhaps closer acquaintance with it will change my attitude to the task you've proposed to me – although I very much doubt it. . . . In all probability your programme could indeed serve as a design for a symphonist inclined to imitate Berlioz . . . but for the present it leaves me completely cold, and if the heart and imagination are not warmed, it's scarcely worth setting about composing. To please you I might, perhaps – to use your expression – *make an effort*, and squeeze out of myself a whole series of more or less interesting episodes, in which you'd meet conventionally gloomy music to reproduce Manfred's hopeless disillusionment, and a lot of effective instrumental flashes in the Alpine fairy scherzo, and sunrise in the violins' high register, and Manfred's death with pianissimo trombones. I would be able to furnish these episodes with harmonic curiosities and piquancies, and I would then be able to send all this out into the world under the sonorous title: *Manfred – Symphonie d'après*, and so on. I might even receive praise for the fruits of my labours, but such composing in no way attracts me.[6]

He followed this by dismissing his own *Francesca da Rimini* and *The Tempest*, both so admired by Balakirev, and concluded by observing that his love for Schumann's *Manfred* made it impossible for him to conceive this subject in musical terms other than those already created by Schumann.

And there the matter remained for two years. But then something occurred to revive the *Manfred* project. Exactly what we will probably

---

[4] *BVP*, p. 165; *TZC3*, p. 51; *DTC*, p. 409.
[5] *BVP*, p. 167; *TZC3*, p. 53; *DTC*, p. 410.
[6] *TLP11*, pp. 280–1; *BVP*, pp. 167–8; *DTC*, p. 410 (partial).

never know, though we may guess. In the autumn of 1884, as we have
seen, Tchaikovsky had to be in St Petersburg for the new production of
Eugene Onegin. On 11 November, during this visit, Balakirev wrote to
him.

> Dear Pyotr Ilich,
>   I'm sending you the programme sheet copied out for me by
> Vladimir Stasov, and furnished with my notes. I sincerely wish and
> hope that *Manfred* will be one of your pearls.
>   It was so pleasant for me to talk with you today that, if only it is
> convenient for you tomorrow, don't refuse to come to the Chapel at
> the same time (11 o'clock). By then I shall have arrived and, taking
> you for a walk, will tell you much of great importance which I
> completely omitted today. I shall be disappointed if anything pre-
> vents you giving me a couple of hours during the morning . . . May
> Christ preserve you!
>
>   Ever yours,
>   M. Balakirev[7]

The two men had talked about religion. It was a subject which had
occupied Tchaikovsky's thoughts a good deal during the previous
months. In March he had read Tolstoy's *Confession*, still forbidden by
the spiritual censor, but which was circulating in manuscript. 'The
impression it made on me was all the stronger because the torments of
doubt and tragic perplexity through which Tolstoy has passed, and
which he expresses so amazingly well in his *Confession*, are known to me
also,' he had written to Nadezhda von Meck on 25 March. 'But
enlightenment came much earlier for me than for Tolstoy, probably
because my head is more simply constructed. . . . Every hour and every
minute I thank God He has given me faith in Him. In my faintheated-
ness and my talent for losing heart to the point where I yearn *for oblivion*
because of some trivial blow, what would I be if I did not believe in God,
and did not submit to His will?'[8] Significantly this year he had attended
Easter services in Moscow with particular assiduity. But his response to
such rituals was primarily aesthetic and sentimental, and his religious
belief was largely self-persuasion which might bring certainty to counter troubling perplexities and assure final deliverance from irrepressible guilt. The confession made to his beloved cousin, Anna Merkling, a
few weeks later came much nearer the truth. 'What is needed is not to

[7] *BVP*, p. 170.
[8] *TLP*12, p. 336; *TPM*3, p. 266; *TZC*2, pp. 630–1.

be afraid of death. In this respect I have no grounds for complacency. I am not so imbued with religion as, with certainty, to see in death the beginning of a new life, nor enough a philosopher to reconcile myself to the abyss of non-existence into which I shall have to plunge.'[9]

Balakirev, however, no longer suffered from such uncertainties. Formerly he had been a free-thinker, but in the early 1870s he had come under the influence of a soothsayer, and had developed a very intense and eccentric brand of Christian faith. Might not that same Balakirev who, fifteen years before, had performed him such musical service, now also show him the way to spiritual salvation, delivering him from his sexual guilt, perhaps even thwarting his fate? Such must surely have been Tchaikovsky's thoughts. Certainly he had listened to Balakirev with longing and, perhaps, with renewed hope. The next day he replied.

> I was deeply moved by our conversation of yesterday. How good you are! What a *true* friend you are to me! How I wish that that *enlightenment* which has come to your soul would also descend on me. I can say in all truth that more than ever I *thirst* for solace and support *in Christ*. I shall pray that faith in Him may be confirmed in me.[10]

It was within the closeness bred by this single religious exchange that Balakirev had reintroduced the *Manfred* project, and Tchaikovsky had agreed to compose it. Unfortunately the further meeting both men wanted could not materialize, for Tchaikovsky had now received his urgent summons to Switzerland to visit the dying Kotek. Nor does it seem that the further conversations which he and Balakirev planned ever took place. But this time he held to his resolve about Balakirev's other gift.

Tchaikovsky had now received two communications containing the *Manfred* programme.[11] In presenting his first version two years earlier, Balakirev had copied out Stasov's scheme, lightly paraphrasing it and fleshing out one or two details; upon remembering Astarte in the first movement Manfred 'calls upon her in vain', but 'only the echo from the cliffs repeats her name', while her appearance in the finale was to be 'the same as was in D major in the first movement, except that there this idea was fleeting, like a memory, and was immediately engulfed by Manfred's mood of suffering; here this same idea now appears in its full

[9] *TLP*12, p. 363; *TZC*2, p. 641.

[10] *TLP*12, p. 470; *BVP*, p. 172.

[11] The version of 1882 is printed in *BVP*, pp. 165–6, *DTC*, pp. 409–10 and *TZC*3, pp. 51–2.

and finished form'. Manfred's death would be preceded by a sunset. Far more important than such programmatic details had been the musical prescriptions. Balakirev had confirmed Stasov's requirement of an idée fixe recurring in all four movements, and had specified that the first movement was to begin in F sharp minor and end in F sharp major, while the Astarte music in between was to be in D. The second movement would be an Adagio pastorale in A major – and here Balakirev had added a caveat: 'Of course you should first have a hunters' tune, but in doing this, you must be *particularly careful not to fall into triviality*. God preserve you from vulgarities like German fanfares or Jägermusik!' The Alpine fairy movement would be a *Scherzo fantastique* in D, and the finale would begin in F sharp minor. Astarte's appearance would use her D major music from the first movement, though now in D flat.

When Balakirev sent Tchaikovsky the *Manfred* scheme for the second time, he enclosed Stasov's original hand-written programme (see above, pp. 296–7), and some of his own musical requirements had undergone changes. His obsession with keys not only of two sharps but of five flats had resurged; the symphony was to be in 'B flat minor without B flat major', while Astarte's first movement music was to begin in D major as before, but be repeated in D flat. The Adagio pastorale in A major was now envisaged as a Larghetto in G flat which, however, 'will not be difficult since the tempo is slow, and as supporting keys you can take B flat major and A major'. For some reason the scherzo was no longer *fantastique*, though the key remained, and Balakirev added that the idée fixe should provide material for the trio. The finale would begin in B flat minor, Astarte's music would still be in D flat, though now muted strings were stipulated, and the whole piece would end with a requiem (ideally with organ) and a final B flat major chord.

As significant as these revised musical supplementations was the list of 'helpful materials' which Balakirev supplied. In his 1882 directions he had reminded Tchaikovsky that the programme was like those of Berlioz's Symphonie Fantastique and *Harold en Italie*; now he specified particular pieces which he judged would help Tchaikovsky in each movement.

For the first and last movements:
Francesca da Rimini by Tchaikovsky
Hamlet by Liszt
Finale from *Harold* by Berlioz
Preludes in E minor, E flat minor and C sharp minor (No. 25, separate from the others) by Chopin

For the Larghetto:
Adagio from the Symphonie Fantastique by Berlioz
For the Scherzo:
La reine Mab [from *Romeo and Juliet*] by Berlioz
Scherzo (B minor) from the Third Symphony by Tchaikovsky

Before leaving for Switzerland to attend Kotek, Tchaikovsky bought
a copy of Byron's *Manfred*. He reflected that finding himself among the
Alps might stimulate him to begin work, except that the distress at his
friend's condition would probably make this impossible. But he did
read the poem at Davos, and reaffirmed to Balakirev his intention of
composing the symphony. He did not start composition until April
1885 at Maidanovo, however. The evidence of progress is very con-
flicting. Various notes on the sketches are themselves confused ('End of
the symphony: 25 May – but before the end a very great deal still needs
to be done. . . . Today's 18 July, but I still haven't gone very far. . . .
And today's 12 August – and yet, oh, how far it is to the end!'[12]). In the
full score the individual movements are clearly dated (first – 24 June;
second – 3 August; third – 23 September; fourth – 24 September); yet
the final date for the whole symphony is recorded as 4 October.
Tchaikovsky's letters written during the period of composition sometimes seem to tell yet another story; what they do confirm is the labour
which went into composition. He had intended to heed Balakirev's
counsel not to rush, and first made only a few preliminary sketches. But
by the end of June the urge to compose with his more characteristic
intensity was beginning to grip him, though his feelings about the work
he was forming were still equivocal. 'After some hesitation I've decided
to compose Manfred, for I feel that, until I've fulfilled the promise I
imprudently gave Balakirev during the winter, I shall not be at ease,' he
confessed to Taneyev on 25 June. 'I don't know what will come out, but
for the moment I'm dissatisfied with myself. No! It's a thousand times
pleasanter to compose without a programme.'[13] But, as had happened
many times before, as the labour progressed, so his feelings changed.
'Now I can't stop,' he told Emiliya Pavlovskaya on 1 August. 'The
symphony's come out enormous, serious, difficult, absorbing all my
time, sometimes wearying me in the extreme; but an inner voice tells me
that I'm not labouring in vain, and that this will perhaps be the best of
my symphonic compositions.'[14] Three weeks later, though he feared his

---

[12] *Avtografi P. I. Chaykovskovo v arkhive Doma-Muzeya v Klinu: Spravochnik* (Moscow/
Leningrad, 1950), p. 28.

[13] *TLP*13, p.101; *TZC*3, p. 50; *YDGC*, p. 348; *DTC*, p. 411; *TTP*, p. 124.

[14] *TLP*13, p. 118; *DTC*, p. 411 (partial); *YDGC*, p. 350 (partial).

involvement in the work was turning him into a Manfred himself, he was acknowledging to Emiliya even greater confidence. 'I'm extracting a promise from you that, when it's played in St Petersburg, you'll go to hear it. I'm very proud of this work, and I want those persons whose sympathy I value most in the world (and you are in the first rank of these) to experience, when they hear it, a reverberation from the joy with which I wrote this piece.'[15]

But it was still 25 September, a month later, before he could write to Balakirev.

> I have carried out your wish. *Manfred* is finished . . . I think you will be somewhat displeased at the speed with which I've composed it . . . but the point is that I cannot do otherwise . . . I've sat over *Manfred* – not getting up from my seat, I may say – for nearly four months (from the beginning of June until today). It was very hard work – but also very pleasant, especially when, having begun with some effort, I got carried away. Of course, I cannot predict whether this symphony will please you or not, but *believe* me, never in my life have I tried so hard and become so weary from my work. The symphony is written in four movements in accordance with your programme. But I ask your forgiveness: I have not been able to keep to the keys and modulations you indicated, even though I wanted to . . . This piece is very difficult and demands a large orchestra – that is, a lot of strings. . . . Of course *Manfred* is dedicated to you.[16]

What followed was precisely what might have been expected after the history of *Romeo and Juliet* nearly sixteen years earlier: Balakirev pressed to be shown the piano-duet version so that he might suggest improvements, and promptly told Tchaikovsky what sort of piece he should compose next. Tchaikovsky tactfully but firmly parried this attempt to take over his creative plans yet again, but he conceded that Balakirev's opinion might be useful on details of pianistic layout in the duet transcription, even though he had already sought the help of Hubert's wife, whose advice on such matters he had always found sufficient. Yet just as, when composing the piece, he had shown himself perfectly prepared to ignore many of Balakirev's prescriptions, so now he declined point-blank to listen to any requirements Balakirev might have regarding the content of the piece.

Tchaikovsky felt that his confidence in his Manfred Symphony was confirmed when the première under Erdmannsdörfer took place in

---

[15] *TLP*13, pp. 125–6.
[16] *TLP*13, pp. 145–6; *BVP*, p. 176; *DTC*, pp. 411–12.

Moscow at an RMS concert on 23 March 1886, the fifth anniversary of Nikolay Rubinstein's death. There had been five rehearsals and an 'excellent' performance. 'The first movement proved undoubtedly the best,' he wrote to Balakirev two days later. '*The scherzo* was taken very quickly, and when I heard it I didn't experience disenchantment as I frequently have. . . . The *Andante* doesn't sound bad. *The Finale* gains *very much* in performance, and proved to be the most effective movement *with the audience.*' Yet though at rehearsals the players had given increasingly open demonstrations of approval, he still felt the public had not much liked the symphony, while his friends were divided, some enthusiastic, others feeling that Tchaikovsky had concealed himself behind a mask. 'But I myself think it's my best symphonic work,' he continued defiantly, 'though because of its difficulty, impracticability and complexity it is doomed *to failure and to be ignored.*'[17] It was indeed the most extended orchestral piece he had yet written, using the largest complement of players, and bristling with formidable difficulties. Because of this complexity he had already offered it to Jurgenson free of charge.

Events quickly disproved his gloomy prediction. Before the end of the year it had been performed three times in St Petersburg or at nearby Pavlovsk; it had even reached New York. There was some very warm critical reaction, and Cui for once was full of praise, especially for the first movement.

But once the Manfred Symphony had begun to become history, and the composer himself could view it with some detachment, his satisfaction turned to hatred. In October 1888 he wrote blisteringly of it to the Grand Duke Konstantin Konstantinovich.

Without any wish to make a mere show of modesty, I will say that it is an abominable piece, and that I loathe it deeply, *with the one exception of the first movement.* Moreover, I must say to Your Highness that within a short time, with the agreement of my publisher, I shall destroy completely the remaining three movements, very poor as music (the finale in particular is something loathsome), and out of a large symphony which is quite impossibly long-winded I shall make a *Symphonische Dichtung.* Then I am sure my *Manfred* will be capable of pleasing. Indeed, it must be so: the first movement I wrote with enjoyment – the remaining ones are the result of straining from which, I remember, I felt myself for some time very unwell.[18]

[17] *TLP*13, pp. 298–9; *BVP*, p. 182; *DTC*, p. 414.
[18] *TLP*14, pp. 542–3; *TZC*3, pp. 274–5; *DTC*, p. 416 (partial).

Thankfully, nothing more was heard of Tchaikovsky's destructive intentions towards the last three movements.

When Tchaikovsky came to know Byron's *Manfred* for himself in the days after giving his second promise to Balakirev, there might have seemed no reason why he should not have ended in rejecting the subject as before. Yet he did not, for Balakirev's new choice had been as inspired as that of *Romeo and Juliet*. True, its conventionally grand Alpine setting, its bevy of supernatural beings against whom the Abbot stands as representative of the other side of the spiritual equation – even its Chamois Hunter as a pattern of common humanity – probably left Tchaikovsky little stirred. But the figure of Manfred gripped him. Here was an outsider who from childhood had felt himself apart from other mortals. His solitariness had grown ever greater, his gloom ever deeper, his longing for forgetfulness was as strong as it was vain. Fate ruled his life; above all, Tchaikovsky must have perceived that Byron's hero was haunted by a very special sin – that he had been guilty of unnatural love. Byron had been impelled to write *Manfred* by his own attraction to his half-sister, Augusta, and though there is only bare mention of the wrong committed by Manfred with Astarte ('the only thing he seem'd to love – as he, indeed, by blood was bound to do'), it is clear that it was incest:

> Thou lovedst me
> Too much, as I loved thee: we were not made
> To torture thus each other, though it were
> The deadliest sin to love as we have loved.

There was, of course, no hint of this aberrant love in the programme Balakirev had transmitted. Stasov had obviously selected his elements to bring the scheme as close as possible to that which a moderately lively imagination might extract from Berlioz's *Harold en Italie*, as Tchaikovsky cannot have failed to notice, for as in *Harold* the first movement was to be concerned with the hero and his affairs, the second (in Tchaikovsky's sequence) shifted to a world outside that of the hero (religious in Berlioz, supernatural in Tchaikovsky), while the third returned to the plane of everyday life and simple mortals. The finale of both works was an orgiastic tableau of unbridled energy disrupted by the entry (or intimations) of the hero and, in the case of Manfred, ending in his death. Certainly Tchaikovsky seems to have heeded well Balakirev's admonition to take account of this other musical incarnation from Byron when setting about his own, and the acute-eared listener will find a variety of tiny musical moments in it which would

probably not have come into being, but for the existence of Berlioz's
Harold. Most striking of these is the clear echo of the harmonic structure
supporting the second phrase of Berlioz's idée fixe (Ex. 202c), both at
the opening of the trio in the Alpine fairy scherzo (Ex. 202a) and for the
main theme of the slow movement (Ex. 202b; this harmonic parallel
draws attention to the kinship of Tchaikovsky's themes, whose contours also seem not altogether unconditioned by those of Berlioz's first
phrase (Ex. 202d)).[19]

Ex. 202

It was also to be expected that since Manfred, like Harold,
stands apart from the other personalities and events of the drama,
Tchaikovsky should have retained the musical personification of his
hero unchanged throughout. The combination of an immutable theme
with the material proper to the movement into which it has intruded
could pose technical problems as great as were the expressive rewards
to be reaped from such a confrontation of differing worlds and materials, for the idée fixe was likely to be at variance in pace, metre – and,
consequently, in phrase structure – with its new, brief companions. The
skill with which Berlioz had answered these challenges in the central

[19] Coincidentally the same progression was used by Bach in his C major keyboard
prelude for which Gounod devised his Ave Maria obbligato, and which Tchaikovsky
appears to quote at the beginning of Manfred's death scene (see below, p. 309).

movements of *Harold* is not the least impressive feature of that symphony, and was both a model and an inspiration to Tchaikovsky when
he inserted Manfred's theme into the trio of his own scherzo. Yet
elsewhere such combinations are mostly avoided – and here we begin
to touch on the differences between the two pieces. Harold has the
singularity of the individual, not the misanthropy of the recluse; his
customary role may be that of detached observer, and he does not
merge into a scene, but he can find a quiet corner to observe it from
inside. Not so Manfred; he intrudes roughly (as did fate in the Fourth
Symphony), for a moment sweeping aside other material – a scowling
spectator, impotent to become part of the world he has briefly entered,
and quickly forgotten by it.

For the fact is that *Harold en Italie* and the Manfred Symphony are
really very different works, and nowhere is this more apparent than
in the finale of each, in *Harold* the most implicitly, in the Manfred
Symphony the most explicitly programmatic movement. While the
Manfred Symphony is a fully romantic work of the 1880s, *Harold*
remains a post-classical conception of the 1830s, and even the listener
who is implacably convinced that the *Orgie de brigands* is a series
of extra-musical representations will surely recognize that what
prompted Berlioz to begin by recalling material from all three preceding movements was the example of Beethoven's Ninth Symphony as
much as any pictorial purpose. So, too, when the brigands are at last
allowed to sweep Harold aside and proceed to business, they organize
their activities to shape out the events in a kind of abbreviated sonata
structure. Only the startling recollection of the *Marche de pélerins* after
all these spirited proceedings brings a reminder that the movement is
not controlled simply by musical considerations. If there is a model for
Tchaikovsky's bacchanal, it is more the *Songe d'une nuit du Sabbat* in
Berlioz's earlier Symphonie Fantastique; that much is suggested by the
combination later devised between the two main thematic ingredients.
Yet this is effected almost coincidentally, rather than because it might
provide the movement's musical climax, as in Berlioz. In fact, almost
the sole arbiter of events is Stasov's programme.

Yet the weakness of this finale derives less from the absence of any
larger musical coherence than from the feebleness of the melodic
material. Intended to be terse, this is merely short-winded. That
abundant rhythmic variety, which had encouraged such a diversity of
phrase structure in Berlioz's wild tableau, is here confined mostly to
simplistic rhythmic restructuring of the initial phrase. Turning this
orgy into a bacchanal was Tchaikovsky's idea, but the boozy impro-
prieties of such occasions rarely have the spice of true villainy or the

relish of an honest hellish debauch, and the invention soon becomes all too redolent of the colourful gopaks of Tchaikovsky's operas. The best of the music which here represents Manfred comes straight from the first movement, though when Astarte appears she adds a few poignant touches to her earlier material. Tchaikovsky's own brief summary of events in his autograph score claims erroneously that Manfred is finally forgiven, and this must explain the complacent rosiness in the death scene. If the opening of this sounds suspiciously like a quotation from Gounod's Ave Maria obbligato on Bach, with one note added to incorporate the contour of the first Manfred theme (compare x in Ex. 202e with the opening of Ex. 208a), there can be no doubt about the explicit appearance of the 'Dies irae' in the bass some bars later.

The central two movements have been far more successful. In substance both are mainly of the world of the suites, though much elaborated. As in the finale, Tchaikovsky rejected Balakirev's directions on key, selecting B minor for the scherzo and G for the slow movement. He also decided on andante con moto as the speed of the latter and called it *Pastorale*, though this label is rendered redundant by the opening oboe solo in compound duple time. The mood and material of this movement are certainly conditioned by those of the Adagio in the Symphonie Fantastique, but its structure owes nothing to Berlioz. As early as the slow movement of his First Symphony and as recently as the first movement of his Third Suite Tchaikovsky had shown an impressive capacity for organizing melodic materials into schemes whose totalities are rather more than the sum of their parts. As Ex. 203 shows, this *Pastorale* has a wide variety of materials in a large number of sections strung out with refreshing unpredictability. The brief intrusion of Manfred is external to the design, but it serves the useful function of breaking the movement into two clear but unequal parts. After this interruption, much of the earlier material is systematically recalled, the two A sentences and a fragment of F being blended to make a particularly extensive paragraph, while the fleeting demisemiquaver appendage to D is expanded to provide the first part of a tiny coda; this ends with echoes of the opening melody, now shaped to conform exactly with the last melodic contour of Berlioz's *Scène aux champs*. Most striking of all these modifications in this second half is the reharmonization of C, a horn theme based upon only three notes. On its first two appearances in this slow movement it had been harmonized by a sustained A minor triad, but now its repeated three-pitch cells are supported by a magical progression of chromatically related chords (Ex. 204b); enchantment, it seems, touches even the world of artless mortals – always assuming, that is, that this theme truly *is* the hunter's emblem, for with its

Ex. 203

MANFRED SYMPHONY: THIRD MOVEMENT

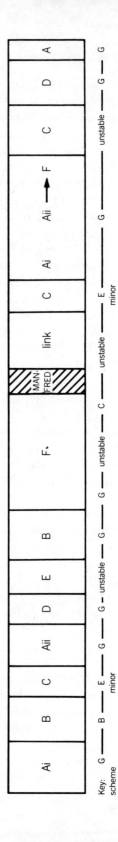

affiliations to a horn passage in the first movement (Ex. 204a), it might be yet another facet of Manfred himself. This is far from the only instance of thematic ambiguity in this symphony, as we shall see.

Ex. 204

This slow movement is decorated with all sorts of picturesque touches: a shepherd's musette, occasional bird-song, the 'sweet bells of the sauntering herd'. But enchantment had been the very essence of the preceding scherzo. Balakirev had said that Manfred should appear in the trio, and he intrudes twice, first merely as observer of the spirit he has conjured ('to look upon thy beauty – nothing further'), then as despairing interlocutor. Perhaps the main theme of the trio is indeed Tchaikovsky's personification of the 'Witch of the Alps', as Byron called her, but the similarity already noted between this cheerful theme and the oboe melody of the following *Pastorale* (see Ex. 202a and b) might suggest that it also contains intimations of the world of ordinary mortals. Yet within any study of Tchaikovsky's evolving style the materials of the scherzo itself and their presentation are of prime interest. The ten years which had passed since the scherzo of the Third Symphony provide a perspective which clarifies the novelty of that earlier movement. Like the Manfred scherzo its orchestration is critical

to its effect. But Tchaikovsky's craft has developed immensely in the
intervening years, and the two movements really share nothing except
their key. The 1875 scherzo had been a relatively simple affair – a single
line of undulating semiquavers presented in constantly changing colours as background to a variety of crisp phrases. Nothing as crystalized
as these stands out in the Manfred scherzo. Instead it spins a web of
intricate yet impeccably clear textures, unfolded on harmonic structures of great simplicity, as the opening demonstrates (Ex. 205); two
bars of tonic alternating with submediant follow upon two bars which
select components of a dominant ninth, delicately fragmented and
spiced with appoggiaturas.

Ex. 205

Nevertheless, though that fastidious variety of colour already exploited in parts of the Second and Third Suites is in this scherzo evolved into a chiaroscuro of a myriad fineness new in Tchaikovsky's music, it would be wrong to assume that this movement is merely a stream of bewitching orchestral sound. It displays a simple yet effective motivic growth; for instance, the slurred-note feature soon grows into a three-note cell which is first heard as accompaniment to the tiny melodic figure of which it is a simplification (bars 31ff.), then as a foreground motif of flexible contour (bars 39ff.) in a passage which reminds us that Naina's spiky dartings in *Ruslan and Lyudmila* are as much behind the hatching of this music as Berlioz's *Queen Mab* or Tchaikovsky's Third Symphony scherzo. As for matters of tonality, the listener is hard put to specify the key in force, once Glinka's witch has really taken possession, and it is only after much elusiveness that B minor is at last allowed to regain and confirm its hold. And just as, at the trio's opening, the Alpine fairy had seemingly materialized from the pulsing F sharp at the spellbound conclusion of the scherzo, so at the movement's end, as Manfred again stands as observer and his theme is heard for a third time, the spirit with 'hair of light and dazzling eyes of glory' vanishes upwards in the dying flickers of a B minor chord.

Tchaikovsky prefaced his autograph score of the first movement with a quite detailed account of its content, diverging a little from Stasov's prescription in both substance and emphasis.

Manfred wanders in the Alps. Tormented by fateful questions of existence, tortured by the burning anguish of hopelessness and memory of his guilty past, he experiences cruel spiritual torments. Manfred has penetrated deeply into the secrets of magic and communicates imperiously with the powerful forces of hell, but neither they nor anyone in the world can give him the *oblivion* which he yet vainly seeks and craves. Memories of his ruined Astarte, whom once he had passionately loved, gnaw and eat at his heart, and there is neither Grace nor an end to Manfred's boundless despair.[20]

It may seem curious that, though Tchaikovsky added Manfred's involvement in magic arts, there is no firm trace of those specific musical idioms of enchantment which he had used so pointedly in, for instance, *The Tempest*. In fact, it is a measure of his especially serious approach to this movement that he should have felt that such essentially ornamental elements, which had found a ready place elsewhere in the symphony, would be inept here, and the very existence of this more

---

[20] *DTC*, p. 408.

elaborate programme substantiates the importance he attached to this Lento lugubre. Balakirev, too, must have perceived it as the most significant part of the symphony, and he specified for it the longest list of pieces he felt might help Tchaikovsky's own thoughts to stir, for the only item which was obviously to relate to Tchaikovsky's finale was the brigands' movement from *Harold*. The other two orchestral works, Liszt's *Hamlet* and Tchaikovsky's own *Francesca da Rimini*, were musical portraits, as Tchaikovsky's first movement was to be. *Hamlet* seems to have left no direct marks on Tchaikovsky's invention, but *Francesca* may have bequeathed its ternary structure in which the heroine's music forms the centre. As for the preludes by Chopin, it could hardly be expected that pieces as idiomatically pianistic as those in E flat minor and C sharp minor could offer much, though the Largo in E minor was a different matter, and this gently melancholy piece may have played some part in forming the passage for solo horn (see Ex. 204a); both melodies are in E minor and are tightly confined, and both are supported by harmony proceeding solely by stepwise movement, often chromatic.

Yet it seems likely that Tchaikovsky selected his own models for the distinct musical worlds associated with Manfred and Astarte. He had already confessed to Balakirev his profound admiration for Schumann's incidental music for *Manfred*, and his determination to avoid its influence is suggested by the studied absence of any detectable connection between the earlier score and his own. Except, that is, for one small but crucial link: the hesitant and tender invention through which Tchaikovsky introduces Astarte in his first movement (Ex. 206a: andante) has a striking general affinity with the tiny, widely spaced phrases, also for muted strings, with which Schumann had punctuated Manfred's first words in the melodrama he devised to support Astarte's corresponding appearance (Ex. 206b). And if, by contrast, a musical antipathy should have driven Tchaikovsky to his choice of 'helpful material' for Manfred's own music, this need hardly cause surprise. Byron's hero had destroyed the woman who had become involved with him; Tristan, too, had been guilty of a kind of

Ex. 206

treachery in love, and Isolde had died. There any similarities
Tchaikovsky may have thought he could perceive with that tale ended;
nevertheless, as his creative urges prepared their incarnation of Manfred, their attention seems to have turned towards the music which
introduces the hero in Wagner's opera (Ex. 207a). There is the same

Ex. 207

bluntness in the unaccompanied phrases on the well-reeded wind, the same gruffness in the trenchant string chords which follow. Moreover, somewhere among Tchaikovsky's thoughts there seems to have lingered a memory of the theme (Ex. 208e) which underpins Fricka's denunciation in *Walküre* of another act of incest: the union of Siegmund and Sieglinde. Indeed, when Tchaikovsky widens the falling fourths to fifths at Manfred's first climactic outburst (Ex. 208d), Wagner's contour is exactly matched. Yet Tchaikovsky's music (Ex. 207b) is all his own. Though opening firmly in E minor, resolution into a triad is rigorously avoided until the ninth bar, the dissonances which promote the absolute ascendency of the seventh chord arising almost entirely from aggressive passing notes or appoggiaturas. Its terse masculinity is consolidated when the strings present a rising line (bar 14) initiated by a plunging seventh which steepens the contour of Manfred's very first

Ex. 208

notes, constituting a second Manfred theme (Ex. 208b), and confirming this as the toughest music Tchaikovsky had yet composed.

This process of thematic evolution is fundamental to the music of
Manfred himself, and in the following quieter passage it is pursued at a
motivic level when the twice-heard figure of three adjacent notes in the
work's opening phrase (y in Ex. 208a) becomes an undulating quasi-
ostinato thread (Ex. 208c) upon which is strung a series of new, brief
ideas. Yet the progressive disclosure of a personality which such
thematic unfolding admirably suggests is soon to be opposed by an
obsessiveness which has already been foreshadowed in the nagging
repetitions of this Manfred cell (y), though this is held in check until the
entire first section has, Liszt-like, been repeated, now opening in the
tonic key, and finally passing to yet another restatement of the symphony's first two bars, but with their contours widened, and with the
second Manfred phrase annexed (Ex. 208d; further forms of these
materials are set out in Ex. 208f and g).

But now, abruptly, thematic amplification suffers a reverse. Passages
of great dynamic and expressive force had occurred before in
Tchaikovsky's music. That last impetuous eruption of the lovers' music
in *The Tempest* is but one example; yet the theme, once stated, had
been allowed to range freely, then give place to other material. Not so
this second Manfred phrase, for it is caught into a series of obsessive
repetitions made more intense by diminution, and more frustrated by
being trapped within a single chord which batters them with increasing
violence. When at last Manfred's desperate writhings burst through
these confining bonds, he can do no more than complete the earlier
broken course of his original theme, then sink back exhausted towards
E minor.

Some may feel that the dramatic analogies of the preceding prose are
overheated. Yet one thing is surely clear from this music: even the most
tempestuous passages in *Francesca* and the fiercest stretches of the
Fourth Symphony had held back from the sheer violence which
momentarily attends the climax of this first section. Without a readiness to hear such music as transmitting signals in addition to those
received from the purely musical operations of the materials, it is
doubtful whether the impact of this first movement could even be
tolerated. This challenge to the listener's neural fortitude (the term is
not used facetiously) is more powerful still after Manfred's music has
detonated again to end the movement. Now enduringly marked by his
encounter with his beloved, he returns morosely towards the original
form of his opening phrase (Ex. 209a), restates it a fourth higher, then
continues with a phrase impregnated by memories of Astarte's music –

by the descending fate-scale pattern which had proliferated so abundantly at the climax of her scene, above all by the two-quaver feminine ending which had emerged unobtrusively when her opening music had been heard for the second time (see z in Ex. 206c), and which had become a stronger feature as her paragraph had unfolded (see Ex. 210). It might be suspected that the brevity of this concluding section would balance inadequately the earlier spacious deployment of Manfred's material. But Tchaikovsky knew perfectly well what he was about. After his vain pleas to Astarte, Manfred can but collapse into hopeless and, finally, frantic misery, and this he does when the opening notes of the Astarte-stamped phrase are broken off (Ex. 209b, bar 8) to be repeated and decorated with ever-shortening note values while the accompaniment pounds against it with increasingly brutal force. After the trumpet scream which crowns this tumult, despair can go no further; frenzy is bordering on hysteria, and Tchaikovsky's swift conclusion is as right as it is necessary.

Ex. 209

There remains Astarte's music. Her first notes issue in the most natural way out of the brusque sounds which Manfred had uttered before falling into a characteristically abrupt silence (see Ex. 206a), for besides echoing his last two pitches, her first fragile phrase grows above yet another statement of his cell. The other moment when their worlds touch is in that last emotional vortex of the whole movement, both in the phrase which her music had so deeply conditioned (Ex. 209a, bars 8ff.), and even more when it is truncated (Ex. 209b) and so becomes yet another derivative of the three-note Manfred cell. Of all the thematic ambiguities of this symphony, this is the most subtle and perhaps the most significant. Yet otherwise Tchaikovsky could not conceive Astarte's music as anything but distinct from Manfred's, not simply because of the programme's requirements, but because to him it signified something far more poignant and pointed than anything in the literary subject. What had made Tchaikovsky's response to Manfred himself so strong was the irresistible invitation it provided for self-projection, and in the music he conceived for Byron's hero that autobiographical strain, so important in Tchaikovsky's work but for so long muted, reasserts itself with a vengeance. Nevertheless, an equally significant strand running through Tchaikovsky's work – and one which invariably lifts the level of his inspiration, sometimes to its greatest heights – is that of the suffering woman, almost always young and vulnerable, and almost always innocent – or, at least, enduring torments far greater than her failings. This strand goes back to his first important piece – that precocious student work, *The Storm*, where Katerina is destroyed through one lapse in love. In *Undine*, his second opera, the water nymph languishes and perishes through the faithlessness of her human lover, while in his next opera, *The Oprichnik*, it is the Boyarïna, tough and courageous in suffering, yet finally unable to survive the ordeal of her son's execution, who drew by far the strongest response from Tchaikovsky. In his orchestral music the suffering woman resurges powerfully in *Francesca da Rimini*. Nor should we forget Odette in *Swan Lake*: her final catastrophe inspired Tchaikovsky to a symphonic tableau of almost disconcerting power. In the years immediately following his marriage, with no more symphonic poems coming from his pen, the image lives on in his operas. After Tatyana comes Joan in *The Maid of Orléans*, for like her even more favoured predecessor in *Onegin*, it was she who prompted the opera's best music. Next Mariya in *Mazepa*, torn between her father and his murderer, the husband she loves: nothing in the nominal hero could rouse in Tchaikovsky a response as powerful as that stirred by Mariya's final crazed and hopeless predicament. And now Astarte. Insubstantial, yet still wonderfully beautiful, she haunts her lover's thoughts in the loveliest and most heartfelt music Tchaikovsky had discovered within himself since Tatyana had opened for him his richest and most personal vein some eight years before. Her floating ascent into Manfred's consciousness is exquisitely captured in the slender opening phrases (see Ex. 206a, bars 5ff.), each suggesting a brief delicate movement which is checked into a motionless silence. Then, as the phrases and the silences shorten, the tonal mists begin to lift and D major strengthens its pull in a string texture filled with the most telling chromatic detail and rich in seventh chords, though these now suggest a wistful yearning quite different from their abrasive contribution to Manfred's glowering appearance at the symphony's opening. But the ground is not even brushed; there is no hint of cadential resolution before the gentle ghost glides upwards to vanish as she receives renewed incarnation in the woodwind. The following duet for first violins and cellos (Ex. 210) has all the eloquence of that plangent dialogue which had formed the most memorable passage in the Piano Trio, though it possesses a more affecting simplicity of phrase, and combines in the most natural way with a fragment of Astarte's earlier music until both are swept aside by invading scales of fate. The re-entry of Astarte's first music as the climax of this outburst has a surprising vehemence: her sufferings still truly match those of Manfred. Finally, in a single line which faintly

Ex. 210

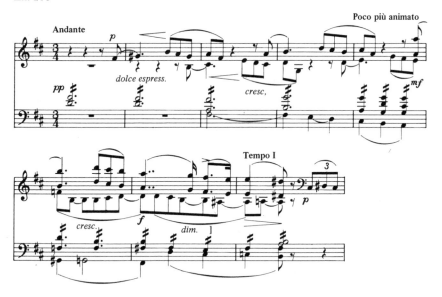

foreshadows a portion of that phrase which is about to bear the full burden of Manfred's response, she sinks down again to linger only in the recesses of her fateful lover's memory.

In November 1882, when Tchaikovsky had rejected the newly offered Manfred programme, his letter to Balakirev had also contained a dispirited assessment of his own achievement.

> Despite my venerable age and my considerable experience in composing, I must confess that *I am wandering* still in the boundless field of composition, trying vainly to discover my true pathway. I feel that such a pathway exists and I know that, once I find it, I shall write something really good – but some fateful blindness constantly leads me astray, and God knows whether sometime I shall hit upon where I ought to be going. . . . From time to time it's happened that I've come close to 'the pathway', and then pieces have emerged of which, to the end of my life, I shall not be ashamed, which please and maintain in me the energy for work. But this has happened rarely, and in no way can I number *Francesca* and *The Tempest* among these few exceptions. Both these pieces are written with affected ardour, with false pathos, with a pursuit of purely external effects – and at bottom they are cold, false and weak in the extreme. Their failings stem from the fact that these compositions of mine in no way *recreate* the given subject, but are only written *à propos* of it – that is, the kinship of the music and the programme is not an inner one, but external, incidental.[21]

It was, of course, a verdict too severe. Uneven as both pieces are, they contain, in the music of Miranda's love or Francesca's misery, passages which speak truly from the heart, though it is no surprise that Tchaikovsky would not wish (or, perhaps, have the capacity) to admit this, even to himself. Yet his assertion that other stretches of these works were no more than efficient responses to elements within his subjects was well founded, and his unsparing repudiation in 1888 of the last three movements of the Manfred Symphony was an equally valid recognition that, whatever the qualities of some of their musical invention or the craft with which this was deployed, they also were, as counterparts of Byron's poem, merely synthetic. In 1882 he had even censured *Romeo and Juliet* on the same grounds of non-commitment, even though only two years earlier he had felt sufficient regard for it to think it worth expending some of his creative energies upon a further

[21] *TLP*11, p. 281; *BVP*, p. 168.

revision. Yet he continued to recognize that the first movement of the Manfred Symphony was something different, and three years after completing it his pride and trust in it remained as firm as ever, for he must have perceived that this time his identification with the subject had been total. The quality of the musical ideas and their application may be a matter for debate, but of one thing there can be no doubt: in this movement of such expressive extremes, Tchaikovsky was fully himself again.

And so, for a second time, Balakirev had rendered invaluable service. Yet for all the new hopes Tchaikovsky may in November 1884 have placed in his old mentor as a guide to personal salvation, his ambivalence remained. 'I have again taken a cordial farewell of Balakirev. He's a strange man (between ourselves, be it said, a *madman*), but all the same, essentially a wonderful person,' he had written to Jurgenson on 19 November, a week later.[22] It was predictable that Tchaikovsky should have wished to avoid direct contact with Balakirev while the Manfred Symphony remained unfinished; nor is it surprising that afterwards he should have done nothing to foster face-to-face encounters between himself and this autocrat who, with the symphony done, had promptly signalled that his next work should be a piano concerto in F sharp minor or C sharp minor, and who was threatening to pressurize him into making changes in *The Tempest* when they next met. In January 1886, when Tchaikovsky paid a visit to St Petersburg, they did consult over details of the piano-duet transcription of the symphony, but their religious exchanges do not seem to have been renewed.

The disintegration of their relationship is charted in their few remaining letters. Always it is Balakirev who attempts to engineer meetings. 'I'm inviting you . . . to my place on Thursday evening,' he wrote on 6 November 1886, when Tchaikovsky was in the city. 'But I won't tell anyone about this; I don't know whether you want to be completely alone, or whether you want me to invite anyone else. You'll tell me on Tuesday.'[23] It was the same four months later on Tchaikovsky's next visit. The party would include a few old friends they had in common – but 'if there's any of them you don't want to see, then let me know; it shall be as you wish, and the secret will remain *between us.*'[24] Whether they had met in November is unknown, but on this second visit Tchaikovsky simply could not face an encounter. 'I

[22] *TLP*12, p. 480; *TPJ*2, p. 20; *YDGC*, p. 329.
[23] *BVP*, p. 182.
[24] *BVP*, p. 183.

haven't the strength to bear any longer my extreme weariness and nervous derangement, and today I've decided to go away into the country,' he pleaded. 'I'm very distressed I shan't be a witness to your triumph [the silver jubilee concert of the Free Music School which Balakirev was to conduct the next day]. Please, old chap, don't be angry. God knows, I have no more strength.'[25]

In November 1888, Balakirev tried for the last time. He had attended the première of Tchaikovsky's Fifth Symphony which the composer had conducted three days before, and he was determined to extract an answer to his invitation for the following Thursday. 'I shall send for a reply,' he promised on 20 November, 'so don't go out without leaving one for me.'[26] But again Tchaikovsky excused himself.

A three-year silence followed. Then in October 1891 Tchaikovsky wrote to Balakirev on behalf of a choirboy from St Sofiya's Cathedral in Kiev who had been inexplicably dismissed by the Metropolitan, despite possessing an unusually beautiful voice; perhaps Balakirev might have a place for him in the Imperial Chapel. But Balakirev wrote that he could offer no help. Their last two letters were exchanged some seven weeks later when Tchaikovsky was in St Petersburg to participate in a concert. Their tone and content tell all.

Wanting to hear your Slavonic March played by an orchestra, I earnestly beg you to inform me when your last rehearsal will be, and by *approximately* what time I need to come to the hall to hear the Slavonic March without having to waste more time than necessary. You will greatly oblige me by fulfilling my request.

Yours ever,

M. Balakirev[27]

Three days later, on 11 December, Tchaikovsky answered.

At today's rehearsal (it's the last one) the Slavonic March will be played second. I shall begin with the overture *exactly at 1 p.m.*; consequently the march will be played *at approximately* 1.20, since the

[25] *TLP*14, p. 61; *BVP*, p. 183.
[26] *BVP*, p. 184.
[27] *BVP*, p. 185.

overture's not especially long. The rehearsal's taking place in the hall of the Assembly of the Nobility.

Sincerely devoted to you,
P. Tchaikovsky[28]

Not a hint of personal exchanges – not a hint of an invitation, nor even of a wish to meet. Their relationship was finally over.

---

[28] *TLP*16A, p. 285; *BVP*, p. 186.

INDEX OF WORKS

ARRANGEMENTS

MAJOR LITERARY WORKS

INDEX OF PERSONS